MINING AFRICA:
Law, Environment, Society and Politics in Historical and Multidisciplinary Perspectives

Edited by

Artwell Nhemachena &
Tapiwa V Warikandwa

Langaa Research & Publishing CIG
Mankon, Bamenda

Publisher
Langaa RPCIG
Langaa Research & Publishing Common Initiative Group
P.O. Box 902 Mankon
Bamenda
North West Region
Cameroon
Langaagrp@gmail.com
www.langaa-rpcig.net

Distributed in and outside N. America by African Books Collective
orders@africanbookscollective.com
www.africanbookscollective.com

ISBN-10: 9956-764-32-9

ISBN-13: 978-9956-764-32-7

© Artwell Nhemachena & Tapiwa V Warikandwa 2017

List of Contributors

Artwell Nhemachena holds a PhD in Social Anthropology; Master of Science in Sociology and Social Anthropology and Bachelor of Science Honours Degree in Sociology. He has lectured at a number of universities in Zimbabwe before pursuing his PhD studies in South Africa. Currently he lectures in the Sociology Department at the University of Namibia. His current areas of research interest are Knowledge Studies; Development Studies; Environment; Resilience; Food Security and Food Sovereignty; Industrial Sociology; Conflict and Peace; Transformation; Science and Technology Studies, Democracy and Governance; Relational Ontologies; Decoloniality and Anthropological jurisprudence. He has published in the areas of social theory, research methods, democracy and governance; conflict and peace; relational ontologies; industrial sociology; development; anthropological jurisprudence, environment, and knowledge studies; transformation and decoloniality. He is a CODESRIA Laureate since 2010 and has been participating in the CODESRIA Democratic Governance Institute.

Tapiwa Victor Warikandwa holds Doctor of Laws, Master of Laws, and Bachelor of Laws degrees from the University of Fort Hare in South Africa. Currently, he is a Senior Lecturer in the Faculty of Law at the University of Namibia. He specializes in International Trade Law, Labour Law, Indigenisation Laws, Mining Law and Constitutional Law amongst other disciplines. Prior to coming to Namibia, Dr. Warikandwa worked as a legal officer and later legal advisor in the Ministry of Public Service Labour and Social Welfare. Key amongst his duties was legal drafting. Dr Warikandwa worked with the law reviser of the Ministry of Justice in Zimbabwe in reviewing laws administered by the Ministry of Public Service Labour and Social Welfare. Dr Warikandwa also completed an ordinary and advanced training in Labour Law Making at the International Labour Organization's International Training Centre in Turin Italy. On numerous occasions, Dr. Warikandwa was actively involved in the activities of the Cabinet Committee on Legislation on behalf of the Ministry of Public Service Labour and Social Welfare. Dr.

Warikandwa has since written books on labour law and women's rights in South Africa and Namibia respectively, as well as publishing articles in accredited peer reviewed journals such as Law, Development and Democracy, Speculum Juris, Potchefstroom Electronic Law Journal, Comparative International Law Journal for Southern Africa and the African Journal of International and Comparative Law, amongst others. Dr. Warikandwa has also been awarded a number of merit based scholarships and has served as a Post-doctoral Fellow with the University of Fort Hare in South Africa. He has also worked as a senior lecturer at the University of Fort Hare and presented papers at conferences in and outside South Africa.

Christopher Dick-Sagoe is a development specialist. He recently completed a Doctor of Philosophy programme in Public Administration in India, where his thesis examined the efficiency of decentralised local governments in providing public services in Ghana. Before starting the PhD programme, he headed the research and development unit of the Ghana Technology University College, Takoradi campus. He taught research methodology and supervised Masters' theses of students in the same University. His previous position was a junior lecturer in Ashesi University College in Ghana. His academic qualifications span from Bachelor of Science Development Planning, Master of Philosophy in Development Studies and PhD Public Administration. Dick-Sagoe is a proud author of more than 12 peer reviewed papers and has made several presentations at international conferences in different countries. He has special enthusiasm for researches in the fields of poverty, decentralization, rural sustainable livelihoods, environment and local governance and accountability. Currently, his research has concentrated more on improving the efficiency of decentralised service provision to achieve sustainable poverty reduction in Ghana. He has peer reviewed papers for Public Administration Research Journal of the Canadian Centre of Science and Education.

Jean-Pierre Wome is a CODESRIA fellow and doctoral candidate in the department of Criminal and Procedural Law in the Faculty of Law of the North West University, South Africa. He holds an LLM in conflict management from the University of Fort Hare, South Africa, and, an LLB from the University of Buea, Cameroon. He has authored many articles in the areas of international law and constitutionalism. Presently, his research interest is focused towards the challenges facing the International Criminal Court.

Tembo Moment is a PhD student at North West University, Potchefstroom Campus at the Bench Mark School for Corporate Social Responsibility (CSR). His research area is mining and development focusing on the impact of Corporate Social Investment on communities in the mining industry. He is a holder of a Bachelor of Sociology (Honours) from the University of Fort Hare and a Masters in Development Studies from Nelson Mandela Metropolitan University. He is studying for a Post-graduate diploma in Risk Management at the University of South Africa and currently working as a Researcher and risk Manager at Acmeret Solutions Consultancy.

Njabulo Chipangura is employed by the National Museums and Monuments of Zimbabwe as an archaeologist and is based in Eastern Zimbabwe at Mutare Museum. His research interests include looking at the configuration and reconfiguration of museum collection and exhibition practices within colonial and post-colonial settings. He has also carried out research on the hosting of cultural festivals at heritage sites specifically looking at the dissemination of public culture at these festivals and how they give communities a sense of heritage ownership. His other research focus is on the different classifications of heritage in Zimbabwe with an interest on the category of colonial historic buildings and he has looked at how it has lost relevancy in the present conservation discourse. This research saw him critically analysing the emergence of the category of liberation war heritage in the country and how it has seemingly supplanted all the other forms of heritage in terms of conservation priority. This research was extended to take an inside look at liberation war heritage and he analysed the narratives that have emerged from exhumation exercises of liberation war fighters in which he has been involved as an archaeologist. He has thereafter argued that the process of monumentalisation in Zimbabwe is increasingly becoming synonymous with the rituals of exhuming human remains of liberation war fighters scattered across the country. He is currently a Wenner Gren PhD Fellow in the Anthropology Department at the University of Witwatersrand in South Africa. His PhD research looks at the archaeological, ethnographic and historical characteristics of artisanal and small scale mining of gold in the Eastern Highlands of Zimbabwe. In this research, he intends to establish the historical connection between ancient gold mining and contemporary artisanal mining by 'illegal miners' who are presently exploiting the gold reef around Mutanda cultural landscape.

Phefumula Nyoni is an anthropologist and sociologist; lecturer and researcher who is currently attached to the University of the Witwatersrand as a Research Associate. He is currently actively involved in research on artisanal mining with a specific focus on *zamazama* experiences and livelihoods as well as finding strategies for community development through artisanal mining and state approaches to artisanal mining. He has also been involved in research on small businesses in South Africa which is the focus of his PhD thesis. His other previous research has also focused on cultural practices, migration and employment in the construction industry among others. He is also involved in advocacy work in support of marginalised communities in South Africa.

Michelle Munyanduki is an LLB graduate from the University of Namibia with notable academic achievements. She attained a distinction for her dissertation paper on mining law. In addition she was awarded a certificate for best second year law student as well as best in criminal and contract law. Outside the academic realm, Michelle served as the Law Faculty representative in her third year and in her final year as the Speaker of Parliament in the Student Representative Council. She is an avid believer in the potential Africa has as far as growth and development are concerned and aims to be a significant contributor to this end. On the strength of her solid law background Michelle is currently working in the legal department of a renowned construction company overseeing legal matters which consists of managing construction contracts and dispute avoidance. Michelle continues to monitor advances on sustainable mining in Namibia and from an international perspective and follows trends in international best practices. Her drive to make her input to the mining discourse makes her an upcoming individual to look out for.

Janet Munakamwe is a Doctoral candidate at the African Centre for Migration & Society (ACMS), University of Witwatersrand and an Alumnus of the Global Labour University (GLU), South Africa. In 2014, she was awarded an International Centre for Development and Decent Work Research fellowship at Chris Hani Institute where she conducted research on illegal/ informal mining in South Africa as part of her doctoral studies. Her work attempts to reconcile the link between the formal and non-formal economy through seminal findings which reveal the destination of illegally mined gold. In addition, Janet has documented some of the lived experiences of 'illegal' miners popularly known as zamazama (meaning we are trying to earn a living) in her efforts to ensure that these uncelebrated workers' voices are heard by policy makers (through the academic space) as part of the process towards decriminalisation and transformation of their precarious (working) conditions.

Ndatega Victoria Asheela is a Lecturer in the Department of Commercial Law at the University of Namibia. She holds the degrees B.Juris, Bachelor of Laws (LLB) (Unam) and Master of Laws (LLM) (Pretoria). Ndatega is currently a doctoral candidate in the Faculty of Law at the University of Pretoria, writing a thesis on the creditworthiness assessments under Namibian consumer credit law. Ndatega joined the University of Namibia in February 2013 as a part-time lecturer in the Department of Commercial Law. In August 2013, she was appointed as a full-time lecturer in the same department. She is responsible for teaching competition law, insolvency law and income tax law to LLB students. Her main research areas of interest are on consumer protection, consumer credit law, insolvency law, investments and securities law. Ndatega was accredited as a mediator of the High Court of Namibia in May 2014. In July 2015 she was appointed as a member of the Magistrates' Commission of Namibia.

Howard Chitimira is a Professor of Law who holds an LLB (*cum laude*) degree and LLM degree in Corporate Law from the University of Fort Hare. He also holds an LLD degree in Securities and

Financial Markets Law from the Nelson Mandela Metropolitan University. Prof Chitimira is a reviewer and editorial board member for several local and international law journals. He is also an external examiner for LLB modules; LLM and LLD programmes for several local and international universities. His expertise and research interests include Corporate & Financial Markets Law; Corporate Governance; Commercial Law; Mercantile Law; Insolvency Law; some aspects of Competition Law; related aspects of Intellectual Property Law; related aspects of Banking and Financial Law and aspects of International Trade Law. Prof Chitimira is a Y2 NRF Rated Researcher in Securities and Financial Markets Law an NRF Grant Holder in Securities and Financial Markets Law. Prof Chitimira is currently an Associate Professor in the Faculty of Law at North West University.

Oliver Mtapuri is a Professor who holds a PhD in Development studies (UKZN) and an MBA degree from the University of Zimbabwe. He is an Associate of the Institute of Chartered Secretaries and Administrators. Before joining the academe, Oliver worked for 12 years in the Government of Zimbabwe as a Labour Economist/Researcher in the Ministry of Labour and Social Welfare. Prior to joining UKZN, Oliver was a full Professor at the University of Limpopo. Oliver's areas of research interest include poverty, redistribution and inequality, community-based tourism, public employment programmes, research methodologies, financial management, climate change and project management. Recently he has taken a keen interest in the nexus between the environment and poverty and the "Anthropocene" particularly in light of the surfacing of many 'poverties' and many 'inequalities' afflicting contemporary societies. Oliver was the Editor in Chief (Founding) of the *Journal of Business and Public Dynamics for Development.*

Esther Dhakwa holds a Bachelor of Science Honours Degree in Sociology from the University of Zimbabwe. She is currently pursuing a Masters Degree in Sociology. Her areas of interest include Environment, Health, Human Security as well as Development studies.

Table of Contents

Foreword

While mining and environmental issues have been written on, there is a general dearth of multidisciplinary and multi-temporal perspectives that would otherwise provide holistic coverage of the issues. Such holistic perspectives are not only necessary for scholars, researchers, activists and students to grasp the pertinent issues related to mining but also assist in multi-sectoral policy planning by African governments, particularly those whose economies are heavily reliant on mining and environmental resources. Such perspectives are clearly essential given the fact that in spite of Africa being richly endowed with minerals, the continent continues to suffer revolting levels of poverty and conflicts over mineral resources. These challenges have led some scholars to depict Africa as resource-cursed. Broadly, the book seeks to critically interrogate, refine and or create theories and practices on mining on the continent of Africa. The approach taken is multidisciplinary in that issues of mining and environment will be examined from different disciplinary perspectives such as law, archaeology, geography, sociology, African studies, anthropology, history, economics, development, security studies, politics and human ecology. The book also examines mining and environmental ideas, and practices from pre-colonial eras on the African continent. It interrogates the ways in which these ideas and practices can possibly feed into contemporary debates on mining, environment, "modernity", science and "tradition", development, ecology, economics and transformation on the African continent.

The book also proposes a shift from the free market based mining regulatory practice in Africa to a Pan-African regulatory framework. The underlying rationale of this approach is that African mineral resources have been used to develop and sustain development in Western and Asian countries yet Africans remain trapped in chronic impoverishment. If African countries could focus on value addition before trading in their mineral resources, Africa could have realised greater development. However, due to the fact that the mining education that Africans are subjected to is Western or recently Asian in content, African graduates who are supposed to drive transformation using the mining sector are ill-equipped to provide African solutions to African problems. As such, the book also points to the flaws in Western Emperors' template on business, the environment, as well as mining education and proposes an African oriented mining education system.

Artwell Nhemachena & Tapiwa V Warikandwa

Chapter One

On the Challenges of African Mining and Environments in the New World Order: An Introduction

Artwell Nhemachena and Tapiwa V Warikandwa

> *The secret of great wealth with no obvious source is some forgotten crime, forgotten because it was done neatly* (de Balzac H 1991: 103).

Africa's Resources and Western Conjurations of a New World Order

The contemporary hype about an emergent New World Order (Hagger, 2013; Garcia, 2010), needs to be understood in relation to sad colonial histories of what invading Europeans similarly called the New World. Although some scholars in the contemporary era present the New World Order as a necessity and as beneficial to all peoples in the world, the history of what the Europeans called the New World underlines that what is commonly presented as new is not *ipso facto* beneficial, or necessarily so to those that become sacrificial victims in the crucibles of (neo) imperial creation of history. Indeed the enslavement and colonisation of Africans was at some point in imperial history, marketed as new, as ushering change, transformation and transitions. Yet when these terms such as new, change, transformation and transition are pronounced, they sometimes appear to have so powerful magical qualities that even the, supposedly most intelligent, imperial sacrificial victims themselves are petrified to the point of blindness to the fact that even death, dispossession, enslavement and exploitation are often alluringly presented as new things, as change, transformation and transition. In the religious sphere Africans are being wooed into what are being popularised as New Age Spiritualties that bear on supposedly new ontologies [that deny the existence of the Heavens] of the environments; in the political realm Africans are being courted to new ways to conceive and do politics that bear on supposedly new

1

ontologies [that deny African autonomy and sovereignty over their resources], new notions of being and becoming; in the academies Africans are wooed to supposedly new theories and ways to understand the world bearing on supposedly new ontologies and new epistemologies [that exploit distorted notions of indigenous knowledge to blindfold Africans into the New World Order]; in the realm of law, environment, politics, and culture, Africans are being courted into supposedly new assemblages [wherein they lose their autonomy and sovereignty over their resources]. But what is seldom questioned are the gospels and catchwords-'new', 'change', 'transformation', 'transition' that have been present since the colonial era but without necessarily bettering the lives of Africans who remain dispossessed, exploited, enslaved and in the (neo-)colonial zones of what Fanon (1963), in his book 'The Wretched of the Earth', calls 'zones of nonbeing'.

In other words, "secular" gospels about the new, change, transformation and transition in Africa have tended to paradoxically summon immense suffering by the dispossessed and exploited since the colonial era some of who unfortunately continue to be flattered by the evangelists of gospels of the [inorganic and cancerous] newness, change, transformation and transition. At a time when the dispossessed and exploited, who in addition to being dispossessed of their resources have been dispossessed of the Heavenly God of Creation *ex nihilo*, have intensified their search for Godly newness, change and transformation, the secularists have tactfully designed "new" immanentisms to further deny the Heavenly God that the dispossessed are hankering for. In spite of the existence of massive evidence that the [inorganic] (neo-)colonial gospels of newness, change, transformation and transition are vacuous and in fact cancerous, seldom asked are questions such as transition or transformation to where/what and to whose destination? Thus, the fact that right from the beginning of colonisation, territories that were being colonised by Europeans where described by them as the New World shows that even colonisation of other people is appealingly described as new and as change or transformation. In all these, the challenge is that even those that are being colonised and dispossessed often become bandwagonist and celebrate the songs about the need for the new, for transformation and transition even if they remain ignorant of the destination of the transitions, transformations and changes. For this reason, Africans have since the colonial era been dispossessed, exploited and impoverished using linguistic and ideological decoys of change and the bringing in of new things, as if the new is *ipso facto* good. The ideological and linguistic decoys about the, supposedly unquestionable, necessity of [inorganic] newness and change have, right from the onset of such ideologies, legitimised the rejection of the ["old"] God of Creation and justified the birth of European gods of the violence of the Big Bang (Nhemachena and Mawere, 2017). In other words, with the over-glorification of (neo-)imperial newness and change, the subaltern have been cultured into dissatisfaction with the God of Creation whose worldly Creation is presented as old and in need of the detonations that are considered imperative in New World Order quests for the new and for change. Transformation or change since the era when the God of Creation was rejected has become coterminous with Big Bang violence, disorder, dispossession and exploitation of others.

The point here is that some Africans, whether elite or not, have so far tended to act like passengers [in a world driven by the agendas of others in the global north] who do not care to critically ask about the destinations of agendas on the supposed newness, change, transformation and transition. In other words, if (neo-)empire merely changes the side by which it is pressing on Africa [turned into an imperial bed], the change of side would ordinarily not warrant the celebration as change or newness by those that are still pressed, except that (neo-)empire has been careful enough to, over the years, popularise [often dangerous] cosmetics that have normalised satisfaction with mere appearances. Thus, failure to ask critical questions about the agenda of colonial "civilisation" including "education" missions has led many Africans into (neo-)imperial zombiehood lacking rights to own their resources, including their own minds (Nyamnjoh, 2012; Nhemachena, 2016; 2017). Critical minds would notice that Euro-American gospels about newness and change witnessed the enslavement and colonisation, involving dispossession and exploitation, of Africans and other peoples of the world. So, with reference to the Euro-American imperial evangelisation of the New World, Nellis (2013: 1) notes that:

> Between the sixteenth and nineteenth centuries, the people of Africa, America and Europe were linked to form new societies in what historian Robin Blackburn calls the "American crucible". During that time, while Native American populations were displaced, assimilated, or exterminated, millions of Europeans and African people cross the Atlantic, the majority of the later without consent as African slaves.

Apart from deliberately introducing diseases as strategy to decimate the native people in the New World that was subjected to colonisation (Stannard, 1993), MacMillan (2006: 18) observes that Euro-American laws were used to justify, claim and maintain imperium and dominium. MacMillan (2006: 24-33) notes thus:

> At the same time, then that the English were turning their attention towards the New World, the concept of a monarch as an independent, or absolute sovereign ruler (emperor) free from all external human control within his or her own territories (empire) had become commonplace…this common, pluralistic interpretation of sovereignty was essential in determining how English crowns claimed and maintained imperium and dominium in the New World…The English New World colonies were part of the English King's composite monarchy of diverse dominions…

Thus, the New World was 'created' and exploited at the expense of the natives of the colonised world who were shocked by massive killings at a time when Europeans sought to exterminate New World adversaries by introducing diseases (Cook, 1998: 17; Stannard, 1993: vii). Stannard (1993: vii) reports graphically that:

> …barrage of disease unleashed by the Europeans among the so called "virgin soil" populations of the Americas caused more deaths than any other single force of destruction. However by focusing almost entirely on disease, by displacing responsibility for the mass killing onto an army of invading microbes, contemporary authors created the

impression that the eradication of those tens of millions of people was inadvertent…

Much as the ideology of the New World served to legitimise the colonisation, dispossession and exploitation of the colonised and enslaved people in the world, the contemporary hype about the New World Order aims to legitimise capitalism's complete and definitive global sway (Panitch et al, 1992). Thus, the ideology and conjurations of the New World Order are aimed at ensuring planetary hegemony by the Western transnational corporations that trawl for resources home and away. Much as the imperial New World ideologies were not about freedom for the enslaved and colonised, the ideologies of the New World Order are not necessarily about freedom or protection of the enslaved and colonised (Story, 2007). Thus, the New World Order has been understood as a worldwide conspiracy to effect Western complete and total control over the planetary resources (Mentan, 2010).

Although Mentan (2010) addresses the contemporary New World Order as a *worldwide* conspiracy, it is understood by other writers as in fact a conspiracy by a *secret society* called the illuminati that historically monopolise control over mining corporations, international banking corporations and institutions, including international media and education institutions. So, Hagger (2013) states that, the former American President, Bush made much use of the phrase 'New World Order' and that the New World Order (NOW) came in the 1990s to mean a world government imposed by the syndicate, led by "Rothchilds" and "Rockefellers" which would completely own and control the world's natural resources. For Lloyd (2015), the illuminati [secret society] oligarchs control politicians, the courts, the educational institutions, the food, the natural resources, the foreign policies, the economies and the money of most nations, in addition to controlling the media. Lloyd (2015) argues that the end game of the current hype about the New World Order will be a One World Government presiding over the earth for the benefit of the global oligarchs and their superclass functionaries, leaving the mass of humanity as serfs, to serve the elite, while suffering impoverishment and immiseration. In the New World Order or One

World Government envisaged by the illuminati, all laws will be uniform under a legal system of world courts practising the same unified codes of laws, backed up by a One World Government police force and a One World Unified military (Lloyd, 2015). This illuminati's quest to control world resources is noted by Lloyd (ibid) as involving the development of antifertility vaccines by Rockefeller Foundation working with John D Rockefeller's Population Council, the World Bank, the United Nations Development Programme, the Ford Foundation and others working with World Health Organisation.

The Rothchilds that some writers like Hagger (2013) implicate in the New World Order are also noted by other scholars like Zagami (2016) as controlling 80% of uranium supplies in the world; besides, Kubicek (1991: 68) notes that: "By the end of the 1980s, the largest De Beers' shareholders with over 30 000 each were the London Rothchilds…Rhodes held 20 000 or less, Beit and Wernher together owned about 20 000". The Global Research (5 October 2015) traces the secret society to 1891 when a secret plan was drawn between the architect of colonisation of Africa Cecil John Rhodes, Lord Rothchilds, Salisbury, Roseberry and Milner who insisted on a secret society and drew a plan to bring all inhabitable portions of the world under their control. It is further reported that the meeting in 1891 was in fact the birth of the New World Order and so: "Rhodes…sought to amass great wealth into his secret society in order to achieve political ends, to buy governments and politicians, buy public opinion and the means to influence it".

Similarly, All Africa (2 April 2015) notes world conspirators stating thus:

> Why should we not form a secret society with but one object: the furtherance of the British Empire and the bringing of the whole uncivilised world under British rule, for the recovery of the United States, and for the making of the Anglo-Saxon race but one empire? Africa is still lying ready for us, it is our duty to take it. It is our duty to seize every opportunity of acquiring more territory and we should keep this one idea steadily before our eyes: that more territory simply means

more of the Anglo-Saxon race, more of the best, the most human, most honourable race the world possesses…

While Lichtenstein (2005) notes that giant corporations are the most important institutions shaping the character of the world; Hagger (2010: 110) contends that the Rothchilds and Rockefeller corner the world's natural resources including gas and oil; they control central banks of many countries. Hagger (2010: 110) states that: "….the syndicate has planned to reshape the world and reduce its population to a "sustainable" figure by encouraging local wars, spreading diseases and exploiting famine so that it can control the world and loot the earth's natural resources for the benefit of its own select band of relatively few oligarchs…" For this reason, Bienefeld (1994) observes that the New World Order is witnessing a more open and explicit form of imperialism, in which some countries' national sovereignty is more readily overridden by a hegemonic power pursuing its own self-defined national interest and the neoliberal policy will be imposed on the more monolithic world with potentially serious effects on developing countries. In fact, there are already traces of New World Order bandwagonism by some African and Asian leaders who as the Mail & Guardian (23 April 2015) reports, called for a "New Economic World Order" at a recent Asian-African conference.

The African bandwagonism in the New World Order is partly explained by the fact that the transnational [mining] corporations and the secret society that is deemed to be at the head of such corporations have established universities, often out of the sweat and stomachs of the enslaved and colonised (Global Research, 5 October 2015) in order to control the minds of those they have dispossessed. Thus, while noting the formation of the transnational mining corporation, London and Rhodesia Mining and Land Company (LONRHO) which has been renamed, in 1999, as Lonmin, Global Research (5 October 2015) points out that:

> Rhodes' network of stolen wealth also helped set up universities such as Rhodes, Witwatersrand, Pretoria and Cape Town. Rhodes University came into existence through a "donation' from the Rhodes

Trust, and UCT was built on land 'donated' by Rhodes…In fact…Rhodes proposed to build the university mainly from profits-about 10 000 pounds a year-of the kaffir compound system of DeBeers Mines and joked that, 'he meant to build the university out of the kaffirs' stomachs.

In this vein, it is important to note that not only universities or academies have been established by transnational corporations using proceeds from the dispossession and exploitation of Africans; international institutions and organisations also have their financial support from the transnational corporations that are exploiting Africans. This could be why even the United Nations (UN) is implicated in the constitution of the New World Order that is financially supported by the wealthy secret society in the world (New American, 11 October 2012). It is further argued that the UN and its affiliated institutions are usurping [from nation states] legislative, executive and judicial powers including taxing, policing, and military powers; it is doing so with the approval, funding and support of the 'globalists'. The New American (11 October 2012) states thus:

> Besides putting in place a vast civil service of administrators and bureaucrats to run the planned world government, the ever expanding UN system has created a huge global constituency of local and national politicians, corporations, and NGOs that benefit from the UN's presence and can be counted on to lobby for its continued expansion…The UN's rapidly growing organisational footprint is most jarringly visible throughout the Third World, where offices of UN agencies, the IMF, and World Bank dominate the political and economic landscape, and UN trucks, UN tent cities, blue-helmet UN peacekeepers, and UN civilian staff are ubiquitous.

The imbrication of the UN in the secret society and the New World Order is suggested in its paradoxical nature in so far as it often professes to be a guardian of democracy and human rights including, inclusivity and equality while at the same time its supreme Security Council [with veto powers] comprises of states in the global north and excludes the majority of African states. States that constitute the

Security Council are themselves not voted into those positions by the majority in the world. In other words, there is no democracy within the UN system that paradoxically purports to be the guardian of world democracy and human rights. Furthermore, the funding for the UN system comes from the resilient dispossession and exploitation of peoples of the global south; and from the transnational corporations that are culprits of the (neo-)colonial dispossession and exploitation of Africa and the rest of the global south. If transnational corporations, as indicated above, are owned and controlled by the secret society, it then follows that the secret society funds the UN in so far as the funds that sustain the UN system comes from transnational corporations exploiting resources across the entire planet. In addition, the lacklustre attention of the UN in the indigenous struggles for restitution and reclamation of their resources can be understood in terms of the fact that the UN system itself is a beneficiary of the dispossession and exploitation of Africans and the rest of the global south. For these reasons, Nhemachena et al (2017) have argued that the contemporary discourses about African state failure, simply underscore bias against Africa because the failures of the United Nations for many decades after independence of Africa to champion the restitution and compensation of Africans for enslavement and colonisation is paradoxically not made as visible. Nhemachena et al (2017) further argue that even the civil society organisations have failed to facilitate restitution and compensation of African victims of enslavement and colonial dispossession; thus it is contended that the targeting of African states alone as having failed is part of the ideologies of the New World Order [One World Government] that is set to demonise and hack down African sovereigns and then monopolise resources and thrive on ensuing chaos, anarchy and absence of states in Africa.

The fact that funding of the UN systems comes from countries erroneously described as rich, wealthy and developed rather than correctly described as dispossessors, looters and robbers (Nhemachena, 2016), explains the absence of democracy within the UN systems even as it paradoxically purports to be a guardian of democracy. The kind of what we call *cul-de-sac* Western 'democracy' that the UN system is a guardian of is sadly supposedly deemed, in the scheme of world governance, to be superior to restitution and reclamation struggles.

Analysing the façade of Western democracy, Garcia (2010) argues that in the light of the fact that there has always been a significant royal factor in aspirants to the white house, democracy is in fact a case of kissing cousins who stage elections and the false right-left paradigm. For Garcia (2010), the American royalty are tied to other ruling families of the Western world in what is a New World Order familial conspiracy, perpetuated by 'wealthy' elites who have centralised wealth and power by intermarrying among themselves'. What this entails is that while Euro-American states purport to be champions of democracy their democracy is in fact a façade. Also underscored in the façade of Western democracy is the vacuity of contrived linkages between democracy and development; it is erroneously purported that the West is developed because it is highly democratic. The fallacies in arguments that presuppose that the West developed because of excellence in democracy are meant to hide the fact that the West developed because it looted resources and exploited colonised and enslaved people in the global south (Nhemachena, 2016) whose resources have not been restituted and compensated despite independence and affiliation to international organisations that claim to champion global human rights. Given the absence of democracy in the UN system of which Security Council, dominated by the global north, dictates to the rest of the world, it would be myopic to argue that the West is democratic and that it is excellence in democracy that explains its developed state. Western democracy is simply a front, cosmetics applied onto the face of the leviathan of a capitalist system that continues to dispossess, rob, loot, kill and exploit peoples of the global south.

The fallacy of Western democracy is apparent when one considers how much African states and governments and even socio-cultural institutions are demonised for lack of democracy and equality yet firms including private security companies managed from the West are paradoxically tolerated even as they dispossess and exploit Africans monopolising their gold, oil, diamonds and so on (see for instance Global Policy Forum, March/April 1998). So, companies like Executive Outcomes (EO) which is one of more than 18 firms

10

including international oil, gold and diamond mining ventures and offshore financial management services, roam around the world in order to exploit not only resources but also people. If, as Marxists would have it, the states are superstructural reflections of the infrastructural base in the world, then the African states risk being servants of the global capital that owns and controls the infrastructural bases. Therefore expecting the states alone to be democratic is akin to expecting the servant to be democratic in a context where the global [capitalist] master is allowed to be autocratic even to the point of failing to respect the geographies of continental and state boundaries. African states, some of which were avowedly socialist at independence, have been co-opted particularly via neoliberal reforms into the International Monetary Fund (IMF) and World Bank capitalist structural adjustment programmes. Yet, sadly and paradoxically the IMF and the World Bank that have, particularly since the neoliberal era, intensified capture and control of African states are not subjected to the rubrics of democracy. Furthermore the problem of African impoverishment is presented narrowly and erroneously as the problems of African states and governments rather than as *a fortiori* the problem of transnational corporations and institutions, which dispossess and exploit without restitutions and compensation. Thus, with a vision to set up the New World Order or One World Government that would open up the entire planet to transnational corporations' unencumbered exploitation of resources, it is only African states and states in the global south that are problematized and considered as warranting political excision, rescission and circumcision by the global north that operate via mafia of various shades of missionaries (Nhemachena et al, 2017).

As tools for effecting the New World Order, Western ideologies of democracy [which are sponsored by the dominant and secret society in the world] are being used to justify postmodern [revolutions] coups in the global south. Paradoxically, these postmodern colour revolutions only target states that are also demonised as repressive, autocratic and undemocratic and as having failed; the colour revolutions do not target international or transnational capital that is dispossessive, oppressive, and undemocratic and has failed to restitute and compensate for colonial

11

and enslavement crimes. Thus, Global Research (3 June 2014), reports about the field testing of post-modern coups which are funded by some Western organisations [democracy guerrillas] including those that evade paying taxes in the global south. Global Research (3 June 2014) further points out that The [U.S.A] National Endowment for Democracy (NED) and its primary arms, the National Democratic Institute for International Affairs (NDI) and International Republican Institute (IRI) play central roles in the revolutions.

Such sponsored postmodern coups that target African states and states in the global south, rather than the centuries old dispossession, exploitation and hegemony of the transnational corporations in fact facilitate recolonisation of [unwary] Africans that are made to erroneously believe that postmodernism entails freedom, when in fact postmodernism supports projects of the New World Order including the flattening of Africa and the creation of anarchy or order in chaos. Ideologies in support of the New World Order are being deployed to deterritorialise Africans by dissipating, disembedding and displacing their subjectivities from their territories and communities including from their resources (see for instance Tomlison, 2012; Patton, 2010). By disembedding and displacing African subjectivities from their territories and from their resources, the subjectivities are transposed from their territories to the realm of the global and transnational in which territorial resources are locally devalued, and therefore left to transnational exploitation. Deterritorialisation of African subjectivities also displaces and disembeds African states whose power is increasingly replaced with the more virulent power and hegemony of the transnational corporations and institutions whose ambition is unbridled planetary profits (Ortiz, 2016).

Thus, while contemporary scholars like Deleuze and Guattari call for an absolute form of deterritorialisation that would be "called the creator of a new earth", of a new land-of a new land, a universe (Crockett, 2013: 173), deterritorialisation often relies on terror including the instigation of civil wars and internal conflicts, directly or via proxies (Lunstrum, 2009). Looked at more closely, processes of deterritorialisation began with the colonisation of Africa when colonial and imperial ideologies such as about presence of savagery, barbarity, backwardness, underdevelopment, poverty, helplessness etc. were meant to displace African subjectivities from their attachments with territory, resources and with African institutions. So, to frighten Africans out of commitment and attachment to their communities, societies, cultures, polities and resources, (neo-)imperialism uses ideological terrorism that involves presenting frightening media images about often exaggerated African problems (Nhemachena, 2016). In other words, colonial and imperial processes and ideologies that were meant to cause disaffection between Africans, about Africans' own institutions etc. were effectively deterritorialisation processes with the aim of displacing and disembedding Africans' subjectivities from one another and from their own institutions as part and parcel of the colonisation process, that needed Africans to open up their psychological spaces [and not only physical ones] for effective penetration by colonists. Openness of Africa, for [physical and psychological] penetration and economic dispossession and exploitation has been crucial for colonists and it is still supported and funded by organisations such as the Soros Foundation's Open Society Initiative (Sundstrom, 2006; Peizer, 2005; Fosshagen, 2014; Silova et al, 2008; Sudetic, 2011). Thus, with reference to the Arab spring, Fosshagen (2014: 13) notes:

> The US government allegedly spent $334, 3 million on NGOs in Egypt over 14 years, and in 2010 alone the NED spent around $2 million on grants to youth organisations...In Tunisia and Egypt, Western foundations, such as Freedom House, the International Republican Institute, the Ford Foundation, the Open Society Foundations (founded by Soros and until 2011 known as the Open Society Institute), and NED, substantially funded NGOs working for regime change in the years leading up to the uprising...

One of the contemporary forms of deterritorialisation, and disembedding of Africans from their national, cultural and continental contexts, is underscored by the Global Research (3 June 2014) as involving the use of social media. Global Research (3 June 2014) states thus:

What is new about the template bears on the use of the internet (in particular chat rooms, instant messaging and blog sites) and cell-phones (including text messaging), to rapidly steer angry and suggestible "Generation X" youths into and out of mass demonstrations and the like-a capability that only emerged in the mid-1990s…the US military and National Security Agency subsidized the development of the internet, cellular phones, and software platforms. From their inception, these technologies were studied and experimented with in order to find the optimal use in a new kind of warfare. The "revolution" in warfare that such new instruments permit has been pushed to the extreme by several specialists in psychological warfare…This new philosophy of war,…as enhanced by modern technologies, is intended to aid both military and non-military assaults against targeted states through what are, in effect, 'hi tech' hordes" [youth movement insurgencies]…states with traditional cultures could be destabilised, thereby creating the possibility of a global civilisation. There are two requirements for such a transformation…building internationally committed networks of international and locally committed organisations and creating global events through the transformation of a local event into one having virtually instantaneous international implications through mass media…In the aftermath of such youth deployments and media operations more traditional elements come to the fore that is, the forceful, if covert, intervention by international institutions and governments threatening the targeted regime, and using well-placed operatives within the targeted regimes' military and intelligence services to ensure no countermeasures can be effectively deployed.

The deterritorialisation of Africans and other peoples of the global south does not only involve the imposition of transnational, unelected, unaccountable regimes on formerly independent states without a semblance of public consent (New American, 1 September 2014); it also involves setting up international institutions including international courts that displace and disembed state and continental institutions. The constitution of the troubled International Criminal Court and the recent constitution of the "International Tribunal for the Rights of Nature and Mother Earth" (Maloney, 2015; The Guardian, 10 December 2014; Christina, 2010) speak to efforts to

14

deterritorialise African states and African people as well as the generality of peoples of the global south by effacing their own institutions.

Couched as the protection of rights of nature, even if paradoxically such international institutions are funded by transnational corporations that exploit nature, the institutions often hide the real goal which is to deterritorialise, displace and disembed African subjectivities from their territories while offering the façade that the funding transnational corporations and institutions serve to protect diversity of life in the former colonial states. Unfortunately the contemporary Western [alias international] protectionism simply replicates the [now] discredited colonial ideologies of protection and protectionist treaties, on African people that they sought to colonise. The setting up of extraterritorial institutions including courts can be likened to the colonial ideologies that presumed that Africans and their environments could only be saved by colonial [extraterritorial] protectionism. Similarly, subsumed under the emergent 'International Tribunal for the Rights of Nature and Mother Earth' are colonial animistic assumptions. To the extent that animistic assumptions hold that Africans cannot be distinguished from their environments, including animals (Christina, 2010), contemporary international institutions premised on animistic assumptions replicate the colonial caricaturing of Africans [and people of the global south] as brutes, animals, savages, raw, barbaric, incapable of ownership of their resources, lacking scientific knowledge etc. (Nhemachena, 2016).

In order to pre-empt African struggles for ownership and control over their resources, there is increasing popularisation of colonial ideologies of animism that seek to put Africans and their natural resources on the same plane, as is evidenced by the emergent theorisations around what is called symmetrical anthropology (Latour, 2005). While there is popularisation in some scholarship of the notion that the environmental problems in the world originate from anthropocentrism and binaries, it is clear from African struggles for restitution and reclamation that the problem for them is in the failure by (neo-) imperial people to restitute and return what they have been looting since the enslavement and colonial eras (see also

Nhemachena, 2016). Efforts to legitimise colonial ideologies of animism are being made across disciplines in various academies where ideologies that portray nature as 'mother', 'father', 'God' etc. are being proliferated in disciplines such as environmental law/jurisprudence where there is also increasing popularisation of what is called 'Earth Jurisprudence' (Pelizzon, 2015; Maloney, 2015), Rights of nature; in environmental studies where nature and human beings are collapsed together as actors or as having agency; in science and technology studies where ideologies of posthumanism are being proliferated. Thus, Pelizzon (2015) notes that there is emerging legal theory known as Earth Jurisprudence and that one of the novel proposals of this theory is the granting of subjective legal status to nature and the consequent foreclosure of claims to property by some human beings in the world. The point here is that the supposed recognition of the subjective status of nature is meant to foreclose increasing African claims to their environment, minerals, water, forests etc. as their property. In this sense, the supposedly new jurisprudence and new ontologies that are being popularised have recursive and indeed atavistic effects in so far as they forestall redress to colonial looting of African resources and property.

International civil society organisations, some of which are funded by the same transnational corporations purporting to protect African resources have been increasingly deployed to influence [in the direction of deterritorialisation] the domestic legislative processes in Africa. In this vein, Global Research (13 April 2007) states that: "The United States also directly funds a number of civil society organisations (NGOs) and provides them with training and technical assistance to help them to advocate...In other words so called civil society organisations are being paid and trained to influence legislation in an amenable manner for Western interests". In this vein, armies of civil society organisations populate the African territories to ensure that Africans sign "neoprotectionist" treaties in the form of the ICC and the new 'International Tribunal for the Rights of Nature and Mother Earth' and in all this, little if any cognisance is taken of the resilient logics of colonial "protectionism". Thus, Maloney (2015) notes that the newly created 'International Tribunal for the Rights of Nature and Mother Earth' was created by

International Civil Society Network called 'The Global Alliance for the Rights of Nature', formed in 2010. Maloney further notes that the tribunal has emerged from civil society organisations and not from state-centred international law. While Maloney (ibid) celebrates civil society networks in the setting up of the 'International Tribunal for the Rights of Nature', Global Research (15 March 2016) shows connections between organisations such as Amnesty International, Human Rights Watch etc. with top state officials. Global Research (15 March 2016) states thus: "…it's also a well-documented fact that America's CIA and Pentagon intelligence departments have used an array of charities, and organisations, and even religious missionary organisations as fronts for conducting espionage overseas, and with the prime directive to further foreign policy objectives".

Instead of correctly understanding the problem in terms of African and other people in the global south's calls for restitution and reclamation of resources, the civil society organisations erroneously portray the problem in terms of anthropocentrism wherein the erroneous solution suggested is the creation of assemblage of earth community of humans and nonhumans. Thus, rather than recognising the right to restitution and reclamation, the decoy of rights of nature simply states that all beings have the right to exist, right to habitat or a place to be and the right to participate in the "earth community" (Maloney, 2015). Much like in the colonial era, the rights that are mooted in the supposed Earth Jurisprudence and in the tribunal, that some celebrate, deny Africans the right to own their property- thus Africans [put by such ideologies on the same plane with animals] are simply permitted to exist, to have habitat, to have places to be and to participate in the "earth community" but without rights of restitution and ownership of their resources.

Similarly, much like during the colonial era when precolonial African states were dismantled and disarmed as a precursor to colonisation, contemporary antipathy against African states are hidden in discourses about the outdatedness of the Westphalian principle, from which African states are erroneously narrowly deemed to originate (Fidler, 2004). Thus, the intended dismemberment, 'excision' and 'circumcision' of the African states is being legitimised in terms of Westphalian ideologies that erroneously presume that no states existed in Africa prior to colonialism. Cast in terms of Westphalianism, African states are now being coaxed and coerced to demilitarise and demobilise; the states are paradoxically being replaced with transnational private military corporations and private security corporations (Singer, 2006; Pingeot, 2014; African Business, 22 November 2012; Fulloon, n.d.; News24, 29 March 2015) that are owned and controlled by the same transnational corporations some of which spearheaded the original colonial process. Thus, Singer (2006) notes that more weapons are now in private hands than in public stocks and the number of areas of instability have increased mainly because there is a shift towards the outsourcing and privatisation of state services including provision of military and security services.

'Order in chaos' or **order out of disorder** or *ordo ab chao* is the name that has been given to what will increasingly transpire as the Western architects of the New World Order hack down African states while at the same time heralding the supremacy of their transnational corporations plus their private armies that are already rearing their heads on the continent. From computer studies, mechanics, engineering, medical management, architecture, geometry, astronomy, physics, criminology to politics one witnesses the increasing popularisation of chaos theories [together with turbulence, anarchism, catastrophe theory, quantum mechanics etc.] (Milovanovic, 1997; Kellert, 1993; Berdichevsky, 1997; Hayles, 1991; Peters, 1996; Augulis et al, 2010; De Boer, 1999; Haken, 1985) that effectively prepares the world of the global south for ensuing induced chaos. Important to note in all this popularisation of chaos, anarchy, catastrophe, turbulence etc. is the presence of resilient logics of the centuries old Big Bang theories and Western logics that assume that creation only comes out of disorder, chaos, anarchy and the Big Bang; rather than from Godly orderly Creation *ex nihilo*. Important to note also in the popularisation of theories of order in chaos is that theories of chaos and anarchy were deployed by Westerners to justify their original colonisation of Africa which they falsely historically portrayed as in a precolonial chaotic Hobbesian state of nature (Nhemachena, 2017). In this respect, the popularisation of theories of anarchy, chaos, catastrophe etc. particularly at a time when there

18

is the new scramble for Africa and for its resources (Southall et al, 2009) is a cause for profound worry. The rehashing and (re-)popularisations of such theories speak to recolonisation and to the resilience of colonial templates. In other words, the New World Order threatens to be in fact an intensification of the Old Colonial World Order that is coming back in the guise of newness and transformation.

Locating Africans Back in the Mine Compounds: On the Resilience of Colonial Templates

The resilient colonial templates thrive on a form of invisibility or invisible absent presence (Nhemachena, 2016) which is hardly recognised by scholars who erroneously presume that it is only indigenous [people] knowledge and ownership of resources that have been rendered invisible by colonisation. Colonisation and recolonisation inherently thrive not merely on openness and visibility but also on invisibility and illegibility, and this is precisely why Marxist scholars wrote about ideologies being employed to create false consciousness: false consciousness underscores the fact that truth is rendered invisible and often inaccessible, through ideological machinations. In addition to making indigenous people and their knowledge invisible in the 'formal' domains, colonists sought to make their own colonial practices invisible, in what we call 'dual invisibilities'. The colonial decimation of indigenous people through conjurations of diseases as pointed out above underscores the colonists' reliance on invisible occultic actions at a distance. Whereas scholars like Ndlovu-Gatsheni (2013; n.d.) notes the existence of the invisible global matrix of power that continues to smoother and suffocate Africa, scholars like Gibson-Graham (2005) focus on indigenous epistemologies that have been rendered invisible by colonial epistemologies and practices. In this respect, scholars on transformation need to keep in mind these 'dual invisibilities' if they are to create meaningful transformation for Africans, and the global south more generally. It is a new world, as Gibson-Graham (2005: 5) argues that would utilise the sociology of absences [but including the absent presence of invisible global matrices of power] to resurface what has been rendered invisible: "The task of sociology of absences is to focus on what has been 'disqualified and rendered invisible, unintelligible, or irreversibly discardable" and to make the non-credible, the non-existent present as alternatives to hegemonic experience".

When empire portrayed Africans and other people of the global south as indistinct from animals, as savages, barbaric, bestial etc. (Magubane, 2007; Nhemachena, 2016), it sought to render intelligible and invisible its abuses [including dispossession and exploitation] of African human rights during the enslavement and colonial eras. Similarly when more recent writers and scholars propose to put nature including animals [in the guise of granting liberal personhood rights to nature] on the same plane with people of the global south (Stone, 1972: 456), the ultimate effect is to repeat the colonial denigration of such people's human rights by collapsing them together with animals and the rest of nature, and thus deny them property rights. In other words, considerations of Africans and other peoples of the global south as indistinct from animals are replicated by some contemporary scholars that, in this era of the new scramble for African resources (Southall et al, 2009) seek to deny Africans autonomy and sovereignty over their resources by collapsing them together with animals and nature in general. Thus, in the guise of protecting African and other environments in the global south, and in the guise of extending [juristic] personhood to animals and the environment in the global south, the West via its networks of "civil" society organisations is effectively collapsing indigenous people of the global south back into the colonial epoch in which they were treated as indistinct from animals and in which they were considered incapable of owning property of their own including livestock, land, rivers, trees, mines etc. The proponents of such changes are in effect re-enacting and reperforming the colonial templates at a moment when Africa is wary of the new scramble for its resources, and the increasing antipathy to its sovereignty and autonomy over its resources. Whether African persons are [erroneously] described as animals as during the colonial era or animals are described as African persons as in this contemporary era, the effect [which is to collapse them together] is the same and it has deleterious effects as colonial and enslavement histories testify.

While some have celebrated the granting of [juristic] personhood rights to rivers as in the recent cases of the Indian Ganges, Yamuna, jungles, streams, lakes, air, forests, wetlands, grasslands, glaciers, springs and waterfalls (BBC News, 5 April 2017) and the recent case of the New Zealand national park (New York Times, 13 July 2016); the effect of granting these rights do not differ from colonial practices. The fact that states and peoples of the global south would have to relinquish ownership of their resources that are deemed to have been granted juristic personhood and thus to have ceased to be resources or property (BBC News, 5 April 2017; New York Times, 13 July 2016; Stone, 1972) underline (neo-)colonial logics of expropriation of African property but via the guise of granting [juristic] personhood to the resources. Thus, the New York Times (13 July 2016) notes about the land in New Zealand that, the land became a legal entity and so the government had to give up formal ownership rights, powers, duties and liabilities of a legal person and that: "The settlement is a profound alternative to the human presumption of sovereignty over the natural world...Personhood means, among other things, that lawsuits can be brought on behalf of the land itself..." Similarly, arguing against human New Zealanders' claims to ownership of property, Vernon (2017) reports that: "The crown will not own the river bed. The river will own itself. That's the world leading innovation for a river system".

This denial of ownership of property to indigenous people via pretences of granting rights to nature is in stark contrast to the [apartheid style] planetary ownership and control over resources by transnational corporations some of which corporations even control the United Nations system (Teitelbaum, 2007; Korten, 2012; Inter Press Service News Agency, 22 September 2015). Given that some CEOs of transnational corporations meet over lunch at the UN with UN leadership to establish partnership and influence UN policy (Korten 2012), it is little wonder that the UN is accused of failing to control planetary dispossession, exploitation and abuses by TNCs. Thus, Teitelbaum (2007) argues:

The close collaboration with transnational corporations is institutionalised within the United Nations via the Global Compact, an alliance between the Secretariat of the UN and large corporations, many of which have long histories of human rights violations and corruption…heavy influence which transnational corporations have on the United Nations system. Institutionalised via the Global Compact, this is also exerted through private funding of UN programmes, projects, organs and organisations including the United Nations High Commission for Human Rights, which receives two thirds of its funding from the voluntary donations of nation states and private institutions…influence that transnational corporations have over some aspects of so-called "civil society"…

Thus, what has been made invisible by (neo-)colonial establishments is not only indigenous knowledge and indigenous people but Westerners also render invisible and unintelligible their processes of global apartheid and (re-)colonisation. Africa's mineral richness (Holl, 2000) is rendered invisible and unintelligible by Western discourses about the continent as irredeemably poor. Similarly African science is rendered invisible and unintelligible by Western discourses that portray Africans as mired in superstitious beliefs without any scientific rationality or logic of their own. While contemporary critiques of Cartesian dualisms and science purport to speak to decoloniality, the critiques begin from erroneous assumptions that Africans did not have their own science with own dualisms prior to colonisation (Nhemachena, 2016).When Westerners use their epistemologies to theorise African knowledge merely in terms of diffusion from other regions of the world (Holl, 2000: 8), these Westerners effectively render invisible and unintelligible precolonial African scientific mining knowledge. For purposes of this book, what is paradoxical is that scholars who utilise diffusionism to construe African knowledge about mining do not also apply diffusionism to construe Western knowledge; rather, the West is assumed to be the [natural] oracle of knowledge that it supposedly circulates to other parts of the world. The point here is, if African knowledge is not inherent but a result of diffusion, from where did the Western knowledge about mining diffuse also?

If Westerners did not require diffusion of knowledge from other parts of the world, why would Africans require such diffusion as the source of their knowledge? If Westerners own resources including outside their own Western states and hemisphere, why should Africans not also own their own [mining] resources? When postdevelopment scholars and thinkers encourage Africans to consider *alternatives* to Western development (Ziai, 2007; Gibson-Graham, 2005; Escobar, 2002) they in fact render invisible and unintelligible African quests for restitution and reclamation; in other words seeking alternatives presupposes forgetting about African resources and knowledge including about mining that have been stolen and looted by Westerners from Africa. To insists on alternatives as is often done by some scholars is akin to advising victims of dispossession, exploitation, raping and theft to simply forget about the rape, theft, dispossession, exploitation and merely focus on seeking alternatives to what has been looted, lost, expropriated and so on. It is an unsound solution that not even the Westerners would embrace if they suffered the same fate of enslavement and colonisation. To consider 'Western' knowledge to be indisputably Western is in fact to perform erasure of theft of knowledge and other resources because as Harding (1994) rightly observes, Western science has grown and developed by preying on the sciences of other people in the world.

Rendering the colonisation, dispossession and exploitation of Africans invisible and unintelligible, Western colonisers like the French have forced some West African countries since the 1960s to agree that they are indebted to French colonialism, which is considered by the French to have brought about development to Africa (Koutonin, 28 January 2014). While colonisers such as the French hold that Africans benefited from colonisation for which they are forced to pay debts, Lenoir (1 February 2004) states that:

> Millions of people on the continent and throughout the world have concluded that it is the countries of the Global North that are heavily indebted to African countries for over centuries of exploitation…the call for cancellation of the debt is increasingly being coupled with the demand that governments, corporations and leading institutions of the

23

Global North repair the harm to African nations and peoples of African descent for the effects of slavery, colonialism, and neoliberalism. Reparations-in particular, monetary damages for past wrongs-has been posed as a moral and legal obligation...The conference, held in Abuja, Nigeria, spelled out Africa's case for reparations. The Abuja Proclamation declared that the injury caused by slavery, colonialism and neo-colonialism is not a thing of the past, but is painfully manifest in the damaged lives of contemporary Africans from Harlem to Harare, in the damaged economies of the black world from Guinea to Guyana, from Somalia to Surinam....Jubilee partners in the global south note that a greater debt is owed to the south by northern nations as a result of slavery, the colonial and neo-colonial extraction of mineral wealth and other resources, and environmental damage resulting from northern policies and lifestyles.

Colonisers such as the French who have forced West African states since the 1960s to pay colonial debts to the French forget that even French economies were built on the backs of enslaved and colonised Africans and using the African [mining] resources that were looted. In fact, it has always been a strategy of the colonists since the beginning of the colonial era to consider Africans to be indebted to them. Colonial mine and farm owners who dispossessed and exploited Africans as cheap labour would grant "credit" to such Africans to purchase from the colonists' local stores, so that they would be "indebted" and bound to serve as cheap labour longer (Beckman, 2017). Also, much as colonists secured mining and other concessions from some African precolonial chiefs on the basis of vacuous promises to provide security, ammunition, monthly payments and so on; in the contemporary era, Western states and institutions are trying to win the hearts and minds of Africans but extending "phantom" aid that nevertheless creates senses of indebtedness by Africans to the West. As much as 60% of all donor pledges constitute phantom aid that does not materialise (VOA, 29 October 2009; The Guardian, 27 May 2005).

Thus, to argue as postdevelopment thinkers and scholars do (Andreasson, 2007; Escobar, 2014), that Africa and the global south simply need to adopt alternatives to [Western] economies and development is in fact an apology for colonisers such as the French that think they brought development and economies to Africa. It is in fact to argue that development was brought to Africa by Westerners and that Africa did not have its [subsequently usurped] development, economies and growth prior to colonisation. If transnational corporations are, as some of them are doing, looting African mineral resources, evading taxes, smuggling African minerals and other resources; holding onto and hiding African mineral exploration data (Mail & Guardian, 12 November 2012; Bulawayo24 News, 6 July 2014; BBC News, 14 March 2016; Lusaka Times, 16 Jan 2017; Ndikumana, 2013; Rego, 2003: 808-11; BBC News, 4 Dec 2012; Kwaramba et al, 2016a; Kwaramba et al, 2016b; The Guardian, 2 June 2015; Mail and Guardian, 15 July 2015; Institute for Security Studies, 5 July 2011; Mail and Guardian, 20 Sept 2014); the question for postdevelopment thinkers and scholars is why Africans should simply be encouraged to look for alternatives to development and to economic growth? The situation advocated for by postdevelopment thinkers and scholars is akin to advising a victim of robbery and looting to simply look for alternatives to what has been stolen. In essence it is akin to naturalising and ossifying colonial theft and robbery by advising the victims not to seek restitution and reclamation but instead to look for alternatives.

Africans whose precolonial economies, families, religions, education systems and states were destroyed by colonists (see for instance Fenske, 2012; Posselt, 1935; Austin, 2004; Jerven, 2016) are simply encouraged by some scholars and thinkers to seek alternatives to what was stolen. In fact what is happening in practice is that colonisers who have not made any apologies let alone payments of compensation for their debts of colonisation and enslavement (The Guardian, 20 August 2005) sponsor some academies (Warikandwa et al, 2017) to popularise considerations of alternatives to seeking restitutions and reclamation. Paying attention to such academies that do not privilege African aspirations, Nyamnjoh (2012) describes them as *excelling in irrelevance* on the continent of Africa. In the context of this book, the million dollar question for scholars that always emphasise on Africans adopting alternatives is; what alternative resources can Africans own in a world where their own resources have been looted since the beginning of colonisation and in a world where capital continues to trawl the world, including in space, to lay claim to whatever is valuable?

Much as during the colonial era when colonially dispossessed, exploited and estranged Africans were compensated through colonial liberal freedoms to have sex, to prostitute, to engage in homosexuality, bestiality and so on (van Onselen, 1976: 175-6 cited in Epprecht, 2013), empire continues to extend [mere] liberal freedoms of these sorts to Africans whose rights to restitution and reclamation the imperial powers do not want to acknowledge and effect. Indeed (neo-)imperial liberal freedoms to have sex, to prostitute, to engage in homosexuality, to engage in bestiality and so on have come to foreshadow rights to materialities including restitution and compensation for colonial and enslavement era looting and exploitation. Thus, Epprecht (2013: 9) notes:

> For van Onselen, sex in the service industry helped to secure a relatively docile labour force with minimal expenditure on wages, social services, and urban infrastructure-distracted and presumably demoralised by sexually sordid affairs,…the men were disabled from organising effective resistance against appalling working and living conditions…Nongoloza, alias Jan Note, had purportedly ordered his men to have sex with each other or with boy servants rather than with women sometime in the mid-1890s.

Similar ways in which liberalisation of sexual freedoms cushioned early imperial economies in South Africa are noted by Thusi (2015: 210-1) thus:

> Sex work kept the morale of the seamen high after long voyages…an officer warned about the potential for unrestrained homosexuality where there were restrictions on male seamen's sexual interactions stating, 'far more than half of the young men quartered [in a barrack that banned concubinage] were guilty of practising unnatural vices [including male-male sex]'…Sex work was in this way encouraged although feared, because colonial authorities did not want men to resort to homosexuality because they were not provided with

alternative forms of sexual release…Engaging sex work ensured that men would not lose all their "sensibilities" by delving into homosexual absence from Europe.

Thus, Africans and the global south more generally that has been dispossessed, exploited and estranged are often compensated using liberal freedoms so as to distract their attention from reclaiming their resources. So, busy with free sex, homosexuality, bestiality, prostitution and other liberal [idealistic] *cul-de-sac* freedoms, Africans are supposed to fail to wake up to the gargantual material dispossession and exploitation to which they continue to be subjected. In fact (neo-)empire does not stop multiplying liberal forms of entertainment [with their own forms of frustration] for Africans that would hopefully keep them busy and distract attention from transnational looting of mineral and other resources, despite independence. Even though they are granted the right to life and the right to freedoms of movement, Africans are not even allowed to migrate to Euro-American countries [some of which have erected hi-tech systems of fences and detection devices at their borders] where paradoxically their looted resources go; as is evident in contemporary efforts to curb African migrants to Europe and to America (Reuters, 13 October 2016; The Guardian, 26 January 2017; Kohnert, 2007). Thus, Kohnert (2007: 12) observes that: "Because of more rigid migration controls of EU member states, the sealing off of its southern borders and of the coastal line between Morocco and Mauritania against the increasing influx of irregular migrants, migration routes shifted increasingly to sea-born alternatives, notably from Senegal, Gambia and Guinea to the Spanish Canary Islands…"

Granted imperial (neo-)liberal [phantom] freedoms except to get restitution and own their resources, Africans are so enslaved that they continue in the postcolonial era to pay colonial debts to those that have enslaved and closed them for centuries, in the vain belief that the colonists brought real freedom to Africa. It is not only the West African French colonies that continue to be mortgaged resource-wise and to pay debts for being enslaved and colonised but the entirety of the global south is currently paying debts for being colonised and enslaved. Openshaw et al (2015: 44-5) for instance examine similar logics of odious debts that Zimbabwe inherited at independence from the colonial Rhodesian government; much of this debt had been accumulated during the later years of the Rhodesian regime, after it had been ostracised by the international community and repeatedly denounced as "illegal" and "racist" by both the UN General Assembly and the Security Council. Similarly, Toussaint et al (2010) examine odious debts, which Africa continues to pay, incurred within the framework of the devastating International Monetary Fund's structural adjustment programs. In Southern Africa, News24 (22 April 2014) examines the agreement negotiated between the apartheid regime and Mandela's ANC that allowed whites to keep the best land, the mines, manufacturing plants, and financial institutions and to export vast quantities of capital while the ANC inherited the burden of apartheid era debts [to the tune of billions annually]. It is stated by News24 (ibid) thus: "As a consequence, the state cannot grow its economy and create jobs because huge chunks of GDP goes to the IMF and most of the profits generated by mines and banks in South Africa are invested offshore as part of the conditions of the loan taken by the apartheid government and the political opportunist Council of a Transitional Government called the TEC".

Although African Renaissance has been launched in a context where the United States of Africa and Pan-Africanism are increasingly popularised (Maloka, 2001; Nyerere, 1963; The Guardian, 21 January 2013; Reuters 27 January 2010), some of the outspoken proponents [such as the late Gaddafi; Kwame Nkrumah and Nyerere] of United States of Africa, African unity and Pan-Africanism have attracted the condemnation of the imperial order from which, for instance, Gaddafi sought to delink Africa. The fact that African leaders who genuinely make efforts to transfer ownership of [mineral] resources and their proceeds to the African people are subjected to coups and assassinations is not difficult to understand particularly when one takes into account the fact that international institutions that purport to be guardians of peace and human rights get funding from the same transnational corporations that monopolise and exploit Africans and their [mineral] resources. The murder of the nationalist Burkinabe leader Thomas Sankara; the murder of the Congolese leader Patrice Lumumba and the staging of a coup against Kwame Nkrumah (de Witte, 2002; Kini-Yen, 2015; Owusu, 2006), [all of them genuinely bent on reversing the colonial (neo-)imperial establishment in the interest of the African people] can be understood in terms of (neo-)imperial resistance to changes that would reverse the old colonial order of dispossession and exploitation of Africans.

Despite the recent slant towards American nationalism by the American President Donald Trump, (Daily Mail, 21 February 2017; The Guardian, 21 February 2017), African nationalism, Pan Africanism and African Renaissance continue to be demonised as promoting nativism, [which allegedly promotes the much maligned 'essentialist' African identity and culture] rather than cosmopolitanism (Mbembe, 2014). This Western opposition to African nationalism and nativism is paradoxical in that the same Western states that are critical of African nationalism and nativism defend their own borders, block African migration to Euro-American regions, in other words they defend their own Western nations and variants of [predatory] nativism. In other words, Westerners whose nationalism and nativism, are by virtue of being predatory, erroneously described as the international are paradoxically virulent in criticising African nativism and nationalism even if these, latter, are not as cancerous as the forms of Western nationalism and nativism that do not obey their borders and boundaries.

It would be inequitable to expect Africans to uncritically open up to Western cosmopolitanism in a context where the supposed cosmopolitans [who after all trawl for African resources] are shutting their borders in the faces of Africans, seeking to enter them. As Vambe et al (2007) argue; critiques of nativism trivialise the overall contributions of the politics of nativism in struggles for liberation of Africans. While noting the shortfalls of Black Economic Empowerment and indigenisation that benefit only the elite, Ndlovu-Gatsheni (2007: 12-23) similarly argues that:

> For one to understand the meaning and essence of nativism, intellectual care is needed that goes beyond the present, ahistorical dismissals of nativism as a 'catalogue of epistemological error, of

essentialist mystification, as masculinist appropriation of descent, as no more than anti-racist racism…Pan-Africanism also entails notions of 'regeneration', 'awakening', or 'renaissance' of Africa as well as the 'dream' of an Africa united in social, cultural, economic, and political spheres, predicated on the overarching spirit of solidarity among people of African descent.

As hinted above, it is not easy to realise African renaissance, Pan Africanism and the United States of Africa in a context where the subjectivities of Africans are manipulated including at a distance, by those in the world who stand to lose in the event of successes of African Renaissance, unity and Pan-Africanism. Entire Foundations and international institutions have been set up and deployed to deterritorialise and disembed the subjectivities of Africans from their states, communities and continent, including from their [mineral] resources (News24, 27 February 2013; Dice, 2014). While some may think that the Foundations' training of African and Asian bloggers in digital security, video making, message development and digital mapping is an act of philanthropy, the training is in fact meant to assist in poking revolutions such as in Egypt where young Egyptian activists were referred to as YouTube Generation" and supported by Freedom House to enhance their outreach, advocacy and effectiveness (News24, 27 February 2013). The idea, as Dice (2014) argues is to create a more technocratic era that entails the gradual appearance of a more controlled society dominated by a global elite with continuous surveillance over every citizen and to maintain an up-to-date, complete files, containing the most personal information about health or personal behaviour of the citizen in addition to the more customary data.

This emergent contrived New World Order is argued to be premised on Euro-American "full spectrum dominance" (Ryan, 2013; Korybko, 2015; Global Research, 21 May 2015) which is being operationalised via irregular [marked by protestors and insurgents across the world] warfare in the world. The ways in which full spectrum dominance is being effected are well captured by Korybko (2015: 9-25) thus:

Fifth columns will be formed less by secret agents and covert saboteurs and more by non-state actors that publicly behave as civilians. Social media and similar technologies will come to replace precision-guided munitions as the "surgical strike" capability of the aggressive party, and chat rooms and Facebook pages will become the new "militants' den". Instead of directly confronting targets on their home turf, proxy conflicts will be waged in their vicinity in order to destabilise their periphery...Ideology is another name for a human software virus...The virus "infects" individuals by working to change their political sentiments, and the idea is that once it finds one "victim", this individual will then actively "spread" their new ideas to others, leading to a political contagion...At its core, hybrid war is managed chaos. It begins as a virus that upends the social system of the targeted state...

Although the Pentagon is actively searching for ways to maximise the social media use to infiltrate the minds of many unaware future participants (Korybko, 2015: 33), there is also deployment of conventional military power across the world in an effort to secure and protect resources for Western transnational capital (Global Research, 21 May 2015). The Global Research (21 May 2015) observes that:

The Pentagon has become the primary resource extraction service for corporate capital. Whether it is Caspian sea oil and natural gas, rare earth minerals found in Africa, Libya's oil deposits or Venezuela oil, the U.S's increasingly hi-tech military is on the case...Russia has the world's largest deposits of natural gas and significant supplies of oil. The U.S has recently built military bases in Romania and Bulgaria and will soon be adding more in Albania. NATO has expanded eastward into Latvia, Lithuania and Estonia; right on Russia's border...calls for the break-up of Russia into many smaller pieces thus giving Western corporations better access to the vast resources available there...The entire U.S military empire is tied together using space technology. With military satellites in space the U.S can see virtually everything on the earth, can intercept all communications on the planet at any time.

Russia and China understand that the U.S military goal is to achieve "full spectrum dominance" on behalf of corporate capital.

Outlines of the Chapters

The chapters in this book offer both theoretical and empirical arguments and data that are necessary to critically approach the domain of African mining and environment in this age of transformation. The book dissects the entire spectrum from the everyday lives of miners to the global, transnational corporations and institutions that often fiddle in African mining.

In chapter two, Artwell Nhemachena and Esther Dhakwa forcefully argue that Africans, who have from as far back as the precolonial era, had their own mining, melting and smelting industries, have often been erroneously dismissed as unproductive and economically sterile, reduced to beneficiaries of Western humanitarian assistance, often receiving contentious and toxic genetically modified food handouts. They argue that Africans are deeply excluded from owning their own resources on the continent; and this exclusion is sadly ideologically legitimised by some bandwagonist media houses and some academics on the continent that also paradoxically evangelise political and social inclusion, but minus inclusion in ownership of material resources. In this sense, discourses that reduce Africans to beneficiaries of Western humanitarian assistance and that [presumed] inability, impotence and sterility of Africans to exploit their own resources have come to constitute discursive dispossession. Their chapter argues that dispossession of Africans since the era of enslavement and colonisation has not only involved direct physically violent and visibly evident expropriation of resources from Africans; it also argues that colonists have also used and still use carefully concocted discourses to legitimise and oil-up the processes of dispossession of Africans. In other words dispossessing people materially requires, as a correlative, dispossessing them also in ideological, epistemic, social, cultural, spiritual and political senses so that they become [cognitively] demobilised and defused for battling for repossession.

The chapter understands such cognitive demobilisation and diffusion as leading to what Bourdieu calls misrecognition or *meconnaissance*. Misrecognition refers to social practices of individual or collective misattribution made invisible through a displacement of understanding. Misrecognition is understood as referring to an everyday and dynamic social process where one thing is not recognised for what it is because it was not previously 'cognised' within the range of dispositions and propensities of the habitus of the persons confronting it. Instead the thing is attributed to another available realm of meaning, and in the process interests, inequities or other effects may be maintained whilst they remain concealed.

Njabulo Chipangura's chapter three critically examines the archaeological objects that the author recovered during excavations at Mutanda site in Zimbabwe. He argues that these objects confirmed that the major economic preoccupation of the residents at this site was linked to high temperature production activities associated with the making of gold. The argument in this chapter is that the high temperature technologies at Mutanda signify the use of the site predominantly for gold processing activities of the past. This seems highly likely because the site is located within the productively rich Manica- Mutare- Odzi (MMO) gold belt. As a result, the Mutanda cultural precinct is surrounded by artisanal and small scale miners (*makorokozas* in local parlance) who are exploiting this rich reef gold belt. Thus the second argument in this chapter is that since, in the first place, colonial miners displaced African precolonial miners from the site, contemporary African *makorokoza*s who are sadly described by other scholars as "illegal" miners can be understood simply as reclaiming these ancient sites of mineral wealth. There are several contemporary gold mining claims dotted throughout the range which are being reworked on by *makorokozas* and constitutes part of the ancient mining landscape of Mutanda. *Chikorokoza* is a popular Shona buzz word that has been used to describe gold mining by small scale miners who are themselves in local parlance referred to as *makorokozas*.

In chapter four, Phefumula Nyoni unpacks the identities and ways in which *zamazama* or small scale African miners derive livelihoods within the precarious conditions they find themselves in.

The chapter is based on research carried out in a mining site around Johannesburg that is, Roodepoort. Qualitative research in the form of key informant interviews with a number of participants found within the mining context was employed. The question of identities and connections of *zamazamas* is also being explored, that is, from the perspective of their lived experiences. Strategies on how the artisanal miners deal with the various challenges they face are also pursued in this work. The historical overview of mining practices in Africa, influence of contemporary mining practices on the sustainability of the mining activities as well as the questions of gender, "illegality" and "informality" are also considered. Whilst conventional literature has tended to project *zamazama* activities as tainted with 'illegality' and instability, the reality points to a group of persons successfully deriving their livelihoods from this form of mining and who have drawn from various forms of agency in dealing with the challenges frequently encountered.

Janet Munakamwe's chapter five powerfully argues that while non-formal mining plays a central role in poor households' livelihoods, it is a great concern that a lot of attention is given to the criminal aspect of the mining activity but not the destination of the 'illegally' mined minerals. Her research examined the issue of cross-border migration, with particular reference to the working lives and career aspirations of women and men who are finding a livelihood by working in abandoned and closed mines in Durban Deep, Johannesburg, South Africa. The chapter documents the activities involved, socio-economic dynamics including aspects of power and resistance as they relate to the non-formal economy. Janet's ethnographic research which is the basis of this chapter included direct observations and in-depth interviews with participants and key players in the gold mining value chain which occurs outside of formal mines. Preliminary findings showed that there is a symbiotic link between formal and non-formal mining as the two come to a convergence between level 3 and 5 of the commodity value chains which are international markets and elite multinational companies. She argues that non-formal mining activities are as a result of economic exclusion including inequalities and that by engaging in such activities, zamazama are reclaiming what belong to them through passive resistance. The research also demonstrated that while these workers lack a formal political voice, they however, have developed their own strategies of passive resistance to police brutality as they also demand gold trading licenses.

In chapter six, Artwell Nhemachena and Christopher Dick Sagoe critically examine the conventional notion that transnational mining corporations constitute investments for Africa. They argue that the transnational corporate mining activities often involve competition with local farmers over the use of fertile land meant for crop farming. The authors argue that to simplistically consider such transnational corporate mining activities as investments ignores the fact that their activities often destroy the livelihoods of the local people in most mining communities in Ghana, and the rest of Africa. Thus, the more corporate mining activities there are, the greater the risks for the local people who lose their autonomous local livelihood activities. In this way, there is a paradox in that corporate mining activities which destroy local economic autonomy and sovereignty are conventionally deemed to constitute investments for Africa. Further, while the law is ordinarily expected to balance interests and rights of citizens, Ghanaian mining laws and state institutions which regulate the activities of corporate mining companies, enforce environmental laws and protect the interest of the indigenous people have sometimes failed to protect the interests of the local indigenous people. This failure results in intensive environmental degradation with further negative implications on the livelihoods of the local people who depend heavily on the natural environment.

Oliver Mtapuri's chapter seven valiantly argues that because of the importance of mining to communities, a counter narrative is required on the kind of freedom and liberation that enables current and future African generations to benefit from those resources, with impunity for themselves and their posterity in order to ignite a new form of accumulation which he calls emancipatory accumulation by re-possession. Emancipatory accumulation by re-possession is characterised by the accumulation of assets, mineral wealth, biodiversity, and flora and fauna for the benefit of indigenous communities. Repossession means taking back what belongs to the 'sons and daughters of the soil' by all means possible led by an indigenous intelligentsia with community interests at heart in an organic process of indigenisation. Mtapuri argues that it was during the colonial times when African possessions were forcefully confiscated and seized with no compensation. The land, the flora and fauna and the creatures that crept on them, the sheep, the goats, cows, the ducks, their wildlife and all livestock and harvests were all appropriated by colonists with unprecedented brute force and ruthlessness. Mtapuri laments the fact that when the indigenous communities tried to reclaim what belonged to them, they were labelled thieves for their harvests, livestock and land; and poachers for their wildlife - in their own lands. The changed landscape was reinforced by the proclamation of laws and regulations that sanctified property rights to the extent that indigenous communities were stripped of their rights to their property and all that belonged to them, to induce total dispossession. Those rights were unjustly and illegally transferred to the colonists and their children. Therefore, Mtapuri argues, repossession without compensation and no regrets becomes imperative in the interest of social, economic and emancipatory justice.

Tapiwa V Warikandwa and Ndatega V Asheela's chapter eight critically focuses on the creation of a Pan-Africanist mining regulatory framework and how Africans can draw lessons from the precolonial customary law based mining practices. The authors argue that it is regrettable that the customary law regulated, traditional community-centred mining practices were supplanted and replaced by exploitative neo-liberal, free market-based mining regulatory frameworks which focus on the natural resources benefiting foreign investors with little accruing to communities from which such resources have been mined. Warikandwa and Ndatega proceed to argue that while the argument has often been that African countries cannot do without the capital injection from Western investors, as mining is a capital intensive business venture, other African leaders have rightly been critical of dependence on Western lending institutions. They use the example of Burkina Faso under the leadership of the robust Pan-African president, Thomas Sankara, who proved that African countries can become independent of traditional Western lending institutions such as the International

Monetary Fund (IMF) and World Bank (WB) and run their economies through positively exploiting their mineral resources in the best interest of their people.

In chapter nine, Howard Chitimira and Moment Tembo examine corporate social responsibility and the adequacy of mining laws in Zimbabwe. They argue that Zimbabwe has made considerable efforts to enact some relevant environmental and other related mining legislation prior to, and subsequent to 1980. They give the example of key legislation such as the Mines and Minerals Act and the Environmental Management Act that were enacted. They also note that the government's efforts to enhance the protection of the environment and minerals were recently buttressed by the entrenchment of environmental rights in the current Zimbabwean Constitution. In spite of these accolades, Chitimira and Tembo remain critical about the fact that the growth of the Zimbabwean mining sector has been consistently impeded by the enactment of inadequate mining laws, poor enforcement of such laws by the enforcement authorities, corruption and the lack of robust CSR related mining policies since 1980.

Jean-Pierre Wome's chapter ten critically examines natural resource partitioning and exploitation by the Cameroonian Government in relation to speculated economic output. Wome notes that the identification and classification of targeted mineral reserves within the country's geographical territory has been a subject of consideration from the birth of the independent state of Cameroon. However, colonial administration prevailed prior to this period and it contributed significantly in developing formal administrative structures governing natural resource exploitation in the modern state of Cameroon. For Wome, with the aid of the formal administrative structures, targeted mineral reserves have been identified and programmed for present and future exploitations. Thus, Wome critically examines the policies and political interplays affecting resource partitioning and exploitation in Cameroon.

In chapter eleven, Michelle Munyanduki provides an evaluation on how Namibia currently deals with the social and environmental aspects of sustainable development with a particular focus on the corporate social responsibility (CSR) and rehabilitation in the uranium mining industry. Her central question is; to what extent is the current status of the mining industry aligned with sustainable development?

Tapiwa V Warikandwa and Artwell Nhemachena's chapter twelve argues that the minerals sector in Africa still remains a fundamental component for realising sustainable development on the continent. The authors argue that these mineral reserves are largely unexplored and offer unique opportunities for Africa to realise significant economic growth. Warikandwa and Nhemachena proceed to argue that this serves as a reason why Africa is constantly being courted by suitors who are looking for reliability and security of supply of mineral commodities. The authors point out that all the suitors have a clear and focused strategy on what they want from Africa; to exploit African resources and maximise on their gains at little or no cost. The suitors' interest is not on the welfare of poor Africans or the development of the continent. It is in this regard that Africa has to develop a coherent strategy in response to the exploitative agenda set by the foreign investors as assisted by global monetary institutions such as the World Bank and the International Monetary Fund. Warikandwa and Nhemachena further argue that Africa must leverage the increased competition for its natural resources and maximise on such opportunities to realise development. However, for this to happen there is need for a paradigm shift. Africans must realise that they are capable of running the mining industry on their own without relying heavily on the West and Asia. Investing in a Pan-African mining education and regulatory regime would be the starting point.

References

African Business, (22 November 2012). Is Private Security Taking Over? Africanbusinessmagazine.com/uncategorised/is-private-security-taking-over-africa/

Al Africa., (2 April 2015). South Africa: The Fall of Cecil John Rhodes and the Rise of Blackpower, allafrica.com/stories/201504031520.html

AllAfrica, (25 Feb 2016). Africa: Tackle Tax Evasion to Fuel Africa's Development, allafrica.com stories/2016 02261373.html

An Dorp, M., (2016). *How Shell, Total and Eni Benefit from Tax Breaks in Nigeria's Gas Industry: the Case of Nigeria Liquefied Natural Gas Company (NLNG)*. Amsterdam

Andrae, G. *et al.*, (1999). *Union Power in the Nigerian Textile Industry: Labour Regime and Adjustment.* Transaction Publishers: New Brunswick

Andreasson, S., (2007). Thinking Beyond Development: the Future of Postdevelopment Theory in Southern Africa, Prepared for the British International Studies Association Annual Conference, University of Cambridge 17-19 December 2007

Augulis, R. *et al.*, (2010). Quest for Order in Chaos: Hidden Repulsive Level Statistics in Disordered Quantum Nanoaggregates, in *The Journal of Physical Chemistry Letter* vol 1 (19): 2911-2916

Avant, D. D., (2005). *The Market for Force: The Consequences of Privatising Security.* Cambridge University Press

Avant, D., (2012). Mercenaries, in Blackwell Encyclopedia of Globalisation. DOI:10.1002/9780470670590.wberg

Baum, J. A. C. *et al.*, (2009). Outsourcing War: The Evolution of the Private Military Industry After the Cold War, Rotman School of Management, University of Toronto, Ontario: 1-53

BBC News, (4 Dec 2012). Corporate Tax Avoidance: How Do Companies Do It? www.bbc.com/news/business-20580545

BBC News, (14 March 2016). Zimbabwe's Robert Mugabe: Foreign Companies 'Stole Diamonds' www.bbc.com/news/world-africa-35720912

BBC News, (28 June 2010). Diamonds: Does the Kimberley Process Work. www.bbc.com/news/10307046

BBC News., (5 April 2017). Could Making the Ganges a Person Save India's Holiest River? www.bbc.com/news/world-asia-india-39488527

Beckman, R., (2017). *Colonial and Postcolonial Africa.* New York: The Rosen Publishing Group, Inc.

Bisson, M. S., (1982). Trade and Tribute: Archaeological Evidence for the Origins of States in South Central Africa, in *Cahiers d'etudes africaines* volume 22, No 87: 343-361

Boaduo, N. A. P., (2012). African Renaissance in the Contemporary Era of the African Union: Re-Thinking Strategies for Africa's Industrial and Economic Development, in *International Journal of Developing Societies* vol 1 (3): 124-132

Boehringer, G., (2016). Rights of Nature and Human Rights vol 41 (4), in ALTL J: 285

Botes, A., (2013). The History of Labour Hire in Namibia: A Lesson for South Africa vol 16, No 1 PER/PELJ: 507-536

Boyle, F. A. (2013). *Destroying Libya and World Order: The Three Decades U.S Campaign to Terminate the Gaddafi Revolution.* Atlanta: Clarity Press Inc.

Bulawayo24News, (6 July 2014). Canadian Firm Hides Zimbabwean Mineral Data, bulawayo24.com/index-id-news-sc-national-byo-50116.html

Butler, J. et al., (2013). *Dispossession: The Performative in the Political.* Polity Press: Cambridge

Caroline, V., (2010). Mercenaries and the State: How the Hybridization of the Armed Forces is Changing the Face of National Security, PhD thesis, The London School of Economics and Political Science

Christina, A., (2016). *Defending Human Rights and Democracy in the Era of Globalisation (Advances in Religious and Cultural Studies).* IGI Global

Chukwuemeka, E. *et al.*, (2011). African Underdevelopment and the Multinationals-A Political Commentary, in *Journal of Sustainable Development* vol 4, No 4

Cook, N. D., (1998). *Born to Die: Disease and New World Order, 1492-1650.* Cambridge University Press

Crockett, C., (2013). *Deleuze Beyond Badiou: Ontology, Multiplicity and Event.* Columbia University Press

Daily Mail, (21 February 2017). Zimbabwe's Mugabe Praises Trump's America First Policy Because it Resonates with His Own Thinking and Urges the World to Give Him Time, www.dailymail.com/uk/news/article-4244554/zimbabwe's-mugabe-turns-93-says-stand-2018-polls-html

De Balzac, H., (1991). *Pere Goriot [A new Translation by A J Krailsheimer].* Oxford: Oxford University Press

De Boer, J., (1999). Order in Chaos: Modelling Medical Management in Disasters, *EUR J Emerg Med* vol 6 (2): 141-8

de Leon, N. *et al.*, (1998). Order in Chaos and the Dynamics and Kinetics of Unimolecular Conformational Isomerization, in *The Journal of Chemical Physics*, vol 91 Issue 6

de Witte, L., (2002). *The Assassination of Lumumba*. London and New York: Verso

Dean, J. *et al.* (2004). *Empire's New Clothes: Reading Hardt and Negri*. Routledge

Dice, M., (2014). *Inside the Illuminati: Evidence, Objectives, and Methods of Operation*. The Resistance

Edoho, F. M., (2015). Entrepreneurship Paradigm and Economic Renaissance in Africa, in *African Journal of Economic and Management Studies* vol 6 Issue 1: 2-16

Eko, S. S., (2015). *Being Black Not Much Has Changed: Then, Now and the Way Forward*. Dorrance Publishing

Epprecht, M., (2013). *Hungochani: The History of Dissident Sexuality in Southern Africa*. Montreal: McGill-Queen University Press

Escobar, A., (2010). Worlds and Knowledges Otherwise: The Latin American Modernity/Coloniality Research Program, in Mignolo W D *et al*, (eds). *Globalisation and the Decolonial Option*. Routledge: London: 33-64

Escobar, A., (2014). Degrowth, Postdevelopment, and Transitions: a Preliminary Conversation, in Sustain Sci Springer DOI. 10.1007/s11625-015-0297-5

Fenske, J., (2012). Ecology, Trade and States in Pre-Colonial Africa, University of Oxford Dept of Economics MPRA Paper No 37372

Fosshagen, K., (2014). *Arab Spring: Uprisings, Powers, Interventions*. New York: Berghahn Books

Frye, E. L, (2005). Private Military Firms in the New World Order: How Redefining "Mercenary" Can Tame the "Dogs of War", in *Fordham Law Review* vol 73, Issue 6, Article 4, http://ir.lawnet.fordham.eedu/flr/vol73/iss6/4

Fulloon, M., (n.d). Non-State Actors: Defining Private Military Companies, in *Strategic Review for Southern Africa* vol 37, No 2: 29-51

Fyle, M. C., (1999). *Introduction to the History of African Civilisation: Precolonial Africa vol 1*. University Press of America, Inc. New York, Oxford

Garcia, Z., (2010). *Awaken to the New World Order*. Zen Garcia

Gibson-Graham, J. K., (2005). Surplus Possibilities: Postdevelopment and Community Economies, in *Singapore Journal of Tropical Geography* 26 (1): 4-26

Global Policy Forum (March/April 1998). Footsoldiers of the New World Order https://www.globalpolicy.org/component/content/article/190/39260.html

Global Policy Forum, (2 November 2011). Kimberley Process https://www.globalpolicy.org/the-dark-side-of-natural-resources-st/diamonds-in-conflict/kimberley-process.html

Global Research, (14 January 2015). France's Colonial Tax Still Enforced for Africa: Bleeding Africa and Feeding France" www.globalresearch.ca/frances-colonial-tax-still-enforced-for-africa-bleeding-africa-and-feeding-france/5547512

Global Research. (15 March 2016). Smart Power and "The Human Rights Industrial Complex" www.globalresearch.ca/smart-power-and-the-human-rights-industrial-complex/5514739

Global Research, (21 May 2015). The Pentagon's Strategy for World Domination: Full Spectrum, from Asia to Africa www.globalresearch.ca/the-pentagons-strategy-for-world-domination-full-spectrum-dominance-from-asia-to-africa/5397514

Greer, A., (2014). Confusion on the Commons, in Books and Ideas, 8 December 2014. http://www.bookssandideas.net/confusion-on-the-commons.html

Hagger, H., (2010). *The World Government*. John Hunt Publishing Washington

Hagger, N., (2013). *The Secret American Dream: The Creation of a New World Order with the Power to Abolish War, Poverty and Disease*. Watkins Publishing: London

Haken, H., (1985). Order in Chaos, in *Computer Methods in Applied Mechanics and Engineering*, vol 52, Issue 1-3: 635-652

Hammel, A *et al.*, (2000). Precolonial Mining in Southern Africa, in The Journal of the South African Institute of Mining and Metallurgy Jan/Feb: 49-56
https://www.saimm.co.za/jorunal/v100n01p049.pdf vol 100, issue 1

Hardt, M. and Negri, A., (2000). *Empire*. Cambridge: Harvard University Press

Hashim, Y. *et al.*, (1999). Cross-Border Trade and the Parallel Currency Market-Trade and Finance in the Context of Structural Adjustment: A Case Study from Kano, Nigeria Research Report No 113, Nordiska Afrikainstitutet Uppsala

Holl, A. F. C., (2000). Metals and Precolonial African Society, in Bisson M S *et al.*, (eds) *Ancient African Metallurgy: The Sociocultural Context*. Oxford: Lanham

Institute for Security Studies, (5 July 2011). Copper and Capital Flight: How Corporate Debt Becomes Public Debt https://issafrica.org/iss-today/copper-and--capital-flight-how-corporate-debt-becomes-public-debt

Inter Press Service News Agency. (22 September 2015). U.N Manipulated by Transnational Corporations, New Study Charges, www.ipsnews-net/2015/09/u-n-manipulated-by-transnational-corporations-new-study-charges/

Isla, A. *et al.*, (2014) Report of the Climate Change Conference (COP20), Lima, Peru, *Canadian Woman Studies* vol 31, No 1, 2: 44-49

Jerven, M., (2016). Capitalism in Pre-Colonial Africa: A Review: African Economic History Working Paper Series No 27/2016, Norwegian University of Life Sciences

Jun, N. *et al.*, (2011). *Deleuze and Ethics*. Edinburgh University Press

Kellert, S. H., (1993). *In the wake of Chaos: Unpredictable Order in Dynamical Systems*. Chicago and London: University of Chicago Press

Kini-Yen, K. F., (2015). *Pan-Africanism: Political Philosophy and Socio-Economic Anthropology for African Liberation and Governance*. African Book Collective

Klerck, G., (2003). Labour Market Regulation and the Casualisation of Employment in Namibia, In *South African Journal of Labour Relations*, vol 27, Issue 2: 63-95

Klerck, G., (2008). Industrial Relations in Namibia since Independence: Between Neo-Liberalism and Neo-Corporatism? In *Employee Relations* vol 30, Iss 4: 355-371

Klerck, G., (2009). Rise of Temporary Employment Industry in Namibia: A Regulatory 'Fix', in *Journal of Contemporary African Studies* vol 27, Issue 1: 85-103

Kohnert, D., (2007). African Migration to Europe: Obscured Responsibilities and Common Misconceptions, GIIGA Working Papers No 49

repec.giga-hamburg-de/pdf/giga_07_wp49_kohnert-pdf

Korten, D. C. (2012). The United Nations and the Corporate Agenda, in American Diplomacy.

www.unc-edu/depts/diplomat/AD_issues/amdip/_5/korten.html

Korybko, A., (2015). Hybrid Wars: the Indirect Adaptive Approach to Regime Change, Project of the Institute for Strategic Studies and Prediction PFUR, People's Friendship University of Russia

Kubicek, R. V., (1991). Mining: Patterns of Dependence and Development 1870-1930, in Konczacki Z A et al., (eds) *Studies in the Economic History of Southern Africa vol I* Frank CASS & Co Ltd. Abingdon: 64-86

Kwaramba, M. *et al.*, (2015). Capital Flight, Natural Resources and Institutions in Zimbabwe, Centre for the Study of African Economies (CSAE) Conference Oxford, UK, On Economic Development in Africa, 1-38

Kwaramba, M. *et al.*, (2016). Capital Flight and Trade Misinvoicing in Zimbabwe, in *African Development Review*, vol 28, Issue Supplement SI: 50-64

Kwaramba, M. *et al.*, (2016). Tax Rates, Economic Crisis and Tax Evasion: Evidence Using Zimbabwe and South Africa Bilateral Trade Flows ERSA Working Paper 593 Economic Research Southern Africa

Latour, B., (2005). *Reassembling the Social: An Introduction to Actor-Network Theory*. Oxford: Oxford University Press

Lenoir, G., (1 February 2004). Debt and Reparations: Probe International: Rethinking Foreign Aid, Restoring Accountability Reinvigorating Economies, http://journal.probeinternational.org/2004/02/01/debt-and-reparations/

Likuwa, K, (2014). Contract Labour System and Farm Labourers' Experiences in Pre-Independent Namibia, Historical Reflections, Perspectives and Lessons, BAB Working Paper No 2, Presented at Basler Afrika Bibliographien, Switzerland

Lloyd, J., (2015). *The Truth: New World Order.* Ebozon Publishing

Lunstrum, E., (2009). Terror, Territory, and Deterritorialization: Landscapes of Terror and the Unmaking of State Power in the Mozambican "Civil" War, in *Annals of the Association of American Geographers* vol 99 Issue 5: 884-892

Lusaka Times, (16 January 2017). Zambia Revenue Authority to Audit Large Mining Firms for Tax Compliance https://www.lusakatimes.com/2017/01/16/zambia-reenue-authority-audit-large-mining-firms-tax-compliance/

MacLean, R., (2015). Iron Working and the Iron Age in Africa, in Oxford Bibliographies, www.oxfordbibliographies.com/view/document/obo-9780199846733

MacMillan, K., (2006). *Sovereignty and Possession in the English New World: The Legal Foundations of Empire, 1576-1640.* Cambridge

Magubane, B . M., (2007). *Race and the Construction of the Dispensable Other.* Pretoria: UNISA

Mail & Guardian Africa, (15 July 2015). 'I Call that Robbery': Rich-Poor Tax Dispute Overshadows Key UN Development Summit in Ethiopia, mgafrica.com/article/2015-07-15-this-is-robbery-rich-poor-tax-dispute-oershadows-key-un-deelopment-summit-in-ethiopia

Mail & Guardian, (12 November 2012). Report Accuses Zimbabwe of Stealing Diamond Money, mg.co.za/article/2012-11-12-report-accuses-zimbabwe-of-stealing-diamond-money

Mail & Guardian, (20 September 2014). Inquiry into Lonmin Fee Transfer to Tax Haven, mg.co.za/article/2014-09-20-inquiry-into-lonmin-fee-transfers-to-tax-haven

Mail & Guardian, (21 Nov 2014). Clampdown on Tax Avoidance mg.co.za/article/2014-11-20-clampdown-on-tax-avoidance

Mail & Guardian, (22 August 2014). Iron Age Mining Links Ancient South Africa to the World mg.co.za/article/2014-08-15-iron-age-mining-links-ancient-sa-to-the-world

Mail & Guardian, (28 March 2013). Central African Republic: Is this What Our Soldiers Died For? Mg.co.za/article/2013-03-28-00-central-african-republic-is-this-what-our-soldiers-died-for

Mail & Guardian, (6 July 2016). How Much Do Governments Rake In? Mining Giants Come Clean on Taxes, mg.co.za/article/2016-07-06-00-mining-giants-come-clean-on-taxes

Mail & Guardian., (25 January 2016). Colonial Legacy of Mining Pioneers Poses a Dilemma for South Africa, https://mg.co.za/article/2016-01-25-colonial-legacy-of-mining-pioneers-poses-a-dilemma-for-south-africans

Maloka, E. T., (2001). The South African "African Renaissance" Debate: A Critique in *Polis/R.C.S.P/C.P.S.R* vol 8, Special Issue 1-10

Maloney, M., (2015). Finally Being Heard: the Great Barrier Reef and the International Rights of Nature Tribunal, in *Griffith Journal of Law & Human Dignity* vol 3, No 1: 40-58

Mbadlanyana, T, (n.d). Moral Politik and Realpolitik: Seeking Common Ground on the Use of Private Military and Security Companies, in Gumedze S, (ed) *From Market for Force to Market for Peace: Private Military and Security Companies in Peacekeeping Operations*, ISS Monograph no 183

Mbeki, M., (2000). Issues in South African Foreign Policy: The African Renaissance is Souls, in *Spring* 200 p 76-81

Mbembe, A., (2014). Ways of Seeing: Beyond the New Nativism, Introduction, *African Studies Review* vol 44, Issue 2: 1-14

Mbindwane, B, (25 May 2015). Soldiers for Hire: SA's Great Security Risk, in Daily Maverick https://www.dailymaerick.co.za/opinionsta/2015-05-25-soldiers-for-hire-sas-great-security-risk/

Mbindwane, B, (25 May 2015). Soldiers for Hire: SA's Great Security Risk, in Daily Maverick https://www.dailymaerick.co.za/opinionsta/2015-05-25-soldiers-for-hire-sas-great-security-risk/

Mentan, T., (2010). *The New World Order Ideology and Africa: Understanding and Appreciating Ambiguity, Deceit and Recapture of Decolonised Spaces.* Bamenda: Langaa RPCIG

Milovanoic, D., (1997). Postmodernist versus the Modernist Paradigm: Conceptual Differences, in Milovanoic D., (ed) *Chaos, Criminology, and Social Justice: the New Orderly (Dis)order.* London: Praeger

Mosley, P., (1977). Review, in *The Journal of Modern African Studies* vol 15, No 2: 328-330

Murray, A., (2015). Invisible Power, Visible Dispossession: The Witchcraft of a Subterranean Pipeline, in *Political Geography* 47: 64-76

Mzamane, M. V., (2001). Where there is no Vision the People Perish: Reflections on the African Renaissance, Hawke Institute Working Paper Series No 16, University of South Australia

Ndikumana, L, (2013). The Private Sector as Culprit and Victim of Corruption in Africa, Working Paper Series No 330

Ndlovu-Gatsheni, S. J., (2007). Tracking the Historical Roots of Post-Apartheid Citizenship Problems: The Native Club, Restless Natives, Panicking Settlers and the Politics of Nativism in South Africa, ASC Working Paper 72 African Studies Centre, Leiden, The Netherlands

Ndlovu-Gatsheni, S. J., (2013). *Coloniality of Power in Postcolonial Africa: Myths of Decolonisation.* Dakar: CODESRIA

Ndlovu-Gatsheni, S. J., (n.d). Global Coloniality and the Challenges of Creating African Futures, in *Strategic Review for Southern Africa* vol 36 (2): 181-202

Nellis, E., (2013). *Shaping the New World: African Slavery in the Americas, 1500-1888.* New York: University of Toronto Press

New American, (1 September 2014). Globalist Henry Kissinger Outlines "New World Order"
https://www.thenewamerican.com/world-news/item/19030-globalist-henry-kissinger-outlines-new-world-order

New American, (11 October 2012). The United Nations: On the Brink of Becoming a World Government, http://www.thenewamerican.com/world-new/item/13126-the-united-nations-on-the-brink-of-becoming-a-world-government

New Zimbabwe, (30 December 2014). Zimbabwe Still Fighting for Diamonds Seized in Belgium. www.newzimbabwe.com/news-19714-zimbabwe+still+fighting+for+seized+diamonds/news.aspx

News24, (29 March 2015). Private Security Industry Under Fire. www.news24.com/Archives/city-press/private-security-industry-under-fire-20150429

News24, (22 April 2014). How Mandela's ANC Sold Out the Economic Struggle. www.news24.com/elections/opinionand analysis/how-mandela-anc-sold-out-the-economic-struggle-20140422

News24, (27 February 2013). What we Can Learn from the Illuminati and Other Conspiracy Theories, www.news24.com/myNews24/What-we-can-learn-from-the-illuminati-and-otheer-conspiracy-theories-20130227

Nhemachena, A. (2015). Envisioning African Democracy in the Twenty-First Century: Mwana Washe Muranda Kumwe and the Coloniality of Contrived Democracy, in Mawere, M. and Mwanaka, T R. (eds) *Democracy, Good Governance and Development in Africa*. Bamenda: Langaa RPCIG

Nhemachena, A. (2016). Animism, Coloniality and Humanism: Reversing the Empire's Framing of Africa., in Mawere M *et al*. (eds) *Theory, Knowledge, Development and Politics: What Role for the Academy in the Sustainability of Africa?* Bamenda: Langaa RPCIG

Nhemachena, A. (2017). Hearing the Footfalls of Humanoid Robots: Technoscience, (Un-)employment and the Future of Development in Twenty-First Century Africa, in Mawere, M, (ed) *Underdevelopment, Development and the Future of Africa*. Bamenda: Langaa RPCIG

Nhemachena, A., (2016). (Post-)development and the Social Production of Ignorance: Farming Ignorance in 21st Century Africa, in Mawere M., (ed), *Development Perspectives from the South: Troubling the Metrics of [Under]development in Africa*. Langaa RPCIG: Bamenda p 77-118

Nhemachena, A., (2016). Double-Trouble: Reflections on the Violence of Absence and the Culpability of the Present in Africa in Mawere, M. and Marongwe, N, (eds), *Politics, Violence and Conflict Management in Africa: Envisioning Transformation, Peace and Unity in the Twenty-First Century*. Bamenda: Langaa

Nhemachena, A. and Mawere, M. (2017). Introduction: Theorising Fundamentalisms and Fetishisms in the 21st Century, in Nhemachena A and Mawere, M., (eds) *Africa at the Crossroads: Theorising Fundamentalisms and Fetishisms in the 21st Century*, Langaa RPCIG: Bamenda

Nicholas, J. E, (2012). A Conflict of Diamond: The Kimberley Process and Zimbabwe's Marange Diamond Fields, in *Denv.J.Int'L L & Pol'y* vol 40 (4): 648-688

Nyamnjoh, F. B. (2012). Potted Plants in Greenhouses: A Critical Reflection on the Resilience of Colonial Education in Africa, in *Journal of Asian and African Studies,* 47 (2): 129-154

Nyerere, J. K., (1963). A United States of Africa, in *The Journal of Modern African Studies* vol 1, No 1: 1-6

Openshaw, K. S. *et al.*, (2015). Zimbabwe's Odious Inheritance: Debt and Unequal Land Distribution in *Openshaw and Terry* vol 11, No 1: 43-86

Ortiz, D. R., (2016). Reterritorializing Deterritorialization, in Virginia Public Law and Legal Theory Research paper No 2016-61, http://papers.ssm.com/sol3/papers.cfm?abstract_id+2859599

Oskarsson, P., (2012). Dispossession by Confusion from Mineral-Rich Lands in Central India, Talk at the Australian National University, 14 November 2012

Owusu, R. Y., (2006). *Kwame Nkrumah's Liberation Thought: A Paradigm for Religious Advocacy in Contemporary Ghana*. Eritrea: Africa World Press

Pambazuka, (15 October 2008). Sankara 20 Years Later: A Tribute to Integrity, https://www.pambazuka.org/pan-africanism/sankara-20-years-later-tribute-integrity

Patton, P., (2010). *Deleuzian Concepts: Philosophy, Colonisation, Politics*. Stanford University Press: Stanford, California

Peizer, J., (2005). *The Dynamics of Technology for Social Change: Understanding the Factors that Influence Results: Lessons Learned from the Field*. iUniverse

Pelizzon, A., (2015). The Sentience of Plants: Animal Rights and Rights of Nature, *in AAPLJ* 11: 5-13

Pingeot, L., (2014). Contracting Insecurity: Private Military and Security Companies and the Future of the United Nations, Global Policy Forum Report https://www.globalpolicy.org/pmscs/52579-new-gpf-report-contracting-insecurity.html

Promskaya, A, (25 September 2015). West Africa: France Still Robbing Its "Former" African Colonies, in All Africa. allafrica.com/stories/201509281230.html

Promskaya, A., (25 September 2015). France Still Robing its "Former" African Colonies, in Pambazuka News. https://www.pambazuka.org/goernance/france-still-robbing-its-former-african-colonies

Rego, S. O, (2003). Tax-Avoidance Activities of U. S Multinational Corporations in *Contemporary Accounting Research* vol 20, Issue 4: 805-33

Reters, (13 October 2016). Africa's Population Boom Fuels 'Unstoppable' Migration to Europe www.reuters.com/article/us-europe-migrants-africa-analysis-idusk CN12DIPN

Reuters, (27 January 2010). We can Build United States of Africa, Gaddafi Says, www.reuters.com/article/us-africa-summit-gaddafi-idUSTRE66Q70620100

Reuters, (27 July 2010). We can Build United States of Africa, Gaddafi Says www.reuters.com/article/us-africa-summit-gaddafi-idUSTRE66Q70620100

Rubinowicz, P., (2000). Chaos and Geometric Order in Architecture and Design, *Journal for Geometry and Graphics* vol 4 (2): 197-207

Ryan, M., (2013). Full Spectrum Dominance: Donald Rumsfeld, the Department of Defence, and U.S Irregular Warfare Strategy, 2001-2008, in *Small Wars and Insurgences* vol 25, issue 1: 41-68

SABC News, (2 October 2014). Task Team Set Up to Probe Demilitarisation of SAPS, www.sabc.co.za/news/a/af840d8045ae5548c85/task-team-set-up-to-probe-de-militarization-of-SAPS

Sagafi-nejad, T. *et al.* (2008). *The UN and Transnational Corporations: From Code of Conduct to Global Compact (United Nations Intellectual History Project Series).* Indiana University Press

Scheidel, W. *et al.,* (2002). *The Ancient Economy.* Routledge

Shaw, I. G. R., (2016). *Predator Empire: Drone Warfare and Full Spectrum Dominance.* Minneapolis: University of Minnesota Press

Singer, P. W, (2006). Humanitarian Principles, Private Military Agents: Some Implications of the Privatised Military Industry for the Humanitarian Community, in Wheeler et al., (eds) *Resettling the Rules of Engagement: Trends & Issues in Military-Humanitarian Relations,* HPG Report 22

Southall, R. *et al.* (2009). A New Scramble for Africa, in Southall R *et al.* (eds) *A New Scramble for Africa? Imperialism, Investment and Development.* University of KwaZulu Natal Press

Stannard, D. E., (1993). *American Holocaust: The Conquest of the New World.* New York: Oxford University Press

Stone, C. D. (1972). Should Trees Have Standing? Towards Legal Rights for Natural Objects, in *Southern California Law Review* 45: 450-501

Story, C., (2007). *The New Underworld Order: Triumph of Criminalism: Dark Actors Playing Games.* Stranger Journalism

Sudetic, C., (2011). *The Philanthropy of George Soros: Building Open Societies.* Publisher Public Affairs

Sunday Times, (12 February 2017). Flexibility Needed to Realise BEE Dream.
www.tiemslive.co.za/sundaytimes/businesstimes/2017/02/12/flexibility-neded-to-realise-BEE-dream1

Sundstrom, L. M., (2006). *Funding Civil Society: Foreign Assistance and NGO Development in Russia.* Stanford University Press

Teitelbaum, A. (2007). United Nations and Transnational Corporations: a Deadly Association, in Transnational Institute
https://www.tni.org/en/article/united-nations-and-transnational-corporations-deadly-association

Terray, E., (2006). Long Distance Exchange and the Formation of the Sate: the Case of the Abron Kingdom of Gyaman, in *Economy and Society* vol 3, Issue 3: 315-345

The African Economist, (20 June 2013). France Has Economically Enslaved West African Countries, theafricaneconomist.com/economically-enslaved-west-african-countries-by-france/

The Chronicle, (8 December 2014). Zimbabwe Recovers $45 m Diamonds Seized by South African Company, www.chronicle.co.zw/zimbabwe-recoers-45m-diamond-seized-by-sa-company/

The Guardian, (2 June 2015). Tax Dodging by Big Firms "Robs Poor Countries of Billions of Dollars a Year, https://www.theguardian.com/global-deelopment/2015/jun/02/tax-dodging-big-companies-costs-poor-counties-billions-dollars

The Guardian, (24 March 2014). The Kimberley Process is a "Perfect Cover Story for Blood Diamonds https://www.theguardian.com/sustainable-business/diamonds-blood-kimberley-process-mines-ethical

The Guardian, (20 August 2005). The Wealth of the West Was Built on Africa's Exploitation http://theguardian.com/politics/2005/aug/20/past.hearafrica05

The Guardian, (10 December 2014). Fracking and Lima Climate Talks Slammed at Nature Rights Tribunal http://www.theguardian.com/environemt/andes-to-the-amazon/2014/dec/10/fracking-redd-lima-climate-talks-slammed-nature-tribunal

The Guardian, (17 January 2011). Patrice Lumumba: the Most Important Assassination of the 20th Century https://www.thegaurdian.com/global-development/poerty-matters/2011/jan/17/patrice-lumumba-50th-anniversary-assasination

The Guardian, (21 February 2017). Robert Mugabe 93rd Birthday With Praise for Donald Trump https://www.theguardian.com/world/2017/feb/21/robert-mugabe-93rd-birthday-zimbabwe-president-donald-trump

The Guardian, (21 January 2013). Mugabe Revives Gaddafi's United States of Africa, Dream https://www.theguardian.com/world/2013/jan/21/mugabe-gaddafi-united-states-africa

The Guardian, (26 January 2017). Europe's Crackdown on African Immigration is Hitting Vulnerable Refugees https://www.thegaurdian.com/commentisfree/2017/jan/26/europe-crackdown-africa-immigration-vulnerable-rfugees-sudan-eritrea

The Guardian, (27 May 2005). Scandal of Phantom aid Money, https://www.theguardian.com/business/2005/may/27/development.debt

The Herald, (12 August 2015). Yoked Francophone Africa Must be Pitied, www.herald.co.za/yoked-francophone-africa-must-be-pittied/

The New York Times. (13 July 2016). In New Zealand, Lands and Rivers can Be People (Legally Speaking) https://www.nytimes.com/2016/07/14/world/what-in-the-world/in-new-zealand-lands-and-rivers-can-be-people-legally-speaking.html?_r=0

Thusi, I. G., (2015). Policing Sex: the Colonial Apartheid, and New Democracy Policing of Sex Work in South Africa, *Fordham International Law Journal* vol 38, No 1 Article 4: 205-243

Tomlison, J., (2012). *Deterritorialisation*. John Wiley & Sons, Ltd

Tousaint, E. *et al.*, (2010). *Debt, the IMF, and the World Bank: Sixty Questions, Sixty Answers.* New York: Monthly Review Press

Traub-Merz, R., (2006). The African Textile and Clothing Industry: From Import Substitution to Export Orientation, in Jauch H., (ed) *The Future of the Textile and Clothing Industry in Sub-Saharan Africa.* Bonn: Friedrich-Ebert-Stiftung

Turse, N. (2015). *Tomorrow's Battlefields: US Proxy Wars and Secret Ops in Africa.* Chicago: Haymarket Books

Vambe, M. T. *et al.*, (2007). Notes on Theorising Black Diaspora from Africa, in *African Identities* vol 5 No 1: 5-32

Vernon, T. (2017). What Does it Mean to Make a River a Legal Person? https://vernontava.com/2017/03/18/what-does-it-mean-to-make-a-river-a-legal-person/

VOA, (20 June 2011). Zimbabwe's Marange Diamonds Put Kimberley Process to the Test. www.voanews.com/a/zimbabwe's-diamonds-put-kimberley-process-to-the-test-124310334/160985.html

VOA, (29 October 2009). Global Charity: 60 Percent of International Aid is Phantom, www.voanews.com/a/a-13-07-2005voa/o/-67394527/275669.html

Warikandwa, T. V., Nhemachena, A., and Mpofu, N., (2017). "Double Victimisation? Law, Decoloniality and Research Ethics in post-colonial Africa", *Africology: The Journal of Pan African Studies* volume 10(2), (forthcoming April 2017)

Watts, M., (2009). Oil, Development, and the Politics of the Bottom Billion, in *Macalester International* vol 24, Article 1

West, H. G., (2003). "Who Rules Us Now"? Identity Tokens, Sorcery, and Other Metaphors in the 1994 Mozambican Elections, in West H G *et al.*, (eds) *Transparency and Conspiracy: Ethnographies of Suspicion in the New Wold Order.* Duke University Press: Durham and London

West, P., (2016). *Dispossession and the Environment: Rhetoric and Inequality in Papua.* New York: Columbia University Press

Zeleza, P. T., (2009). What Happened to the African Renaissance? The Challenges of Development in the Twenty-First Century, in *Comparative Studies of South Asia, Africa and the Middle East*, vol 29, No 2: 155-170

Ziai, A, (2007). Development Discourse and its Critics: An Introduction to Post-development, in same, (ed) *Exploring Post-development: Theory and Practice, Problems and Perspectives.* Routledge: London and New York: 3-18

Zimbabwe Independent, (23 January 2017). Government Collaborated with Illegal Panners at Marange, https://www.theindependent.co.zw/2017/01/23/govt-collaborated-illegal-panners-marange/

Chapter Two

When Did the Rain Start to Beat Us? Discursive Dispossession and the Political Economies of Misrecognition about African Mining

Artwell Nhemachena and Esther Dhakwa

In May 2000 the Economists, the haughty British magazine, published a notorious cover story that contemptuously called Africa "the hopeless continent". What followed was an avalanche of bad history, discredited anthropology, questionable sociology, sterile economies, and, vulgar political science about Africa's inhospitable environments, endemic "tribalism", vacuous states, ferocious tyrants, deformed psyches, and beneficent but misguided donors. The story provoked widespread outrage in the Pan-African world (Zeleza, 2009: 156).

Ethnic, tribal and racial sentiments through the use of divide and rule strategy were used as a weapon to shift the minds of Africans to defending their ethnic and tribal hegemony at the expense of fighting for economic and industrial development (Asante, 1987 cited in Boaduo, 2012: 125).

Past renaissance efforts shared a common failing in that they did not prioritise the economy as the principal arena of struggle...African renaissance is fully realised when attention is paid to the economic plight of the majority of Africans that live in abject poverty and under dehumanising conditions" (Mzamane, 2001: 12).

Introduction

Contemporary discourses about 'inclusion' are misplaced for the majority of the people in the global south who have been dispossessed, robbed and looted, without restitution, only to be mollified by those that have dispossessed them with the false global (neo-)liberal ideological comfort of the emergence of an "inclusive but skewed world". To be "included" as global underdogs in a world characterised by the material and ideological machismo of those that have stolen material, cultural, epistemic and historical spaces and resources of others is in fact to live on facades or lullabies. In fact contemporary discourses of "inclusion" are no different from old colonial and neo-colonial discourses of civilisation, Eurocentric modernisation and development particularly in so far as these purported to bring or include Africans in 'civilisation' projects, 'modernisation' and 'development' projects that in fact meant dispossessing peoples of the global south. Thus, the paradox is that in a world that claims to be increasingly inclusive, Africans are increasingly being excluded from owning their own resources that are still being grabbed by transnational corporations trawling the world, in the logics of global hunter-gatherers. In fact Africans are increasingly treated as foreigners in their own countries and on their own continent [where descendants of colonial establishments are paradoxically ingraining and affirmatively repositioning themselves as the indigenous] that is increasingly privatised and owned by foreign transnational corporations with Africans coming in only as underdog or appendages of transnational capital and Western institutions masquerading as innocent international institutions. In these countries and on the continent of Africa, mineral and other resources are still owned by colonists and or their descendants who have benefited from the proceeds of colonial looting, and from proceeds arising from the massive exploitation of African labour since the eras of enslavement and colonisation.

Erroneously dismissed as unproductive and economically sterile, Africans have been reduced to beneficiaries of Western humanitarian assistance, often receiving contentious and toxic genetically modified food handouts (Nhemachena and Mawere, 2017). They are deeply excluded from owning their own resources on the continent; and this exclusion is sadly ideologically legitimised by some bandwagonist media houses and some academics on the continent that also paradoxically evangelise political and social inclusion, but minus inclusion in ownership of material resources. In this sense, discourses that reduce Africans to beneficiaries of Western humanitarian assistance and that [presumed] inability, impotence and sterility of Africans to exploit their own resources have come to constitute discursive dispossession. This chapter argues that dispossession of

Africans since the era of enslavement and colonisation has not only involved direct physically violent and visibly evident expropriation of resources from Africans; it also argues that colonists have also used and still use carefully concocted discourses to legitimise and oil-up the processes of dispossession of Africans. In other words dispossessing people materially requires, as a correlative, dispossessing them also in ideological, epistemic, social, cultural, spiritual and political senses so that they become [cognitively] demobilise and defused for battling for repossession. This chapter understand such cognitive demobilisation and diffusion as leading to what Bourdieu calls misrecognition or *meconnaissance* (see James, 2015: 100). Misrecognition refers to social practices of individual or collective misattribution made invisible through a displacement of understanding. Thus, for Bourdieu, misrecognition refers to an everyday and dynamic social process where one thing is not recognised for what it is because it was not previously 'cognised' within the range of dispositions and propensities of the habitus of the persons confronting it. Instead the thing is attributed to another available realm of meaning, and in the process interests, inequities or other effects may be maintained whilst they remain concealed. Understood from a reading of Celikates (2012: 162), in misrecognition, agents do not really know what they are doing and so they are really prisoners of an ideology that masks their situation and their interest. Celikates (2012: 163) points out thus: "The doxa of participants in a practice guarantees that they misrecognise the conditions of their thought and action, and do not ask any questions for which there is no immediate and 'official' answer".

Thus, historically, (neo-)colonial dispossession has been cloaked as progress, development and civilisation such that the material dispossession of Africans has been ideologically masked as [material] progress. The cultural, social and epistemic dispossession of Africans has similarly been masked as progress and civilisation whose dictates required Africans to abandon their [secure] social, cultural and epistemic moorings. The colonial invention [and fanning] of "tribal" and ethnic wars on Africa, much as the invention [and fanning] of African intergenerational and other conflicts constituted colonial discursive forms of dispossession aimed at preventing the solidarity of the dispossessed (neo-)colonised. *A fortiori*, (neo-)colonial forms of discursive dispossession effectively prevent the dispossessed from uniting and sharing their intergenerational knowledge including about restitution, mining, extracting, processing and trading their own resources. In a context where generations of youths have increasingly turned against their elders that since colonialism are deemed to be backward (see for instance Colson, 1971), the knowledge and expertise about mining that elders have is not being transferred to new generations that are paradoxically struggling to get funds to enter formal education. In other words, youths who have been trained since the colonial era to turn against their elders [who as will be discussed below had expertise on mining, melting, smelting and trading] are paradoxically financially finding it difficult to enter into formal education to acquire the knowledge and skills that they have lost.

The much maligned African social, cultural, religious, political, epistemic and economic institutions are in fact resources about which colonial settlers have always endeavoured to discursively dispossess Africans, in addition to material dispossession. Although some scholars consider Western critiques of African institutions to be acts of philanthropy for hapless Africans deemed to be trapped in the supposedly incorrigibly [oppressive] African institutions, it is important to note that colonisation also came in the guise of philanthropy. The paradox in all this is that some Westerners who have used their institutions including cultures to colonise other people do not see the oppressive nature of their own cultures and other institutions which they continue to impose on the global south, in spite of independence. Instead many in the West continue to primarily demonise African institutions, including cultures as oppressive even if these African institutions have never been used to colonise, at least to the extent that Westerners have done with theirs, other people. Much like in the colonial era, African peoples and their cultural, social, legal, political, epistemic and economic institutions that have not been used to colonise other people are demonised paradoxically and principally by foreign (neo-)colonial Western institutions, and in some African academies beholden to Western epistemologies. The question that is seldom asked by Western

58

epistemologies is how much more oppressive are the acts of (neo-)colonisation and the structural violence that comes with imposed global institutions? The point here is that the indiscriminate demonisation of African institutions including cultures is part and parcel of the (neo-)colonial discursive dispossession that seeks to depose not only African cultures but also epistemologies including expertise about mining, smelting, melting and commerce which are embedded in the cultures.

Although there has been a deafening outcry about the fact that the statue of Cecil John Rhodes was smeared, by angry students at the University of Cape Town, with human waste (Nyamnjoh, 2016), little regard is taken of the centuries old smearing of Africa with (neo) colonial [ideological and cognitive] waste that is accountable for the self-hatred by Africans many of whom no longer stand in the podiums of [relevant] excellence in the world. Little regard is paid to how much waste Rhodes and other colonialist smeared on Africans for centuries. The colonial ideological and cognitive waste, calculated to demean, dehumanise, defuse, demonise and animalise Africans has not been cleared partly because the African academies that provided rays of hope, at independence, have no sufficient ideological and cognitive ablution facilities. Having been deprived, by colonists such as Cecil Rhodes, who owned some colonial mining companies, of their precolonial industries including mining, some Africans have sadly come to believe that all their did during the precolonial era was to produce, hunt and gather for subsistence.

Thus, while Africans have come to be conflated with subsistence sectors of the economy, there is evidence that Africans had their own [mining] industries including commerce in the precolonial era; while Africans are often treated as 'illegal' miners, without knowledge of mining melting and smelting ores, there is evidence that precolonial Africans could mine, melt, smelt and even weave cloths and produce guns (Ellert, 1984; Chirikure, 2010). So, while Africans have come to be portrayed as without their own heritage of the science of mining and processing minerals, there is evidence that Africans have always had scientific knowledge of mining even during the precolonial era. With an eye on debates about Pan-Africanism and African Renaissance, the chapter situates African mining in colonial discourses that have up to now sadly portrayed Africans as freaks of nature with neither industries nor commerce of their own. The chapter contextualises African mining in resilient colonial discourses that have erroneously conflated Africans with subsistence economies and therefore portrayed them as lacking the rudiments of industrialisation. It is also argued that processes of (neo-) colonial discursive dispossession have effectively generated misrecognition such that some Africans have come to regard themselves as gate-crashers of industrialisation rather than as legitimate and privy to mining, and indeed broader industrialisation processes on the continent.

Such resilient colonial discursive practices that constitute Africans as gate-crashes and mere beneficiaries of Western industrialisation account for the incessant wretchedness of Africans, who have come to believe that they are hopeless beneficiaries of Western grace, even in the postcolonial era. In Francophone West African countries for example, France has forced the Francophone African states to sign colonial pacts in which those countries are held to be indebted to French colonisation for which they are paying compensation. Thus, instead of former colonial masters such as France paying compensation to Africans whom they enslaved and colonised, it is the African victims of Western enslavement and colonisation that are made to pay for the supposed benefits of enslavement and colonisation. In spite of the fact that the economies of Europe and America (Fanon, 1963) were built on the backs of colonised and dispossessed Africans, Koutonin (28 January 2014) notes that since the 1960s, West African countries such as Benin, Burkina Faso, Guinea Bissau, Ivory Coast, Mali, Togo, Senegal, Cameroon, Central African Republic, Chad, Congo Brazzaville, Equatorial Guinea and Gabon have been forced by their former colonial master, France, into the colonial pacts. Apart from paying debts to France for the supposed benefits of colonisation, these countries are also forced to deposit their national monetary reserves in French Treasury over which they have no control; France holds that the Africans should pay for the infrastructure built by France during colonisation, African leaders who refuse to do so are killed or subjected to coups. Much in the logic of Western sanctions on errant

African leaders that refuse to tore the line, those that refuse to pay the supposed 'colonial debts' attract Western fury; everything that [former] colonists call 'benefits of colonisation' is destroyed- medicine, public buildings, cars, research institutes, cows, warehouses and food reserves have been destroyed or poisoned for those that refused to pay the so called 'colonial debts' (Promskaya, 25 September 2015; Global Research, 14 January 2015; The African Economist, 20 June 2013; The Herald, 12 August 2015).

Similarly, the International Monetary Fund and the World Bank claim that Africans, who have been enslaved and colonised by the West for centuries, are indebted to the Western institutions; this is another instantiation of logics of colonial pacts all over the Global South. Besides, recently, a high ranking member of the opposition party Democratic Alliance (DA) in South Africa argued that South Africans were indebted to colonialism that [in spite of actually dispossessing and exploiting Africans] is erroneously argued to have brought benefits of independent judiciary, transport infrastructure, piped water, specialised healthcare and medication (Al Jazeera, 16 March 2017). Thus, colonial pacts are not isolated or exclusive to West African Francophone countries but they are more widespread on the African continent where colonial discursive dispossession reigns. The issue here is that logics of colonial pacts are evident in African academies where, cognitively speaking, some intellectuals have come to simplistically believe that Western epistemologies and ontologies are better than African ones; logics of colonial pacts are also evident among Africans that have come to believe that Western institutions are naturally and always unquestionably better than African ones.

As a result of [ideological and cognitive] colonial pacts, some Africans have also sadly started to believe that they owe debts to the West that has paradoxically enslaved and colonised them for centuries without compensation (Nhemachena, 2015). The evangelisation of African indebtedness and helplessness has historically served to legitimise the enslavement of Africa: Western slave-drivers for instance spread the gospel that they were actually saving the Africans, who they in fact enslaved, from their own despotic kings and chiefs back home. The colonists, who exploited

African [as cheap labour] labour, similarly claimed that they were actually saving African youths from the despotism of their own elders who made them work on family farms (Colson, 1971). Enslavement and colonisation of Africans therefore depended on colonial conjurations of the paradoxical psychologies of indebtedness of Africans to those that exploited them. Traces of these colonial logics are still evident including at the global level where Western institutions still evangelise African indebtedness to their looters and exploiters. Western civil society organisations also still presuppose the indebtedness of Africans to Western civility. Thus, Thomas Sankara's (Pambazuka, 15 October 2008) call on African countries to form powerful fronts against the continent's illegitimate and immoral debt [which he saw as modern enslavement] and to collectively refuse to pay it, is germane here.

It is contented in this chapter that discursive dispossession and the attendant politics of misrecognition are purveyed through academies including African ones that are beholden to resilient colonial ideologies and epistemologies that for instance conceptualise [the majority of] African miners as 'illegal', 'informal' and often 'criminals' while paradoxically celebrating multinational and transnational corporations as legitimate indispensable salvific *foreign investors;* forgetting in the process that transnational corporations come to Africa primarily to exploit resources, maximise the repatriation of profits to their home countries and often evade taxation by African governments. Much like Aristotle argued that [natural] slaves belong to the master and are tools for praxis rather than making (Garner, 1994; Scheidel et al, 2002; Pangle, 2013), some Africans have been turned into Western slaves via discursive dispossession that explains the interminable pandering of some, on the continent, to dispossessive and exploitative Western corporations. From physically enslaving individual bodies, to enslaving entire nations by physical force as well as by ideological discursive dispossession, the West has moved on to enslaving entire regions and continents by insidious discursive means that also materialise in, and perpetuate, the material dispossession of Africans. The weapons of mass destruction and enslavement are not merely the physical weapons that we have been cultured by the West into searching for; rather the weapons of mass destruction and enslavement also include (neo-)colonial ideological and epistemic discursive practices that have resulted in some Africans including highly educated intellectuals (Ngugi Wa Thiongo, 1986) giving away not only their kith and kin, to enslavement, but also giving away their cognitive selves that have been consequently thoroughly cognitively deterritorialised from the continent, and turned into zombies.

Much like in witchcraft discourses, in which witches are understood to take away the souls of their victims and replace them with different souls that are nonorganic and alien, discursive dispossession effects displacements of souls and minds of African victims. The subjects or victims' nonmaterial aspects and identities are manipulated as means to dispossessing them of their abilities to resists (neo-)colonial imperial formations. These (neo-) colonial imperial formations have entailed long invisible (neo-)imperial networks of exploitation of Africans, which invisible networks have been likened to witchcraft. Scholars like Murrey (2015: 64) have pointed out thus:"... dispersed geographies of extraction (including the ways in which pipeline infrastructure, oil wealth and consortium employees and representatives fluctuate between invisibility and visibility) are understood by people...through epistemologies of witchcraft...Invisible actors and materials are associated with evil, wrongdoing, suspicion and distrust".

While Western scholars hold that precolonial African economic activities were irrational, superstitious and pervaded with witchcraft and sorcery, the colonisers are held by Africans noted by Murrey (2015) to be so irrational and occultic [if via material and discursive dispossession] as to engage in the evils of dispossessing and exploiting Africans on their continent. In other words, Western economies that have been described by some scholars as rational and as involving rational individuals are not necessarily rational if seen from the points of view of the Africans who were dispossessed and exploited with the advent of such Western economies and individuals. From this point of view, to say Western economies are rational would amount to legitimising colonial economies, including the dispossession and exploitation that they occasioned on Africans. Arguments that posit the rationality of such exploitative and dispossessive economies risk generating misrecognition and producing ignorance among Africans: colonial economies cannot logically be regarded as rational without distorting or erasing the histories of colonial dispossession and exploitation. To say that (neo-)colonial economies are rational is by extension unfortunately to legitimise (neo-)colonialism; it amounts to rationalising and legitimising the dispossession, exploitation and looting that are inherent to (neo-)colonial economies into which Africa has been drawn. The challenge here is that African academies that continue to teach African students about the purported 'rationality' of inherited (neo-)colonial economies have forgotten to correct or change their templates upon independence. By extension such academies continue to legitimise and rationalise the dispossession and exploitation of Africans from whose taxes the same institutions paradoxically thrive.

A closer look at material and discursive dispossession reveals that Africa was not backward, as has sadly become standard in Eurocentric representations of the continent.

(Dis-)possessing the 'Possessed'? On the Material and Discursive Dispossession of Africans

While Foucault holds that discourse is a powerful means of enabling forms of critique and resistance (Hook, 2001), in a world where transnational capital monopolises the control of and sets the agenda in the media, schools, colleges, academies and in various forms of technology that enable action at a distance; inequalities define the terrain of discourse as the impoverished are excluded or conscripted into the agenda of powerful others. For this reason, Young (1981) cited in Hook (2001: 2) argues that "...the effects of discursive practices is to make it virtually impossible to think outside them; to be outside of them is, by definition to be mad, to be beyond comprehension..."

If discursive practices are understood as making it impossible to think outside them, it then follows that discourses enhance possession in the sense of the subjects of the discourse becoming possessions or possessed by the dominant others who own the media through which discourse takes place. For instance, Africans that got possessed by colonial ideologies and epistemologies have started to believe in the colonial ideologies that precolonial Africans had no scientific knowledge to mine, melt and smelt minerals for instance. Similarly, Africans possessed by colonial ideologies now believe that there was no commerce, no forms of money, no industries and no modernity in precolonial Africa. The fact that colonialism pre-empted African modernity that included existence of mining industries (Taiwo, 2010; Chirikure, 2010) and the fact that colonialism destroyed African industries (Ellert, 1984) have been foreshadowed by (neo-)colonial ideologies to the effect that precolonial Africans were hopeless. In other words, as Young (1981) cited in Hook (2001) underscores, trapped in (neo-) colonial discursive practices, some Africans can no longer think outside these (neo-)colonial discursive practices since to think outside them would appear as madness and beyond comprehension to those that have been captured by the colonial discourses.

Whereas other scholars like Foucault (Hook, 2001) would link discourses to knowledge, it can be argued that colonial discourses did not necessarily produce knowledge [but rather ignorance] for Africans that were dispossessed, exploited and deskilled as a result of colonial appropriations of their material, cultural, epistemic and social resources (Nhemachena, 2016). In this vein, Said (1983: 21) cited in Hook (2001: 6) states thus: "The will to exercise…control in society and history has also discovered a way to clothe, disguise, rarefy and wrap itself systematically in the language of truth, discipline, rationality, utilitarian value, and knowledge". These (neo-)colonial discursive practices are not merely meant to manufacture consent in Gramsci's (1971) sense but we argue here that as far as Africans are concerned the practices are aimed at discursively dispossessing Africans. To simplistically argue that they are aimed at manufacturing consent would be to play down the dispossessive history of coloniality in Africa. In other words, the problematic in the connections between Africa and the West is not located in the simplistic discourses of 'manufacturing of consent' but rather in the dispossession of the peoples of the continent. Scholarship that focuses on Gramscian discourses about 'the manufacturing of consent' risk occluding the more material issues of dispossession or looting of African material and cognitive resources. Thus, in analysing Africa in relation to the West, it is necessary to be cautious about the terms that are used. For instance, standard Marxist terms like oppression, exploitation, alienation, class struggle hardly speak to the core issue of dispossession of Africans; in any case Marxism originated from analyses not of the colonial conditions of African societies, economies, laws, histories and experiences but rather European ones where alienation, separation, oppression, class struggles were arguably more central than were questions of dispossession. Thus, remedies to Marxist concerns about alienation, class struggle, separation, oppression, exploitation do not include at their core repossession and restitution as would be the case where African problems are clearly analysed using the Africans' own colonial historical experiences of dispossession as springboards. So, while Marxist concerns about alienation, separation, exploitation, oppression can help resolve some issues in Africa, the Marxist concerns circumvent or play down the core issue of (neo-)colonial and imperial dispossession of Africans. Life changing struggles in Africa are not necessarily between classes as Marxists would have it; they are rather between the dispossessed and colonised on the one hand and the colonisers and dispossessors on the other hand. All other struggles make up sideshows that do not really change the lives of Africans beyond the tapestries of (neo-)imperial nets.

Although it has been pointed out that the remedy for discursive dispossession is discursive repossession (Apter, 1992), other scholars note immense challenges posed by discursive dispossession. For instance, Medina (2006: 126) argues that:

> Power relations are established in our discursive practices through our everyday activity of playing language games…and if these power positions and relations are to be sustained across generations, they have to be sedimented by means of their transmission through processes of enculturation that brings new generations into the discursive practices.

Discursive dispossession as constituted via nonmaterial forms of dispossession (West, 2016) is harder to recognise even though these nonmaterial forms of dispossession also often materialise as material dispossession. Through rhetoric and ideology, Povinelli (2011) contends, we can see that the material and economic are always underpinned and presupposed by the ideological discursive and the semiotic. Thus, for Povinelli (2011) processes of accumulation and dispossession are understood to rest on the discursive, semiotic and visual production of countries and continents as outside the natural order of things with the assumption that the natural order of things is a kind of linear progression fantasy in which everyone, globally, has come to live, or should have come to live, in urban cosmopolitan ways. This clearly connects discursive dispossession as articulated through the rhetoric of the frontier with the material dispossession of Africans.

When the Mozambicans were baffled about who ruled them in postcolonial postwar scenario of the 1990s (West, 2003), their confusion can be understood in terms of the frontierism that Africa is constituted into by Western discourses with an eye to dispossessing them. Western discourses often portray Africans as incapable of governing themselves in spite of Africans' struggles for independence from the same Westerners. These discourses together with other discursive practices that rely on human rights and humanitarianism constitute not necessarily Western philanthropy but Western mechanisms for discursively dispossessing Africans, by maintaining foothold on the continent, whose mineral and other resources the West cannot do without. Paradoxical Western discursive dispossession involves popularisation of discourses of decolonisation even as the same Westerners are busy setting up transnational institutions and corporations that they are using to rule Africans despite 'postcolonialism'. The use of human rights and humanitarian discourses as pretexts to invade other countries (Boyle, 2013) and to *de facto* recolonize those countries, indicate that these are in fact tools for discursive dispossession of contemporary Africa. For this reason, Gillespie (2016) argues that dispossession is a strategic response that employs a range of physical-legal and discursive mechanisms.

One can similarly argue that the generation, by colonists, of confusion among Africans about their identities-the labels such as savages, barbarians, animists, animals, and heathen and so on were meant to create discursive confusion to facilitate the dispossession of Africans. If, as Nhemachena (2016) argues, possession of clear identities is crucial in matters of (re-)possession, the colonial and neo-colonial discourses about African hybridisation of identities are in fact tools for generating discursive confusion and discursive dispossession of Africans. The Africans afflicted by such discursive confusion have first and foremost to lose their identities as Africans and then next they have to lose their material possessions that constitute the heritages of Africans. So, when empire celebrates hybridisation of African identities or the confusion of identities of Africans; or when empire celebrates multiplicities of identities, this need not be understood as generosity or philanthropy-it is in fact part and parcel of discursive dispossession that facilitates imperial material dispossession of Africans. If, as is the case, African modes of ownership of resources [including mineral resources] are part and parcel of African cultures and religions, social institutions and polities, it becomes clear why Euro-American epistemologies are antithetical to these African institutions. The ultimate idea is to discursively and materially dispossess Africans by first of all distorting and confusing their institutions within which regimes of ownership of resources are premised. The contention therefore is that Euro-American critiques of African institutions is not out of philanthropy but the quest to continuously dispossess Africans; after all academies and other Western institutions that lead in the critiques are sponsored by global capital ever keen to maximise profit rather than to maximise philanthropy.

Thus, contemporary efforts to generate identity confusion speak to Oskarsson's (2012) observation that dispossession by confusion involves creating uncertainties. The colonial discursive constructions of Africans as inhuman legitimised the loss of African life to colonial violence; the logic of colonial discursive constructions of Africans as inhuman also legitimised the imperial material dispossession of Africans. Similarly, the contemporary scholarly discursive practices about the need to pull down African sovereignty and autonomy represent (Nhemachena, 2017), efforts at discursively dispossessing Africans of institutional belonging and protection. Equally, the contemporary discourses on deconstruction of African institutions and identities also represent discursive dispossession by generating confusion among Africans. If Africans get to a point where they thoroughly believe (neo-)colonial ideologies portraying them as indistinct from animals for example, the implications are quite unfortunate as far as ownership and control of their mineral and other resources is concerned (Nhemachena, 2016). Internalisation of the ideologies of animism and claims of absence of distinctions between Africans and animals negate African claims to ownership of their resources. Similarly, acceptance of colonial ideologies about absence of distinctions between Africans and animals legitimises destruction of Africans' institutions of marriages, families, cultures, polities, and above all lineages that were historically crucial in passing knowledge and expertise about mining from one generation to the other.

The upshot of the above is that contemporary epistemic and activist deconstructive efforts directed at African institutions and orders are aimed at creating confusion and anarchy that are historically foundational to discursive and material dispossession. Discursive dispossession necessarily relies on creating confusion, in the institutions of the targeted victims, as a step to dispossessing them in the material sense. As Greer (2014) observes, Africa was colonised partly via discursive mechanisms wherein the continent was portrayed as open commons and hence free for all including and especially for the coloniser-outsiders. Thus, Greer proceeds to argue that although collective, the commons were very much property and like all property, they were fundamentally about exclusion. They were not public lands open to the entire human race, but were maintained for the use of local residents only. In this vein, dispossession of the colonised occurred through operations of the commons, or through imposition of settler-centric forms of common property in place of the existing indigenous commons.

Looked at more closely, Africa did not match the colonial discourses of backwardness, absence of industrialisation and modernity and absence of scientific knowledge; Africa did not only have subsistence economies; African societies were not isolated and remote as is presented in popular Western colonial discourses on remoteness of Africa. Thus, Hashim et al (1999: 22-3) state that:

In the centuries before colonialism, the Hausa states of what is now Nigeria were linked to the rest of the continent, as well as to the outside world, by a range of interregional trading circuits. Trade was based largely on ecological and artisanal specialisation, although routes were also influenced by levels of tolls and taxation…To the north, the trans-Sahara trade routes linked urban centres in the desert and savannah areas of West Africa to Tripoli…Exports from the Hausa areas of the central Sudan included slaves, hides and skins, local textiles, leather goods, small quantities of condiments, and in the 19th century, ostrich feathers.

The observations that Africa was not all about subsistence economies is supported by the Mail & Guardian, (22 August 2014) noting that "…by the beginning of the 18th century, metal goods-from iron hoes to copper bangles-were widely consumed across southern Africa and fed into a global trading system that linked the Indian Ocean rim, from the Mozambique Coast to the Middle East, India and as far as China". In West Africa Kano was the largest precolonialcity; it was the commercial capital of Sokoto Caliphate and it became the largest state in the region (Austin, 2004). Kano, Austin (2004) further notes, was the largest centre of production in West Africa especially of cotton cloth, which was among the commodities traded over far and beyond. Markets were mainly in Europe. Cotton textiles, salt, currency media (such as cowrie and metal bars) were the basis of most goods traded along with weapons-horses, guns and ammunition. Other scholars have also noted that farming was supplemented by long distance trade; and that although the focus of the trade networks had a regional emphasis, there was also long distance trade across the Indian Ocean about 2000 years ago (Schoeman et al, 2013; Fyle, 1999). Supporting these observations, Jerven (2016: 24) argues that:

> …in precolonial Africa there was production for the market, there was wage labour, exchanges took place, and there was economic growth in Africa before 1850. The term 'subsistence economy' has been proven to be a misnomer, even food crops were exchanged on local markets, higher end consumer goods were exchanged in regional

trade, and these markets linked with and benefitted from external market growth.

With respect to African scientific knowledge related to the extraction, melting and smelting of minerals, Schoeman et al (2013: 86) note that knowledge of iron, copper and gold production is traceable to about 2000 years ago and these metals were clearly produced by Africans and not by foreigners as is proposed by some writers. Similarly Fyle (1999: 58-9) notes that:

> By the start of the second millennium AD, many of the Shona settlements in present day Zimbabwe were beginning to come together in state-like organisation...those same areas have yielded information on concentrated metal working in gold, bronze and iron, and long distance trade...Evidence of gold mining in this area dating to about 1000 AD indicate that the mines were worked to depths of as much as 100 feet below the surface. After breaking the rock cover by alternately heating and cooling, they used iron picks to break the ore, which was then crushed and panned at the streams...The gold mining fed international trade through the port of Sofala on the East African Coast, part of the Swahili coast trade...

Similarly noting the knowledge and expertise in mining, melting and smelting minerals are scholars like Garson (n.d); Ofosu-Mensa et al (2011); Matambalya (2015). Noted is the fact that even 'Bushmen' were acquainted with iron oxides, manganese compounds and that copper was mined from as early as 200AD in Zimbabwe and Zambia. Also noted is the fact that in precolonial times, gold mining was one of the mainstays of the economies of Ghanaian Asante, Denkyira, Akyem, Wassa and many other Akan states. Thus, Matambalya (2015: 9) argues that: "...industrialisation in Africa was possible and indeed, Africans did experiment with industrialisation. The precolonial industrial development efforts produced different results in different parts of the continent, with comparatively high progress in certain types of industrial activities and in some parts (regions) and little progress in others".

Thus, while scholars show that smiths produced implements such as spearheads, arrow tips, tools such as burins, axes, needles, sticks and palettes (Holl, 2000: 15), there are also indications that women and children participated in the activities. For instance, Ofosu-Mensa et al (2011: 9) state that:

> The most common and defective method, however, seems to have been for the women and boys to scoop holes in the alluvial earth or gravel on the river banks or in whirlpools on the shallow sides...Organised on a family basis, panning for alluvial gold in stream beds in the forest areas and along coastal shorelines was primarily the work of women, adolescent girls and boys.

Similarly, Schmidt (1992: 51-52) notes about the Shona people of Zimbabwe that:

> Women were also involved in gold mining and washing for alluvial gold during the slow periods in the agricultural cycle...Recovered skeletons of precolonial miners, killed in mining accidents, indicate that the miners were about equally male and female...Given the importance of female labour in the production of gold, women were crucial to the long distance trade in luxury goods, firearms and ammunition,...Shona women were also highly respected artisans and skilled workers. Like their male counterparts, skilled craftswomen such as potters and beer brewers were called by the honorific title, *mhizha*. Similarly skilled dancers and musicians of both sexes were called *nyanzi*.

Writing about the expertise of [precolonial] African men and women in mining and smelting at the Lolwe Mine in South Africa; the Mail and Guardian (22 August 2014) points out that they engaged in smelting, melting and processing of minerals. It is further stated that there is evidence to suggest that the men and women were specialist producers with a high degree of mastery. It is noted thus:

> The residues of metals that stuck to the edge of furnace walls and copper crucibles show that these metallurgists knew a great deal about the conditions and temperatures needed to refine copper metals from

this complex ore body…There were also 1000 year-old trading items such as spindle whorls for spinning of cotton, glass beads of Asian origin and cowrie shells from the Indian Ocean coast.

Africans had expertise in making tools including guns, razor blades, knives and bullets, and making copper currencies such as in the form of ingots called handa (Ellert, 1984; Bisson, 1982: 350). Apart from expertise in precolonial mining industries, Africans also had expertise in textiles industries some of which produced for export (Traub-Merz, 2006: 12). Traub-Merz (2006: 12-13) states thus:

Heinrich Barth, the famous German Africa traveller gave a vivid picture of the cotton fields in the Sahel region and the size of the Kano weaving industry in the middle of the 19th century. Most weaver households were still linked to agricultural activities and produced their basic needs of food. But during nonfarming seasons they supplied textiles in such quantities and with such skilled labour that markets for them stretched from today's Senegal to Chad and many entered the Trans-Sahara-Trade to North Africa and were even sold in Europe. Barth estimated cotton textiles to have made up some 30% of all Kano exports… Most of the local spinning and weaving industry in West Africa was destroyed between 1880 and 1930…Between 1900 and 1960 the colonial regimes ensured that Africa supplied European markets with unprocessed raw materials whilst being a selling ground for fully processed consumer goods. As a result Africa's economy suffered: its craft industry was destroyed and auto-centric processes of economic development were turned back.

The precolonial Africans' expertise and knowledge show that Africa's industrial and economic development dilemma is not due to lack of talents as suggested by some scholars (Boaduo, 2012: 127) but it is due to the resilient colonial modes of discursive and material dispossession that continue to rein in the contemporary era. Colonial impositions destroyed much of the regional and long distance trade (Andrae et al, 1999: 84). Thus, scholars who argue that the problem with Africa is lack of knowledge and entrepreneurial talents (Edoho, 2015), appear to be missing the point that the real challenge for Africa is the fact that colonists expropriated and destroyed African industries as well as evidence of the existence of such precolonial African industries. In fact, the colonists could have acquired knowledge of mining from Africans (Oxland et al, 1974: 245). Thus, Hammel et al (2000: 49) note that:

> Smelting operations have often left behind tangible evidence in the form of a product such as an ingot or the remnants of a constructed furnace...The perceived value of many ancient mines, however, has been predominantly that they indicate the location of deposits and thus they...have often been destroyed by colonial prospecting and mining. Compounding this problem of destroyed evidence is the fact that the southern African region lacks an indigenous written record and much of the knowledge conveyed through the oral tradition was truncated with the coming of colonialism...One troubling aspect of this lack of evidence is that it opens the door to unfounded theorising which fail to acknowledge the innovations and achievements of indigenous metal workers.

Exposing (neo-)colonial ideologies about African hopelessness thus, Matambalya (2015: 11) states that: "During this period, home-grown industrial development initiatives were largely, de jure and de facto suppressed and replaced with models that propagated dependence to colonial centres. The primary goal of colonialism was to integrate the colonies into the international capitalist system, managed by the colonial powers". The colonial destruction of African industries is especially evident in colonial Zimbabwe where colonists did not only suppress African midwifery, salt production, herbalism, weaving and beer brewing but they also prohibited, through the Gold Trade Ordinance in early 1900s, Africans from mining and trading in gold (Schmidt 1992: 91). Schmidt (1992: 91) states thus: "The Gold Trade Ordinance specifically prohibited Africans from buying or selling gold. Company police and officials of the Native Department enforced this measure by patrolling the eastern frontier and arresting traders who attempted to transport gold into Portuguese territory".

Arising from the above are challenges for scholars like Andreasson (2007) that are arguing for postdevelopment.

Postdevelopment is held to offer new solutions to challenges of orthodox development practices; postdevelopment is considered to move beyond orthodox development "as externally imposed". Despite these arguments by postdevelopment scholarship, there is evidence to show that development has always been taking place [and was extant] in Africa including in the precolonial era. Therefore Africa does not necessarily need to move away from development or from growth: Growth and development are not necessarily inherently Western but what is Western is a predatory variant of "development and growth" that thrives on dispossessing other people of other continents in the world. Precolonial Africa has had development and growth that were however not premised on dispossessing and colonising other people. It is therefore the Western kind of development and growth that is and should be the subject of critique by Africa scholars. Although other scholars like Escobar (2014) have argued for a postdevelopment approach that seeks "alternative worlds", the "pluriversal perspectives", the dissolution of binaries and the movement towards "recognition of the rights of nature", meaningful African development and growth requires close attention to the history of the continent from enslavement and colonial eras through to postcolonial era including the dispossessive and exploitative imperial networks that the Africans have suffered. Any perspective that does not factor in this history would be flawed right from the start.

Africans need to retrace their history to find out where the rain started to beat them. The challenges in Africa are not simplistically traceable to lack of alternatives among Africans but to (neo-)colonial expropriation and dispossession of Africans; including dispossession of resources such as mines. Similarly, the challenges in Africa are not simplistically traceable to lack of diversity or recognition of multiplicities; rather the challenges are traceable to colonial expropriation, dispossession and destruction of African mining and other industries. The challenges in Africa are not necessarily traceable to Cartesian problematics of binaries (Nhemachena, 2016) but rather to colonial expropriations, dispossession and destruction. Indeed problems in Africa are traceable to the resilient colonial networks that explain the externalisation of currencies; the transnational corporations' evasions of taxes and to the repatriation of profits from Africa to home countries, by the multinational corporations(see for instance Mail & Guardian, 12 November 2012). Neither is the African problem simplistically one of the existence of their states because states have always existed including in precolonial Africa and such precolonial states regulated and facilitated the mining, processing and trading of African minerals, by Africans.

The point is that discursive dispossession [distracts and] creates [ideological and epistemic] confusion so that within the attendant mist and myths, capital can make super-profits while the dispossessed sections of humanity are kept busy discussing peripheral matters including in the academies of which existence on the continent is yet to assist the dispossessed Africans. The scenario is akin to a situation where the victims of theft and looting are kept busy in discussions or conversations that operate as decoys; by the accomplices while their colleagues do the actual looting and externalisation of materialities. The fundamental challenge for Africa, as indeed the Global South, is therefore that academies are funded directly or indirectly by capital and there is the risk of witting or unwitting collusion in global capital-inspired discursive dispossession. Awareness of the fact that global capitalist systems funds academies makes plain the need to be extra careful so as to avoid being engaged in discussions or conversations that are in fact epistemic and ontological decoys meant to distract the attention of otherwise critical Africans from what Bond (2006) call the 'looting of Africa'.

One way in which we may expose how Africans are discursively dispossessed, including via the use of Western constructions of time, is to look more closely at the whole (neo-)colonial discourse on the supposed backwardness of hunter-gatherers. In the discourses, there are underlying suppositions that hunter-gatherers were living in history and that their hunting and gathering economies were becoming anachronistic. In all this it should be noticed that the multinational or transnational corporations themselves are enamoured in logics of global hunting and gathering; and this includes slashing and burning those regions particularly in the global south from which the transnational corporations maximise the repatriation of profits to home countries.

Global Hunter-Gatherers and the Question of Security for Capital? Multinational Corporations of Private Security and Private Armies

Scholars have for a long time focused their scholarly eyes on what they called African hunter-gatherers, derided as unsettled and hence primitively engaged in archaic modes of life [threatened by Western modernity with extinction] premised on hunting and gathering. The unfortunate thing is that scholarship has not been able to make it possible for us to clearly see the hunting and gathering parallel logics in so called modern Western modes of economic life. Veiled by the façade of Western temporal constructs that presume that time marches inexorably in linear fashion, scholars have so far been unable to render epistemically visible the hunter-gatherer multinational [mining] corporations that hop from one country to the other prospecting for and exploiting minerals. In other words, scholarship has not shown us the fallacies of the logics of Western economies that purport to be modern and contemporary even as they have foundations in ancient practices of hunting and gathering. In fact the footloose transnational corporations have simply replaced hunter-gatherers as they were known in Africa: the corporations have become large scale hunter-gatherers on a world scale. They hunt and gather on a world scale and they have replaced small scale African hunter-gatherers. Looked at more closely the question of linear time is therefore a façade that hides the more fundamental resilient logics of hunting and gathering within the corporations.

When Cecil John Rhodes and his company, the British South African Company (BSACo) headed off to what is now Zimbabwe, to look for minerals they were obviously motivated by logics of hunting and gathering. When Cecil John Rhodes set up the DeBeers Company to mine diamonds in Africa while at the same time partaking in the British market, the foundational logics are those of hunter-gatherers, hunting and sending or repatriating profits back home. As large scale hunter-gatherers, Western corporations have historically carved out spheres of influence [understood more properly here as hunting grounds] that they deceptively claimed to be civilising when in fact they have been hunting and gathering, collecting from those 'spheres of influence'. From hunting and gathering human African beings during the era of enslavement the West resorted over time to hunting and gathering of African minerals, land and other resources. In all this, the West used ideological discursive facades of progress, development, civilisation and modernisation when in fact they have been engaged in large scale hunting and gathering on the African continent.

In order to gather as much as possible from Africa, the early colonial corporations including companies like Consolidated Diamond Mines (CDM) in Namibia exploited Africans through extensive contract labour system (Cooper, 1999; Hishongwa, 1992; Likuwa, 2014; Botes, 2013). Equally to maximise their hunting and gathering from Africa, the corporations hunted down Africans who were then forced to work for nothing or for next to nothing; and these Africans who were hunted down for purposes of forced labour were regarded and treated as indistinct from animals (Likuwa, 2014: 4; Botes, 2013: 511; Mosely, 1977). Captured Africans who refused to work for the corporations in the forced labour system had their huts, including granaries, burnt down by the colonial settlers. Deprived of their resources and their means of subsistence, the captured Africans were allowed to engage in liberal [black-market] sex and drugs, alcohol and football matches and dance competitions so that they could channel off their energy and drain them of the steam to resist colonial dispossession and exploitation (Mosely, 1977).

Salient in the foregoing is the fact that discursive practices often constitute baits, in this case by transnational corporations that are mining Africa. Discursive practices, in this case around liberal freedoms to sex, drugs, alcohol, constituted baits with which to deceive Africans into believing that colonial settlers brought freedom when in fact Africans were being pillaged of their [mineral] resources while they engaged in liberalised sexual activities, alcoholic and drug consumption that colonists yielded them as liberal "freedoms" from "traditional" cultural constraints. It is of course safer for global capital to concede liberal sexual, and other freedoms from [supposedly] constraining cultural taboos and ethics than it is for capital to grant Africans liberties to own their material resources such as mines and land. Granting such liberal freedoms against supposedly constraining cultural constraints helps to distract attention from global transnational corporations' monopoly over ownership of African resource. In other words, capital concedes sexual and other such [ordinarily materially derivative] freedoms so that it can continue to plunder African material resources while Africans are engrossed and engaged in the liberalised sexual congresses. The liberal freedoms are meant to rechannel and detour the energies of the dispossessed and hence defuse tensions and attendant resistance to capitalist penetration, exploitation and expropriation. In other words, the underlying logic of capital's liberalisation of sexual and other such realms is that while Africans liberally penetrate one another in the sexual congresses, including in manners that have been lamented by some Africans as unnatural penetration (Apprecht, 1998; 2013), capital would in the meantime also be busy penetrating them, mining and expropriating material resources. In other words, liberal freedoms are part and parcel of the discursive dispossession that has greased up the material dispossession of Africans by global capital.

Thus, the challenge with many of the civil society organisations on the continent is that they have facilitated more discussions on liberal rights than they have facilitated restitution of African mineral and other resources (see for instance Voice of America, 20 June 2011; BBC, 28 June 2010; The Guardian, 24 March 2014). So, much like in the colonial era when Africans were conceded sexual and other liberal freedoms, in lieu of restitution and ownership of their material resources, postcolonial civil society organisations tend to focus on similar liberal freedoms in their engagements with Africa. But then the question is what use are sexual freedoms to Africans that have been deprived of their material resources such as mines on which their livelihoods are based? Similarly, the question is what use is freedom of movement to Africans who have been historically dispossessed of their material means of subsistence such as mining activities? In the same vein, the question is what use is freedom of conscience to Africans who have been colonially dispossessed of their material means of livelihood such as mining activities? What use is the notional right to life for Africans that are starving because capital has dispossessed them of their material means of livelihood? In other words, the challenge is that fundamental rights do not deal with the fundamental and ongoing issues of dispossession by capital and the correlative necessity of restitution. Similarly civil society organisations are often more spirited in dealing with African diamonds as contentious bloody diamonds but they do not deal with the more fundamental questions of ownership of resources by Africans. In the light of the history of colonial exploitation, dispossession and the resilient structural violence perpetrated by global capital on disinherited Africans, one can argue that global capital is itself bloodier than African bloody diamonds.

In a context where Africans are agitating for restitution of their land and other mineral resources (Nhemachena, 2016; Moyo, 2008), it is strange that civil society groups focus on narrow issues, such as bloody diamonds and liberal freedoms. There are reports for instance that "grassroots" movements on "bloody diamonds" have sought to combat trade in bloody diamonds through the Kimberley Certification Scheme (Global Policy, 2 November 2011; Howard, 2016: 137; Nicholas, 2012: 648). Yet there is not as much grassroots mobilisation to support Africans agitating for indigenisation, restitution and repossession of their resources from capital that has, for centuries, perpetrated structural violence as well as fanned wars in Africa. The salience of questions of restitution and repossession of African resources is underscored by Mbeki's (2000: 77) observation that:

> For the African Renaissance to happen, Mbeki identified several necessary pre-conditions. He identified the emergence of a new, unionised 'proletariat class' that is not only concerned with traditional issues such as working conditions and wages, but that is also involved in ownership and enterprise management as one of those preconditions. He also identified the emergence of a large urban professional and entrepreneurial middle class that is property-owning and is an active participant in the development of small and medium enterprises as the second precondition.

Capital is seriously threatened by the majority of Africans who having suffered historical dispossession including recent neoliberal retrenchments, devaluation and deregulation of prices have realised that their security does not lie in seeking [unstable and insecure] employment in multinational corporations but in ownership of their resources. Africans who have realised the insecurities of global capital's regimes that render flexibility to capital while extending insecurities to African employees (Klerck, 2008; Klerck, 2003) are now poised for indigenisation and restitution struggles. To defuse indigenisation and restitution struggles, capital can only fund epistemological shifts and ideologies that allow it to retain what it has expropriated, and create opportunities for new cycles of dispossession. Contemporary discourses on 'privatisation' as the panacea for African economic challenges are part of the discursive dispossession of African publics who are forced to cede or sell what they collectively own to 'private' capital in the [erroneous] hope that capital is a better manager of economies. These discourses erroneously assume that what "private" Western capital owns or possesses is "private" property when in fact it is property looted over centuries by colonists from African publics. In this sense, the escalation of security systems in Euro-modern societies is not necessarily a function of progressive or development conscious mentalities but it is a function of realisations that stolen property needs stronger fortifications lest the victims of (neo-)colonial looting help themselves to their stolen property.

Western discourses and practices show increasing concerns about 'insecurities' in Africa to such an extent that Western corporations and governments are deploying their private security companies and private armies to African countries (News24, 29 March 2015; Avant n.d; African Business, 22 November 2012; Fulloon n.d; Caroline, 2010). For purposes of this chapter, it is argued here that the increasing Western concerns about insecurities in Africa are less about the security of African people than about the security of transnational corporations and institutions in Africa. The fact that these concerns about insecurities are increasing at a time when Africans are increasingly fighting for indigenisation and restitutions of their resources, including mining, underscores that what constitutes the greatest insecurity for global capital is African restitution and indigenisation. It is not necessarily African dictators, autocrats, or democratic deficits that threaten global capital; rather it is the upwelling of the historically dispossessed who reclaim and fight for restitution. Notions of democracy are arguably meant to constitute apparatuses for discursive dispossession or to operate as decoys in the planetary games of dispossession; the fact that the West broods over a form of democracy that does not facilitate restitution of what was looted is proof enough that the term is just a notional decoy.

With African states increasingly supporting popular indigenisation struggles, transnational capital can no longer bank on the African states to provide security for them, hence the recent preference to constitute private security and private armies for deployment on the African continent. To get African states out of the way so as to privilege private security and private armies, there are increasing discourses about African state 'weakness', 'failure' etc. but there is hardly any comprehensive and deep reflection that could expose the fact that African states are being demonised primarily for failure and for being too weak to protect transnational capital against indigenous people, [some of who are being labelled as terrorists] restless and reclaiming their resources. The contemporary discourses about the supposedly unviable and supposedly anachronistic notions of state sovereignty need to be understood in terms of the interests of transnational capital that feels so threatened by African states supporting restitution for African majorities that they would rather support the exit of those states and create spaces for their [transnational corporations] own private security and private army firms. Apart from threatening and challenging African state security and sovereignty (Caroline, 2010), these private security companies and private armies [some of which are owned by Western governments] replicate the old mercenary activities associated with colonial companies such as the British South African Company and East Indian Company that came as chartered companies to establish colonies and engage in long distance trade (Avant, n.d).

Some of the private security companies and private armies are hired for criminal purposes such as destabilisation of legitimate governments (Mbadlanyana, n.d). Destabilising Africa assists multinational [mining] companies [to get rid of indigenising states that they deem to be problematic] that are threatened with African state sanctioned indigenisation, restitution and compensation claims. Indeed some of the private security and militaries such as Executive Outcomes (EO) engage in illegal natural resources exploitation in countries such as Democratic Republic of Congo (Pingeot, 2014). These private security firms do not only protect multinational mining operations, the United Nations, transnational corporations and Nongovernmental Organisations (Frye, 2005); they also protect banks, telecoms, transport (African Business, 22 November 2012). In addition to thousands of private security companies which are foreign owned, Africa is also harassed by the presence of United States of America's AFRICOM which coordinates, from its bases in Africa, all U.S military operations on the African continent, since 2008 (African Business, 22 November 2012; Turse, 2015; Boyle, 2013).

The connection between these private security companies and private military companies and African mineral resources is underscored by Frye's (2005: 2620) observation that: "Executive Outcomes (EO) was formed in South Africa during the transition from apartheid to democracy. The company primarily worked for African states and received as payment mining and oil concessions in these nations. Founded in 1989, EO was linked to the [apartheid era] South African Defence Force and to mining and oil extraction companies". Although EO operates in African countries, it is managed from London yet it has drilling interests for instance in Angola (Global Policy Forum, April 1998).

Thus, although contemporary discourses often juxtapose state security to human security, there is hardly any mention of transnational corporation security that lurks in Africa and that threatens to replace state security with private security and private armies on the African continent. In this sense, both African state security and African human security are threatened by the transnational corporations' private security and private armies that are seldom problematized in discourses on security in Africa. While African state security including armies and police forces are increasingly being problematized in discourses on security, little regard is paid to emergent private security and private armies that constitute mercenaries on the continent. If the contemporary antipathy against African state security is read together with contemporary antipathy against African indigenisation of resources, it becomes clear that the efforts to replace state security with "human security" is in fact a ploy to replace state security with transnational private security, so as to evade threats of indigenisation and nationalisation of resources by African states. In other words, it is the security of transnational corporations that capital is worried about and not necessarily the security of ordinary Africans, who in any case have been victims of (neo-) colonial expropriation, exploitation and structural violence for centuries.

Further, transnational [mining] corporations playing global hunter-gatherers feel immensely threatened by African states that seek to define and fortify their borders particularly against exploitative and dispossessive transnational capital. Contemporary discourses against African borders and boundaries need to be looked at in terms of the interests of global transnational capital that is also sponsoring epistemological and ideological shifts towards borderlessness in the global south, including Africa. Similarly, contemporary civil society projects on creating open societies in Africa must also be looked at in terms of discursive dispossession that supports openness in a world where transnational corporations continue to forage the world, grabbing whatever they find valuable irrespective of place and space. Equally, contemporary antipathy towards African states needs to be understood in terms of the interests of transnational capital that sponsors epistemological and ideological shifts against the African states particularly those that threaten to nationalise and indigenise resources, currently monopolised by transnational corporations. The colonisation of Africa began with the erasure of precolonial African states; this means that contemporary epistemologies and ideologies against African states are not necessarily liberating for Africans. In fact the [intended] erasure of African states is an omen of intense vulnerability to exploitative and dispossessive transnational capital. Through ideological and discursive practices against African states, indigenisation and nationalisation, Africa is being prepared for unmitigated global capitalist vulnerability, and not security as erroneously and insidiously claimed. Contemporary ideologies and discursive practices are preparing Africa on behalf of transnational global appropriators, who detest closure and protective boundaries and hence African states or the African union. Hunting grounds do not have to erect their own borders and boundaries that threaten to foreclose the global hunters and gatherers.

Attracting Foreign Investors or Attracting Foreign Appropriators? Discursive Dispossession and the Political Economies of Misrecognition in Africa

When the South African Police Service gunned down striking miners at Marikana (Institute for Security Studies, 6 December 2012), simplistic arguments would conceive that as protection of national security. Little, if any regard is paid to the fact that the activities by the police amounted to protection of transnational capital in the form of Lonmin whose interests the strikers threatened. Thus, in spite of the fact that the transnational corporations such as Lonmin evade paying taxes to African governments (Mail and Guardian, 20 September 2014), African governments sadly tend to prioritise attracting and protecting foreign corporations even when these corporations operate against the interests of ordinary citizens. Although in the Marikana case, calls were subsequently made for the de-militarisation of the South African Police (SABC News, 2 October 2014; Institute for Security Studies, 6 December 2012), demilitarisation of national police forces would not necessarily help in a context where transnational corporations are themselves constituting and bringing in private security and military companies that also threaten the security of African citizens. The problem is transnational capital that apart from historically dispossessing Africans pays them starvation wages while at the same time evading payment of taxes to African governments. In other words, the South African state failed to notice the fact that it shared a lot with the striking miners that the police force gunned down: both the miners and the South African state were not paid their dues-whether in the form of wages or taxes- by Lonmin. Thus, the Mail and Guardian (20 September 2014) reported that there have been transfers of over R2, 3 billion in fees from Lonmin to two of its subsidiaries, with one located in a tax haven. Thus Lonmin is alleged to have transferred, between 2008-2012, $160m (R1, 2 billion) in commission fees to a subsidiary, Western Metal Sales Limited, based in Bermuda (a well-known tax haven). It is said that the amounts were shifted from Lonmin's South African Operations so that it would be kept away from financing wage demands, social labour commitments or so that it would not be absorbed into taxable income.

Although in conventional economics, transnational corporations are often described as foreign investors worth attracting, the [profit maximising and repatriating] transnational corporations have not necessarily helped host African nations to develop (Chukwuemeka et al, 2011; Bulawayo24 News, 6 July 2014). As aptly argued by Warikandwa and Osode (2016) capitalist markets often perpetrate injustice, expose financial systems of developing countries to unpredictable global business environment and the vigorous competitions for foreign investors result in lowering of African labour standards. Some transnational corporations decline to hand over data about mineral exploration to African governments (Bulawayo24 News, 6 July 2014) and still other transnational corporations have also swindled and smuggled African resources (BBC News, 14 March 2016). In spite of the fact that some of these transnational corporations sponsor civil society organisation in Africa to promote openness, transparency and accountability, the same transnational corporations are not transparent; they under-invoice, under-price and smuggle African minerals (Mail & Guardian, 12 November 2012). Some transnational corporations engage in profit shifting and tax abuse which deprive developing countries of resources (The Guardian, 2 June 2015; Institute for Security Studies, 5 July 2011; Rego 2003).

Thus, The Guardian (2 June 2015), states that:

> Tax abuse by multinational corporations increases the tax burden on other taxpayers, violates corporations' civil obligations, robs...countries of critical resources to fight poverty and fund public

services, exacerbates income inequality, and increases developing country reliance on foreign assistance...A recent report by the UN conference on Trade and Development estimated that profit-shifting by multinational companies costs developing countries $100 billion a year in lost corporate income tax. Another report by International Monetary Fund (IMF) researchers, estimated that developing countries may be losing as much as $213 billion a year to tax avoidance...Multinational companies, many with headquarters in the UK and other G8 countries, are cheating African countries out of billions of dollars in vital tax revenues that could help vulnerable people get descent health care and send their children to school...

Similarly, the Institute for Security Studies, (5 July 2011) states that:

Capital flight is a significant obstruction to Africa's development. Each year, the continent loses US $148 billion-four times the amount of foreign aid it receives-in this way. Corporate profits, generated from the sale of Africa's natural resources, are rarely adequately taxed, leaving governments with little to fund national budgets. Such shortfalls must be addressed, either by raising revenues from already overburdened citizenry or by accepting conditional loans from multinational institutions. Either way it is the ordinary Africans who must service this debt, effectively plugging the holes in the national budget left by transnational corporations, and indirectly contributing to their massive profit margins.

Comparing multinational corporations and local companies, Rego (2003: 808) argues that:

Multinational corporations are able to avoid income taxes that domestic-only companies cannot. They avoid income taxation by locating operations in low-tax countries, by shifting income. Multinational corporations have opportunities to avoid income taxation by locating operations in low-tax countries, by shifting income from high tax locations to low-tax locations, by exploiting differences

87

between the tax rules of different countries, and by taking advantage of tax subsidy agreements with host countries.

The challenges above are also evident in Zambia where the Lusaka Times, (16 Jan 2017) reported that: "Recently, financial intelligence centre (FIC) assistant director Clement Kapalu disclosed that Zambia is losing US$3 billion annually due to illicit financial flows mainly perpetrated in the minerals subsector where tax evasion malpractices such as transfer pricing, over and under-invoicing and trade mispricing are rampant".

Thus, while civil society organisations have tended to focus on criticising African governments for corruption (Ndikumana, 2013), African leaders are calling on multinational corporations to stop dodging tax and from engaging in illicit money flows (Mail and Guardian, 15 July 2015). Thus, while the transnational corporations' evasions of tax amount to more than the aid which the West claims to be giving to Africa per year, Western countries continue to popularise the idea that Africa is a beneficiary of Western assistance. For instance, Global Research (13 April 2007) notes that in September 2001 the International Monetary Fund declared Zimbabwe [that expropriated land from white farmers from the year 2000] ineligible to use its general resources and in 2001 U.S.A former President, George Bush's, Zimbabwe Democracy and Economic Recovery Act (ZIDERA) of 2001 directed U.S treasury to instruct U.S members of international institutions to oppose and advocate against any extension of any loan, credit or guarantee to Zimbabwe. It is further noted that British Foreign Secretary, Jack Straw, revealed that he was "building coalitions" against Zimbabwe and he stated that Great Britain would oppose any access by Zimbabwe to International Financial Institutions. Also, British officials threatened to eliminate financial assistance to southern African nations unless they imposed sanctions on their neighbour, Zimbabwe.

What all this means is that transnational corporations are not necessarily investors but they are appropriators of African resources of which proceeds they maximally externalise. And of course in order to externalise, the transnational corporations have to construct roads, railways, air and other forms of transport and communication but these cannot be simplistically described as investments as they are in fact routes for appropriating and externalising African resources. While in Africa there are conceptions that Africa got independence, this is actually misrecognition of the continuing invisible exploitative global matrix of power which explains coloniality (Ndlovu-Gatsheni, 2013). Because African "independence" was often negotiated by corporations including mining giants such as Consolidated Goldfields (Mail and Guardian, 7 October 2008), some Western corporations still monopolise resources. Although strategic mineral reserves and production capabilities of the world are concentrated in the former Soviet Union and in Africa (Butts, 1993), it is the Rothchild family in the West that controls 80% of uranium supplies around the world (Zagami, 2016) and the late Cecil John Rhodes's DeBeers diamond cartel towers in the mining and exploitation of diamonds (Dice, 2014).

The paradox here is that those that monopolise the world [mineral resources] claim to be global champions of equality, human rights, transparency, accountability and democracy. The question then is whether Africa should continue to adhere to the templates or scripts that are produced by the Janus-faced monopolists or must Africa instead read what is not said in the templates or scripts rolled out to the world from the empire? Evidence presented in this chapter shows that Africa had from the precolonial era, its own mineral extraction, melting and smelting and other industries that were supplanted by colonial settlers who wanted to impose their own political, economic, social, cultural, epistemic and legal templates on the dispossessed Africans. These colonial templates, which continue to be used, unfortunately erroneously presuppose that Africans were completely blank on economic, political, legal, social, cultural and epistemic terrains.

Thus, Africa needs to revamp the education system so that the colonial templates, that perpetuate discursive and material dispossession, are jettisoned. It is via the resilient colonial epistemologies that the emerging New World Order is creating lacunae for new, more virulent forms of colonial domination that deny [African] humanity its overdue pre-eminence; it is through resilient colonial education that the New World Order perpetuates the old colonial ideologies and practices that legitimise Western quests for planetary dominance. There is thus need for Africans to hold fast to their struggles for humanisation that recognises their creativity and innovativeness as well as their imperatives of owning and controlling their resources. Besides, there is need for Africa to shy away from emerging Western ideologies about animism and ideologies that problematic African anthropocentrism. Such ideologies simply replicate colonial and enslavement logics. When (neo-)colonists enslaved, dispossessed and exploited Africans, the underlying logic of their project was that Africans are no different from animals. Colonists and enslavers did not bring anthropocentrism to Africa as is implied by some contemporary scholars; indeed, colonisation reduced Africans to the level of animals-colonists pulverised African autonomy, sovereignty and anthropocentrism and therefore the contemporary critiques of African anthropocentrism are in fact symptoms of colonial hangover in the 21st century.

Conclusion

It has been argued that discursive dispossession thrives on creating confusion and misrecognition about Africa; it creates misapprehensions among those that are targeted for dispossession. Contrary to Gramscian arguments holding that ideologies 'manufacture consent', discursive dispossession serves to create not necessarily consent but misapprehension, misrecognition and confusion all of which are foundational to (neo-) colonial dispossession and exploitation of Africans. Discursive dispossession is also productive of discursive disposal where the objective is to dispose of other people's forms of knowledge, cultures, laws, beliefs, economies and polities. It has been argued that colonists engaged not only in material dispossession of Africans but they also engaged in discursive dispossession at ideological, cognitive and epistemic levels. Some Africans who have been effectively discursively dispossessed have come to erroneously believe that Africans had no knowledge, no science of mining in the precolonial era; they have come to believe that Africans had no knowledge and science of melting, smelting, trading or commerce prior to colonisation; they have come to believe that Africans were mere subsistence producers prior to colonisation and that therefore Africa had no modernity of its own. Discursively dispossessed and constituted thus, Africans have been discursively disposed to the margins of humanity where their economic activities have come to be considered as 'illegal', 'blackmarket', 'informal' and so on. There is thus need to ask more serious questions such as about how and at what point the majority of African economic activities have come to be regarded as 'illegal', 'blackmarket', 'informal' and so on, when in fact Africans have mined and engaged in such activities for centuries prior to colonisation without attracting such derogatory sanctions. Thus, rather than understanding Africans as trapped in cycles of poverty as other scholars have posited, it is more productive to understand Africans as trapped in cycles of global capitalist dispossession. To conceive Africans as simply trapped in cycles of poverty would be to misrecognise the reality of their historical and contemporary position as prey to capital. Africans are necessarily poor as is often simplistically argues; *a fortiori* they are dispossessed of their [mineral] resource and exploited.

References

African Business, (22 November 2012) Is Private Security Taking Over? Africanbusinessmagazine.com/uncategorised/is-private-security-taking-over-africa/

Al Jazeera., (16 March 2017) Outrage Over Helen Zille's Colonialism Tweets, www.aljazeera.com/news/2017/03/outrage-heln-zille-colonialism-tweets-170316154748367.html

AllAfrica, (25 Feb 2016) Africa: Tackle Tax Evasion to Fuel Africa's Development, allafrica.com stories/2016 02261373.html

Andrae, G. et al., (1999) *Union Power in the Nigerian Textile Industry: Labour Regime and Adjustment*, New Brunswick: Transaction Publishers

Andreasson, S., (2007) Thinking Beyond Development: the Future of Postdevelopment Theory in Southern Africa, *Prepared for the*

British International Studies Association Annual Conference, University of Cambridge 17-19 December 2007

Apter, A., (1992) *Black Critics and Kings: The Hermeneutics of Power in Yoruba Society,* Chicago and London: The University of Chicago Press

Austin, G., (2004) Markets With, Without, and In spite of States; West Africa in the Precolonial Nineteenth Century, Working Paper No ¾, London School of Economics, March 2004

Avant, D. D., (2005) The Market for Force: The Consequences of Privatising Security

Avant, D., (2012) Mercenaries, in The Wiley-Blackwell Encyclopedia of Globalisation. DOI:10.1002/9780470670590.wberg

Baum, J. A. C. et al., (2009) *Outsourcing War: The Evolution of the Private Military Industry After the Cold War,* Rotman School of Management. University of Toronto: Ontario

BBC News., (14 March 2016) Zimbabwe's Robert Mugabe: Foreign Companies 'Stole Diamonds' www.bbc.com/news/world-africa-35720912

BBC News., (28 June 2010) Diamonds: Does the Kimberley Process Work. www.bbc.com/news/10307046

BBC News., (4 Dec 2012) Corporate Tax Avoidance: How Do Companies Do It? www.bbc.com/news/business-20580545

Bisson, M. S., (1982). Trade and Tribute: Archaeological Evidence for the Origins of States in South Central Africa, in *Cahiers d'etudes africaines* Volume 22, No 87: 343-361

Boaduo, N. A. P., (2012). African Renaissance in the Contemporary Era of the African Union: Re-Thinking Strategies for Africa's Industrial and Economic Development, in *International Journal of Developing Societies* vol 1 (3): 124-132

Bond, P., (2006). *Looting Africa: The Economics of Exploitation*. Zed Books

Botes, A., (2013). The History of Labour Hire in Namibia: A Lesson for South Africa vol 16, No 1 PER/PELJ: 507-536

Bulawayo24News, (6 July 2014). Canadian Firm Hides Zimbabwean Mineral Data, bulawayo24.com/index-id-news-sc-national-byo-50116.html

Butler, J. et al., (2013). *Dispossession: The Performative in the Political*, Cambridge: Polity Press

Butt, K. H., (1993). Strategic Minerals in the New World Order, in Strategic Studies Institute

Caroline, V., (2010). Mercenaries and the State: How the Hybridization of the Armed Forces is Changing the Face of National Security, Unpublished PhD thesis, The London School of Economics and Political Science

Celikates, R., (2012). 'Systematic Misrecognition and the Practice of Critique: Bourdieu, Bottanski and the Role of Critical Theory', in Bankowsky, M. et al., (ed,) *Recognition Theory and Contemporary French Moral and Political Philosophy*. Manchester University Press: 160-172

Chirikure, S., (2010). *Indigenous Mining and Metallurgy in Africa*. Cambridge University Press

Chukwuemeka, E. *et al.*, (2011). 'African Underdevelopment and the Multinationals-A Political Commentary', in *Journal of Sustainable Development* vol 4, No 4

Colson, E., (1971). *The Social Consequences of Resettlement: The Impact of the Kariba Resettlement Upon the Gwembe Tonga*. University of Zambia Institute

Cooper, A. D., (1999). The Institutionalisation of Contract Labour in Namibia, *Journal of Southern African Studies* vol 25, No 1: 121-138

Dice, M., (2014). *Inside the Illuminati: Evidence, Objectives, and Methods of Operation*. The Resistance

Dorp, M., (2016). *How Shell, Total and Eni Benefit from Tax Breaks in Nigeria's Gas Industry: the Case of Nigeria Liquefied Natural Gas Company (NLNG)*, Amsterdam

Edoho, F. M., (2015). Entrepreneurship Paradigm and Economic Renaissance in Africa, in *African Journal of Economic and Management Studies* vol 6 Issue 1: 2-16

Ellert, H., (1984). *The Material Culture of Zimbabwe*. Longman: Harare

Epprecht, M., (2013). *Hungochani: The History of a Dissident Sexuality in Southern Africa*. McGill-Queen's Press

Escobar, A., (2010). 'Worlds and Knowledges Otherwise: The Latin American Modernity/Coloniality Research Program', in Mignolo

W D *et al*, (eds) *Globalisation and the Decolonial Option*, London: Routledge 33-64

Escobar, A., (2014). 'Degrowth, Postdevelopment, and Transitions: a Preliminary Conversation', in *Sustain Sci Springer* DOI. 10.1007/s11625-015-0297-5

Fanon, F., (1963). The Wretched of the Earth. New York: Grove Press

Fayemi, J. K., (1998). The Future of Demilitarisation and Civil Military Relations in West Africa: Challenges and Prospects for Democratic Consolidation, *in fri.Polit.Sci* vol 3, No 1: 83-103

Fenske, J., (2012). Ecology, Trade and States in Pre-Colonial Africa, University of Oxford Dept of Economics MPRA Paper No 37372

Frye, E. L., (2005). Private Military Firms in the New World Order: How Redefining "Mercenary Can Tame the 'Dogs of war', in *Fordham Law Review* vol 73, Issue 6, Article 1

Frye, E. L., (2005). 'Private Military Firms in the New World Order: How Redefining "Mercenary" Can Tame the "Dogs of War", in *Fordham Law Review* vol 73, Issue 6, Article 4, http://ir.lawnet.fordham.eedu/flr/vol73/iss6/4

Fulloon, M., (n.d). Non-State Actor: Defining Private Military Companies, in *Strategic Review for Southern Africa* vol 37, No 2: 29-51

Fulloon, M., (n.d). Non-State Actors: Defining Private Military Companies, in *Strategic Review for Southern Africa* vol 37, No 2: 29-51

Fyle, M. C., (1999). *Introduction to the History of African Civilisation: Precolonial Africa* vol 1, New York, Oxford: University Press of America, Inc.

Garson, N., (n.d). The Development of Mining and Minerals Processing in Southern Africa www.sarpn.org/mmsd/vol 1/mmsd-2 pdf

Garver, E., (1994). 'Aristotle's Natural Slaves: Incomplete Praxeis and Incomplete Human Beings', in *Journal of the History of Philosophy* vol 32, No 2: 173-195

Gillespie, T., (2016). 'Accumulation by Urban Dispossession: Struggles over Urban Space in Accra, Ghana', in *Transactions of the Institute of British Geographers*, Vol 41 (1): 66-77

Global Policy, (April 1998). Foot Soldiers of the New World Order https://www.globalpolicy.org/component/content/article/190/39260.html

Global Policy Forum, (2 November 2011). Kimberley Process https://www.globalpolicy.org/the-dark-side-of-natural-resources-st/diamonds-in-conflict/kimberley-process.html

Global Research, (13 April 2007). The Battle Over Zimbabwe's Future www.globalresearch.ca/the-battle-over-zimbabwes-future/5373

Global Research, (14 January 2015). France's Colonial Tax Still Enforced for Africa: Bleeding Africa and Feeding France" www.globalresearch.ca/frances-colonial-tax-still-enforced-for-africa-bleeding-africa-and-feeding-france/5547512

Gramsci, A., (1971). *Selections from the Prison Notebooks of Antonio Gramsci*. New York: International Publishers

Greer, A., (2014). Confusion on the Commons, in Books and Ideas, 8 December 2014. http://www.bookssandideas.net/confusion-on-the-commons.html

Hammel, A. *et al.*, (2000). Precolonial Mining in Southern Africa, in *The Journal of the South African Institute of Mining and Metallurgy* Jan/Feb: 49-56 https://www.saimm.co.za/jorunal/v100n01p049.pdf vol 100, issue 1

Hashim, Y. *et al.*, (1999). Cross-Border Trade and the Parallel Currency Market-Trade and Finance in the Context of Structural Adjustment: A Case Study From Kano, *Nigeria Research Report* No 113, Nordiska Afrikainstitutet Uppsala

Hishongwa, N. S., (1992). *The Contract Labour System and its Effects on Family and Social Life in Namibia: A Historical Perspective*. Gamsberg MacMillan

Holl, A. F. C., (2000). 'Metals and Precolonial African Society', in Bisson M S *et al*, (eds) *Ancient African Metallurgy: The Sociocultural Context.*, Oxford: Lanham

Hook, D., (2001). 'Discourse, Knowledge, Materiality, History: Foucault and Discourse Analysis', in *Theory and Psychology* 11 (4): 521-547

Howard, A., (2016). Blood Diamonds: The Success and Failure of the Kimberley Process Certification Scheme in Angola, Sierra Leone and Zimbabwe, in *Washington University Global Studies Law Review* vol 15, Issue 1

Institute for Security Studies, (5 July 2011). Copper and Capital Flight: How Corporate Debt Becomes Public Debt https://issafrica.org/iss-today/copper-and--capital-flight-how-corporate-debt-becomes-public-debt

James, D., (2015). 'How Bourdieu Bites Back: Recognising Misrecognition in Education and Educational Research', in *Cambridge Journal of Education*, 45 (1): 97-112

Jerven, M., (2016). Capitalism in Pre-Colonial Africa: A Review: African Economic History Working Paper Series No 27/2016, Norwegian University of Life Sciences

Kautonin, M. R., (28 January 2014). African Countries Forced by France to Pay Colonial Tax for the Benefits of Slavery and Colonisation, in Silicon Africa www.siliconafrica.com/france-colonial-tax

Klerck, G., (2003). 'Labour Market Regulation and the Casualisation of Employment in Namibia', in *South African Journal of Labour Relations*, vol 27, Issue 2: 63-95

Klerck, G., (2008). 'Industrial Relations in Namibia Since Independence: Between Neo-Liberalism and Neo-Corporatism?' In *Employee Relations* vol 30, Iss 4: 355-371

Klerck, G., (2009). 'Rise of Temporary Employment Industry in Namibia: A Regulatory 'Fix', in *Journal of Contemporary African Studies* vol 27, Issue 1: 85-103

Likuwa, K., (2014). 'Contract Labour System and Farm Labourers' Experiences in Pre-Independent Namibia, Historical Reflections, Perspectives and Lessons', BAB Working Paper No 2, Presented at Basler AfrikaBibliographien, Switzerland

Lusaka Times, (16 January 2017). Zambia Revenue Authority to Audit Large Mining Firms for tax Compliance https://www.lusakatimes.com/2017/01/16/zambia-reenue-authority-audit-large-mining-firms-tax-compliance/

MacLean, R., (2015). Iron Working and the Iron Age in Africa, in Oxford Bibliographiess.com/view/document/obo-9780199846733

Mail & Guardian Africa, (15 July 2015). 'I Call that Robbery': Rich-Poor Tax Dispute Overshadows Key UN Development Summit in Ethiopia, mgafrica.com/article/2015-07-15-this-is-robbery-rich-poor-tax-dispute-oershadows-key-un-deelopment-summit-in-ethiopia

Mail & Guardian., (12 November 2012). Report Accuses Zimbabwe of Stealing Diamond Money, mg.co.za/article/2012-11-12-report-accuses-zimbabwe-of-stealing-diamond-money

Mail & Guardian., (20 September 2014). Inquiry into Lonmin Fee Transfer to Tax Haven, mg.co.za/article/2014-09-20-inquiry-into-lonmin-fee-transfers-to-tax-haven

Mail & Guardian., (21 November 2014). Clampdown on Tax Avoidance mg.co.za/article/2014-11-20-clampdown-on-tax-aoidance

Mail & Guardian., (22 August 2014). Iron Age Mining Links Ancient South Africa to the World mg.co.za/article/2014-08-15-iron-age-mining-links-ancient-sa-to-the-world

Mail & Guardian., (6 July 2016). How Much Do Governments Rake In? Mining Giants Come Clean on Taxes, mg.co.za/article/2016-07-06-00-mining-giants-come-clean-on-taxes

Schoeman, A. *et al.*, (2013). Final Thoughts, in Mapungubwe Institute for Strategic Reflection (MISTRA) Research Report, Mapungubwe Reconsidered: Exploring Beyond the Rise and Decline of the Mapungubwe State

Mbadlanyana, T., (n.d). 'Moral Politik and Realpolitik: Seeking Common Ground on the Use of Private Military and Security Companies', in Gumedze, S., (ed) *From Market for Force to Market for Peace: Private Military and Security Companies in Peacekeeping Operations*, ISS Monograph no 183

Mbeki, M., (2000). Issues in South African Foreign Policy: The African Renaissance is Souls, in *Spring* 200: 76-81

Mbindwane, B., (25 May 2015). Soldiers for Hire: SA's Great Security Risk, in Daily Maverick https://www.dailymaerick.co.za/opinionsta/2015-05-25-soldiers-for-hire-sas-great-security-risk/

Medina, J., (2006). *Speaking from Elsewhere: A New Contextualist Perspective on Meaning, Identity and Discursive Agency*, Albany: State University of New York Press

Mentan, T., (2010). *The New World Order Ideology and Africa: Understanding and Appreciating Ambiguity, Deceit and Recapture of Decolonised Spaces*. Bamenda: Langaa RPCIG

Mosley, P., (1977). 'Review', in *The Journal of Modern African Studies* vol 15, No 2: 328-330

Moyo, S., (2008). *African Land Questions, Agrarian Transitions and the States: Contradictions of Neoliberal Land Reforms*. Dakar CODESRIA

Murray, A., (2015). 'Invisible Power, Visible Dispossession: The Witchcraft of a Subterranean Pipeline', in *Political Geography* 47: 64-76

Mzamane, M. V., (2001). Where there is No Vision the People Perish: Reflections on the African Renaissance, Hawke Institute Working Paper Series No 16, University of South Australia

Ndikumana, L., (2013). The Private Sector as Culprit and Victim of Corruption in Africa, Working paper Series No 330

Ndlovu-Gatsheni S. J., (n.d). Global Coloniality and the Challenges of Creating African Futures, in *Strategic Review for Southern Africa* vol 36, No 2: 181-202

Ndlovu-Gatsheni, S. J. (2013). *Coloniality of Power in Postcolonial Africa: Myths of Decolonisation*. Dakar: CODESRIA

New Zimbabwe, (30 December 2014). Zimbabwe Still Fighting for Diamonds Seized in Belgium. www.newzimbabwe.com/news-19714-zimbabwe+still+fighting+for+seized+diamonds/news.aspx

News24, (29 March 2015). Private Security Industry Under Fire. www.news24.com/Archives/city-press/private-security-industry-under-fire-20150429

Ngugi wa Thiongo, (1986). *Decolonising the Mind: The Politics of Language in Africa Literature*. Heinemann

Nhemachena, A., (2015). Envisioning African Democracy in the Twenty-First Century: Mwana Washe Muranda Kumwe and the Coloniality of Contrived Democracy, in Mawere M *et al.*, (eds), *Democracy, Good Governance and Development in Africa.* Bamenda: Langaa RPCIG

Nhemachena, A., (2016). Animism, Coloniality and Humanism: Reversing the Empire's Framing of Africa, in Mawere M *et al.*, (eds), *Theory, Knowledge, Development and Politics: What Role for the Academy in the Sustainability of Africa?* Bamenda: Langaa RPCIG

Nhemachena, A., (2016). Double-Trouble: Reflections of the Violence of Absence and the Culpability of the Present in Africa, in Mawere M *et al.*, (eds), *Violence, Politics and Conflict Management in Africa: Envisioning Transformation, Peace and Unity in the Twenty-First Century.* Bamenda: Langaa RPCIG

Nicholas, J. E., (2012). 'A Conflict of Diamonds: The Kimberley Process and Zimbabwe's Marange Diamond Fields', in *Denv.J.Int'L L &Pol'y* vol 40 (4): 648-688

Nyamnjoh, F. B., (2016). *#RhodesMustFall: Nibbling at Resilient Colonialism in South Africa.* Bamenda: Langaa RPCIG

Ochonu, M. E., (2015). The Wangara Trading Network in Precolonial West Africa: An Early Example of Africans Investing in Africa, in Ochonu, M. E., (ed) *Africans Investing in Africa: Understanding Business and Trade, Sector by Sector.* Palgrave Macmillan

Ofosu-Mensa, E. A., (2011). Gold Mining and the Socio-Economic Development of Obuasi in Adanse, in *African Journal of History and Culture* vol 3 (4): 54-64

Oskarsson, P., (2012). Dispossession by Confusion from Mineral-Rich Lands in Central India, Talk at the Australian National University, 14 November 2012

Oxland, J. O. *et al.*, (1974). Ancient Mining Practices in the Rooiberg Area, in *Journal of the Southern African Institute of Mining and Metallurgy* vol 74, Issue 6: 245

Pambazuka, (15 October 2008). Sankara 20 Years Later: A Tribute to Integrity, https://www.pambazuka.org/pan-africanism/sankara-20-years-later-tribute-integrity

Pangle, T. L., (2013). *Aristotle's teaching in the 'Politics'*. Chicago and London: University of Chicago Press

Pingeot, L., (2014). *Contracting Insecurity: Private Military and Security Companies and the Future of the United Nations*, Bon: Global Policy Forum Report https://www.globalpolicy.org/pmscs/52579-new-gpf-report-contracting-insecurity.html

Povinelli, E. A., (2011). *Economies of Abandonment: Social Belonging and Endurance in Late Liberalism*. Durham and London: Duke University Press

Promskaya, A., (25 September 2015). France Still Robing its "Former" African Colonies, in Pambazuka News. https://www.pambazuka.org/goernance/france-still-robbing-its-former-african-colonies

Promskaya, A., (25 September 2015). West Africa: France Still Robbing Its "Former" African Colonies, in All Africa. allafrica.com/stories/201509281230.html

Rego, S. O., (2003). 'Tax-Avoidance Activities of U. S Multinational Corporations', in *Contemporary Accounting Research* vol 20, Issue 4: 805-33

SABC News, (2 October 2014). Task Team Set Up to Probe Demilitarisation of SAPS, www.sabc.co.za/news/a/af840d8045ae5548c85/task-team-set-up-to-probe-de-militarization-of-SAPS

Scheidel, W. *et al.*, (2002). *The Ancient Economy*. Routledge

Schmidt, E., (1992). *Peasants, Traders and Wives: Shona Women in the History of Zimbabwe, 1870-1939*. Harare: Baobab

Singer, P. W., (2006). 'Humanitarian Principles, Private Military Agents: Some Implications of the Privatised Military Industry for the Humanitarian Community', in Wheeler, *et al.*, (eds) *Resettling the Rules of Engagement: Trends & Issues in Military-Humanitarian Relations*, HPG Report 22

Taiwo, O., (2010). *How Colonialism Preemptied Modernity in Africa*. Bloomington: Indiana University Press

Terray, E., (2006). 'Long Distance Exchange and the Formation of the Sate: the Case of the Abron Kingdom of Gyaman', in *Economy and Society* vol 3, Issue 3: 315-345

The African Economist, (20 June 2013). France Has Economically Enslaved West African Countries, theafricaneconomist.com/economically-enslaved-west-african-countries-by-france/

The Chronicle, (8 December 2014). Zimbabwe Recovers $45 m Diamonds Seized by South African Company, www.chronicle.co.zw/zimbabwe-recoers-45m-diamond-seized-by-sa-company/

The Guardian, (2 June 2015). Tax Dodging by Big Firms "Robs Poor Countries of Billions of Dollars a Year, https://www.theguardian.com/global-deelopment/2015/jun/02/tax-dodging-big-companies-costs-poor-counties-billions-dollars

The Guardian, (24 March 2014). The Kimberley Process is a "Perfect Cover Story for Blood Diamonds https://www.theguardian.com/sustainable-business/diamonds-blood-kimberley-process-mines-ethical

The Herald, (12 August 2015). Yoked Francophone Africa Must be Pitied, www.herald.co.za/yoked-francophone-africa-must-be-pittied/

Traub-Merz, R., (2006). 'The African Textile and Clothing Industry: From Import Substitution to Export Orientation', in Jauch, H., (ed) *The Future of the Textile and Clothing Industry in Sub-Saharan Africa*, Bonn: Friedrich-Ebert-Stiftung

Van Onselen C., (1980). *Chibaro: African Mine Labour in Southern Rhodesia, 1900-1933*. London: Pluto Press

VOA, (20 June 2011). Zimbabwe's Marange Diamonds Put Kimberley Process to the Test. www.voanews.com/a/zimbabwe's-diamonds-put-kimberley-process-to-the-test-124310334/160985.html

Warikandwa, T. V. and Osode, P. C., (2016). 'Exploring the World Trade Organisation's Trade and Environment/Public Health Jurisprudence as a Model for Incorporating a Trade-Labour Linkage into the Organisation's Multilateral Trade Regime: Should African Countries Accept a Policy Shift?' In *African Journal of International and Comparative Law*, 25 (1): 47-65

West, H. G., (2003). "Who Rules Us Now"? Identity Tokens, Sorcery, and Other Metaphors in the 1994 Mozambican Elections', in West, H. G. *et al.*, (eds) *Transparency and Conspiracy: Ethnographies of Suspicion in the New Wold Order*, Durham and London: Duke University Press

West, P., (2016). *Dispossession and the Environment: Rhetoric and Inequality in Papua*, New York: Columbia University Press

Zeleza, P. T., (2009). 'What Happened to the African Renaissance? The Challenges of Development in the Twenty-First Century', in *Comparative Studies of South Asia, Africa and the Middle East*, vol 29, No 2: 155-170

Ziai, A., (2007). 'Development Discourse and its Critics: An Introduction to Post-development', in Ziai, A., (ed) *Exploring Post-development: Theory and Practice, Problems and Perspectives*, London and New York: Routledge: 3-18

Zimbabwe Independent, (23 January 2017). Government Collaborated with Illegal Panners at Marange, https://www.theindependent.co.zw/2017/01/23/govt-collaborated-illegal-panners-marange/

Chapter Three

Archaeological Technologies of Gold Mining and Processing and their Relationship to Contemporary *Chikorokoza*: The Case of Mutanda Site, Mutare, Zimbabwe

Njabulo Chipangura

Introduction

Mutanda is a multi-component cultural precinct with evidence of successive human settlements and is located 56km north west of the city of Mutare, Eastern Zimbabwe. The site is perched on Mutanda mountain range and comprises of a circular free standing perimeter wall with one entrance and an inner wall with two entrances. It has both freestanding and retaining walls constructed in a rough style format. There are at least five semi-circular raised platforms within the wall and thick furnace fragments were found scattered around these platforms. The archaeological objects that I recovered during the excavations at this site confirmed that the major economic preoccupation of the residents at this site was linked to high temperature production activities associated with the making of gold. Any ceramic used in metallurgical and other high temperature operations such as metal production, or glass making is generally referred to as 'technical ceramics'. The argument in this chapter is that the high temperature technologies at Mutanda signify the use of the site predominantly for gold processing activities of the past. This seems highly likely because the site is located within the productively rich Manica- Mutare- Odzi (MMO) gold belt. As a result, the Mutanda cultural precinct is surrounded by artisanal and small scale miners (*makorokozas* in local parlance) who are exploiting this rich reef gold belt. Thus the second argument in this chapter is that since, in the first place, colonial miners displaced African precolonial miners from the site, contemporary African *makorokozas* who are sadly described by other scholars as illegal miners can be understood simply as reclaiming these ancient sites mineral wealth. There are several contemporary gold mining claims dotted throughout the range which are being reworked on by *makorokozas* and constitutes part of the ancient mining landscape of Mutanda. *Chikorokoza* is a popular Shona buzz word that has been used to describe the often called 'illegal' gold mining by small scale 'illegal' miners who are themselves in local parlance referred to as *makorokozas*.

The archaeological data from the excavations coupled with an analysis of the material culture has so far revealed that the site was used as a protected cultural precinct dominated by gold processing activities. Furthermore, the ethno-archaeological information obtained from interviewing *makorokozas* adds up to the argument that there has been a long duration of *chikorokoza* in the area from historical times. Within this long duree framework, the interactive nature of human activity, past and present can be structured and ordered chronologically (Bene & Zvelebil, 1999:79). The chaîne opératoire concept was applied as in this research as an analytical approach in reconstructing archaeological technological systems at Mutanda. The findings from the excavations at Mutanda revealed that the technical activities associated with gold processing transcended beyond the hardware (tools/objects) to social activities enacted through the process of social agency. Such technologies were centred on the relationship or process existing between the intentions of the makers and the things they make (Dobres & Hoffman, 1994: 229). Gold processing objects were made and used within the specific social contexts at Mutanda and the knowledge of identifying mining the ore from the reefs and making the gold from this 'dirt' was an important precursor to material objects.

A summary of the archaeological excavations at Mutanda Site - S 18° 59' 49.2" E 032° 19' 27.84", Elev. 1089m.

The excavation work at Mutanda provided the much needed contextual information to place the high temperature metal extraction processes in a socio-cultural context using the chaîne opératoire framework. The excavations involved the uncovering of objects and other traces to provide clues on activities related to ancient mining technologies and ultimately leading to reconstructions of past events. Two trenches and one test pit were excavated to investigate the high temperature technologies of this site. Trench 1 (TR1) measured 3 by 1 metres with an additional 1 m extension. Trench 2 (TR2) also measured 3 by 1 metres and Test Pit T 1 (TP1) measured 1 x I m. Technologies used in the past can be reconstructed from the contextual objects obtained from excavations and the use of scientific techniques will in turn provide additional information through laboratory analysis (Banning 2002:2).

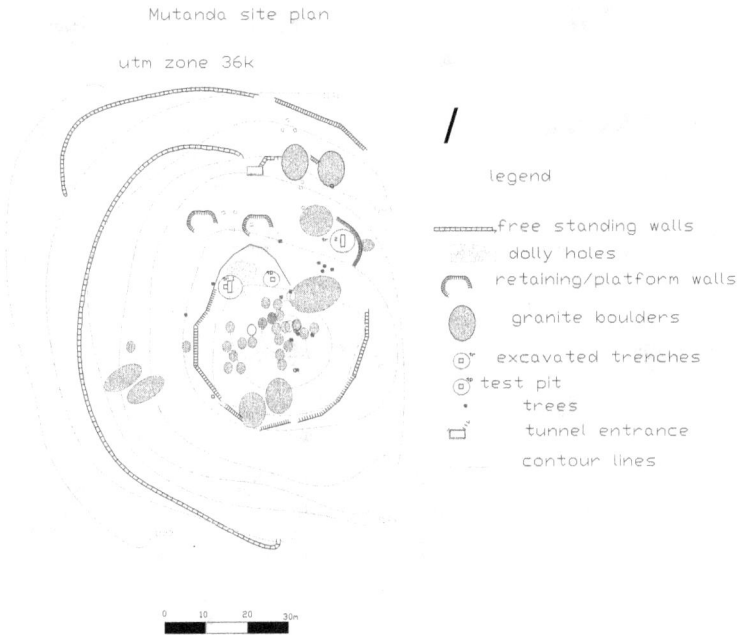

Figure 1. *Lay out plan showing the archaeological components of Mutanda and the excavated areas.*

The selection of TR1 for excavation was informed by the visible dense concentration of material remains on the surface. Excavations were carried out using trowels, hand picks, paint brushes, dust pans at 10cm spits levels from the surface. The excavation was documented in field notes as wells as in aerial photographs using the Phantom DJI 3 camera. Still photographs were also taken using the Nikon D3200 single lens reflex digital camera (18-55mm 1:3.5-5G11) in order to produce a comprehensive pictorial record of the archaeological phenomena. The finds were sorted and bagged in plastic bags according to context and artefact category in the field. Each artefact was bagged separately during the excavation so as to avoid edge damage and chemical contamination. Uncontaminated charcoal samples were collected for radiocarbon dating process with trowels. The table below provides a summarised view of the excavations:

Context	Depth	Soil Colour	Finds	Comments
TR1 SC	surface	humus	FF	Collected for analysis
TR1A L1	0-10cm	light grey soil	HS, DPT	Collected and bagged for analysis
TR1B L1	0-10cm	dark grey soil	UPT, DPT, HF	Collected and bagged for analysis
TR1C L1	0-10cm	dark grey soil	HS, AS, HF , UPT	Collected from the trench and bagged for analysis
TR1A L2	10-20cm	light grey soil	UPT, HF, BN	Collected from the 10mm sieve
TR1B L2	10-20cm	dark grey soil	AS , HF, UPT,	Collected after sieving
TR1C L2	10-20cm	dark grey soil	AS, UPT, BNF	Collected after sieving
TR1A L3	20-30cm	sterile layer with light grey soil on the bedrock	2 HS	Collected from the trench
TR1B L3	20-30cm	sterile layer with dark grey soil on the bedrock	CH, HF	Collected after sieving
TR1C L3	20-30cm	sterile layer with light grey soil on the bedrock	GB, DPT	Collected after sieving
TR1B EX L1	0-10cm	light grey soil	FF, UPT, DPT, 2 HS	Collected from the trench and the sieve
TR1B EX L2	10-20cm	dark grey soil	UPT, HF, FF, BNF	Collected from the trench and the sieve
TR1B EX L3	20-30cm	dark grey soil on a sterile bedrock	HF, CH	Collected from the sieve
TR2A L1	0-10cm	dark grey humus soil	UPT, DPT, CS	Collected from the sieve
TR2B L1	0-10cm	dark grey humus soil	CRF, FF	Collected from the trench
TR2C L1	0-10cm	dark grey humus soil	CRF, FF	Collected from the trench

TR2A L2	10-20cm	white grey soil	HFF, IS, HF	Collected after sieving
TR2B L2	10-20cm	white grey soil	UPT, HFF, CR	Collected from the trench
TR2C L2	10-20cm	white grey soil	HFF, DPT, UPT	Collected after sieving
TR2A L3	20-30cm	light grey soil	HF, HS	Collected from the trench
TR2B L3	20-30cm	light grey soil	UPT, FF	Collected from the trench and the sieve
TR2C L3	20-30cm	light grey soil	BFF, UPT, HS BNF, CH	Collected from the trench and the sieve
TR2A L4	30-40cm	sterile layer with stones	UPT, SL, FF, RO, BNF	Collected from the trench and the sieve
TR2B L4	30-40cm	sterile layer with stones	HSL, BD, SL	Collected from the sieve
TR2C L4	30-40cm	sterile layer with stones	CH, SL, BN, RO,GF, UPT	Collected after sieving
TP1 L1	0-10cm	grey humus soil	CH , IP	Collected after sieving
TP1 L2	10-20cm	light grey soil	BNF, UPT, FF,CH	Collected after sieving
TP1 L3	20-30cm	dark grey soil with stones	2 GB, BN,FF, UPT	Collected after sieving
TP1 L4	30-40cm	sterile layer with stones	SL	Collected after sieving

TR = Trench , L1 = Level 1, TP = Test Pit, SC = Surface Collection , HS = Hammerstone , DPT = diagnostic potsherd , UPT = undiagnostic potsherd , HF = Hearth Floor , AS = Ash , BN = Bone , BNF = Bone fragment , CH = Charcoal , GB = Glass bead , FF = Furnace fragment , CS = Carbonised seed , CRF = Crucible fragment , HFF = Highly fired furnace fragment , BFF = Base of furnace fragments , SL = Slag , RO = Red ochre , HSL = Hammerslag , BD = Bead, GF = Glass fragment , IP = Iron piece

The chaîne opératoire of Mutanda Cultural Precinct

The operational chain refers to all the processes involved in people's use of raw materials from the discovery, the selection, and processing of raw materials, through manufacture, use and rescue of artefacts, to recycling and eventual discard of the artefacts, their remnants and the debris from their manufacture (Banning, 2012:141). The process also considers the strategies that people use in these processes, the decisions they make at each stage and the gestures they learn through an immersion with their culture. It alludes

107

to the sequence of actions involved in the production of an object. The study of operational sequences through which material culture is created permits an understanding of techniques and what they represent about the social relations involved (Dobres & Hoffman, 1994:220). The chaîne opératoire methodology also permits us to understand that any technological act is the sum of technical facts, physical facts and cognitive and perceptual motor facts. The chain of operations starts at the ore deposit with the mining of the ore, followed by technological steps in the smelting process when slag, raw materials and other intermediate products are produced (Hauptmann, 2000:7). According to Dobres (2000), the concept of the chaîne opératoire can be traced from the writings of Leroi-Gourhan whose works perceived the importance of studying the technical sequences of material operations by which resources are acquired and transformed into cultural commodities. Since the chaîne opératoire emphasises on actions and choices that informs the creation of material culture, it moves the centre of attention to culture rather than techniques and materials (Lemonnier 1993, Pfaffenberger, 1988, Childs, 1994, Dobres, 2000).

Chirikure (2005:24) further argues that "this approach provides a sharp contrast with the technocentric models that separated human industry from the social relations that produce them relegating human beings to the side-lines in ancient technologies". It thus provides a distinct advantage in the study of ancient technologies and for Mutanda Site it enabled me to consider all the phases involved in the making of the gold from mining dirt, through smelting to the use and discarding of processing artefacts (Chirikure, 2005:25). Through this chain the historical chronology of mining and metallurgy in Eastern Zimbabwe over the millennia was established as well as the spatial organisation and social pattern of mining and metal production. According to Hauptmann (2000: 7), "the metallurgical chain describes single steps of human activities and the transformations of materials beginning with the extraction of ores from the deposit to the production of a finished product that was possibly traded and which then may finally be unearthed in an archaeological context". The movement of the archaeological material at Mutanda possibly suggest that this ancient mine was evenly distributed with different activities linked to gold processing being undertaken at different spaces. The flow path of such activities was unlocked using the chaîne opératoire model in order to understand vital raw materials procurement and processes that lead to the making of gold from dirt at this site.

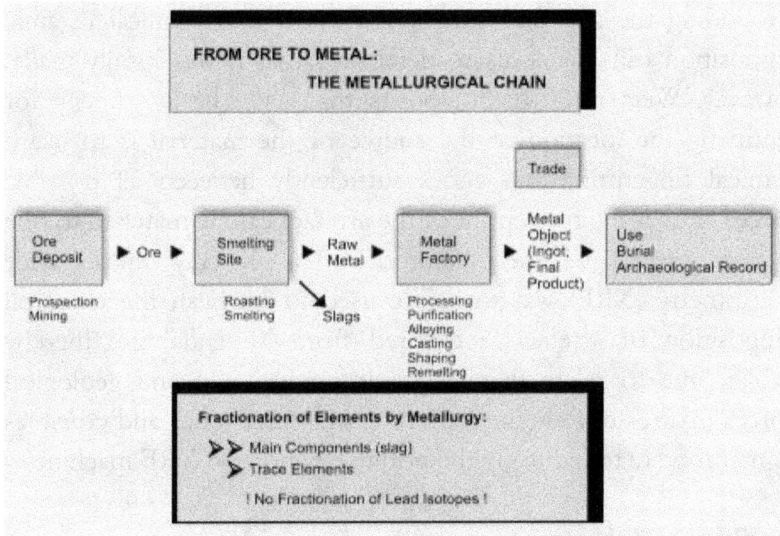

Figure 2: The Metallurgical chain, adopted from Andrea Hauptmann, The Archaeometallurgy of copper, Springer; New York, 2000, 7.

In the chain of operations technological changes can be attributed to economic and seasonal differentiations while the ratios of some characteristic elements of gold are correlated to the geological origin (Liritzis & Zacharias, 2011:124). Moreover, mining and processing are two different activities that were previously collated together with no clear cut distinctions. Within this old understanding mining is treated as a simple process that merely entails the extraction of the ore followed by the production of the metal. This is despite the fact that there are chains of operations in the processing stages which need to be understood differently and distinguished from the actual mining. It is thus important to differentiate mining, smelting and processing using the chains of interaction because these steps are controlled by different factors in the production line. (Hauptmann, 2000:8). Mining is closely bound to ore deposit while smelting and processing are more dependent on the framework of the settlements and were carried out under different social conditions (Hauptmann, 2000:8). Provenance which refers to the identification of the location where the major materials that were used to make the metals were obtained from is also captured in the metallurgical chain (Weiner, 2010:198). The unique characteristics of possible sources of raw materials within the area surrounding the site that corresponds with the technical ceramic composition can enable us to determine that it was locally made. However, Weiner (2010: 36) posits that, "the basic strategy for identifying the location of the source of the material is to use a chemical fingerprint that varies sufficiently between all possible sources so that the fingerprint of the artefact can be matched to one or only several of these sources". The X- ray fluorescence spectrometry (XRF) was therefore used to establish the chemical composition of artefacts recovered from Mutanda Site thereby enabling me to relate them to their original kiln and geological sources (Torres & Rehren, 2007:120). Hammerstones and crucibles fragments were tested using the portable hand held XRF machine.

Crucibles and the archaeometallurgical evidence

A crucible is a vessel used to hold a metal while being melted. Crucibles come in various shapes and sizes from thimble-sized to larger than pint beer mug sized (Bayley, 1988; 1990). Crucible clay was usually tempered with fine sand and organic materials. A number of interesting research questions have been formulated concerning crucibles that were used in metallurgy and other high temperature processes (Thodhlana, 2013:237) Small quantities of metal can become chemically bound in the crucible surface, or physically trapped as droplets of metal. Thus chemical analysis is often the only way of determining the process in which the crucible was used. Much of the gold (Au) mined within Mutanda Site was found in quartz veins. The presence of Au on crucible fragments recovered from the site varying between 2ppm – 5ppm (parts per million) undoubtedly confirms that they were used for metallurgical purposes. The fragments were tested for their chemical composition using the pXRF and tiny traces of gold were detected. One question that bedevilled the excavation work at Mutanda was the absence of complete crucible vessels on a landscape that was heavily filled with fragmented pieces. This probably suggests that the crucibles were deliberately destroyed soon after use and also gives a hint on the social organisation of the gold processing activities at this site. The occurrence of numerous fragments indicates that the processing was done by well organised groups or bands of people on the protected precinct who deliberately shredded the crucible as a ritual meant to protect the sanctity of the site. Smelting activities have largely been viewed as ritualised practices that took place in secluded area away from the habitation sites just like at Mutanda. The recovered crucible fragments were heavily highly fired and hardened. They invariably became grey or black as a result of intense firing. One of the most difficult questions that has been raised about crucibles metallurgy be it for smelting or melting is whether the source of the heat was internal or external (Bayley & Rehren, 2007; Thornton *et.al*, 2010). This is because some crucibles were used primarily for smelting of metals from ores whilst some were used to refine, melt, alloy and cast metals (Thodhlana, 2012: 238). Thus determining the use or uses of the crucibles involves the analysis of probable designed features and an identification of residues as well as use related residue (Banning, 2012: 161).

Figure 3. *A reconstructed crucible from the fragments recovered from Mutanda Excavations, note the greyish- black colour and the little holes (voids) which results from the addition of tempers.*

The presence of voids with a distinctive shape in the fabric is evident in most of the tempered crucibles, and this is the result of the burning out of the organic temper during firing (Banning, 2012:167). The temper alters the physical characteristics of the fabric and prevents the pot from collapsing under its weight before and during firing, controls shrinkage during drying and increases the porosity and resistance to cracking by the finished product (Banning, 2012: 164). However, tempers were sometimes added for ritual reasons. Crucibles were usually made from refractory ceramics and because they were exposed to high temperatures, the clay was sometimes partially vitrified. Vitrified surfaces were produced by a high temperature reaction between the clay lining of the furnace and the alkaline fuel ashes or slag. The outer parts are usually orange (oxidised-fired), while the inner zone is grey or black (reduced firing) and often vesicular with a glassy surface' (English Heritage Handbook, 2001: 10). The clay was often modified with large amounts of temper, such as small stones and organic material. Sand was sometimes added to the clay for repairing the high temperature zones of the furnace to make it more temperature resistant (English Heritage, 2001). Typological studies of crucibles in Southern Africa reveal that only bronze, gold and brass were worked in crucibles (Bandama et.al, 2016). Technical ceramics can therefore provide valuable information about clay selection and preparation as well as the potential contribution of the ceramics to the slagging process and their ability to withstand high temperatures (Thodhlana, 2012:132). An analysis of the chemical composition of these ceramics in combination with other data infer the source of the raw material, the place where the ceramics were made and the technologies used (Banning, 2012: 3).

In their study of a well preserved ancient gold working site at Putushio in Ecuador Rehren and Temme (1994) identified a cultural linkage between an agglomeration of archaeological materials and gold mining. They found remains of a burned bowl-shaped clay installation and lithics materials at the site and conducted X- ray diffraction and microscopic analysis. The analysis confirmed that these materials were used for gold processing. Neither slags nor finished gold objects were found during the excavations (Rehren and

Temme, 1994: 272). I can draw similar parallels with my own excavation work at Mutanda Site where no gold objects were found in the archaeological record. However, XRF and microscopic analysis and examination of lithic remains (hammerstones) from Mutanda Site showed traces of gold on them which means that they were processing gold. The lithics as well as the high temperature ceramics excavated from Mutanda are related to metallurgy due to adhering streaks and drops of gold revealed through the chemical analysis using the XRF machine. The archaeometallurgical investigations at Mutanda site thus provided evidence on the nature and scale of mining, smelting, refining and allowed for an understanding of other structural and artefactual evidence. Surveying ancillary areas is useful and can increase an understanding of the spatial distribution of the working sites and how raw materials were obtained. Mutanda Site 2 (S 18° 59' 27.4 " E 032° 19' 12.4", Elevation 1156m) was surveyed and 21 lower movable grinding stones were recorded. This site is on the other side of the mountain range and must have been as an ancillary site which provided the ore which was processed at the main site. The surveyed site is located close to an area which is being worked on by *makorokozas* which again suggest that the ore was obtained in the same vicinity even in the past as is identifiable in the archaeological record.

MUTANDA RANGE RECORDED SITES

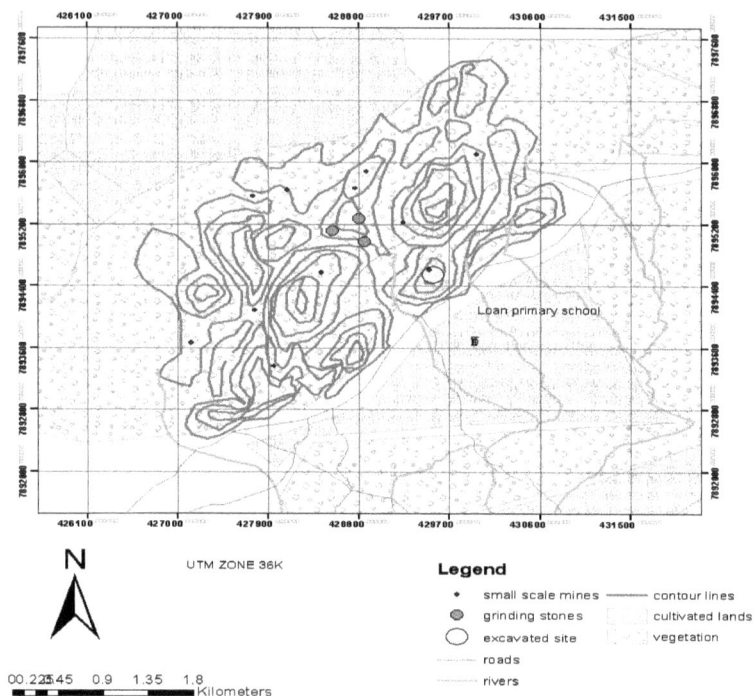

Figure 4. *Map showing the excavated site in relationship to the small scale artisanal gold mines and the ancillary site where 21 lower grinding stones were found.*

The connection between hammerstones and dolly holes

Apart from the crucibles, the other archaeometallurgical activities at Mutanda were supported by the presence of dimpled hammerstones and multiple dolly holes on exposed granite surfaces. These lithics were used for pounding, crushing and pulverising the ore. The hammerstones are ovoid, doom shaped stones with a fairly flat or convex ventral use surface and a convex dorsal arch that is high enough to provide a useful grip (Banning, 2011:153). Some are bifacial and used both the surfaces and sides. Striations on the surface may help us decipher the motion of use and whether this was unidirectional, circular or multidirectional. Because pounding and especially grinding are abrasive processes, the hammerstones experienced pronounced use wear. The rock converted into a hammerstone would not have been prepared before it was used for grinding and thus these hollows are a result of long use (Swan, 1996). These hammerstones range from a mere smoothing of the rock surface to dimpled grinding hollows in the middle.

Figure 5. *Showing hammerstones recovered at Mutanda site, note the deep hollow/dimple in the middle as well as the side of the stones*

These hammerstones have shallow hollows on the surface representing the portion where the quartz powder in the dolly holes was reduced to fineness required for washing (Hall and Neal, 1972). Quartz is the principal host of free gold in Zimbabwe, and when pounded using a hammerstone it was hard enough to have eroded the deep circular hollow. Hall and Neal (1972: 78) argue that the ancients used large granite or diorite stones for crushing gold ore which can be discerned from the ordinary corn crushing stones, though many of such stones could have at a later stage been used to grind corn after having been abandoned by the ancient. Thus if grinding holes also known as dolly holes on exposed granite surfaces are for grinding ore, not grain, then hypothetical scenarios of large scale agriculture are not supported. Swan (1996:73) weighed into the debate by explicitly stating that "circular hollows are reputed to be associated with mining in Zimbabwe, but so far no coherent argument for the connection has been documented". In a way this chapter is advancing the argument that there is a connection between the hammerstones and dolly holes together with the other material evidence from Mutanda which supports the gold processing functions of these features. Results from the XRF analysis of the hammerstones confirmed that they were used for gold processing. Traces of Au were found on the dimpled sections and they varied from 6ppm – 9ppm. The outer surface was also tested and the Au levels ranged from 12ppm – 14ppm and the higher quantity is a finger print of the pulverizing of the ore which was done on this section.

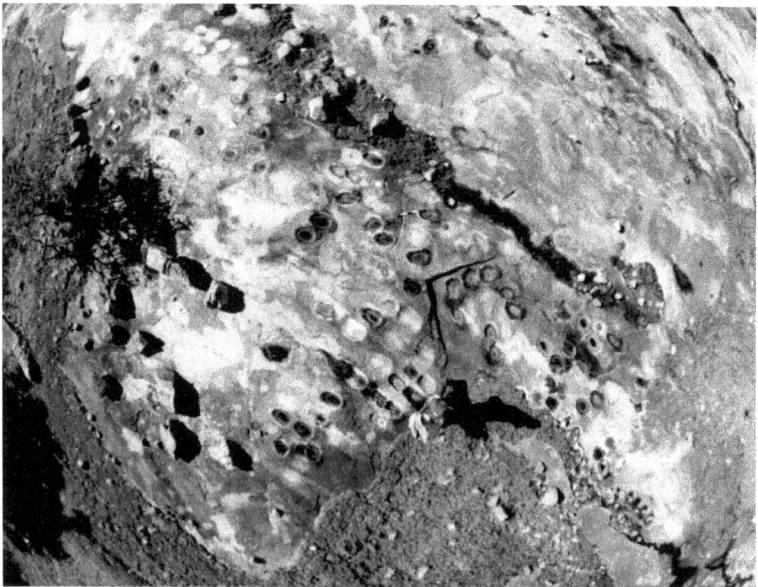

Figure 6. *An aerial picture taken using the Phantom DJI 4 camera (drone) showing the dolly holes at Nyahokwe Site, Nyanga. There is evidence of gold processing as well at this site.*

116

The dolly holes have a circular aperture and are conical or hemispherical in cross section with a very smooth internal surface (Swan, 1996:73). At Mutanda site, there were 16 dolly holes bored into level portions on an exposed granite surface on the eastern end of TR 1. These holes are found at one spot and frequently in batches of ten in two rows of five each (Hall & Neal, 1972) They also varied in size from 8 inches (20.32cm) in depth to 20 inches (50.8cm) and from 6 (15.24cm) to 8 inches (20.32cm) in diameter. The dolly holes on the exposed granite surface at Mutanda evidently shows that they were being used for grinding quartz powder to such an extent that in the course of time they became too deep for the hammerstones to work in them and immediately near them newer and shallow dolly holes can be seen. The inside surface of the dolly holes had score marks scratched lengthwise along them which indicate their use for grinding some particularly hard material (Cooke, 1964). The dolly holes were grouped according to function. Some were used for crushing coarser materials and others would receive the small pieces and ground them into fine powder. This difference was easily recognised at Mutanda from a careful observation of striations on some dolly holes. The dolly holes with striations were adjudged to have been used for pulverising the ore to fine powder. Seemingly supporting this observation, Swan (1996:77) argues that "it is possible that dolly holes might often have started as crushing places on flat rock surfaces, becoming used for grinding after the crushing process had worn a shallow hollow into the rock". The powdered ore was then washed in large open dishes to separate the heavy gold with lighter waste material (Swan, 1996). The overwhelming archaeological evidence at Mutanda thus supports the idea that gold ore milling was the principal cause of circular hollows on the exposed granite surface.

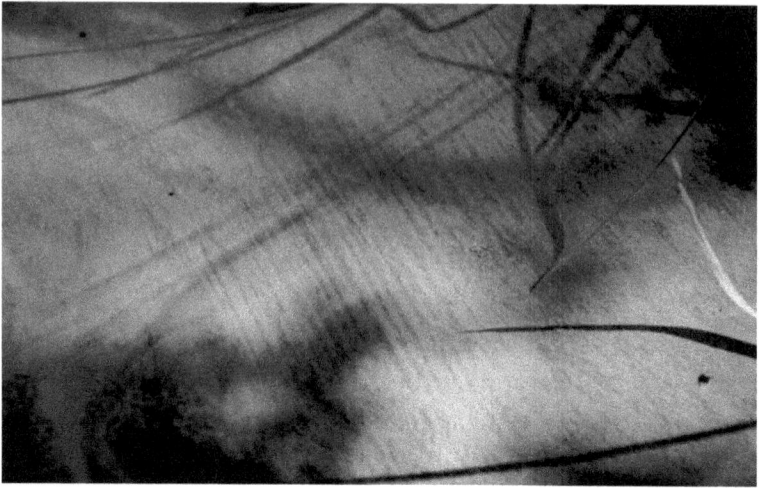

Figure 7. *Striations inside the circular dolly hole at Mutanda, these were a result of pulverising of gold ore*

Early Forms of ASM, trading in Manyika and 'Blanket' Prospecting

Artisanal and small scale mining (ASM) in its very various guises has been an important building block of societies around the world, contributing to the spread of trade routes and the growth of empires (Gibb, 2006:42). From the prehistoric period the Zimbabwean plateau was known to have had fed the East African trade route with gold. This route was controlled by Islamic and Arab traders between the 12th century and 13th century AD (Ellert, 1993, Beach, 1980). Kilwa was famed as the main trading centre on the East African coast that benefited from gold that was coming from the Zimbabwean plateau. Exploitation of gold during this period was done within Nyamukwarara, Mutare and Odzi rivers and it took the form of alluvial deposits. Not only that, major gold reefs were also exploited around within the Manica- Mutare-Odzi (MMO) reef gold belt which has become a hot spot of 'illegal' artisanal mining today. This belt extends into Mozambique and artisanal mining is taking place on both sides of the international boundary (Ellert, 1993). Bhila (1982:2) describing the ancient reef gold mining remarked that , "in order to get gold bearing quartz from a hard reef rock , the Manyika gold

118

miners lighted a fire against a rock and after some time threw cold water on it to enable them to pick out pieces with their little axes".

Portuguese traders later penetrated into the hinterland at the beginning of the 16th century AD to locate the gold sources and subsequently usurped control over trading from the Islam and Arab traders (Miller, Desai, and Thorp, 2000). A number of trading posts and forts were thereafter established by the Portuguese particularly at Masekesa in Mozambique which was close to Manyika where much of the gold was coming from. The gold that was mined in the Manyika kingdom was transported overland to Masekesa and Sofala in Mozambique and then shipped northwards in small boats up to the Swahili coast to Kilwa, where it was loaded onto larger vessels destined for the Indian gold markets (Bryceson *et.al* 014:120). By this period indigenous gold mining, processing and marketing in a pre-capitalist setting were already well established (Miller, Desai, Thorp, 2000). This trading was largely built on an exchange system involving gold that was being mined from the plateau particularly by Shona speaking people in Manyika. Masekesa was to become one of the most thriving Portuguese feira/market which was transformed into a bastion of high gold trading (Ellert, 1993, Mudenge, 1988).

It has been argued that most of the early mining from prehistoric to medieval times was carried out by individuals who lived in agrarian based communities and was conducted during droughts when people were unable to farm (Knapp, 2002). Reef and alluvial gold mining were thus essentially seasonal activities conducted by agricultural communities in the winter seasons. It was a period of the fall of the water table which made reef mining viable at great depths without flooding. Gold washing was done during the same period in order to take advantage of any gold deposit washed by floods at the beginning of the previous summer (Phimister, 1974: 29). Phimister, (1974:29) also asserts that the periodic practise of mining continued into the nineteenth century but however also concedes that this excluded the Manyika district where gold washing was done throughout the year because many of the rivers are perennial. Manyika now forms what is currently called Eastern Highlands of Zimbabwe. Even today, alluvial mining by *makorokozas* within the Eastern Highlands is still being undertaken throughout the year without stoppages.

As already mentioned, gold was coming from ancient mines that were dotted all over the MMO and these are the same spots which are now being reworked by *makorokozas* today. The competency and knowledge of early indigenous Manyika gold miners at detecting gold bearing reefs paved way for easy prospecting by the Europeans who were guided to ancient workings by local Africans (Onselen, 1976, Summers, 1969, Mudenge, 1988, Swan, 1994, Anderson, 1961). As a result most gold mines set up in Rhodesia after 1890 were sited on such old workings. Swan (1994:21) argues that "in fact, the mining companies preferred claims which were staked on land with ancient workings". Early traditional prospecting techniques included a simple panning procedure of the surface soil which would give them an idea whether to continue or not. They also developed intimate knowledge of recognising reef outcrops, however in the absence of such outcrops, there were other indicators notably the presence of acacias or other forms of vegetation associated with the existence of gold (Bhila, 1982:41). With the assistance of local Africans, old workings were located by the British South African Company (BSAC) soon after 1890 and the Africans would receive a blanket as a token of appreciation. 'Blanket prospecting' became a common feature of Rhodesian prospecting in the early days (Anderson, 1961:33). There is archaeological and historical evidence that shows that ancient mining by the Shona speaking people preceded the establishment of a number of mines by colonial gold prospectors between the 19th and early 20th centuries (Kritzinger, 2012). This is indicative of the fact that the later mines were established using early pre-colonial gold mines as yardsticks for the setting up of full operations. Thus claims were pegged on old mines that were considered to be good prospects through 'blanket prospecting'.

ASM, low barriers of entry and ethnoarchaeology

A number of definitions have been proposed as different authors try to set boundaries of what is actually implied when discussing ASM (Gibb, 2006). Laborne and Gilman (1991:1), offer a basic and simplistic definition of ASM by saying: ' although there is no formally recognised definition of artisanal mining ... artisanal mining is characterised mainly by the absence or low degree of mechanization , low safety standards , poorly trained personnel, large influx of migrant workers, low pay scale , low productivity , chronic lack of capital, illegality due to mining without concessions rights , little consideration of environmental impact and unknown mineral reserves'. This form of mining is a relatively open entry activity for *makorokozas* because of a low starting capital requirement. ASM has also been defined as "any operation which extracts and concentrates mineral substances drawn from primary/secondary outcropping or sub-outcropping deposits using manual or traditional methods and procedures" (Gueye, 2001:5). Noetstaller (1995:2) on the other hand is of the view that "artisanal mining could be defined as encompassing all non-mechanised, low –output extraction of minerals carried out by individuals and small groups, frequently on an intermittent basis, employing essentially traditional techniques".

Noetstaller (1995) further conceptualises ASM as fundamentally typified with what he calls barriers to entry which relates to the basic requirements for the starting up of a new operation in terms of skills, investment capital, infrastructure, implementation time and mining reserves. It is thus typically associated with a democratic, social levelling effect in which physically fit, risk taking men from across the social spectrum start working as amateur miners with little or no experience (Bryceson and Geenen, 2016 :7) As such there is no need for specialised training or skill prior to commencement of work. Bryceson and Geenen (2016:7) further argue that "class and educational advantages are not a barrier to work entry, nor decisive for economic success". In Zimbabwe ASM which is called *chikorokoza* in the Shona language is symbolised by the high density of 'illegal/informal' miners dotted around most of the ancient mines in the country which support the low barriers to entry concept. Maponga and Meck (2004:357) argue that it is easier to mine informally than to register a claim legally in Zimbabwe. In addition, the low capital requirements of ASM, shorter lead times and the ability of the sector to exploit marginal and old deposits make it appropriate and an easy activity for *makorokozas* (Maponga and Meck, 2003).

Chikorokoza in the Mutanda Range tend to have a low barrier to entry and under favourable conditions, in most cases it is inclined to the re- exploitation of abandoned or ancient mines with operations capable of immediately commencing with as little as a pick, a shovel and a pan. Moreover, it still takes place in ways that appear to have changed very little from what exists in the archaeological record of pre- colonial mines. Pikirayi (1993:30-31) writing about artisanal mining in northern Zimbabwe says that:

> In autumn and winter, with a return to dry conditions.... some families travel to gold mining areas and open up shafts and tunnels with simple tools. A mining village may grow to accommodate 50-100 miners and their families in a single season. Once a week, gold merchants from established mining concerns come to these villages to buy the unprocessed gold... Traders from places such as Harare bring cloth, beads and other articles of adornment to the mining villages and these products sell quickly.

These modern day activities seem to have a direct correlation with social organisations in pre-colonial gold working settings. ASM processing methods have not significantly changed over years and cannot be divorced from traditional manual mining methods inclined to the use of simple non-industrial implements such as shovels, picks-axes, pans, chisels, hammers and stone tools (Hilson, 2006). Tools such as hammerstones made from granite and dolerite were found in the archaeological record and were used during pre- historic gold mining (Summers, 1969). Miller, Desai, Thorp (2000: 97) argue that "informal artisanal gold mining persists to this day using techniques that are not substantially different from those recorded in early documents and the archaeological record". Today ASM processes are also typically manual and involve the use of wooden ladders, ropes, buckets, calabashes, plastic bags, and transportation of ore using carts and wheelbarrows.

By adopting ethnoarchaeology as methodology, I was able to observe gold production activities by *makorokozas* unfolding in social settings at Mutanda Site. The archaeological record of site clearly shows that the ancients were mining and processing gold.

Archaeological approaches are therefore best suited to study extinct technologies drawing parallels with the present day circumstances (Thodhlana, 2002: 63). Attention was also placed on the social and physical contexts of production technologies, artefact manufacture, use and distribution, stylistic variation, structuring of space and deposition and post-deposition processes (Iles and Childs, 2002:195) However, the working definitions that I have presented above do not encompass the knowledge and the social structures that sustain ASM. A lot of emphasis has been placed on its importance as an economic livelihood with little being said on its normative evolution as a cultural way of life (Bryceson and Geenen, 2016). The contemporary attitude of the Zimbabwean government, as highlighted below, to *makorokozas* sheds light on the normative evolution of *chikorokoza* as a way of life.

Formal or Informal – "Don't arrest gold panners, Mangudya"

The term informal mining has also been used to describe a system in which people engage in mining as a part time activity and in most of the cases these miners will be farmers or wage labourers (Knapp, 2002). It is sometimes used interchangeably with terms like 'illegal' mining. However, in this chapter I seek to problematize the binary that exists between informal/illegal mining and formal/legal mining by breaking it down to show that there nothing neither informal nor illegal about ASM. This is because ASM activities around Mutanda Site exhibit a great deal of systematic organisation evident enough in chains of operations that start from the extraction of the ore to the processing and to the ultimate channelling and selling of the gold into market economies. This binary is not adequate because this study engaged the *makorokozas* in their daily routine activities and established the formal nature of all their operations. This angle is not provided for in the current vocabulary which speaks of ASM as just being illegal and or informal without considering the high levels of its organisation. It has often been defined in terms of what it is not: it is not formalised, not mechanized and not regulated and this kind of victimisation has to be broken (Bryceson and Geenen, 2016). On the contrary, I argue that ASM has always been organised and

123

constituted a formal space in Zimbabwe because all large scale capitalist mining operations were established on old ancient workings with indigenous people assisting in the prospecting. The mining then was a highly organised industry within the limits of the knowledge available at that time and the gold belts were extremely well prospected (Anderson, 1961:26).

In recognition of the formality of ASM, the Reserve Bank of Zimbabwe (RBZ) governor, Dr. John Mangudya announced that the Zimbabwe Republic Police (ZRP) must not arrest artisanal miners for mining and carrying gold (The Sunday Mail, 22 January 2017). In 2016, the total gold output in Zimbabwe was 23 tonnes of which 15 tonnes came through from artisanal miners thus contributing almost US$1billion at a time when the country was desperately yearning for foreign currency (The Sunday Mail, 22 January 17). Thus allowing the *makorokozas to* work freely without the fear of being arrested can alleviate poverty levels in the country as well contribute to sustainable development. According to statistics presented by Mines and Mining Development Minister, Mr. Walter Chidhakwa at the inaugural 2016 Gold Sector Awards, in 2016 gold deliveries from small scale producers amounted to 9,680kgs. ASM is thus slowly becoming an important building block for Zimbabwe's economy as it is generating considerable employment and foreign currency earnings. The *makorokozas* were hailed by the RBZ boss as "heroes of Zimbabwe's economy". The RBZ governor is reported to have said that the police should not enforce wanton arrests on gold panners but rather should consider imposing other penalties such as fines. At the time of writing this chapter the RBZ and the Ministry of Mines and Mining Development were in the process of changing the laws that criminalise artisanal gold mining and possession of gold. Because of its rich endowment with gold, Zimbabwe has been ranked among the top gold producers in continent coming after South Africa and Ghana respectively (The Sunday Mail, 22 January 2017). The *makorokozas* operating within Mutanda Range have also been branded 'illegal' and this was gathered from the ethnographic interview conducted in the area. However, there exist well knitted social organisations in *chikorokoza* which transcend beyond local, regional and cultural differences.

Social practices and the habitus of *Makorokozas*

In *chikorokoza* social differences are kept at bay with emphasis placed on egalitarianism, fairness, camaraderie and democratic potentiality (Bryceson and Geenen, 2016). Bourdieu's (1990) concept of habitus can be usefully applied in trying to explain certain similar behavioural traits of *makorokozas*. This is because they develop a set of internalised structures, common schemes of perceptions, thought and actions that are similar. Such practices are structured by internal schemes which have come into existence in the course of history, as a result of past experiences to which the individual now belongs (Cuvelier, 2010). The habitus thus generates all possible forms of behaviours that become acceptable and are embraced as cultural practices by *makorokozas*. Because *makorokozas* live together, they tend to encounters the same kind of situations, experiences and similar conditions and the assumption here is that they also develop the same habitus (Bourdieu, 1990: 59-60). A team spirit and an atmosphere of camaraderie typically exist among the *makorokozas* that transcend beyond any sense of ethnic difference (Moodie and Ndatshe, 1994). *Makorokozas* naturally acquire mining skills through social contacts and informal apprenticeship at their mining site (Bryceson and Geenen, 2016). The application of Bourdieu's concept within *makorokozas* working at Mutanda Range is valuable because it explain the repetition and reproduction of some social practices throughout space and time. It also helped to make connections between living conditions on the mining site and the advent of particular social practices that condition the behaviour of *makorokozas* (Cuvelier, 2010). Working on the basis of a shared habitus as *makorokozas* many commonalities and scalabilities in many parts of their everyday life emerge (Gratz, 2004).

Makorokozas also engage in a process of labour transformation whereby their skill acquisition, professional norms, ethics and group identity converge in an *ad hoc* fashion while working together (Bryceson and Geenen, 2016). Outside *makorokozas* first apprenticeship on the mining site, they also judge each other on the basis of mining skill and competence instead of place of origin and tribal affiliation (Bryceson and Jonsson, 2010). Writing about tin miners in Bolivia Nash (1979:12) argued that they address each other as brothers with each one having a nickname that captures his characteristic qualities. Argots also develops as a result of the social interactions among *makorokozas,* that is to say their own intimate language cords which they constantly recreate as they work on the mines (Gratz, 2004). At Mutanda buzz words like *tonnera* (tunnel), *bhandi* (quartz vein carrying gold), *mutaka* (ore) and poshto (working place) are common language cords that have been developed as a result of social and working interactions among the *makorokozas.* Looking at the example of ASM in Benin, Gratz (2004:105) illustrated how common codes, symbols, particular neologisms, gestures, speech acts and narratives are developed by miners and thus contributing to the development of distinct modes of interaction and the social creation of meaning. He gave the example of nicknaming which is a common social practice among *makorokozas* with nicknames generally being derived from attitudes, certain events, or circumstances in the biography of a person, or by way of analogy to military ranks, prominent politicians, musicians and actors (Gratz, 2004). Bryceson and Geenen (2016: 5) also argue that while engagement in artisanal mining may be an individual livelihood choice, it initiates a process in which the skill acquisition, economic exchange, psychological reorientation and social positioning of individuals evolve towards a shared occupational identity.

Earnings in *chikorokoza* are sometimes unpredictable because production depends on luck related to various factors most importantly the presence of rich gold veins (*bhandi*), capital to invest, manpower and climatic conditions (Bryceson and Geenen, 2016: 15). Even during low production periods, *makorokozas* are driven by the constant hope of striking gold. More so, these *makorokozas* are known to spend their quick money through daring consumption. This mean that the money earned is spent excessively without aiming for durable accumulation through investments in cattle or buildings (Cuvelier, 2010). *Makorokozas* are prone to spending money on immediate consumption including alcohol, drugs, women and entertainment. However, in the case of Mutanda, some *makorokozas* do their best to develop a more decent lifestyle and transfer part of their money to their relatives back home through Ecocash and Telecash which are popular mobile money transfer platforms in Zimbabwe.

Conclusion

In this chapter, I have looked at the metallurgical chain of ancient gold processing at Mutanda cultural precinct and related it to contemporary artisanal and small scale gold mining. I used the material culture recovered from an archaeological excavation that I undertook at the site to argue that behind the circular wall the ancients were making gold from dirt. This view seems so plausible considering that XRF and optical analysis results of crucible fragments and hammerstones that came from the excavations revealed that these artefacts had signature traces of gold. Historically the Manica – Mutare – Odzi reef gold belt was recorded on numerous Portuguese accounts as having been the source of the gold that feed into the East Africa Coast trade route between the 12th and 13th century AD. Mutanda site is located within the same gold belt and thus the archaeometallurgical evidence from the site presupposes that the high temperature technologies reconstructed were associated with the processing of gold. Within the Mutanda range on which the archaeological site is located, artisanal and small scale miners (*makorokozas*) are also re- exploiting the same gold belt. I thus also looked at ASM in relation to Mutanda site and presented the argument that although *makorokozas* have often been branded as illegal/informal there is a degree of systematic and social organisation of their activities. In fact, *makorokozas* are substantially contributing to the growth of an ailing Zimbabwean economy and in 2016 gold sales from the so called 'illegal mining' realised a revenue of US$1 billion. Social relations were also identified that cut across ethnic, religious and educational differences but rather built by *makorokozas* as they work together with the ultimate goal of striking a rich gold vein. ASM was regarded as open because there are no barriers to entry and in Zimbabwe one can start gold mining with a pick, a chisel and a shovel.

Funding

This chapter is based on fieldwork conducted between 2015 and 2016 at Mutanda Range in Odzi, Eastern Zimbabwe, as part of my PhD research at the University of the Witwatersrand, Johannesburg. It was funded by grants from the Wenner-Gren Foundation-Wadsworth African Fellowship and the National Research Foundation, South Africa (No. 87782 & 85982) provided by my supervisor, Professor Robert Thornton.

References

Anderson, R.B., (1961). The Mining Industry of Southern Rhodesia, Salisbury: Seventh Commonwealth Mining and Metallurgical Congress, 5th edition.

Bandama, F, et.al. (2016). The Production, Distribution and Consumption of Metals and Alloys at Great Zimbabwe. *Archaeometry, Vol* 10, 1-18

Banning, E.B., (2002). *The archaeologist's laboratory; The analysis of archaeological data.* London; Kluwer academic publisher.

Bayley, J. and Rehren, T. (2007). Towards a functional and typological classification of crucibles. In: S. La Niece et.al (eds), *Metals and Mines: Studies in Archaeometallurgy*. London: Archaetype Publications.

Beach, D.N. (1980). *The Shona and Zimbabwe 900-1850*. London: Heinemann.

Bene, J. and Zvelebil, M. (1999). A historical interactive in the heart of Europe: the case of Bohemia. In: Ucko, P.J and Layton, R (eds.), The archaeology and anthropology of landscape, shaping your landscape, London: Routledge.

Bhila, H.H.K. (1982). *Trade and Politics in a Shona Kingdom; The Manyika and their Portuguese and African Neighbours, 1575-1902*. Harare: Longman.

Bourdieu, P. (1990). *The Logic of Practice*. Stanford: Stanford University Press.

Brycesson, D.F and Geenen, S. (2016). Artisanal Frontier mining of gold in Africa: Labour Transformation in Tanzania and the Democratic Republic of Congo, *African Affairs*, pp 1-22.

Brycesson, D.F and MacKinnon, D. (2014). *Mining and African Urbanisation; Population, Settlement and Welfare Trajectories.* London: Routledge.

Chirikure, S. (2005). Iron Production in Iron Age Zimbabwe: stagnation or innovation? Unpublished PhD thesis, University College London.

Cooke, C.K. (1964). Rock gongs and grinding stones: Plumtree area, Southern Rhodesia. *The South African Archaeological Bulletin* 19 (75):70.

Cuvelier, J. (2010). Men, miners and masculinities: the lives and practices of artisanal mines in Lwambo (Katanga Province, DR Congo), PhD dissertation, Katholieke Universiteit, Leuven.

Dobres, M.A and C.R Hoffman. (1994). Social Agency and the Dynamics of Prehistoric Technology. *Journal of Archaeological Method and Theory* Vol.1, No.3, 211-258.

"Don't arrest gold panners, Mangudya", *The Sunday Mail*, 22 January 2017.

Ellert, H. (1993). *Rivers of Gold*. Gweru: Mambo Press.

English Heritage. (2011). Centre for Archaeology Guidelines, Archaeometallurgy

Gibb, M. (2006). Artisanal and small-scale mining in West Africa: An overview of sustainable development and environmental issues. In: Hilson GM (ed), *Small Scale Mining, Rural Subsistence and Poverty in West Africa*. Warwickshire: Action Publishing.

Gratz, T. (2006). Artisanal gold mining in northern Benin: a socio-cultural perspective. In: Hilson G.M. (ed), *Small Scale Mining, Rural Subsistence and Poverty in West Africa*. Warwickshire: Action Publishing.

Gratz, T. (2004). Friendship ties among young artisanal gold miners in Northern Benin (West Africa), *African Spectrum*, Vol 39, No 1.

Gueye, D. (2001). 'Small-scale mining in Burkina Faso', Mining, Minerals and Sustainable Development (MMSD) Working paper 73, *Mining, Minerals and Sustainable Development (MMSD) Project*, London: International Institute for Environmental and Development.

Guy, G.L. (1965). Grooves and stone mortars – Selukwe, Rhodesia. *Arnoldia* 2 (8): 1-4.

Hall, R.N. and Neal, W.G. (1972). *The Ancient Ruins of Rhodesia*, Bulawayo: Books of Rhodesia Publishing Co. (PVT.) LTD.

Hauptmann, A. (2000). *The Archaeo-metallurgy of copper*. New York: Springer.

Hilson, G.M. (2006). Introduction. In: Hilson G.M (ed), *Small Scale Mining, Rural Subsistence and Poverty in West Africa*. Warwickshire: Action Publishing.

Iles, L. and Terry, S. (2014). Ethnoarcaheological and Historical Methods. In: Robert B.W and Thornton C.P (eds.), *Archaeometallurgy in Global Perspective; Methods and Synthesis*. New York: Springer.

Knapp, A.B. (2002). Social approaches to the archaeology and anthropology of mining. In: Knapp B, et.al (eds), *Approaches to an Industrial Past: The Archaeology and Anthropology of Mining*. London: Routledge.

Kritzinger, A. (2012). Pre-colonial mines identified from a Portuguese document with particular reference to Manyika in the Eastern Highlands, *Zimbabwea (10)*, Harare: National Museums and Monuments of Zimbabwe.

Laborne, B. and Gilman, J. (1999). 'Towards building sustainable live hoods in the artisanal mining communities', paper presented at the Tripartite Meeting on Social and Labour Issues in Small Scale Mines, Geneva: International Labour Organisation.

Lemonnier, P. (1986). The study of material culture today; towards anthropology of technical systems, *Journal of Anthropology and Archaeology*, 5, 147-86

Liritzis, I. and Zacharias, N. (2011). Portable XRF of Archaeological Artefacts: Current Research, Potential and Limitations. In: Shackley, S. (ed), *X-Ray Fluorescence Spectrometry (XRF) in Geoarchaeology*. New York: Springer.

Maponga, O. and Meck, M. (2004). Illegal Artisanal Gold Panning in Zimbabwe- A Study of Challenges to Sustainability along the Mazowe River. In: Hilson G.M (ed), The *Socio-Economic Impacts of Artisanal and Small-Scale Mining in Developing Countries*, Tokyo: A.A Balkema Publishers.

Miller, D., Desai, N and Thorp, J.L. (2000). Indigenous Gold Mining in Southern Africa. *Archaeological Society, Goodwin Series* 8, 91-99.

Moodie, T. and Ndatshe, V. (1994). *Going for gold: men, mines and migration.* Berkeley: University of California Press.

Mudenge, S.I.G. (1988). *A Political History of Munhumutapa c1400-1902.* Harare: Zimbabwe Publishing House.

Nash, J. (1979). *We eat the mines and the mines eat us; dependency and exploitation Bolivian Tin Mines.* New York: Columbia University.

Noetstaller, R. (1995). 'Historical Perspectives and Key Issues of Artisanal Mining', Keynote speech at the International Roundtable on Artisanal Mining. Washington D.C: World Bank.

Onselen, C. (1976). *Chibharo, African Mine Labour in Southern Rhodesia 1900-1933.* London: Pluto Press.

Pfaffenberger, B. (1992). Anthropology of Technology. *Annual Review of Anthropology,* Vol 21, pp. 491-516.

Pfaffenberger, B (1988). Fetishized objects and human nature; towards an anthropology of technology, *Man,* 23 (2), 236-52.

Phimister, I. R. (1974). 'Ancient' mining near Great Zimbabwe. *Journal of the South African Institute of Mining and Metallurgy.*

Pikirayi, I. (1993). *The archaeological identity of the Mutapa state: Towards an historical archaeology of northern Zimbabwe.* Uppsala: Societas Archaeologica Upsaliensis.

Pollard, M. et.al. (2007). *Analytical Chemistry in Archaeology.* Cambridge: Cambridge University.

Rehren, T. and Temme, M. (1994). Pre-Columbian Gold Processing at Putushio, South Ecuador: The Archaeometallurgical Evidence. In: Scott, D. and Meyers, P. (eds.), *Archaeometry of Pre-Columbian Sites and Artefacts.* Los Angeles: GCI.

Summers, R. (1969). *Ancient mining in Rhodesia and adjacent areas.* Museums Memoir No.3. Salisbury: National Museums and Monuments of Rhodesia.

Swan, L. (1994). *Early gold mining on the Zimbabwean plateau.* Studies in African Archaeology 9. Uppsala: Societas Archaeologica Upsaliensis.

Swan, L.M. (1996). The use of grinding hollows for ore milling in early Zimbabwean metallurgy, *Cookeia, Zimbabwe* 1 (6): 71-92.

Thondhlana, T.P. (2012). Metalworkers and Smelting Precincts: Technological Reconstructions of Second Millennium Copper

Production around Phalaborwa, Northern Lowveld of South Africa, Unpublished PhD thesis, University College London.

Thornton, C.P and Roberts, B.W. (2014). Introduction. In: Roberts, B.W and Thornton, C.P (eds.), *Archaeometallurgy in Global Perspective, Methods and Syntheses*. New York: Springer.

Torres, M.T and Rehren, T. (2009). Post medieval crucible production and distribution: a study of materials and materiality. *Archaeometry* 51 (1), 49-74.

Towards record gold output, *The Sunday Mail*, 22 January 2017

Weiner, S. (2010). *Microarchaeology, beyond the visible archaeological record*. Cambridge: Cambridge University Press.

Chapter Four

Unsung Heroes?
An Anthropological Approach into the Experiences of '*Zamazamas*' in Johannesburg, South Africa

Phefumula Nyoni

Introduction

This chapter explores the identities and ways in which *zamazamas*[1] derive a living within the precarious conditions they find themselves in. The chapter is based on research carried out in a mining site around Johannesburg that is, Roodepoort. Qualitative research in the form of key informant interviews with a number of participants found within the mining context was employed. The question of identities and connections of *zamazamas* is also being explored, that is, from their lived experiences perspective. Strategies on how the artisanal miners deal with the various challenges they face are also pursued in this work. The historical overview of mining practices in Africa, influence of contemporary mining practices on the sustainability of the mining activities as well as the questions of gender, illegality and informality are also considered. Whilst conventional literature has tended to project *zamazama* activities as tainted with 'illegality' and instability, the reality points to a group of persons successfully deriving their livelihoods from this form of mining and who have drawn from various forms of agency in dealing with the challenges frequently encountered. It is in this regard that the chapter is influenced by post structuralist ideas.

It is important to note that artisanal mining in Africa is not a new phenomenon as it dates back to centuries ago. Whilst the exact figures on the number of artisanal miners are impossible to discern, artisanal miners are growing in number in Sub-Saharan Africa.

---

[1] 'Zamazama' is a label given to the 'informal' miners in South Africa, with the name drawn from an IsiZulu usage literally meaning to 'strive' and 'strive'

According to (Hoadley and Limpitlaw 2004) there is an added challenge related to the inaccuracy of data and information on the actual number of persons who survive on artisanal mining as most of the data is based on assumption. They however note that in South Africa the persons surviving on artisanal mining are estimated to be over 30 000. There is no consensus on what small scale mining entails but the sector is characterised by diversity of actors who are mainly self-regulatory and whose activities lie outside the ambit of the state control. Most artisanal work remains unregulated despite efforts to regulate small scale mining in some African contexts (Jønsson and Bryceson 2009:252). Small scale mining is also said to be characterised by inadequate capital inputs, low level and relatively simpler technology that in some instances hinges upon improvising (Appiah 1998:307).

This work is written in the context of little having been written pertaining to the day to day lived experiences of small scale miners. Despite the scanty literature it is generally agreed that positions of artisanal mines as is the case in formal employment are also characterised by insecurity. Whilst most post-independence migration literature has focused on urban migration and of late forced movement of refugees as well as shifting international migration trends, little or no focus has been paid to miner's mobility as noted by (Jønsson and Bryceson 2009:252). It follows that there is a dearth of literature in relation to miner's mobility as well as the risks that they incur as they pursue livelihoods within a precarious environment that is bedevilled with uncertainties and negative perceptions from large scale players and the state agents who approach has largely left the artisanal miners unfairly labelled "illegal". It is this "illegal" tag that further exposes them to isolation from lawfully accessing the locally available resources. These challenges are worsened by the hostility and punitive approach that states have taken which only serve to fuel tension whilst at the same time alienating the miners from the locally available resources they view as rightful theirs.

This research therefore presents crucial information that has been collected through first hand face to face interviews and direct observations in an attempt to show that beyond notions of illegality and criminality that *zamazamas* have come to be associated with lies a panacea for sustainable livelihood development. It is such a solution that can enhance local economic development whilst at the same time breaking the monopoly by large scale operators whose reasons for the decommissioning of some shafts may not apply to the cause of artisanal miners such as *zamazamas*. In essence this notion of profitability has in some way been exploited as a device by large scale operators to justify laying-off workers whilst holding onto the claims. The chapter therefore seeks to proffer an inclusive progressive regulatory approach that might be adopted by African governments in dealing with *zamazama* activities in a manner that might ensure balance between sustainability in the sector and protection of the environment and mining claims of large scale operators. It is however clear that such an approach may face resistance as it touches on the nerve of monopoly by large scale players who are always reluctant to part ways with any of their claims even under circumstances where the shafts have been decommissioned and lie dormant. The big question remains in relation to how governments will respond to the needs of these unsung heroes who are not willing to budge despite the state's heavy handedness in dealing with them as most of them see no other livelihood alternative hence their preparedness to remain within this space.

Historical overview of mining practices characteristic in African mining systems

The history of gold mining and its trade in Southern Africa has been noted to be dating back to as far as a thousand years with the precolonial scale of gold production being said to be quite extensive (Miller, Desai and Lee-Thorp 2000:91). They further note that indigenous gold production was well established as early as the mid-13th century as reflected in the burials that were accompanied by gold in the Mapungubwe area. Writers as early as 1974 noted that right from the beginning of Southern Africa's recorded history ancient gold mining has been associated with Zimbabwe. In relation to the advent of early mining in Africa, Appiah (1998:307) has revealed the historical existence of artisanal gold mining in the context of the

Gold Coast later known as Ghana for centuries. Government supervised concessions are granted to small groups constituted as family, friends or gangs.

According to (Huffman 1974:240) several places in South Western Zimbabwe such as Kwekwe formerly known as Que Que have displayed evidence of early gold mining. He however makes a significant contribution when he pointed towards the presence of 'ancient dolly holes' that were located a few meters from the current industrial sites of the modern mines, the Globe and Phoenix and the Gaika mines. Although it is debatable as to whether such early installations only related to gold processing and extraction, there is consensus on the fact that these belonged to early miners who valued locating mineral extraction sites near permanent sources of water. The 'dolly holes' have largely been associated with gold ore milling. This same customary milling technology is also used by zamazamas in Roodepoort and as was the case in the early mining practices, with mainly women being involved in the grinding processes using the stone technology which is reminiscent to the 'ancient' technology. Evidence of the 'ancient' 'dolly holes' being located near permanent water supplies also resonates with the location of gold extraction sites in Roodepoort. The backyards of the individuals involved in ore processing are connected to piped water that is supported by 'jojo tanks'[2] that can hold as much as 5000-10000 litres of water that is used during gold extraction. The historical development of Roodepoort formerly known as Durban Deep in the late 1880s has been explored by Nhlengetwa and Hein (2015:1) who noted that within a decade the mining industry of Johannesburg had grown from its artisanal beginnings to become the largest gold producing hub. In defining *zamazamas*, Nhlengetwa and Hein (2015:2) have revealed that '*zamazama*' is a local name that is used in South African circles in reference to 'artisanal' gold miners which can be equated to what is referred to as *galamsey* in Ghana. In other countries such as Zimbabwe the informal miners also get identified as *otsheketsha* or *amakhorokhoza;* labels which embrace the mark of 'illegality' as opposed to legislative right to access.

---

[2] These are plastic tanks of varying sizes that are usually used as a backup facility or else in cases of bulk water usage.

Scholars such as Habashi (2007:11) have noted that prior to colonialism by European powers, African peoples have engaged in the mining of various minerals as well as metallic object extraction using customary practices, including customary laws, since the olden periods. It is in light of such evidence that calls have been made that the current South African government approach is unfriendly towards the indigenous structures and processes as it tends to label them as "chaotic". Regulation of the gold mining and its trade has customarily been through a coterie of local brokers who played leadership and other roles within the gold mining and trade trail. For example gold mining has been widely reported among Egyptians who processed it into artefacts. In addition granite quarrying was carried out together with other semi-precious stones that were made into giant statues and vessels. Similarly in Southern African communities in countries that include Botswana, South Africa and Zimbabwe there has been widespread reports on 'early mining', coupled with evidence of rock breaking, ore grinding, transportation using customary means such as oxen. In addition there have been reports of iron smelting through the use of customary tools that the craftsmen used. In most of these instances the leadership of each group within a particular level was vested on the most senior or skilled individual who also became a gate-keeper, something which is similar to what is taking place in the leadership of various levels of *zamazama* groups be it at the level of miners, entrepreneurs, ore processors, gold buyer and gamblers among others.

Naickera, Cukrowskaa and McCarthy (2003:29) have also chronicled the various gold extraction processes that included the use of mercury amalgam method that related to surface mining, cyanidation in which case finer milling of the ore was required. It is this milling that mainly women still do through the traditional process of grinding using the traditional grinding stone method. This ground powder that has been described by Thornton (2014: 127) as just 'dust and dirt' is then taken to some makeshift backyard treatment plant for extraction. In the Roodepoort context the individuals who engage in this gold extraction process confirmed the use of cyanide in their processes.

Influence of contemporary mining practices on the sustainability of '*zamazama*' mining

Relationships among various actors within the mining communities have generally featured various forms of clashes (Chris and Banks 2003:289). This conflict has taken forms that include ideological clashes and disputes as well as armed conflicts that have resulted in life being lost as well as disruption of livelihoods and the environment. According to Ololade and Annegarn (2013:568), contradictions between environment and development are a common feature in mining communities. It is in line with this argument that they further note that whilst improvements may accompany the mining activities, their likelihood of producing adverse impacts on the environment has been brought to the fore in efforts aimed at highlighting the balancing of benefits against unfavourable consequences of mining practices in an area (Ololade and Annegarn 2013:568). In essence the usage of the concept 'sustainable development' within the mining setting can be defined as being complex (Ololade and Annegarn 2013:568). Researchers who have studied the impacts of mining around the world have revealed the severity of the mining operations on the environment. This is largely the reason why local communities are said to be always suspicious of government and corporate companies operating in their localities.

Many communities found within the vicinity of mining practices have experienced immense disruption and adverse effects. It is local groups who have had to endure the consequences of mineral exploration and mine expansion; they suffer marginalisation both economically and politically (Chris and Banks 2003:289). A plethora of grievances being endured by communities at the hands of the large scale mining companies have also emerged. In addition there have been widespread reports of human rights abuses suffered by local communities on the hands of the large scale companies and state agents. In some African contexts abuses have included unlawful arrests and detention, dispossession of livestock and land as well as livelihood disruption and murder. The Roodepoort case has shown that *zamazamas* do take their business seriously as indicated by the equipment located in the backyard milling and processing sites. One such site is located within a few metres from the mining site and resembles living quarters with well-built houses and some gardening taking place. The millers indicated that their main activities involve processing the gold ore that came from the grinders. Important in relation to the technological depth of the equipment used by millers are the observed pipes that are part of the ore cleaning process, which resemble a modern mill itself.

Another important group that can be used in explaining the risks and sustainability of *zamazama* activities are the buyers. The buyers are usually well aware of the risks of police? raids and hence they usually strategically park their vehicles that act as makeshift buying spaces to ensure that one is able to have a quick escape in case of any raid. They are thus usually positioned by the entrance to the main processing space. The gold buyers are usually viewed as belonging to a higher class as was observed in one of the days in which there were at least six buyers and they were easily identifiable by the luxury cars they were driving, with one on a fancy sports motorbike. This issue of *zamazamas* belonging to different socio-economic strata is reflected in one of the conversations with a 'senior' male buyer in his early 40s who identified himself as 'Sibanda'[3] who comes from south western Zimbabwe. I refer to him as 'senior' as he noted that he has been involved in buying gold for the past 10 years. In what can be said to be an expression of the precarious nature of *zamazamas* despite some like buyers being better off than other individuals within the tier, Sibanda noted that had he been a South African citizen, things could have worked better for him as he could have tried to secure a licence of some sort and entrench his business. The case of Sibanda not only point to the business potential of *zamazama* practices but it further implies that given a proper foundation and support such individuals have potential of leading sustainable livelihoods. To further strengthen this view Sibanda also added that his business as a gold buyer is not just a minor issue as it is his main source of income he has ever known. To show that these individuals are not just clueless armatures without knowledge of markets and prices, he

---

[3] This is a pseudonym just as is the case with all other names for the protection of participant's identities

noted that prices fluctuate but they always offer competitive prices. In essence it is crucial to note that the buyers on site usually represent bigger players in the gold trade as noted by (Gratz 2004) who indicated that petty traders are usually involved in trading on behalf of master traders. This also reflects the way in which the gold trade has historically been handled during the early pre-colonial period.

Zamazama trade does not constitute acts of desperation by individuals. The sentiments echoed by Sibanda and Dhlomo, another Zulu gold buyer from Tembisa as well as the other buyers who were interviewed on the Roodepoort site, underscore the fact that their trade is not a desperate one. In essence Sibanda indicated that in the years that he had been a buyer, he had managed to build a decent home, buy a family and business car and send his children to school just like any formally employed person. In echoing similar sentiments, Dhlomo a South African national and buyer from Tembisa indicated that he is a proud owner of taxis through the buying of the gold from the various sites which he has been doing for more than 10 years. Of importance was his perception that what he did was better than some employment were one gets exploited for small amounts of money. To also show that he is conscious of the market fluctuations just like his other counterparts, Dhlomo noted that there are many of the gold buyers but what is important is to ensure that you pay a 'fair price' and then sellers would be looking for you. It is in light of the preceding arguments related to the sustainability of livelihoods that some writers have come out in support of artisanal mining as a legitimate source of livelihood. They thus noted that although artisanal mining is perceivably widely practiced as a substitute commercial initiative in dealing with livelihood challenges, it is in reality a source of livelihood though with lesser prospects of wealth generation (Hoadley and Limpitlaw 2004).

Identities and the spirit of communalism among zamazamas

In terms of nationalities, *zamazamas* plying their trade in Roodepoort constitute a mixed bag of ethnic groups drawn from countries such as South Africa, Mozambique, Lesotho, Zimbabwe and Zambia. The *zamazamas* do not operate randomly as they tend to organise according to ethnic belonging which in a way further shapes the position that one occupies within the operational chain. In addition to the factor of ethnic belonging, (Gratz 2004) noted that as is the case in Northern Benin, friendship constitutes a crucial social means shaping the communal patterns within mining spaces. He however adds that friendship notions are surprising considering that mining communities are usually associated with notions of selfishness driven by greed, violence and mutual distrust. Another feature of gold mining communities which is commonly noticeable among African groups is that gold mining communities are migrants in general. It therefore follows that the artisanal mining communities depict a scenario in which individuals from different regional and ethnic backgrounds are bonded not just by friendship, though it becomes an important source of the cohesion. This ethnic nature of *zamazama* groups is confirmed by Nabudere (2001:13) who have argued that despite the Janus faced nature of ethnicity, it has shaped the dissention by various groups seeking to reinvent modernity as they fight for broader access to resources traditionally under the control of large scale companies.

It is crucial to note however that in general terms most of the *zamazamas* come from a nearby informal settlement and by virtue of this, they tend to see themselves as constituting a community. What is interesting however is the maintenance of ethnic patterns especially when it comes to the activities they get involved in. There is therefore an indication of the Roodepoort group being constitutive of a community with roles and obligations being handled in a communal way. The various groups which ranged from entrepreneurs who supplied equipment and consumables, miners, processors, buyers and 'security personnel' as well as gamblers were all organised such that they came from similar geographic as well as ethnic backgrounds. The process of going underground is managed communally by a 'committee like structure' and this process is tightly controlled to ensure that all those who enter the particular shaft are legit and registered and would have undertaken all pre-entry procedures. These pre-entry procedures include laid down rules in determining *zamazamas* who could be allowed down a particular shift and were meant to ensure a fair rotation of the shaft exploitation by different groups as well as to keep out the *zamazamas* who do not belong to the group claiming the shaft. The pre-entry procedures further involve conducting bodily searches on all *zamazamas* who intent going underground to ensure they are not in possession of dangerous weapons. The pre-entry procedures constitutes a list of rules that are agreed through consensus by the group laying claims on a particular shaft through what can be termed a communal philosophy. The spirit of communality therefore further manifests itself during the period when miners go underground as they prefer either to go down in pairs or small groups who then cooperate in the underground activities. The miners also cooperate in terms of assisting each other with various items they need underground.

The philosophy of communality also manifested itself in the activities that included a small number of miners who had been observed exiting the shafts with their back packs still strapped onto their backs and with work-suits heavily drenched in dirt from the underground work. Within an eye view distance from this group, a group of miners were also seen preparing to enter the shaft whilst in another corner of the area some miners were seen relaxed and having drinks from their hard earned money. The other groups that were working together and whose formations bore the features of communality was that of women food entrepreneurs, women gold ore grinders, processors of the gold ore, buyers and sellers as well as a multiplicity of other kinds of entrepreneurs selling various items needed by the miners. Informants also noted that working in networks was helpful when they went underground as they shared equipment and sometimes other consumables. They also indicated that working in groups enabled them to carry adequate supplies as failure to do so could compromise their mining efforts since it was difficult to resurface just for supplies considering the distance the miners walked underground to reach the mining spaces. After observing the miners' preparations for going underground one could see the large amounts of consumables taken as supplies. It is therefore important to note that whilst the shaft entrances are located within a particular area where various actors involved in the *zamazama* practices converge, the underground tunnels covered a wider area which has made the mining claim demarcation by large scale

142

companies impossible to establish and let alone to monitor. It follows that whilst the entrances to the tunnels were in Roodepoort, informants indicated that the shafts underground could extend up to the Johannesburg Central Business District. It is also in light of the extensive nature of the underground shafts that informants estimated that the number of persons working on both the surface and underground at any given time could surpass 2000 persons.

Cosmological factors have also been noted to play an important role in relation to how the *zamazamas* negotiated their ways within the precarious space they find themselves in. Important is the fact that scholars such as Hull and Deborah (2012) have noted the embeddedness of economic practices and institutions in the broader cultural milieu, reliance on notions of luck, fortune, fate and many others. It follows that since the *zamazamas* are Africans though from different nationalities, they seem to share common cosmological values and beliefs. This is particularly the case when it comes to the ways they employ in understanding and dealing with the risks they face as they negotiate their way in this precarious space. The notions of fortune and misfortune as well as beliefs in witches' familiars also form a part of the *zamazama's* beliefs. These beliefs and associated rituals are therefore related to the interpretations and mitigatory strategies that are adopted towards challenges that include encounters with the police, rivalry groups, and accidents encountered underground and on the surface, loss of valuables and a plethora of other experiences. It is therefore important to note that there has been an increase in the recognition of the importance of cosmological factors and respect for local beliefs.

Experiences of women artisanal miners

Scholars such as Hintons and Veiga (2006:209) have indicated that women's involvement in artisanal mining differs from context to context. It follows that within the Asian context in general, there are less than 10 per cent miners who are women whilst in the Latin America it's 20 percent (Hintons and Veiga 2006:209). It is however vital to note that women participation in mining activities is highest in Africa where it stands at between 40-50 per cent; it's between 60-

100 percent in some areas (Hintons and Veiga 2006:209). It is also further noted that as the degree of mechanisation increases, it leads to the decrease in the rate of women participation in such activities (Hintons and Veiga 2006:209). It can also be argued that women tend to be most active in small family operations where mining supplements other income as in subsistence agriculture or where mining supplements other income and in instances involving use of low technology mining methods as in the case of Roodepoort where simple traditional grinding stones are used. It can further be noted that women evidently occupy critical roles in artisanal mining though there is scarce information on the actual roles of women in these communities as well as on their experiences within such spaces as noted by Hintons and Veiga (2006:209). The important role that women have notably occupied in *zamazama* mining activities include; 'ancillary roles' as cooks or service providers; transporting and processing materials which have however been considered alienating from the identity of 'miners'. Other writers such as Hoadley and Limpitlaw (2004) have added that high representation of women has implications on the development of artisanal mining.

Women also have a fair share of deriving livelihoods through various activities within the *zamazama* space. One of such women is Olwethu, a 34 year old mother of two and one of the few isiXhosa speaking women in the site and she is accompanied by her younger sister and cousin. Just like other actors who have been pushed into the *zamazama* space by the scourge of unemployment Olwethu, noted that she came to Johannesburg some 10 years ago and has been surviving on piece jobs. She noted that she is a school dropout, a position that even made it difficult to get any better job other than the short stints she had as a domestic worker. On the subject of how she came to join the *zamazamas* she noted that she got to know about the gold ore grinding business from a group of neighbouring women within the informal settlement who happened to come from the Eastern Cape and she decided to try it after noticing that they were getting good money and living a better life. Besides the aspect of ethnic background influencing the composition of the group that Olwethu found herself with, is her view that the skill of grinding wasn't new to her as she had been doing it back home in the Eastern

Cape. This position of women as ore crushers has also been noted by Gratz (2004) who pointed out that women have mostly been employed in the crushing of ore. In relation to how the trade related to sustaining her livelihood needs Olwethu indicated that she makes an average of R400 per day and this becomes more in what she perceives as some 'good days'. In what can be used in highlighting the importance of *zamazama* activities for women actors Olwethu added that ever since she took part in this trade her financial situation has improved. This is further supported by her perception in which she considers the *zamazama* practices to be far much better than the domestic work that she has been doing as she also feels that there is lesser exploitation in this kind of work as she is able to negotiate with each and every miner. Olwethu's view that she and her sibling and cousin can even afford to send some money back home in the Eastern Cape whilst also affording to save and visit during holidays added to the notion of the *zamazama* activities being significant in the sustenance of the actors' livelihoods. In support of what some commentators have alleged as having contributed to the migrant labour system crisis in some sections of South Africa's industries, Olwethu indicated that she gets surprised when some women specifically South Africans shy away from the *zamazama* activities claiming that it is 'dirty'.

The question of 'formality' and 'non-formal' mining practices

The question of formality and informality is crucial in efforts aimed at understanding activities of artisanal miners. In that regard Hull and Deborah (2012) have indicated that the artisanal mining concept denotes ideas of a world outside bureaucracy. (Hull and Deborah 2012) have revealed that in many instances the element of multiple livelihoods represents a combination of formal employment with other forms of income generation. Scholars such as Hull and Deborah (2012) have therefore assisted in the unpacking of classical categories of formality and informality. Focus has thus been on analysing every day activities and survival strategies of the urban poor. It is in light of such arguments that even the narratives of research participants such as Olwethu, have noted that whilst they value the *zamazama* activities as being an important part of their livelihood strategies they have however bemoaned that their work is not only considered illegal but risky and dirty as well.

According to the Government Gazette (2006), the Precious Metals Act No. 37, of 2005 outlines prohibitions related to acquisition, possession or disposal of unwrought precious metal in which case gold is also listed as such. The legal position in the South African context is such that even a mere possession of gold ore which is usually unprocessed is illegal. This is confirmed by an incident in which a miner in his late twenties narrated a very disturbing story of having been cornered by one of the police patrols. During the chase he had to throw away his bag (sawn from sacks) and flee to avoid being caught knowing the price of being caught would have been higher. He alleged that the police may have given chase after suspecting that his bag had gold ore. His story revealed the sad realities that the miners suffer at the hands of state agents. His situation was worsened by the fact that he had borrowed money to buy dynamite and all other consumables and it has all gone down the drain. He however received a lot of sympathy with many people alleging however that he had been affected by misfortune, a highly common way of dealing with the various challenges encountered within the *zamazama* activities.

Scholars such as Thornton (2014:127) have recently studied *zamazamas* in South Africa and come to the conclusion that this group has largely been misrepresented by the government and media among other key players. This misrepresentation has had damaging impacts not only on the identity of this group but this has also negatively influenced the state's approach and policy direction in handling the *zamazamas*. In understanding the sometimes heavy handed approach of the state in dealing with *zamazamas* it is important to reflect on the sector's internal factors that have also resulted in the attraction of such a negative identity through the overt and covert criminal activities that surround *zamazama* mining and related activities. The activities are interwoven into a cog of complex acts that are fluid and difficult to comprehend as the actors not only come from different cultural backgrounds but they also draw from different forms of agency in pursuing their ends. It is within the same line of argument that the post-structuralist idea of Nabudere can be explored (Nabudere 2001:14). This is specifically with respect to his view that modernity in Africa has tended to take a new form in which indigenous persons have tended to reject what one can call the universalistic model of global development linked to the European Renaissance due to its alleged alienative and destructive nature to the environment and livelihoods. In one of the incidences recorded in this chapter is a police and large scale mining company raid of a *zamazama* site. Of particular importance is the informants detailing of the raid by police and private security company officials who had come with bulldozers and caterpillars to destroy the "illegal openings to the shaft". It is therefore such acts that Nabudere (2001:14) projects as creating dissent within indigenous groups whose hopes of modernity seek a more holistic and sustainable locally connected global economy that transcends the quest for human needs by also embracing the needs of the ecosystem.

In most instances "informal" miners usually operate outside of the existing mining legislative frameworks except for the moral ones and are found on the wrong side of a plethora of state laws that govern access to mining rights, payment of royalties to the state, health and safety as well as trespassing on privately owned property. As is noted in how indigenous groups are challenging the dominant and dehumanising developmental features of globalisation as founded on the western canon as noted in the work of Nabudere (2001), it can also be noted that the contemporary legislative framework that is not accommodative of *zamazama* moral regulatory efforts require transformation. In terms of regulation zamazamas appear to be largely self-regulated through a morally defined mutually inclusive code of conduct adopted by a specific group that has claims over that particular shaft opening. It is this lack of clear ownership boundaries that usually provokes turf wars that have in many instances resulted in loss of life. In the different context where zamazamas or *amakhorokhoza*[4] exist, governments have through various state agents resorted to enforcing regulations and resorting to various control means that in the case of Roodepoort have seen

---

[4] This is an IsiNdebele local name that is used in south western Zimbabwe to refer to artisanal miners

policing being tightened as manifested in frequent raids on *zamazama* sites, confiscation of the equipment, detention as well as site demolishment and sealing the shaft entrances used by *zamazamas*. Of importance in this narrative is the reaction and resilience of the *zamazamas* who find it suicidal to abandon the trade despite such state heavy handedness as for most of them this has come to be their only source of what they consider a 'cleaner source' of livelihood. The narratives emanating from the *zamazamas* therefore suggests that even crime levels drop as criminals and gangsters join the informal gold mining camps.

Mutemeria, Walker, Coulsona and, Watsona (2016:655) have pointed out that the challenges towards the regulation of small scale mining emanates from the premise that this sector preceded the beginning of industrial mining in Africa. It therefore follows that the activities of this sector just like what happened to certain indigenous practices have always been adjudged to be an unwarranted mishap that accidentally exists to disrupt the so called 'formal' industrial mining sector. It therefore follows that instead of this sector being viewed as important in the development of communities that rely on it, it has rather come to be seen as a sector that is 'illegally' bent on accessing spaces they do not deserve with the intention of promoting their 'illicit dealings' at the expense of the state and the deserving rightful owners who are the big businesses.

It is also important to deal with *zamazama's* perceptions on police raids as narrated by some of the research participants. It is in that view that Xolani, an informant originally from South Western Zimbabwe indicated that they shared a lot in common with the few South Africans involved in artisanal mining. Important was his perception that what they are doing is not criminal at all. In essence his argument was further enhanced when he noted that prior to them coming up with the idea of mining there was a very high level of crime in the informal settlement whilst adding that this unsafe environment has been resolved by the advent of many former gang members having abandoned the criminal actions for the mining which they considered legit. Another informant, Fikile who is a Zulu from Tembisa, chipped in and indicated that a group of unemployed persons from his area came to the mining area after having decided to abandon the risky criminal activities for jobs as guards of the mine shafts. The participant further bemoaned the police's heavy handedness in dealing with *zamazamas* as it could provoke some former criminals to retaliate especially with respect to allegations that the police seemed to have a network of informers within the mining community which they use for ease of targeting rich picks of gold ore as part of their involvement in the illicit dealings. Key in this conversation was the suggestion by Fikile who noted that, instead of the government exhibiting such a negative attitude towards artisanal mining, they had to regularise the shafts as big companies were no longer using them. After having revealed the significance of the mining for his livelihood in which he noted that some people made an average of about R1000 a day he added that the mining sustained a lot of individuals and families. He thus concluded by noting that it is sad that the government is labelling them illegal as the shafts they are working on have long been abandoned by the big companies and decommissioned for allegedly being unprofitable. These preceding narratives against government's punitive approaches towards artisanal miners tend to outweigh even arguments by scholars such as Hoadley and Limpitlaw (2004) who have levelled the challenges of severe environmental and societal effects on artisanal miners who are further accused of rarely contributing to revenue. Such a position may however be unfairly portraying a negative image on artisanal miners as it has always been noted that large scale companies have always been caught on the wrong side of the law having violated various environmental and even fiscal legislation despite their valuable contributions to government revenue.

Conclusion: Towards an inclusive framework in contemporary African mining systems

A number of researchers have proffered various solutions regarding the subject of 'artisanal mining'. It follows that, scholars such as Nhlengetwa and Hein (2015:3) have shared concerns over the possibility of successfully regulating the sector. They are mainly concerned about the challenges that relate to the various *zamazama* groups laying claims to the shafts which in many instances have led to frequent confrontations between rival groups and state agents. They have further claimed that formalising this sector can open up avenues for illegal immigration whilst at the same time fuelling opportunistic mining with more deaths being recorded in the ensuing rivalry. They further argue that this sector is unfairly posing direct competition to legitimate businesses. Whilst these concerns point to some legitimate challenges that may be encountered in efforts to regulate the activities of *zamazamas*, it is equally important to highlight that the current control and policing approaches by the South African government which tend to be reactive and punitive might just be equated to the planting of a ticking time bomb. In addition to exposing the challenges that may be faced in regulating the *zamazama* activities Nhlengetwa and Hein (2015:2) have correctly noted that the punitive approach by government seems to be beset by a double sword element as it is hardening the *zamazamas* who have devised different overt and covert strategies to counter what they perceive as unprovoked state attacks on 'genuine' livelihood strategies. In light of the connection between *zamazama* activities and rising unemployment and poverty levels among the communities surrounded by the gold fields, it becomes a mirage to think that it is a sector that can be wiped out and replaced by the so called big companies.

It is in light of the preceding concluding statements that this chapter seeks to proffer a number of recommendations in an effort towards finding sustainable means for dealing with *zamazama* activities. At face value *zamazama* activities may appear to be marred by chaos and criminality of epic proportions. It is however important to note that despite the presence of gangsterism and illegality, there is a lot that the various groups have done to ensure order in the various levels within this chain of activities that include entrepreneurs who supply equipment and consumables, the miners, ore processors, grinders who are mostly females, the buyers of the gold as well as those who provide security particularly around the shaft entrances. This chain when looked at closely does give credence to a well organised community with some 'customary regulations' which ensures the smooth running of the activities at the various sites involved particularly in Roodepoort where the study was done. This is a community that is also conscious about the dangers of crime and make efforts to live within the ambits of the law. In essence narratives from research participants have indicated that some *zamazamas* are former members of gangs who saw it better to abandon their criminal activities in pursuit of artisanal gold mining which they deem a 'clean' source of livelihood. Of importance in this argument is the importance of changing perceptions towards these activities. This is especially important in terms of government approach which ought to view this sector as a legitimate source of livelihood whose regulation can benefit all actors involved. The excuse of violence and illegal migrants remains an untenable one as there are other sectors such as the taxi industry where state intervention has progressively helped not only with regulation but also in ensuring that the livelihoods of those involved are secured through various initiatives that have included investments and capacity building. Whilst pockets of violence remain particularly around routes, it has not reached the epic proportions that are seen in the *zamazama* practices. One can only presume that this success within the taxi industry is largely because the sector exists under the ambits of state regulation. It can therefore be argued that applying a similar progressive regulatory approach towards the *zamazamas* can go a long way not only in eliminating the violence and 'illegal' elements but also in ensuring that all actors involved have their livelihoods protected whilst the state also receives direct benefits.

Since the *zamazama* activities and perceptions towards these reactive government approaches seem to be common in many Southern African contexts as well as across Africa, it is important to highlight that the possibility of progressive state regulation can be the most sustainable approach. By virtue of the *zamazama* groups as well as the various expertise being organised on ethnic lines, it is clear that this bears a similar pattern to how the ancient mining and craftsmanship systems were organised. In essence, in as much as the ancient mining activities were regulated through known various leaders who had allegiance and paid tribute to the rulers were the claims lay, it can be argued that such patterns can be adopted in coming up with a regulatory framework. This does not even need one to only draw from the ancient regulatory practices as the situation prevailing in the taxi industry highlights a similar pattern of ethnic orientation and self-governance with government utilising such structures in its interaction with the sector. It is therefore important to do away with liberal philosophy unsustainable notions that seek to portray *zamazama* practices as too wild to be regulated by adopting a progressive approach that will see the *zamazamas* being brought under the ambit of the state whilst maintaining the existing 'communal' structures already effectively being used in the sector. This can see a radical transformation of the local economies which can see the gold production monopoly by large scale operators being broken whilst at the same time empowering communities with resources found in their localities. As the *zamazamas* revealed in their narratives, some of the shafts that they are working on remain rich enough for small scale exploitation which contradicts the reasons those large scale operators proffer in decommissioning them through claims of unprofitability. No matter how genuine these may be, it remains a reality that the zamazamas rely on lighter and cheaper equipment as well as self-employment. These practices may just be dormant opportunities for catapulting local economies into development hubs that modern states are failing to utilise.

References

Appiah, H. (1998). 'Organization of small scale mining activities in Ghana', *Journal of the South African Institute of Mining and Metallurgy*, SA, 0038–223X.

Ballard, C. and Banks, G. (2003). 'Resource Wars: The Anthropology of Mining', *Annual Review of Anthropology*, 32, 287-313.

Gratz, T. (2004). 'Friendship ties among young artisanal gold miners in northern Benin (West Africa)' *Afrika spectrum* 39, (1):95-117, Institut fur Afrika-Kunde, Ham.

Habashi, F. (2007). 'History of mining in Africa. A philatelic review', De Re Metallica, *Sociedad Española para la Defensa del Patrimonio Geológico y Minero* 9, 11-18.

Hinton, J. J., Hinton, B. E. and Veiga, M. M. (eds) (2006). Women in artisanal and small scale mining in Africa in *Women Miners in*

Developing Countries: Pit Women and Others. Lahiri-Dutt, Kuntala and Macintyre: Martha Ashgate Publishing, Ltd.

Hoadley, M. and Limpitlaw, D. (2004). 'The artisanal and small scale mining sector and sustainable livelihoods' A paper presented at the Mintek Small Scale Mining Conference, 2004, 9 September, Nasrec, Johannesburg, Book of Proceedings1-9

Huffman, T. N. (1974). 'Ancient mining and Zimbabwe'. *Journal of the South African institute of mining and metallurgy.*

Hull, E. and Deborah, J. (2012). 'Introduction: Popular economies in South Africa' *Africa* 82, (1): 1–19

Jønsson, J.B. and Bryceson, D.F. (2009). 'Rushing for Gold: Mobility and Small-Scale Mining in East Africa', *Development and change* 40: (2) 249-279.

Miller, D. Desai, N. and Lee-Thorp, J. (2000). 'Indigenous gold mining in Southern Africa', *South African Archaeological Society Goodwin Series*, 8, 91-99.

Mutemeria, N. Walker, J.Z. Coulsona, N. and Watsona, I. (2016). 'Capacity building for self-regulation of the Artisanal and Small-Scale Mining (ASM) sector: A policy paradigm shift aligned with development outcomes and a pro-poor approach', *The Extractive Industries and Society* 3, 653–658

Nabudere, D.W. (2001). 'The African Renaissance in the Age of Globalization', *African Journal of Political Science / Revue Africaine de Science Politique*, 6, (2): 11-28

Nhlengetwa, K. and Hein, K. A.A. (2015). 'Zama-Zama mining in the Durban Deep/Roodepoort area of Johannesburg, South Africa: An invasive or alternative livelihood?' *The Extractive Industries and Society* 2, 1–3.

Naickera, K. Cukrowskaa, E. and McCarthy, T.S. (2003). 'Acid mine drainage arising from gold mining activity in Johannesburg', *South Africa and environs Environmental Pollution*, 122, 29–40.

Olusola, O. Ololade, Harold. and Annegarn, J. (2013). 'Contrasting community and corporate perceptions of sustainability: A case study within the platinum mining region of South Africa', *Resources Policy*, 38, 568–576.

Precious Metals Act, No. 37, 2005, *Government Gazette*, 21 April 2006.

Thornton, R. (2014). 'Zamazama, "illegal" artisanal miners, misrepresented by the South African Press and Government', *The Extractive Industries and Society*, 1, 127–129.

Chapter Five

Zamazama[5] – Livelihood Strategies, Mobilisation and Resistance in Johannesburg, South Africa

Janet Munakamwe

Introduction

While non-formal mining plays a central role in poor households' livelihoods, it is a great concern that a lot of attention is given to the criminal aspect of the mining activity but not the destination of the 'illegally' mined minerals. The research examined the issue of cross-border migration, with particular reference to the working lives and career aspirations of women and men who are finding a livelihood by working in abandoned and closed mines in Durban Deep, Johannesburg, South Africa. The chapter documents the activities involved, socio-economic dynamics including aspects of power and resistance as they relate to the non-formal economy. This research is ethnographic in nature, including direct observations and in-depth interviews with participants and key players in the gold mining value chain which occurs outside of formal mines. Preliminary findings showed that there is a symbiotic link between formally and non-formally as the two come to a convergence between level 3 and 5 of the commodity value chains which are international markets and elite multinational companies. I argue here that non-formal mining activities are as a result of economic exclusion including inequalities and that by engaging in such activities, zamazama are reclaiming what belong to them through passive resistance. The research also demonstrated that while these workers lack a formal political voice, they however, have developed their own strategies of passive resistance to police brutality as they also demand gold trading licenses.

---

[5]Zamazama is a local term which refers to illegal miners and it means 'we are trying'.

The gold mining sector in South Africa has played a critical role in providing employment and livelihoods to thousands of domestic and international households over the last century. According to the Chamber of Mines fact sheet of 2015, mining contributes 500 000 direct and 800 000 indirect jobs resulting in a total of 1.3 million jobs with 16% contribution towards national Gross Domestic product (GDP). Alongside formal mining activities, non-formal mining activities take place and these have created work and income for many in the southern African region in particular cross-border migrants. Approximately, 2-5 billion dollars is claimed to lost in unpaid taxes annually through non-formal mining and clandestine trading activities (Debra et al, 2014: Chamber of Mines 2015).This study investigates the impact of the transformation of the labour migration regime in southern Africa on employment in the mining sector and the subsequent emergence of non-formal mining as livelihoods strategy. Contrary to the public discourse, I argue that non-formal mining is rooted in the political economy of migration and mining and that those involved at the bottom end of this practice are precarious migrants struggling to earn a livelihood.

Existing studies demonstrate that non-formal mining which is usually manifested in the form of small scale artisanal mining plays a fundamental role in poor rural households (Debra *et al* 2014: Lahiri-Dutt, 2011: Zvarivadza, 2014: Perks, 2011: Purevjav, 2011). While many scholars appreciate the significance of artisanal mining in promoting economic development for rural communities, this study provides an insight on how communities in urban spaces earn a living by engaging in non-formal mining activities. Further, I demonstrate that these practices are shaped by the transformation of the labour migration regime in the region and by contemporary realities facing the urban poor in South Africa (see Barchiesi, 2011). Underscoring this argument, I demonstrate how there are two international linkages in this sector: whilst all the attention has focused on the lower end, that of non-formal miners, and on negative factors associated with the people and work that is being done, less attention has been paid to the top end of the sector (see Munakamwe and Jinnah, 2015). Much like the sector itself, it is the predominantly (white) multi-national and transnational wealthy elites who benefit at the expense

156

of poor (black) workers who operate under precarious conditions. While trade unions are constrained from mobilising non-formal miners because of their assumed 'criminal' status, the study revealed that various informal resistance strategies evolved over the years as miners seek to resolve problems which they face in their daily working lives. In some instances, miners resort to worker advice offices (see Wilderman, *et al* 2016) and or commercial legal aid companies like Scorpion for representation in court cases.

The chapter is divided into four parts: part one introduces the background, concepts and literature on the political economy of post-apartheid mining in South Africa; part two focuses on the mining labour process and the precarious conditions of non-formal miners; in part three, I explore the shady world of purchasing and marketing non-formal gold; in part four, I identify the new forms of solidarity and resistance emerging amongst non-formal illegal miners.

Background

In 2011, forty miners died at a non-formal illegal mining shaft in the old mining town of Springs, east of Johannesburg. In 2013, another nineteen miners died at an abandoned shaft ZM[6]. A "volcano" erupted at ZM and the bodies were 'cooked' and charred beyond recognition. No one was willing to risk their lives to go down and extract the dead bodies. The mine was later sealed with the dead bodies inside. In February of 2014, twenty five non formal miners died at Mag[7] shaft in Roodeport, west of Johannesburg. Their colleagues volunteered to retrieve the bodies from underground to ensure a dignified burial for the dead miners. In all three incidents, cross-border migrants constituted the majority of those who perished.

This chapter was triggered by a catastrophic incident of February 2014, which occurred at Mag shaft as mentioned above. Twenty three Zimbabweans (including one woman), one Mozambican and one young Zulu migrant from KwaZulu Natal lost their lives. Three

---

[6] I have used pseudonyms throughout this study to avoid identification of both participants and research sites as this might expose participants to the police.

months later, the municipality and the police in collaboration with an unnamed "owner" of the 'bloody' shaft, sealed the 'mouth' of the abandoned shaft. Despite the dangers and the trauma from the February disaster, two weeks later, *zamazama* reopened the shaft claiming that this was their only source of livelihood in a country where unemployment rate is high (estimated at 27%) and, in the case of foreigners, the rigid and bureaucratic immigration policy which makes it difficult for them to enter the formal labour market.

The chapter was motivated by the need to understand the nature and function of on-formal mining in poor households and further examined the precarious working conditions of zamazama, their resistance and coping strategies including the possibilities of finding a "representative voice" to improve their working and living conditions. These workers operate outside of the formal mines and are classified as non-formal miners based on the activities which they are involved in. Non-formal miners are usually associated with criminality in relation to national laws and policies. It is even worse for immigrants who quite often undocumented. According to the Chamber of Mines (2014: 3), "about 70% of all arrested 'illegal' miners are undocumented immigrants". Indeed, the stereotypes associated with zamazama make it difficult for these workers to seek justice in the face of police brutality and violence or to access critical health services in times of need.

A total of 40 interviews were conducted with women and men involved in the sector; 26 were Zimbabweans, 9 Mozambicans and 4 Sotho and 1 South African from KwaZulu Natal. Of these, 15 were women while 25 were men and all women interviewed were cross-border migrants from Zimbabwe, Mozambique and Lesotho. The profiles of participants varied from individual to individual and nationality. For instance the majority of Zimbabweans interviewed had completed their 'O' levels and some had gone as far as university education. Two of the participants possessed first degrees in geology and marketing but failed to secure jobs in the formal economy because they did not have the right documents to work in South Africa. Ten of the women interviewed were independent migrants[8]

---

[8] Independent migrants in this study refers to those who migrate based on their personal choice other than to join a spouse

and were single parents while five were married. Of the 25 men interviewed, 18 were married while 7 were still single.

Conceptualising non-formal mining

This section aims to unpack the concept non-formal and also deconstruct 'illegality' associated with zamazama activities. In particular it grounds itself on Marxist theories which explain clearly the capitalist constructions of "illegality" and "legality" as ways in which the state and the elite 'ring fence' certain spaces and activities to ensure they are out of bounds for certain categories of people. Things are not naturally "illegal" or "legal" but they are so as a result of social constructions of the powerful and most dominant in the world who use the law as part of their ideological apparatuses. By classifying zamazama activities as non-formal, the study attempts to deconstruct the 'criminality' element associated with economic activities which fall outside of the formal but ironically contribute towards the general economic growth of the country.

Non-formal mining activities could be described as loosely organised and established on individual skills or sometimes guided by experienced personnel such as former retrenched mine workers or immigrants who fail to secure jobs in the formal mines because of restrictive immigration laws. Interesting, many of those involved in non-formal mining acquire tacit skills which they could use to expand chances of employability in the formal mines. A central feature of such mining activities is the use of rudimentary tools as opposed to large machinery used in industrial mining. While they operate in abandoned mines which literally shows a 'grey' area in terms of property ownership between the state and mining companies, the major area of contention is that of space of operation which constitute prosecution based on trespassing of private property. By referring these activities as 'informal', we tend to reinforce existence of dualism yet the products of the mining processes all contribute towards the overall economy in the same manner. Thus, positioning these mining activities as formal and informal creates unrealistic dualisms since in fact the two converge as we shall see later. Again, it tends to blame the poor for claiming their own economic rights in

159

open spaces by labelling them as 'illegal'. Furthermore, given the history in which precolonial African mines were taken over by colonists, I would argue that the (neo-) colonial mining activities have been superimposed on African small scale mining activities such that anything outside of the mainstream capitalist means of accumulation and undertaken by the poor would be rendered 'parallel' or 'illegal'.

In his book "Weapons of the Weak" Scott (1984), contends that

> is it not critical to portray at last this peasant who thwarts the (legal) code by reducing private property into something that simultaneously exists and does not exist? You shall see this tireless sapper, this nibbler, gnawing the land into little bits, carving an acre into a hundred pieces, and invited always to this feast by a petite bourgeoisie which finds in him, at the same time, its ally and its prey…out of the reach of the law by virtue of his insignificance, this Robespierre, with a single head and twenty million hands, works ceaselessly, crouching in every commune… (1984: vii).

The above extract is very critical in my attempt to problematize non-formal mining activities in the context of high levels of inequality between the peasant and bourgeoisie; big mining companies and small scale miners; the elite and the poor in South Africa. Drawing from data gathered in the study, I argue that inequalities in society contribute to the proliferation of non-formal mining activities in existing or abandoned mining shafts and this is not a deliberate choice but that poor people are coerced to engage in such activities as a response to abject poverty and at times restrictive immigration laws in the case of immigrants. While society in general and those in authority, (as guide by state laws) would perceive non-formal economic activities as illegal, from my own observations, engaging in such activities could be an overt form of resistance to domination (see Scott, 1984). It is clear from the study that the state is biased towards big business which thrives on exploitation of poor workers' labour power in exchange for very low wages. Yet, large multinational mining companies generate huge profits from mineral extraction in Africa. This leads us to this very fundamental question: How is it the case that when Africans do such mining they are labelled as 'illegal'

160

yet when foreign transnational corporations do the same they are not labelled as illegal? This question could be better answered by the Marxist theory which shows how the law is used to support capital and foreign capital here as opposed to the poor peasant. Thus, as some of the respondents have confessed, their livelihood activities in abandoned mines do not qualify to be criminalised but constitute mundane ways of earning a living in their everyday lives. To substantiate this argument, some zamazama who were interviewed believe big mining houses are the "real zamazama" as they extract resources in Africa and externalise the benefits and profits out of the country. Some respondents reported that they were tired and discouraged from working for very poor wages and opted out of their formal jobs to embark on entrepreneurial mining activities in abandoned shafts. This on its own demonstrates passive forms of resistance as opposed to direct confrontation as witnessed in the 2012 Marikana Miners' strike which culminated into the death of 34 miners. In our attempt to understand the root causes of non-formal mining activities, we need to understand the experiences of the poor and the marginalised like immigrants and their own understanding of livelihood opportunities within restrictive immigration laws. Equally important to note is that 'non-formality' is a social construct in relation to state laws and is dependent on a country's context. Thus, non-formal economic activities could be described as a reconfiguration of social order under localised conditions. Similarly, the colloquial and derogatory label attached to those involved in non-formal mining activities (zamazama) is socially constructed and identified negatively in relation to the country laws although literally there are no specific laws to prosecute offenders. Accordingly, Scott (1984) asserts that:

> ...All identities, without exception, have been socially constructed ...to the degree that the identity that is stigmatised by the larger state or society, it is likely to become for many a resistant and defiant identity. Here invented identities combine with self-making of heroic kind, in which such identifications become a badge of honour ... (1984: xii –iii).

Evidently so, zamazama seem to have accepted the derogatory name in a much more positive way and accept their economic positioning as formal workers as they believe there is no evidence to suggest that what they do is outside of the law. For them, they are trying to earn a living in the same way in which large mining companies are also exploiting mineral resources. The only difference is that the latter's activities are supported by the state which grants them mining permits and rights; use highly technical machinery; have access to capital and mine at a larger scale whereas zamazama use rudimentary tools; do not possess mining permits and their mining activities are very often undertaken at a very small scale. Ironically, the product of both activities will find their way into the formal economy at some point and this demystifies the binaries between the formal and non-formal (see Chipangura, this volume; Munakamwe 2015). By reconfiguring non-formality alongside formality and through an economic beneficiation lens, the study deconstructs 'criminality' associated with zamazama activities.

While the livelihood activities of zamazama expose the complexities associated with non-formality, they however manifest some elements of inequalities in society which compel the 'have nots' to claim their share outside of formal spaces and at the same time contribute positively towards the overall economy.

Non-formal mining in the context of South Africa

Non-formal mining exists in two forms and is defined in relation to the laws of South Africa. First, it takes place in formal mines where "formal employees engage in criminal activities, either while at work (abandoning their working places) or during their leave periods" (Chamber of Mines of South Africa, 2014:3). *Zamazama* involved in industrial mines spend extended periods of time, between seven days up to six months, underground and sustain themselves through provisions supplied by formal employees. Where strict measures have been implemented to prohibit formal employees to take food underground, a loaf of bread, for instance costs as much as R1000 . In the large operating mines, zamazama are claimed to 'steal' huge blasted gold-rich rocks which generates a lot of income at a time.

This kind of mining is very sophisticated and involves powerful syndicates who aim to make huge profits as opposed to economic survival. The second type of non-formal mining occurs in abandoned or closed mines where miners "use explosives to blast open concrete seals of surface shaft entries" (Chamber of Mines of South Africa, 2014:3). This type of mining usually involves individuals, groups and families and often primary and secondary deposits of minerals are extracted using simple hand tools (Purevjav, 2011: 199).

Neither form should be confused with artisanal mining which is defined as small-scale or subsistence mining and involves gold panning using simple tools but is undertaken within the confines of the law (see Debra *et al* 2014, Zvarivadza 2014: Thornton 2013). While artisanal mining occurs with minerals like sand, clay, precious stones in South Africa, however, this does not occur in gold for the reasons which I will explain later[9]. *Zamazama* do not work for any company and therefore operate independently using their own hand tools and resources. Thornton (2013) describes artisanal miners as those who "produce their own gold using simple techniques" (2013:1). In other countries within Africa, for example artisanal mining is usually undertaken within the confines of the law where individuals are allocated mining claims and licences to trade in gold as in the cases of Zimbabwe, DRC, Tanzania and Ghana (see Zvarivadza 2014: Mutemeri and Petersen 2002). In South Africa, certain minerals not classified under the Precious Mineral Act like sand and clay could be mined within the legal and policy framework (Fakier, 2016). Artisanal mining activities usually contribute indirectly towards a country's overall economy (GDP) because individuals involved usually possess formal gold dealership licences and therefore pay taxes. The study focused on the second type of non-formal mining activities.

---

[9] Interview with Nellie Mutemeri, Anglo-Gold Ashanti, 15/10/2014; Newtown Offices

Part One: The macro and micro political economy of mining in a post-apartheid labour regime

Over the past two decades the mining sector in South Africa has shed hundreds of thousands of jobs, and the composition of its workforce also radically changed from 70% foreign migrant labour in the 1970s originating from neighbouring countries (Lesotho, Mozambique, Zimbabwe in particular), the workforce is now mainly domestic (foreign workers currently represent less than 20% of the workforce), following a political agreement (the Mining Charter) between mining houses and the government..(Crush and Williams, (2010: 11) in Budlender for MiWORC, 2013) Mines have closed leading to job losses and today both locals and foreigners rely on non-formal mining which involves identification of old mining dumps and scraping residual traces of gold left behind by huge mining companies.

The negative structural economic transformation in the mining sector is part of the explanation for the proliferation of non-formal mining in post-apartheid South Africa coupled with independent, individual clandestine mobility of migrant labour into South Africa. Further, while free mobility across the borders increased with the ushering in of democracy, however, rigid immigration policies in particular related to the work permit regime persists. For instance, in my study, I came across a qualified geologist who is in possession of a degree but failed to secure a job in the mainstream labour market because of the bureaucratic requirements and policies which require one to be affiliated to a professional body for their sector. All this is compounded by structural xenophobic tendencies within the very institutions meant to service foreign workers. The aspect of immigration policy has to a greater extent contributed to lack of mobilisation of foreign labour in this particular sector.

Globally, there is a dearth in laws and policies governing mining activities in abandoned mines. However, some relevant international instruments and institutions might be invoked if needed. These include the ten principles of the Council on Mining & Metals [ICMM]; Kimberly Process; Global Reporting Initiative Mining and metals Supplement Mining and the International Labour

Organisation (ILO) Convention 182 on the Worst Forms of Child Labour.

At national level, other than the gold ownership laws and the Mineral and Petroleum Resources Development Act, South Africa does not have explicit laws to prosecute *zamazama* other than drawing from trespassing laws, theft, money laundering or corruption. The country to some extent still relies more on apartheid laws in particular the Precious Stones Act of 1927. According to Chamber of Mines of South Africa, "there is a specific prohibition in the MPRDA on mining without the required statutory authorization (section 5(4) (Chamber of Mines of South Africa Factsheet 2014). South Africa "is about the only country in the world where it is a criminal offense to be in possession of unwrought precious metal without the required statutory authorization" (ibid).

Parliamentary debates on how to deal with illegal mining dominated particularly in 2009 but until today no specific Act has passed through parliament. Policy makers and key players in law enforcement of the country have in the past expressed unorthodox views. Some believe the only way to eradicate non-formal mining is "to rehabilitate the area,"[10]. The then honourable Minister for Minerals and Resources in 2009, Ms Susan Shabangu believed the best way to deal with the problem is through the South African Police Services (SAPS) but this proved to be a short term measure according to the Democratic Alliance, the main opposition party in South Africa. The lack of a clear strategy simply means the government acknowledges the instrumental role played by non-formal, mining in alleviating unemployment and poverty amongst poor communities while at the same time pursuing business interests.

Part Two: The mining labour process: The tools and the division of labour.

This section presents findings based on fieldwork and documents the working conditions of the zamazama. One of the critical issues under investigation was the need to understand the reasons for

---

[10] Col Hennie Flyn of the South African Police Services (SAPS)

individual participants to opt for non-formal mining as a source of livelihood. Immigrants mentioned that they realised there were no jobs when they came to Johannesburg yet they needed money to pay rents and school fees for children:

> Yes I know informal mining is bad but what can I do? I'm a foreigner in a foreign land no one is ready to listen to us.

Further probing on whether he would join a union to assist him, Tomu said:

> Our lives are at risk and we can die anytime, so I can pay union subscriptions then what? I'm ready to join those organisations dealing with social issues like burial society because I know one day I will die and I need a better burial. My fellow countrymen died in the mines and were buried in the bush (meaning South Africa). If I die under the mine and my friends can take my body out, I want to be buried back home.

There are mixed feelings among migrant miners about their preferred places of burial. However, most of them do not really care about their place of burial as long as they receive a decent burial. Sometimes it is difficult to retrieve bodies from rock falls and it is difficult for one to insist that they get buried back in their countries of origin or places of birth for internal migrants. The abandoned mines where zamazama enter were described by participants as "*akaora*" meaning they are "rotten", and very narrow with many dangerous chambers. Miners go to an extent of genderising the mines in their description. They sometimes squeeze through very narrow spaces and had this to say:

> Do you think women's hips can pass through, this is one of the reasons why we say women should not come underground…No women underground…the mines belong to ancestors… the mine has very narrow spaces and we have to move like a snake or chicken.

Miners are sometimes forced to wriggle like snakes for almost a kilometre as one cannot walk straight and this is the reason why they perish when disasters occur.

In terms of tools, miners use rudimentary tools such as hammers, hard- emilites, fuse, ignite and coat chisels, copper cables, simple head torches, horror, drillers, *mugwara* (long chisel), to extract gold underground. Use of modern technology like simple Nokia phones has been introduced of late. A simple Nokia phone is used to 'scan' for gold rich rocks underground. Where a huge concentration of gold is detected, then dynamite or generators are used to blow out the rock. However, the use of such huge machinery is attributed to some extent to rock fall accidents. Very often, "sponsors' buy tools and mercury on behalf of the miners in return for gold. Sponsors play a paternalistic role in the working lives of *zamazama* and thus trust and loyalty is required between miners and sponsors. If a sponsor provides miners with tools and other equipment including food provisions to take underground, the miners are expected to positively reciprocate by selling the extracted gold to their respective sponsors. If miners run out of food or equipment underground, they send one of them to their sponsor (usually buyers) who is also linked to them based on ethnic and nationality lines[11]. Copper cables are used to convey miners in and out where the surface is loose and not stable enough to step on, or else rock fall accidents occur. However, this is the worst form of conveyance as miners mentioned that any slight mistake leads to death.

Mercury plays a very central role in gold processing and is supplied by formal mine workers. This metal is denser than gold hence it is used in the final stages of gold purification to gather together loose gold particles ready for smelting. It is a highly criminalised substance and if one is found in its possession, they will get arrested and imprisoned for at least five years. It forms one of the key exhibits for prosecution in court. A small tube (50ml) costs around R500. Without this metal, gold cannot be extracted from the impurities hence no business. Dark marks on *zamazama* hands are

---

[11]However, this practice seems more like labour brokering of a special kind than sponsorship. The normal practice of sponsorship means someone provides without expecting anything in return!

testimony to the use of this highly volatile metal. Unfortunately, the mercury is negligently disposed of. When rain comes, this is washed away hence poor growth of green plantation around abandoned shafts and surrounding areas including availability of trace metals in vegetables and fruits grown in such areas. This could be another possible cause of a proliferation of cancer-related diseases (see Debra *et al* 2014). In her study of the artisanal and small scale mining in the DRC, Perks (2011: 188) identified miscarriages, still-births and high child mortality rate for those women involved and are exposed to highly radioactive substances such as uranium, copper, mercury and cobalt (ibid).Mercury is smuggled from formal mines by formal miners who collaborate with *zamazama* for exchange of money which they appreciate to subsidise their low incomes. [12]

Ethnicity, nationality and syndicates

Zamazama operate as syndicates based on ethnicity, nationality and sometimes racial lines as people from various racial groups, tend to 'own' particular shafts. Syndicates usually range between three and do not usually exceed eight as this might 'fuel' conflict in particular on allocation of earnings. Brothers can easily turn against each other and the same might apply to friends. Work is usually done collectively although some respondents indicated that they do have non-formal structures and leaders who usually guide them in particular at the distribution of earnings. Leaders also negotiate with other syndicates on common issues such as resistance against police brutality and violence. Violence usually erupts if syndicates trespass shaft rules. The divides and co-operation along ethnic lines would constitute a basis for mobilisation (see Webster, 1985: Milkman 2006).

Gold is extracted by men as according to the miners' taboos, beliefs and superstitions, women are forbidden underground. Miners believe that allowing women to enter underground results in catastrophic incidents as manifested in the 2014 catastrophe which claimed the lives of twenty –five zamazama[13]. Women often work as

---

[12] Interview with National Union of Mineworkers (NUM) M: 16.10.2014. Union Offices

[13] For instance the sole woman who was amongst those who died on the 19th of

processors and transporters of raw material (Perk 2011) and also as service providers in areas of commerce, catering and frequently prostitution (2011: 186). Much of the surface work which involves crushing and refinery of the mineral ore from the rock is also undertaken by women and children. According to Overholt *et al* (1985) cited in Lahiri-Dutt (2011), the gender-based division of labour, as well as access to and control over resources and benefits are likely to differ within a community. Labour is divided based on sex and the same applies to problems and diseases. While respiratory diseases like tuberculosis cuts across both sexes, more women than men suffer from this disease as they get into direct contact with dust particles as they crush and grind gold-rich rocks to extract gold particles. At the same time, women complain of back aches, chest pains and body muscle pains resulting from of rock grinding. Men who go underground complain of flues and sometimes asthma caused by dangerous gases underground. These men's major threat is death due to fatal accidents underground. Babies and toddlers also suffer from tuberculosis as they inhale dust at their mothers' surface 'workplaces'.

Beliefs and Earnings

Zamazama have their own beliefs and superstitions. For instance, they believe that when one gets a large amount of gold at once, then they should never be greedy and go back underground otherwise this means undermining their ancestors. Rather, they are expected to use the money generated as capital to start other surface businesses to avoid ever going back underground. This belief is consistent with the moral economy framework which upholds goodness, fairness and justice and promotes communalism which deters 'greediness' and 'over-accumulation' in order to maintain an equitable society without inequalities (see Moodie 1986). The primary aim of engaging in non-

---

February was blamed for the disaster. The miners believe that *makunakuna (meaning* casual sex) which occurred underground offended the 'gods' of the underworld hence the subsequent disaster. Respondents said there are certain sexual rituals to be observed before they enter underground. Men are not supposed to have sex two days before they go underground and also while they are underground.

formal mining is to earn a modesty living as opposed to self-enrichment, the study has shown.

To economically safeguard themselves from breaching some of the beliefs, some indicated that they invest back home by purchasing livestock and construction of homes in preparation for their future in the event that they might get permanent disabilities through for instance, mine accidents or early retirement which is not compensated for as they do not have employers. Almost all the respondents perceived non-formal mining as a temporary poverty alleviation measure hence poor mobilisation around problems which affect their working lives.

Zamazama do not have a formal employer and their earnings are usually determined by *bhandi* (meaning gold belt) and the stock exchange in relation to gold price for the day. The richer the belt, the higher the earnings. An average of R3 000 is earned per week although some claim to earn as much as R8 000 depending on the size of the syndicate. Women earn between R70-R100 per day which can translate to R700 per week if one works every day. Almost 90% of respondents said they are happy with their earnings of which they compared these to earnings from previous jobs like security, domestic work, farm work, construction and retail work. They claim that at least their earnings in this sector are guaranteed and regular compared to working for some bosses who sometimes underpay them based on their documentation and citizenship. Contrary to many studies (Purevjav 2011: Hinton *et al* 2006; Debra *et al* 2014) which claim that women lack autonomy on their earnings, this study showed that there is a strong link between independent migration of women and autonomy on earnings as single women expressed that they are in control of their earnings. Lahiri-Dutt, (2006) asserts that non-formal mining provides new identities and new senses of the self which women acquire in masculine spaces. Wage disparities are subtle as both women and men earn the same wages for the same work performed on the surface.

However, some expressed that while they are happy with their earnings they are risking their lives as one respondent said:

"I'm not happy about the money because I can die anytime; I know one day I might get underground and never come back."[14]

The aspect of health and safety is a very contentious issue as despite their earnings which are sometimes very high, zamazama do not see the need to purchase highly protective clothing relevant to their kind of jobs. Their priorities are safety shoes and *maperengende* (second hand clothes) which they ironically throw away after each trip. Surprisingly, while they know the negative effects of mercury as evidenced by dark marks on their hands, they do not purchase hand gloves to protect their hands from the hazardous mercury. Woollen hats are used as helmets and these allow them to squeeze through narrow spaces as opposed to helmets (see Thornton 2013). | Women working with dust on the surface do not use masks to cover their noses and mouths from dust and other air-borne impurities. This observation points to a great need for education programmes around the need to observe health and safety in non-formal mining activities.

Part Three: Marketing of gold: Buyers and the destination of gold

Three categories of buyers exist. Primary buyers are those who establish bases at the shafts and buy the gold directly from the miners through the intervention of agents. Agents are directly linked to zamazama and usually live within the community hence they assist primary buyers on security matters. Primary buyers sell their gold to secondary buyers who usually operate in the 'black market'. Secondary buyers sell their commodity to tertiary buyers who are usually linked to big mining companies and possess gold trading licences which then formalises the so-called 'criminally' mined gold. A system of licence brokering exists and one can earn a lot of money without directly involving oneself in gold transactions. Licence brokers sell gold on behalf of buyers who do not possess licences to sell gold directly to the formal refineries. Primary buyers claimed that licence brokers sell gold at the highest price of the day which

---

[14] Interview with Eneristo. 14/09/2014. Site B.

fluctuates between R1, 100 and R1, 200 and they usually pay primary buyers between R500 and R800. The difference between the maximum price and the prevailing market price is theirs and on top of that one has to pay an agreed amount as commission. Clearly, there are no systems of accountability and there exists huge loopholes in the system which allows non-formally mined gold to be legalised along the commodity chain.

An interview with director of security for Company X provided a succinct summary of the value chain of the gold mined by *zamazama* as illustrated in Fig 1 below:

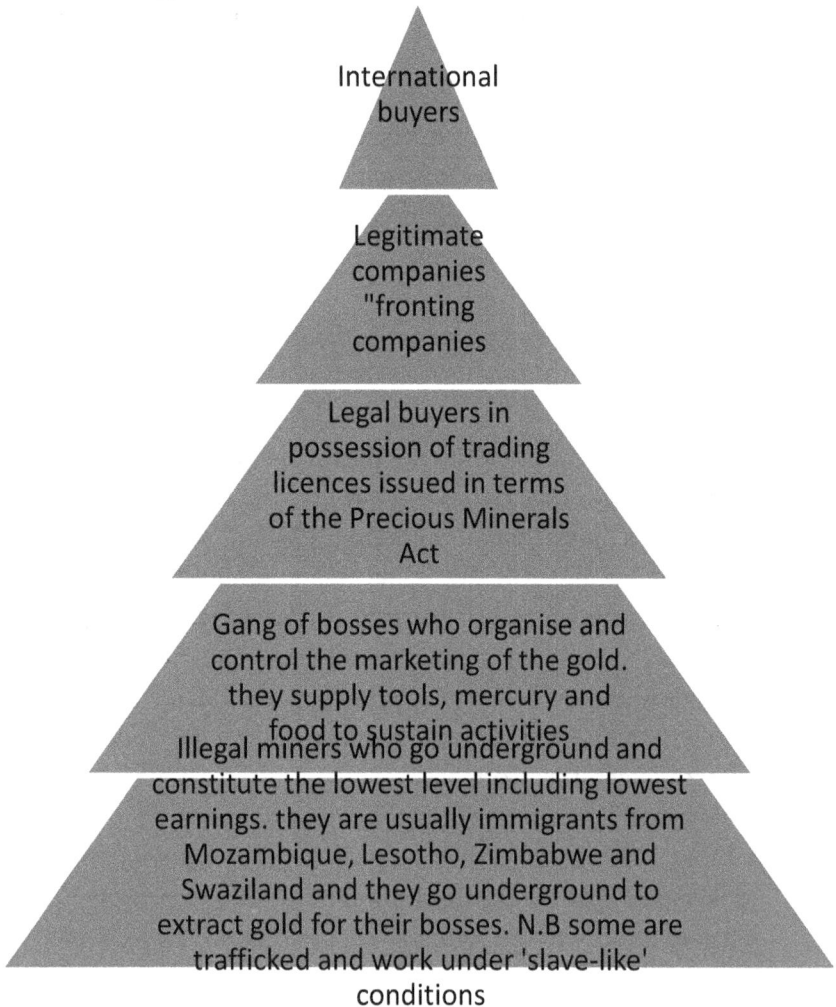

Source: *Interview with Mr P, X Company*

Figure 1: Commodity value chain of 'illegally mined' gold

172

The diagram above clearly demonstrates the relationship between gold mined in the non-formal economy and formal markets. The number of involved individuals becomes smaller as we go up the hierarchy while gold price gets higher at each level. Interestingly, the final destination of gold is at international markets where gold trading is liberalized and formalised. At this stage, no one questions the origin of the product and gold produced in the non-formal economy is legitimized. At level four, gold is sent to the national refinery. Rand Refinery is the largest refinery in South Africa and it is here that gold mined in both formal and non-formal economies subsequently converge beginning at the gold refineries. From credible national refineries, pure gold is exported formally to international markets where it is sold at very high prices usually tenfold compared to what the zamazama on the ground earn after working under risky and precarious conditions. Gold mined by zamazama is claimed to be exported clandestinely through non-formal channels. For example, some experts in the gold trading industry allege that the gold is moulded into personal fashionable chains, rings or bangles.

Primary buyers indicated that they sell gold to some white people in town and they usually shop around before they sell to check who offers the best price on that particular day. Licensed gold dealers are eligible to sell gold to formal refineries within and outside South Africa. Sometimes, buyers from overseas come to buy directly from primary buyers at a higher price as they (international buyers) benefit from the exchange regime.

There are also licensed brokers in possession of formal licenses to trade and deal in gold and its products. While some zamazama who were interviewed claimed to know individuals involved in the buying process, respondents refused to say exactly where these people could be located for interviews. However, they stated that usually buyers are white people who work for registered mines or Indians or Nigerians. However, primary buyers interviewed claim that the later are very 'stingy' and are reluctant to pay the market price. Because of this, most primary buyers prefer white buyers or those who come from overseas but these are difficult to find because they come once in a while.

The commodity chain above involves huge transactions of cash and also demonstrates how South Africa loses billions of rands (estimated at 2 billion a year) to clandestine 'black markets' including evasion of tax. Some key informants admitted that some multinational corporations engage in massive tax evasion through tax havens, and this issue was discussed at length at the 2016 Alternative Mining Indaba[15] The gold market is highly competitive and primary buyers often 'pull down' each other[16]

While zamazama cited police harassment as their major challenge, ironically, primary buyers mentioned robbers (predominantly Basotho) as their main enemies. All the buyers interviewed reported that they hire their own body guards to protect them from robbers. Every gold transaction process involves security guards and these are usually guarding the entrance of the backyard shacks which buyers use as their 'bases'. This raises an interesting issue about the proliferation of private security companies even private armies in Africa including South Africa. In other words, even multinational corporations are increasingly engaging in private security that has become worrisome to African states whose own security systems are being outstripped.

While non-formal mining is very often denounced by governments and large mining companies, its importance for poor communities resides in job creation and alternative livelihoods in response to high levels of unemployment in the country. . In addition, some reported that they consult prophets or *sangoma* for protection. One of the buyers boastfully said *"I got my prophets back home who give me water for protection. Because of this protection I'm untouchable even as small as I am, nobody touches me"*[17]

---

[15] Alternative Mining Indaba is an annual event which brings together civil society, academics, researchers and runs parallel to the Mining Indaba, which is a dialogue platform for government and business. The former advocates for tax justice for communities affected by mining while the later looks at prospects for investments in the mining industry and paves way for collusion between governments and big business in the industry.

[16] Interview with Jackie a gold buyer agent. 27/09/2014. Restaurant in Roodeport.

[17]Interview with Chimbo. 21/09/2014. Site A

Part Four: Risk –taking, Precarity, Solidarity and new forms of resistance

There are a lot of dangers associated with non-formal mining and police harassment tops the list (Munakamwe, 2014). For instance, a pregnant woman fell when running away from police at a 'processing plant' and consequently suffered from a miscarriage. Besides losing her baby, she could not seek recourse through the courts as her colleagues indicated that she is undocumented and at the same time involved in so-called "criminal" activities. [18]

There are syndicates of robbers who also work hand in hand with police. They are said to get guns and ammunition supplies from the police. [19]Sometimes miners are locked up in abandoned mines and struggle to get back to the surface under very hard conditions using a string with the danger of falling down from long heights. In such circumstances, they have to use ropes to travel a distance which takes 45 minutes on a lift in a formal mine.

When people die in the abandoned mines, their colleagues attempt by all means to take out the bodies to the surface so that their spirits cannot haunt the mines. Miners said they do this because they work at night and even sleep underground for many days. If they do not exhume the dead bodies, they believe the mines might get infested with "zvikwinya" which is the same as 'tokoloshe'. So they try to avoid this and where possible they can extract out bodies but where there is a danger of rock falls they cannot risk their lives and prefer to leave the dead body(ies).

Miners cite their families, friends and the local community as key sources of power and inspiration in times of trouble. Sometimes they team up against the police. However, sometimes they are divided as some are very scared of police revenge. They sometimes compromise by paying bribes of at least R500 when police raid their 'bases'. [20] One major barrier to mobilisation is lack of leadership to drive and provide direction. What struck me the most is how the miners choose their leaders and the prioritised qualities? Some said they would

---

[18] Interview with Nina. 04/09/2014. Site A.
[19] Interview with Elyn. 28/08/2014. Site B.
[20] Interview with Mlungi. 06/09/2014. Site A.

choose somebody from the most powerful ethnic grouping while others said they prefer someone who is ready to listen to people and also good at talking.

Very often, miners come together to socialise such as beer drinking during weekends or when there are funerals. They have established burial societies which usually comprise of people from the same country and ethnic groups with leaders like chairman, secretary and treasurer. For instance, when one dies they put together money as families or neighbours to contribute towards burial. Ordinary miners pay R50 and 'buyers' pay R100 or more depending on an individual. If an individual has better-off families then they can repatriate the body back home but if not, they request the municipal councillor for space in the local cemetery to bury the body. Women who work as "crushers or grinders "on the surface claimed that they establish their own women's committees and if somebody dies, they all contribute R20 towards funeral costs. Again, women are socially linked through stokvel collectives whose contributions usually range between R100 up to R500 per week. Miners admitted that they often come together when many people die like with the February 19 catastrophe, but can become enemies anytime and get divided based on earnings.

Power, Representation and Resistance

As mentioned before, zamazama are associated with "criminal" activities and as such lack a voice not because they are docile but because of negative stereotypes attached to their livelihoods. As a result, they prefer passive resistance in order to challenge domination and power. This point is well articulated by Scott (1984) who asserts that "in public those that are oppressed accept their domination, but always question their domination offstage."

The aspect of representation is virtually absent for zamazama yet they are subjected to several risks which would call for trade union representation. The majority are familiar with trade unions from television or street marches and protests. However, a few were union members in their countries of origin while those who once worked in the formal mines have an idea although they admitted not having joined unions for various reasons as this statement reveals:

> You see, in the formal mines we used to see NUM people coming and workers joining. We used to come together as workers but unfortunately, I never joined a union... I was scared because I was using a false ID.[21]

This to some extent divides solidarity and undermines mobilisation amongst workers in particular those of foreign origin who believe that non-formal mining is a temporary measure as shown below:

> Why should I protect and fight for improvements in a sector where I do not intend to spend my entire life. I'm only here to make quick *bucks* (money) and return back to my country of origin. When I go back, I will be able to employ others ...I mean train my siblings on how to buy this mineral...all I will have to do is to sell the stuff I get from country X here in South Africa where I know there is a higher market rate because of the high quality and weight of gold from country X.[22]

Many of the locals who are residents in abandoned and 'ghost' mining settlements are either landlords (popularly known as *masitandi*) or are running some small non-formal businesses like backyard spaza shops, '*pap and chesa nyama*' kitchens, fruit and vegetable markets, welding or fashion industry (which sell second hand clothes or work suits and safety shoes). What this study points to is the fact that unemployed foreigners perceive abandoned mines as their economic safety net but of course exposed with risks of uncompensated mine accidents like rock falls, underground mine violence and slavery; police brutality and violence; mkunzi[23] or 'day light robbery' by police or both local and foreign colleagues.

---

[21] Interview with Chimbo (Observation , to illustrate how politically involved, the respondent was wearing an EFF red beret at the time of the interview)
[22] Interview with Janda. 21/09/2014. Site A
[23] Mkunzi is a township style of robbery as opposed to pick-pocketing. A robber approaches their target with a knife or at gunpoint demanding all their earnings.

Miners are exposed to risks which include police arrests and so they subscribe to commercial legal companies like Scorpion Legal Aid (SLA). The organization provides legal services and assists in bailing out arrested miners. SLA is said to be very efficient in dealing with their cases and has won many cases on behalf of zamazama as shown below:

> At the time when we were arrested for possessing gold... Scorpion helped many of us to get out of prison.[24]

> They (Scorpion Legal Aid) represent us very well and I don't mind paying for whatever amount they ask us to pay. We are all happy. In fact yesterday, they were here busy recruiting.[25]

> Usually, when we get arrested, police officers tell our friends or relatives to call one of the lawyers and that's how we get to know about the organisations.[26]

Members pay monthly subscriptions dependent on the scheme one opts to subscribe to. SLA recently introduced funeral insurance policy. This is because they realised that they are dealing with categories of workers whose lives are prone to death at any given time and would really require such services. Miners also narrated some direct confrontational resistance strategies in response to police like taking videos and photographs which will be used as evidence in court. This tactic scares away unscrupulous police with bad

---

Participants indicated that they are usually 'sold out' by their friends when they extract 'valuable stuff'. There exists a strong sense of mistrust which therefore undermines solidarity. They indicated that they usually stick to their 'blood related siblings' or close friends from their countries of origin for protection. Part of the solution is to establish teams or 'syndicates' to go with underground. However, one participant criticized team from a superstition point of view where he expressed that sometimes you might mix up with somebody "ane zvekumusha kwake zvisingade mari" (meaning you might mingle with somebody who is endowed with bad luck which repels money and as such one can go underground for days and come back to the surface with nothing).

[24] Interview with Achimw. 21/09/2014. Site A.
[25] Interview with Chimbo.21/09/2014. Site A.
[26] Interview with Madube. 13/09/2014. Site B.

intentions to confiscate 'stuff' and miners reported that this has proved very efficient as they cannot always live as victims. Few cases have been narrated where miners converged to devise ways of securing their own gold trading licences as they feel that buyers are 'robbing' them.

Zamazama depend on the communities where they live for solidarity which appropriately explains the concept of moral economy which emphasises goodness, fairness and justice and is more pronounced in small closely knit communities and whereby community members subscribe to the principles of mutuality in a communal economic system. Considering the case of the community, one can argue that there exists a strong cohesive force which binds together both locals and cross-border zamazama as demonstrated by few incidents of xenophobic attacks in those spaces. The poor local community who provide accommodation popularly known as '*mastandi*' mutually benefit from the income generated from non-formal mining activities. In addition, their other sources of livelihoods like small businesses, spaza shops, '*amakitchini*' or second hand business thrive on the same zamazama earnings. Thus, an interruption in the commodity chain of the gold mined by zamazama would affect the entire community as evidenced during my direct observations of the 2014 incident. This, to some extent promotes solidarity and kind of 'an injury to one is an injury to all' when dealing with mine accidents or police raids. The locals forge alliances with zamazama in as far as resistance is concerned. From a moral economy perspective, the workers' power resides in the communities they live in the form of symbolic power. Social movement unionism would be more ideal if unions were to tap on the already existing social networks and solidarity among these workers. However, I would like to caution that the overt unity that exists forged around the intersectionality of race and class does not totally translate into a homogenous society. Of course, other kinds of bad behaviours like robbery and murder tend to divide the community.

Conclusion

To conclude, two kinds of non-formal mining activities mining exist; that which occurs in formal mines and, secondly in abandoned mines. The study showed that the former qualifies to be criminalised under trespassing laws while the latter constitutes part of the non-formal livelihood strategies in abandoned mines which involves the poor 'scrapping' off left over traces of minerals 'dumped' by big business as profits from shafts dwindle. A strong link exists between formal and non-formal mining as the products from both come to a convergence either at the national refineries or at the level of marketing.

In terms of mobilisation, the study reveals that zamazama have shifted their focus and hope from trade unions to private legal aid societies such as Scorpion or Legal Aid Society, Clientele legal, and funeral insurance companies for both legal representation and social support. In the absence of union protection, zamazama rely more on institutional forms of power like the national constitution for protection. Miners have also assimilated and forged strong relations with local communities such that they partner in their action against, for instance, police harassment, as they exercise their societal power (see Dorre et al, 2009).

For social support, workers are organised around social networks or ethnic groupings such as burial societies. Interventions related to social issues such as death are a priority as they claim that their lives are ever at risk underground due to accidents like rock falls or gas emissions and robbery at gun point whilst on the surface. The study thus challenges and tends to deviate from trade union orthodoxy which holds the view that wages constitute a central position in worker mobilisation against capitalism. While these workers lack a political voice (Munakamwe, 2014), they however, have developed their own strategies of resistance to police brutality as they also demand gold trading licenses.

To sum up, the study demonstrates that while intricately linked, it is not easy to transform the non- formal due to complex structural challenges and this calls for "strengthening and extending of workers' rights, protection and benefits" (Horn, 2015:9; see also WIEGO,

2014; Bonner, 2009). While on the one hand, large mining companies to some extent benefit from non-formal mining as revealed by the study, it however holds the view that formalizing non-formal mining will be like promoting an antagonistic gold market hence the need to tighten security. On the other hand, trade unions attribute non-formal mining in formal mines as contributing to very dangerous working conditions and a potential loss of jobs and membership. However, trade unions have no strategy to deal with this sector and have not taken a lead in educating membership on the consequences of collaboration with zamazama which usually results in disciplinary actions or dismissals or in the worst cases imprisonment. Interestingly, both business and trade unions do not concentrate much of their resources and effort in fighting the second type of non-formal mining which occurs in abandoned mines. This is not surprising as some primary buyers claimed that they sell some of their gold to subsidiary companies of large mining houses. Because of the depth of gold mines in South Africa as shown by the study, there is no hope of formalizing non-formal mining activities in this sector in the near future which simply means no formal mobilisation through trade unions will occur, as the latter insists on adherence and compliance to national laws of the country. Mobilising zamazama, in moral terms, according to trade union officials who were interviewed, would mean endorsing illicit mining activities and associated criminal offenses ultimately breaching national laws. From my research, I recommend that the key players in the mining industry explore ways in which a vibrant and small-scale mining industry could be established in South Africa based on the large number of abandoned mines and at the same time ensure protection of workers' rights for those involved.

References

Barchiesi, F. (2011). *Precarious Liberation: Workers, the State and Contested Social Citizenship in Post-apartheid South Africa*, University of Kwazulu Natal: SUNY Press.

Benya, A. (2015). 'Women and subcontracted workers: The new mining labour regime in South Africa's platinum belt'. *A paper presented at the National Research Foundation (NRF) Workshop. 25-26 March 201,* Society, Work and Development Institute, University of the Witwatersrand, Johannesburg.

Bonner C. (2009). 'Collective Negotiations for Informal Workers. Organising in the Informal Economy: Resource Books for Organisers' Number 4, WIEGO and StreetNet, Johannesburg

Budlender, D. (2013). 'Improving the quality of available statistics on foreign labour in South Africa: Strategic recommendations', MiWORC Report, Johannesburg, University of the Witwatersrand.

Budlender (2014). 'Migration and employment in South Africa: Analysis of the migration module in the quarterly labour force survey, third quarter 2012', MiWORC Report, Johannesburg, African Centre for Migration & Society (ACMS), University of the Witwatersrand.

Chamber of Mines of South Africa, (2014). 'Illegal Mining in South Africa Factsheet'. www.chamberofmines.org.za

Crush, J. (2011). 'Complex Movements, Confused Responses: Labour Migration in South Africa'. Southern Africa Migration Project PB 25.

Debra, A.A., Watson, I. and Quansah, D.P.O. (2014). 'Comparison between artisanal and small- scale mining in Ghana and South Africa: Lessons Learnt and Way Forward'. *The Journal of The Southern African Institute of Mining and Metallurgy.* Vol. 114, No.6, pp 1-10.

Dorre, K., Holst, H. and Nachtwey, O. (2009). 'Organising –A Strategic Option for Trade Union Renewal?' *International Journal of Action Research*, Vol. 5, No. 1, pp 33-67.

Fakier, N. (2012). 'Towards equal mining opportunities: Legislative and policy recommendations, Paper presented on behalf of the Legal Resource Centre (LRC)', Artisanal and Mining Workshop. Centre for Sustainability in Mining and Industry (CSMI) and the African Centre for Migration and Society (ACMS), Johannesburg, University of the Witwatersrand.

Forrest, K. (2013). 'Marikana was not just about migrant labour', Mail & Guardian Online; 13 September 2013.

Hinton, J., Barbra, E. and Veiga, M. (eds) (2006). Women in Artisanal and Small Scale Mining in Africa in Lahiri-Dutt, K. And Macintyre, M. *Women Miners in Developing Countries: Pit Women and Others*, Burlington: Ashgate

Horn, P. (2015). 'Collective Bargaining in the Informal Economy – Street Vendors, An updated version of the WIEGO research report on Collective bargaining in the informal economy: Street Vendors', produced for the Solidarity Centre's Global Labour Programme at the end of 2013.

Lahiri-Dutt, K. (ed) (2011). *Gendering the Field: Towards Sustainable Livelihoods for Mining Communities*, Canberra: Australian National University Press.

Lahiri-Dutt, K. (ed.) (2011). 'Gender-based Evaluation of Development Projects: The LAST Method' in Lahiri- Dutt, K. 2011. *Gendering the Field: Towards Sustainable Livelihoods for Mining Communities*, Canberra: Australian National University Press.

Lahiri-Dutt, K. and Burke, G. (ed) (2011). 'Gender Mainstreaming in Asian Mining: A Development Perspective' in Lahiri Dutt *Gendering the Field: Towards Sustainable Livelihoods for Mining Communities*, Canberra: Australian National University Press.

Lahiri-Dutt, K. (eds) (2006). 'Globalisation and Women's Work in the Mine Pits in East Kalimantan, Indonesia' in Lahiri –Dutt, K. and Macintyre, M. *Women Miners in Developing Countries*, Pit Women and Others.

Milkman, R. (2006). *LA story: Immigrant Workers and the Future of the US Labor Movement,* New York: Russell Sage Foundation Publications.

Munakamwe, J. (2014). 'Foreign Zama zamas: Not everything glitters in Egoli', *South African Labour Bulletin*, Vol. 38, No. 1, pp 7-11.

Munakamwe, J. and Jinnah, Z. (2015). 'Mining, and migrancy in the gold sector in South Africa', *Paper presented at the National Research Foundation (NRF) Workshop, 25-26 March 2015,* Johannesburg: Society, Work & Development Institute, University of the Witwatersrand.

Munakamwe, J. (2015). "The interface between the legal and illegal mining processes: unpacking the value chain of illegally mined gold". Paper presented at the Centre for Sustainability in Mining and Industry (CSMI) Artisanal and Small-scale Mining (ASM) Seminar Series. 11 March 2015.

Mutemeri, N. and Petersen, F.W. (2002). 'Small–scale mining in South Africa: Past, present and future', *Natural Resources Forum*, vol. 26, no. 4, pp. 286–292.

Overholt, C., Anderson, M.B., Cloud, K. and Austin, J.E. (eds) (1985). Gender Roles in Development Projects: A Case Book, West Hartford: Kumarian Press.

Perks, R. (2011). (ed) 'Towards a Post-Conflict Transition: Women and Artisanal Mining in the Democratic Republic of Congo' in Lahiri- Dutt, K. *Gendering the Field: Towards Sustainable Livelihoods for Mining Communities*, Canberra: Australian National University Press.

Purevjav, B. (ed) (2011). 'Artisanal and Small Scale Mining: Gender and Sustainable Livelihoods in Mongolia' in Lahiri- Dutt, K. *Gendering the Field: Towards Sustainable Livelihoods for Mining Communities*, Canberra: Australian National University Press.

Segatti, A. and Munakamwe, J. (2014). 'Mobilising migrant workers in the South African post-migrant labour regime: precariousness, invisibility and xenophobia, *Paper presented at the International Sociological Association (ISA) Congress, XVIII ISA World Congress*, Yokohama, Japan, July 13-19, 2014.

The Mining Charter 13 August (2004). Department of Mineral Resources.*www.dmr.gov.za/publications/...charter...mining-charter/0.html*

Thornton, R. (2014). 'Zamazama, "illegal" artisanal miners, misrepresented by South African Press and Government' Blog entry athttp://robertthorntonza.blogspot.com/2013/07/informal-illegal-orartisanal-minin'g-in.htmlandhttp://academia.edu/3893926/Roodeport_Artisanal_Mining_Johannesburg

Scotts, J.C. (1984). Weapons of the Weak: 'Everyday Forms of Peasants Resistance'. New Haven and London: Yale University Press

Thornton, R. (2013). 'Informal, 'illegal', or 'artisanal' mining in Johannesburg. Blog entry athttp://robertthorntonza.blogspot.com/2013/07/informal-illegal-orartisanal-minin'g-in.html andhttp://academia.edu/3893926/Roodeport_Artisanal_Mining_Johannesburg

Von Holdt, K. (2002). Social movement unionism: The case of South Africa. *Work, Employment and Society, 16,* 2, pp283-304.

Webster, E. (1985). *Cast in a racial mould: Labour process and trade unionism in the foundries* Johannesburg: Ravan Press.

WIEGO (2014). Network Platform on Transitioning from the Informal to the Formal Economy in the interests of workers in the informal economy. Discussion Paper circulated at 103rd session of ILO's International Labour Conference in June 2014

Wilderman, J., Munakamwe, J., Tyiso, M. and Riabchuk, A. (2016). 'Worker Advice Offices in South Africa: Exploring Approaches to Organising and Empowering Vulnerable Workers', A report prepared for Chris Hani Institute on behalf of COSATU. Johannesburg: Chris Hani Institute.

Zvarivadza, T. (2014). 'Artisanal and small-scale mining as a challenge and possible contributor to sustainable development', Paper presented at the Mine Closure 9th International Conference on Mine Closure, 1-3 October 2014, Sandton Convention Centre, Johannesburg, South Africa.

Chapter Six

What Indigenous Agricultural Communities Have To Say? Transnational Corporate Social Responsibility and the Mining Environment in Tarkwa Nsuaem Municipality, Ghana

Artwell Nhemachena and Christopher Dick-Sagoe

Introduction: Mining and Relevant Legislation in Ghana

Although transnational mining corporations are considered by some scholars to constitute investments for Africa, the corporate mining activities often involve competition with local farmers over the use of fertile land meant for crop farming. Simplistically considering such transnational corporate mining activities as investments ignores the fact that their activities often destroy the livelihoods of the local people in most mining communities in Ghana, and the rest of Africa. Thus, the more corporate mining activities there are, the greater the risks for the local people who lose their autonomous local livelihood activities. In this way, there is a paradox in that corporate mining activities which destroy local economic autonomy and sovereignty are conventionally deemed to constitute investments for Africa. Further, while the law is ordinarily expected to balance interests and rights of citizens, Ghanaian mining laws and state institutions which regulate the activities of corporate mining companies, enforce environmental laws and protect the interest of the indigenous people have sometimes failed to protect the interests of the local indigenous people. This failure results in intensive environmental degradation with further negative implications on the livelihoods of the local people who depend heavily on the natural environment.

Apart from engaging in agriculture, indigenous Ghanaians have since the pre-colonial era, engaged in mining, smelting of minerals and commerce. Thus, Ofosu-Mensa et al (2011) note that in pre-colonial times gold mining was one of the mainstays of the economies of Asante, Dekyira, Akyem, Wassa and many other African states. The pre-colonial mining and smelting were sensitive both to the environment and to gender since women were involved, [as indeed whole families were involved] and the mining particularly deep shaft mining was done in the dry season. Such mining and mineral processing were done for thousands of years in pre-colonial Africa although it is often erroneously assumed that circumstances in pre-colonial Africa did not favour industrialisation (Matambalya, 2015: 9). The existence of mining industries in pre-colonial Africa is forcefully noted by Botchway (2015: 299) thus: "As far back as the eighth century AD, Arab chroniclers were giving detailed accounts of the gold industry in the sub-region. The industry was one of the main pillars on which the ancient empires that existed in the region were built, namely Ghana, Mali and Soghai".

Such pre-colonial African empires including the Asante, Luba and Lunda Kingdoms were destroyed by Western colonisers (Ofosu-Mensah, 2011: 54; Sanders, 2008; Larmer, 2016). Thus, Ofosu-Mensa et al (2011: 17-8) lament that with colonisation:

> ...small scale artisanal mining which was a respected tradition in Ghana for centuries became a persecuted profession after the British colonised the region in the early 19th century and banned the practice...There is also the argument that artisanal or *galamey* mining operations have exposed the tribal people...to the various risks including mercury poisoning, contamination of rivers and other water sources, deforestation, prostitution, sexually transmitted diseases like syphilis and HIV/AIDS, increased drug use and crime.

In the light of the challenges that are often raised in relation to mineral resource exploitation in Africa, there is the question as to whether mining is a blessing or a resource curse. While noting these arguments about "resource curse", this chapter focuses particularly on the notion of corporate social responsibility, which will be explained in more detail below, in relation to the challenges that are caused by transnational mining corporations onto local indigenous communities. Cognisant of the little integration of transnational mining corporations in local indigenous communities, the chapter argues that there is little that accrues to indigenous communities by way of corporate social responsibility.

This study draws scholarly attention to the operations of the foreign mining companies which have negatively affected the environment and the livelihood of the communities living within the mining catchment area, thereby making them poor. The study seeks to provide evidence to support the debate on environmental policy. It focuses on Tarkwa Nsuaem Municipality, which is a mining hub for foreign mining companies in West Africa.

Although it is the second largest producer of gold in Africa (Kesse, 1980), Ghana's policy of state control of gold mines in the 1960s led to low gold production (Hilson, 2002 and Agbesinyale, 2003). In this case the ownership and control of the mines were solely under the state. Five main gold mining companies were in operation with production of 276,659 ounces in 1983. In 1999, this production level has increased to 2.6 million ounces. The reason is as follows. The economic decline experienced in the 1970s forced the country to accept the World Bank and the International Monetary Fund's (IMF) policy of liberalising and privatising the economy. The result of this policy is the privatisation of ownership and control of gold mines in the country and the removal of import tariffs on heavy machines and equipment for mining. Foreign direct investments began to flow into the country, especially in the mining sector in the 1980s. It is estimated that from 1983 to 2011, $11 billion in the form of foreign direct investment has entered the country (Aidara, 2013). Estimated gold production levels and the number of gold mining companies grew. Aidara (ibid) further states that mining employs 28000 (1 per cent) of the labour force of Ghana, whiles agriculture employs 60 per cent.

Three pieces of legislation have been enacted, between 1986 and 2005, to regulate mining activities. These laws are the Minerals and Mining Law (PNDCL 153) in 1986, the Minerals and Mining Act (Act 475) in 1994, which amends the PNDCL 153 and finally the Minerals and Mining Act (law 703) in 2005. The major provisions in these laws favouring the foreign mining companies, including duty free clearing of imported mining equipment, including heavy mining

189

machinery at the ports of Ghana, payment of only 9 per cent as royalties to the local authorities (like the District Assemblies, Stools and Traditional Authorities) and tax to the state. Mining companies are also allowed to retain 25 per cent or more of their profits in offshore accounts.

The Minerals and Mining Law [favourable to transnational corporations], together with the liberalisation and the privatisation policy attracted foreign direct investments worth US$ 5 billion to Ghana from 1986 to 2002, with 90 per cent going into mining sector (Agbesinyale, 2003). The number of mining companies grew from 5 to 230 during the same period, increasing gold production levels to 2.6 million ounces in 1999 (Trades Union Congress of Ghana, 2007). As a result, 30 per cent of Ghana's land area, which comprises fertile agricultural land, has been allocated to mining companies, of different scale and sizes, for their gold operation (Vital Statistics, 1998). This includes 2 per cent of the, now deforested, forest reserves in Ghana. For example, mining companies in Tarkwa and Prestea have occupied 46 per cent (1083 square kilometres) of the total land area in these two towns, which initially belonged to indigenous farmers. This resulted in loss of agricultural land on the part of the farmers, whose livelihoods have consequently been compromised.

These mining companies have posed several challenges to the livelihoods (which is mainly crop farming) of the communities. Communities within the catchment areas of mines continue to suffer the negative consequences of the mining operations. Mining companies are now competing for land with cocoa farmers and the companies are destroying forest reserves (such as Ajenua Bepo Forest Reserve) at unprecedented rates. Farmer displacement rates in the gold mining towns have been on the increase. For example, within 5 years, Goldfields Ghana Ltd displaced 30,000 farmers. Twenty thousand (20,000) farmers have been displaced by Newmont Ahafo mines and more will be displaced in the near future. Rural communities living in mining towns are now left landless, with polluted water and poor infrastructure. Above all, there is poor compensation from mining companies, as companies pay $9 per cocoa tree which yields $20 per tree per year for a period of 30-50 years, not to factor the labour costs in preparing the land and the crops by the farmers.

It is important to state here that all the gold mines in Ghana are located in fertile agricultural lands where cash crops like cocoa and rubber are cultivated. A specific example is Hilson (2002) who observes environmental pollution from the use of mercury and disposal of an estimated 5 tons mining waste per year causing soil degradation. Soil damage is further worsened by heavy dredging machines. These activities have damaged farmlands and threatened the livelihoods of the farmers. Since the major livelihood of the local people is farming, the subsequent arguments will focus much on the effects of mining on farming, as livelihood for the local people of Tarkwa Nsuaem Municipality. This is in support of Hilson's (2016) assertion that mining and farming are fiercely and strongly related, with an increase in one likely to affect the other.

Problems related to mining and the environment in Ghana: the place of the law

Operations of mining companies, such as emissions, disposal of waste and land degradation threaten livelihoods and health of the local communities (Agyemang, 2010 and Obiri, Dodoo, Essumang, Okai-Sam & Adjorlolo, 2006). Institutions (such as the Environmental Protection Agency, Ghana Chamber of Mines and the Minerals Commission) and laws (such as Minerals and Mining laws, the PNDCL 153 (1986; 2006), Small Scale Mining Law PNDC 218 (1989)) have been very weak in playing their roles of protecting the environment and welfare of the communities living in mining towns (Minerals Commission, 2010; Ontoyin & Agyemang, 2014). In the light of these weak institutions, weak law enforcement on environmental protection and lack of community welfare, there is need to find out what has happened to the sustainable livelihoods securities of these community people subject to the environmental consequences of mining. There is also a question that borders on how these vulnerable communities are coping with such consequences.

The Economic Recovery Programme of Ghana led to the institution of the Mineral and Mining law (PNDCL 153) in 1986. In 1994, this law (PNDCL 153), was amended and replaced by Mineral and Mining Act 475 (Amendment). All these laws regulate mining operations in Ghana. Mining companies are required to pay royalties, corporate taxes at standard rates. PNDCL, used here refers to Provisional National Defense Council Law.

The first amendment to the Mineral and Mining Law favoured the foreign mining companies. This is because while corporate tax ordinarily stood at 45 per cent, a reduction by 10 per cent (thus 35 per cent) was made in favour of the foreign mining companies which also retained other benefits such as duty free imports on mining equipment, machinery and accessories.

To make it more attractive and favourable to foreign mining companies, the Mineral and Mining Act (2005, Law No. 703) was passed by the Parliament of Ghana on December 15, 2005. This new law only made an additional provision to secure the interest of the foreign mining companies which were in competition for gold mining concessions, as they did during the era of the scramble for Africa. The new law provided for the right by companies to demand for written statements from the minister in charge of mining in case their applications for mining concessions were rejected. Further provision is made on duration for an application to be granted.

Some of the major provisions in the Mineral and Mining Laws are:

- Mining companies are given investment allowance of 5 per cent for their first year of operation.
- Free duty imports on mining operations capital equipment, accessories, machinery and plants.
- Mining companies are to pay 45 per cent corporate tax. If the rate of returns exceeds agreed levels, the mining company will pay additional tax. This was later reduced to 35 per cent in 2005, after the passage of the Mineral and Mining Bill (Law No. 703).
- Payment of local property tax (only on immovable property).

- Favourable amortisation levels (75 per cent for the first year, 50 per cent afterwards)
- The government of Ghana receives 10 per cent equity from new mining companies and has the right to purchase additional 20 per cent.
- The law grants the government the power to take a 10 per cent free-carried interest in mining leases.
- Generous retention allowances on foreign profits.
- Payment of royalties to the local government bodies, such as the chief or the district assembly, between 3 to a maximum of 6 per cent of the total amount of mining revenue
- Mining leases should be more or equal to 30 years and renewable once for an additional 30 years.
- Mineral rights land allocation should be done using the cadastral system
- Authorisation for land occupancy, acquisition and use was vested in the Government, on the condition that the land has minerals which need to be mined.

One common feature in these laws is that none of them (among the three) championed the interest and the livelihoods of the communities living in the mining towns. The painful side of the story is that these amendments are only in the favour of the foreign mining companies leaving behind the interest of the country to the extent that the inflows to the country (taxes) received a 10 per cent reduction in 1994. This situation appears to be in accord with what Agbesinyale (2003) and Hilson (2016) describe as 'weak state machinery' securing a good deal under the agreement; or what others brand as selfish politicians, who seek their personal gains against the national interest, as in Brennan and Buchanan's (1980) Leviathan Models of government under the public choice theories.

Underscoring the challenges of corporate social responsibility by companies, some of which are paradoxically granted generous tax concessions, Adjei (2007) observes that mining companies, in neoliberal dispensation, are reluctant to provide alternative livelihoods which are capable of making-up the losses of livelihood security to the local people. This further makes local people vulnerable and it reduces their livelihood security, resulting in impoverishment. There is a disconnection between corporate social responsibilities efforts of these mining companies and sustainable livelihoods legacies for the communities. Thus, Franco & Ali, (2016:1) argue: "lack of regional connectivity in governance and conflict prevents [mining] companies from playing a stronger role in forging sustainable livelihoods".

A brief look at the history of modern mining in Ghana shows the roots of transnational mining corporations that supplanted indigenous miners.

Brief history of (neo-)colonial mining in Ghana

The colonisation of Ghana in the 19th century, by the British, was basically because of the large deposits of minerals such as gold. Two stages of gold rush can be identified in the history of Ghana known as the jungle boom. These boom periods were experienced due to the presence of foreign mining companies in Ghana: they mined gold in the areas endowed with the natural resource (gold) such as Obuasi and Tarkwa. Rivers such as Offin and Pra were also endowed with gold.

Historians such as Ofosu-Mensah (2011) argue that the colonial gold mining in Ghana was pioneered by Thomas Hughes. Thomas Hughes is a late Ghanaian (who hails from the Cape Coast), a trader and civil leader. Hughes was reported to have travelled several times to secure gold concessions in the late 1850s and 1860s at Wassa Amenfi, which is in the Western Region of Ghana. Hughes hired Cape Coast porters to carry imported crushing machines to his mining site (Wassa Amenfi).

J. A. Skertchley, an Englishman, is believed to have been part of the pioneers of colonial mining in Ghana. Skertchley was the first European to take gold concessions in the Tarkwa ridge in 1877. This system of small mining operations of local merchants evolved into a multinational company, targeting the gold rich African countries (Ayensu, 1998). The local people mined old reefs and panned gold in streams before the arrival of the Europeans, and subsequently, there was European engagement in gold mining through foreign transnational companies. While indigenous people appear to have been very sensitive to their environments, transnational corporation are mainly concerned about productivity, generating super-profits that are externalised without care about the endangered livelihoods of indigenous people. For this reason, we argue here that the concern in studies on mining in Africa must not be merely, [even mainly] about mechanisation and high productivity but rather the sustainability of local livelihoods. Being (neo-)colonial corporations, the transnational mining companies were obviously minded on exploiting Africa as fast as possible and before indigenous people regained full control and ownership of their resources. In this vein, the fact that in precolonial Africa the productivity was not as high as after colonisation is not necessarily a weakness: Africans knew the resources were theirs anyway and so they did not exploit them in the kind of haste that has tended to characterise (neo-)colonial transnational corporations trawling African resources. Thus, mechanisation and increased productivity, by transnational mining corporations, do not mean anything for Africans if these do not translate to improvements in their livelihoods in contexts where transnational corporations evade taxes and do not observe corporate social responsibility for instance.

Environmental impacts of mining: The place of corporate social responsibility

Mining activities have impacted negatively on the environment. Large scale mining activity involves the removal of the vegetative cover in ways that leave the land bare. This leads to deforestation and its resultant land degradation. Open pits that result from mining have constituted traps for livestock that are important for the livelihoods of indigenous people. Pits also constitute health hazards for indigenous people. Rain water collects in mining pits, especially the abandoned pits and this results in stagnant water supporting the breeding of mosquitoes and causing malaria. The use of mercury, noise from blasting and dust are all forms of environmental problems from mining (Labonne & Gilman, 1999; United Nations Economic and Social Council, 2003). Disposal of mining waste and the use of chemicals have all posed environmental challenges. Other environmental problems are water and air pollution resulting from discharge of chemicals into water bodies and into the air.

It is in the light of the above observations that we seek to apply the framework of corporate social responsibility (CSR) to analyse the concerns of indigenous Ghanaians about transnational mining corporations. The United Nations Economic Commission for Africa (2011) notes that CSR, which can be voluntary or legislated, enables contributions to wider development objectives. For the United Nations Commission for Africa (2011), the premise of CSR has been that the roles and impacts of these entities go beyond providing revenue, employment and maximising profits: they should be recognised as conscious and influential participants in activities with a broad range of consequences. Thus, it is noted that companies have social responsibility that goes beyond their profit maximisation: they have to contribute to overall sustainability. The United Nations Commission for Africa (2011) further notes that CSR constitutes actions whereby enterprises integrate societal concerns into their business policies and operations, including environmental, economic and social concerns.

The United Nations Commission for Africa (2011: 82) notes that:

> The global growth and institutionalisation of CSR have been strongly driven by the demands and pressures of the growing environmental consciousness of citizens and concerns about the extensive powers and rights that corporations have acquired with economic liberalization. These concerns have been expressed through pressures for ethical investment, social movements on issues such as the environment, fair trade, consumer rights, and humane labour conditions, the rights of indigenous people and greater corporate accountability and transparency.

Thus, notable is a proliferation of CSR frameworks from United Nations conferences, intergovernmental bodies such as United Nations and its affiliate bodies like International Labour Organisation, Organisation for Economic Cooperation and Development (OECD) and the World Bank; national legislations, groups of international private financial institutions, industrial associates and multi-stakeholder bodies have all applied pressures for CSR. In this vein, it is noted with respect to transnational mining corporations that:

> The evolution of CSR has led to the mining industry accepting that implementing community development programmes and behaving as responsible corporate citizens are good business. Mines, particularly when situated in remote areas, require a good relationship with their communities-they need to obtain and maintain a social licence to operate as well as satisfy their company's corporate goals and shareholder expectations. Mining companies now accept that for communities in which they operate to live without basic services such as water, health care, electricity and sanitation is unacceptable for good business (United Nations Commission for Africa, 2011: 84).

In spite of these rubrics on corporate social responsibility, it is important to note here that there are major weaknesses in the operationalization of the principle of corporate social responsibility. At national levels the challenge for African governments is that transnational corporations have significant [financial] power over developing countries [posing challenges in controlling the corporations] whose GDPs and GNPs are extremely low as compared to these footloose corporations. At an international level, the challenge is that these transnational corporations sponsor civil society organisations which then toe their line and therefore cannot conceivably assist in controlling the transnational corporations. Still at an international level, these transnational corporations also fund and sponsor some of the United Nations' programmes (Korten 2012; Global Research, 15 March 2016; Teitelbaum, 2007) and so the United Nations itself is ill placed to effectively control the transnational corporations from which it gets its funding. Even the recently established International Tribunal for the Rights of Nature (Kauffman, 2017) is fatally doomed as it cannot [effectively] control transnational corporations that fund and sponsor the same international institutions that are set up to control them.

In a historical (neo-)colonial context where African societies, cultures, polities, economies and legal orders have been trampled upon and the enslaved and colonised African themselves regarded as indistinct from animals (Fanon, 1963), it would make little sense to simply superimpose corporate social responsibility without first of all reclaiming African social institutions. In other words, to talk about corporate social responsibility in an African context where African societies have been trampled upon for centuries begs the question about whose society is being referred to. In fact increasingly, some scholars are arguing that there is nothing called society (Latour, 2005) and that the world has to recognise posthumanism and postanthropocentrism (Smith. 2011) that sadly further erode the property rights of the colonially dispossessed and exploited Africans, while at the same time regarding them as indistinct from animals and freaks of nature. Transnational mining corporations appear to simply continue the old colonial practices of regarding Africans as without human rights and as indistinct from animals that are without entitlements to their resources, who to be dispossessed, and whose livelihoods are to be wantonly trampled on.

A closer look at matters of livelihoods reveals the shortfalls of the principles of corporate social responsibly in Ghana.

Sustainable Livelihoods and Security

To meet basic necessities in life, households need adequate food, stock and cash (Chambers & Conway, 1992). Livelihoods can simply mean having access to the means of gaining a living. Bhattarai (2005) argues in line with Chambers and Conway, claiming low-income households face vulnerabilities in matters of sustainable livelihoods. Therefore conceptualising livelihood cannot be clear without proper understanding of [rural] impoverishment.

For Carney (1998), livelihood comprises assets (social and materials), capabilities and means of living activities. These assets, (in)tangible in nature are capital, to the individuals or the households, to enhance their well-being. So the assets are capital and the capital takes different forms as natural, human, physical, social and financial.

The World Commission on Environment and Development (1987: 2-5) defines livelihood and sustainability thus: "livelihood is the adequate stock of food and cash to meet basic needs. Livelihood security [refers to two things. These are: first] the access to resources or income earning activity and second, the ownership of resources or income earning activity, reserves and asserts to offset risk, ease shock and meet contingency. Sustainability refers to the maintenance of resource productivity for a long time.

The Department for International Development (DFID) (1999: 1) provides a more current definition and composition of livelihood. To them "...livelihood [includes] the capabilities and activities required for the means of living, [sustainable aspect of livelihood is measured from its ability to] cope ... and recover from stresses and shocks and maintain... its capabilities and assets both now and in the future".

Applying this concept to the mining town, Tarkwa Nsuaem Municipality, it can be said that the livelihood of the local people of Tarkwa Nsuaem Municipality is farming. And because the farming work is erratic, they support their livelihood with other off-season jobs such as driving. Their (local people) livelihood security, to those fertile lands is via ownership and access to the land resource and the food crops providing regular income to them. They are able to maintain their crops and the fertile land for a very long time. However, mining activities have taken their sustainable livelihood security away.

Relationship between mining activities and farm outputs (livelihood)

The local community living in the catchment areas of the mining companies are mainly food crop farmers and subsistence farmers. Therefore farming is their major source of livelihood. Thus a study of this nature which seeks to examine corporate social responsibility in relation to the environmental impacts of mining on the livelihoods of the people living in mining towns cannot avoid studies revealing the relationship between mining and farming. This section of the study reviews studies on mining activity and farming.

Marshall, Ashmore and Hinchcliffe (1997) explain how crop yields are negatively affected by pollution from mines. They further show how mining activities degrade water, soil and air (see also U.S. Environmental Protection Agency, 2012). These forms of degradation negatively affect output of agriculture in the communities within 20 kilometres to a mine. To further explain, 10 per cent reduction is recorded (in agricultural productivity) per one (1) standard deviation in gold production. A simple projection of mining activity from 1997 to 2005 in Ghana implies farming communities, within 20 kilometres of mines, have lost productivity close to 40 per cent, relative to areas further away, for instance 20 kilometres. This situation makes farming unattractive to the local community. This trend has also affected crop yields too. These reductions (in food production and farm productivity) directly affect consumption possibilities of households, increasing poverty in mining areas to 18 per cent (Aragon & Rud, 2015).

Using satellite imagery, Aragon and Rud (2015) observe higher concentrations of nitrogen dioxide (indicating evidence of air pollution) in mining areas and the concentration decreases with distance away from the mines. The regular environmental compliance exercise conducted by the Ghana Environmental Agency, which started in 2009, found that of the nine mines, seven did not comply with the environmental standards (details in http://www.epaghanaakoben.org). These seven mines mismanage and dispose hazardous and toxic waste which creates risk to the environment.

Large emissions of air pollutants, such as ozone (O_3), sulphur dioxide (SO_2) and nitrogen oxides (NO_x, namely NO and NO_2), travel long distances affecting plants and soils. Plants absorbed these emissions directly destroying their tissues: acid rain that is also formed ends up on the soil. Reaction of NO_x or SO_2 and water in the atmosphere forms acid rains with cumulative negative effects (Menz & Seip, 2004). Transportation leakages of mine pollutants, like heavy metal and cyanide, mixed with water form acidic effluent and carried by surface water (Salomons, 1995).

Further, Hilson (2016) describes smallholder agriculture as a less viable enterprise under structural adjustment because mining companies have competed with the farmers over the fertile land for agriculture. Farmers are now left with small holdings of land for farming purposes. Besides, costs of fertile land for farming activity have increased beyond the farmers' ability to pay. Insecurity over fertile farmlands has discouraged farmers to continue with farming activity. An observation made (Hilson & Garforth, 2012) proves undersized plots of smallholder farmers have seen challenges with regard to producing enough crops for the market. Evidently, (Sarris & Shams, 1991), 90 per cent of crops are grown under smallholding cultivation in Ghana. However, from 1970 to 1984, a huge reduction in land holdings for farming purposes was recorded, approximating about 70 per cent (2.4 ha). The authors (Sarris & Shams, 1991) estimate a change from 2,830,000 to 1,879,000 ha in terms of smallholding land.

Description and location of Tarkwa Nsuaem Municipality

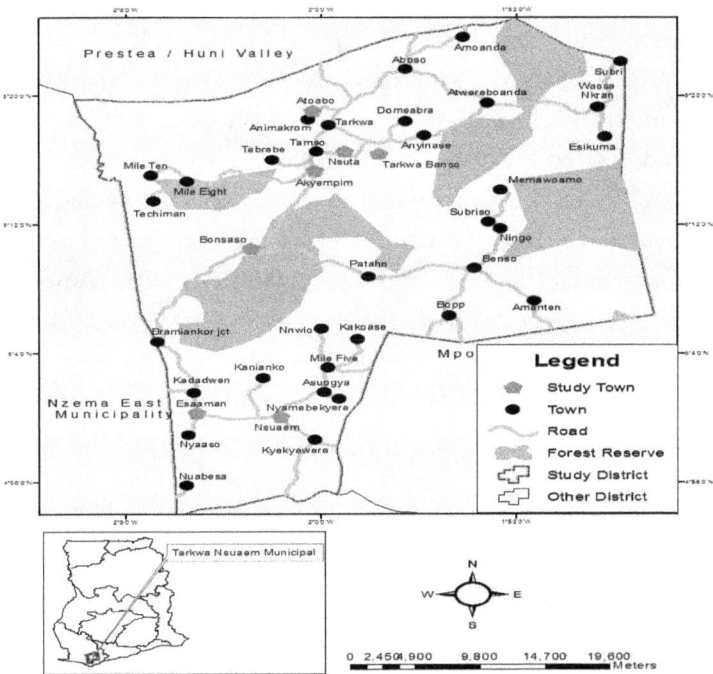

Figure 1: Map of Tarkwa Nsuaem Municipality

Source: Department of Geography and Regional Planning, University of Cape Coast, 2017

Located in the Western Region of Ghana on a land area of 2354 square kilometres, Tarkwa Nsuaem Municipality (Figure 1), is exactly within longitudes 10 45' W and 20 10'W and latitude 400'N and 500 40'N. The boundaries of the municipality are Wassa Amenfi East District, Ahanta West District, Nzema East Municipal assembly and Mpohor Wassa East to the north, south, west and east respectively. The population of the municipality stands at 232,699 (Ghana Statistical Service, 2013). The municipality is a hub to several corporate gold mining and support service companies such as Aboso Goldfields Limited, Ghana Australian Goldfields and Bogoso Gold Limited. The rest are Prestea Sankofa Gold Limited, New Century Mines and Goldfields Ghana Limited. Not forgetting the presence of registered and unregistered artisanal and small scale mining companies, popularly known as *"galamsey"*.

Methodology

The study employed the analytical survey design which shares similar tenets with the quantitative methodology (Gray, 2014 and Bryman, 2012). Sample size used for the study is 100. The justification for the sample size was based on other similar studies like Addai & Baiden's (2014) one which was done in the municipality. The reason for relying on similar studies is lack of available and credible sources of database with the list of the population (sampling frame). However, a sample of 100 respondents from the community was considered large enough to represent the voices of the community members. Data was collected using structured interview guides. Respondents were reached on field using purposive sampling method. Excel and SPSS version 22 became relevant for the analysis of the data.

Methods of data analysis

Likert scale (relative importance index), problem tree analysis and chi-square test were employed for the study.

Calculating the relative Importance Index (RII)

$$RII = \frac{\Sigma W}{A \, x \, N}, \, (0 \leq RII \leq 1)$$

Where:

W – Is the weight respondents attached to a question (options range from 1 to 5)

Sum of weights = W1+W2+W3+ W4+W5

The meanings attached to the weights (1, 2, 3, 4, and 5) have been provided on the data collection instrument

A – The highest weight (in this case is 5) and;

N – Is the sample size

Relative importance index results range from 1 to 0. Where 1 is very important factor and 0 is less important factor.

Chi-square on the other hand measures the differences on livelihoods of the local people before and after the influence of mining activity in the Municipality. Likert scale was used to rank the severity of the effect from insignificant to significant effects of mining on livelihoods.

Effects of corporate mining activities on livelihoods of the people of Tarkwa Nsuaem Municipality

The local people depended on the forest and the fertile lands of the forest for their livelihood. For example, the fertile soil for farming, the forest for food, firewood and medicine. The rivers and the creeks were sources of drinking water for them, their livestock and for irrigation. The rivers also doubled as sources of fish, for food. Now the mining activities have degraded all these resources (land, water and the forest).

Women complained that they were scared of trenches on slopes of hills and deep depressions that resulted from mining activities. These scenes were considered to constitute danger as one had to be careful when gathering firewood around the area for cooking purposes. It posed high risk of falling into the trenches.

Because of low yields, insecurity of agricultural lands and expensive agricultural lands as a result of the mining activities, farming activity has become unattractive, giving rise to artisanal mining (*galamsey*) as a livelihood diversification strategy. This nonformal mining has brought more harm than good. Food insecurity becomes an issue in Tarkwa Nsuaem Municipality where farming should be the main livelihood for local people.

Figure 2 below employs the problem tree analysis to explain the interaction between mining activity and livelihoods of the local people in the municipality. From the figure, mining activity has disposed toxic waste, removed top soil and vegetative cover. These activities have degraded water, soil and air, thus resulting in low crop yields. Mining activity has also competed over fertile agricultural land with local farmers causing high land prices and creating insecurity for fertile land holdings for existing farmers. This has made prices of land to be expensive. Farmers who have lost their livelihoods to mining cannot afford the cost of buying existing new fertile land. Inability to afford existing fertile land, together with lack of security over the new land to mining and environmental pollution reducing crop yields have made the farmers to lose interest in farming activity. All these have resulted in loss of sustainable livelihood security in the municipality. The effects of the loss are poverty and unemployment for those who have decided not to do anything (in terms of coping strategy), increased social vices like robbery, prostitution and so on. Because of impoverishment, bread winners of the families are not able to afford the needs of their families. This has led to loss of control over their families. The situation has also led to the increased adoption of small scale mining.

Since mining has affected particularly farming activity, Table 1 below went further to assess the particular aspects of the mining activity which have been affected by the mining activity. To test the hypothesis that mining has negatively influenced local livelihoods, the study performed a chi-square test. The null and the alternative hypothesis were as follows. Null hypothesis: local livelihoods are the same before and after mining activities were introduced in the Municipality. The alternative hypothesis is: local livelihoods have been negatively affected by mining activities. The chi-square test (reported in Table 1) indicates a significant negative effect of mining activity on the livelihoods of the local people.

Figure 2: Problem tree analysis demonstrating the link between mining and livelihoods

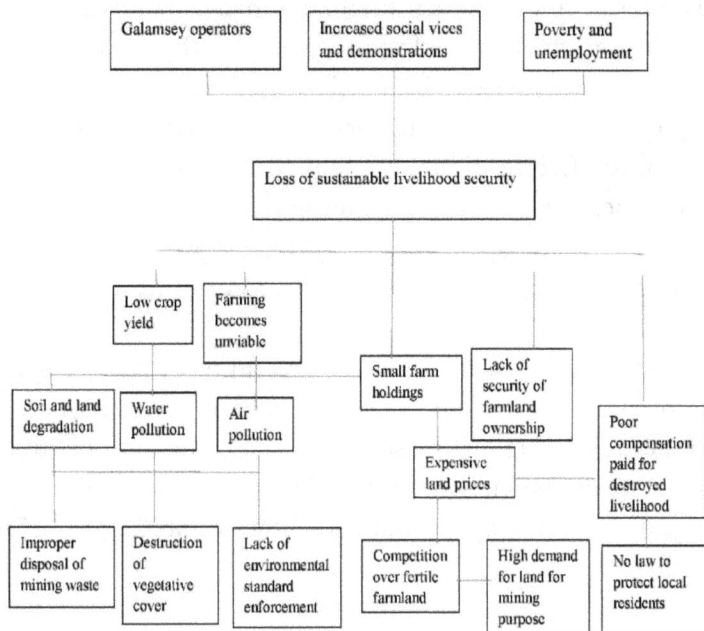

Source: Field survey, 2016

Table 1: Effects of mining activities on the livelihoods of the people

Statement	Strongly disagree	Disagree	Neutral	Agree	Strongly agree	RII	Chi-square
Mining has affected crop farming	0	0	15	20	65	0.90	0.00*
Mining has affected fishing	0	0	6	40	54	0.88	0.00*
Mining has affected hunting	0	0	22	28	50	0.86	0.00*
Mining has affected herbal medicine	0	0	20	40	40	0.84	0.00*
Mining has affected trading business	0	10	25	38	27	0.76	0.00*
Mining has affected firewood gathering	0	8	40	33	19	0.73	0.00*

Source: Computed from Field Data, 2017

*Chi-square value very significant at 0.05 and 0.01 alpha

Further analysis was computed to find which livelihood activity has been severely affected by the mining activity in the municipality. The result has also been presented in the same Table 1 using the result from the Relative Importance Index (RII). The RII scores, the important factors are "1" or close to "1" and "0" or close to "0" indicate least important factors. It was realised that crop farming is the most affected livelihood, followed by fishing, then hunting and medicine. The rest are trading businesses and firewood gathering.

Coping strategies adopted by the community

Naturally, due to the seasonal nature of the farming activity, farmers have learnt strategies of livelihood diversification as coping strategies during off-season. Strategies adopted by the affected households and individuals have been presented in Table 2 below.

Table 2: Coping and livelihood strategies of affected farmers

Statement	Strongly disagree	Disagree	Neutral	Agree	Strongly agree	IRR
Supports/ encouragement words from acquaintances	0	6	22	30	42	0.82
Depending on alternative livelihood programmes of mining companies	10	10	20	20	40	0.74
Adopting to small scale mining	0	23	17	28	32	0.74
Farming on another land	13	20	7	16	44	0.72
Part-time taxi driving	6	28	31	20	15	0.62
Shifting to animal rearing	20	32	8	13	27	0.59
Petty trading	34	17	19	2	28	0.55
Migrating to another city to work	24	33	2	32	9	0.54

Source: Field Data, 2017

Affected individuals and households have resorted to the support from other family members in terms of money and words of encouragement. This is followed by dependence on the alternative livelihood strategies from the corporate mining companies. Others have planned to or begun with artisanal small scale mining activity. The rest of the coping and livelihood strategies of the affected households have been presented in Table 2.

Recommendations

In the light of the fact that transnational corporations are unwilling to invest in meaningful corporate social responsibility, it is necessary to reconsider the hype about attracting foreign investors to Africa. It is clear that the major objective of these corporations is to make super-profits [for repatriation] even as the communities are suffering from the presence of the transnational corporations' mining activities.

It is necessary for the government to render support to indigenous artisanal miners so as to grow them into indigenous mining firms that would most likely be more sensitive and more adapted to the local environments.

Conclusion

Mining is a business and for every business profit making is the key. Mining companies will forever not be willing to invest their profit on the community as corporate social responsibility. It rather takes the effort of strong institutions and law enforcement to make corporate social responsibility effective. This study has examined mining and livelihoods of the local people in Tarkwa Nsuaem in relation to corporate social responsibility. Based on the findings, the study concludes on the following issues.

The study has made it clear that the people have lost capital after the introduction of mining activities in the area. Rural livelihoods are strongly tied to available natural resources. So any activity which takes away access to these resources impoverishes indigenous people. There are also indications that because of low levels of formal education and loss of skills, these community people are not able to take advantage of the employment opportunities created by the transnational mining corporations. Rather people from other parts of the country and foreigners, who are well qualified, get the opportunities. In line with Carney (1998), it is noted here that the local people have lost natural assets, which would otherwise provide livelihoods, as a result of mining activities.

Denial of opportunities and choices results in impoverishment (Labonne & Gilman, 1999). Impoverishment also involves living on vulnerable and/or marginal environments. It can be seen clearly from this study that mining has impoverished the local people (see also Labonne and Gilman, 1999). Denial of ownership and access to sufficient productive and quality resources (forest, good soils, land and water) has impoverished the local people.

Important for improving livelihoods in this municipality is to maintain and improve these resources (land, water, soil, forest) which benefit the impoverished. To further make these livelihoods sustainable implies individual and communities economic needs are integrated into the improvement and maintenance of the environment. Corporate social responsibility has not helped much to better the livelihoods of indigenous Ghanaians whose communities are affected by activities of mining transnational corporations.

References

Addai, K. N. & Baiden, W. B. (2014). Effect of small scale mining on the environment of Tarkwa-Nsuaem Municipality of Ghana, *Journal of Environment and Earth Science,* Vol.4, No.9.

Adegboye, M. A. (2012). Effect of mining on farming in Jos South Local Government Area of Plateau State. *Journal of Soil Science and Environmental Management* Vol. 3(4), pp. 77-83

Adjei, E. (2007). Impact of mining on livelihoods of rural households. A case study of farmers in the Wassa Mining Region, Ghana. An MPhil Thesis submitted to the Department of Geography, Norwegian University of Science and Technology

Agbesinyale, P. K. (2003). Ghana's gold rush and regional development. The case of Wassa West District. *SPRING Research Centre Series*, University of Dortmund

Agyeman, I. (2010). Population dynamics and health hazards of small scale mining activities in the Bolgatanga and Talensi-Nabdam Districts of the Upper East Regions of Ghana. *Indian J, Sci. and Technol, 3 (10)*

Aidara, I. (2013). Mining and its impacts on land and agriculture in Ghana– OSIWA Economic Governance Program Manage. *UNCCD-COP 11*, Windhoek, Namibia

Akabzaa, T.M., & Darimani, A. (2001). Impact of mining sector investment in Ghana: A study of the Tarkwa Mining Region. Draft Report Prepared for SAPRI unpublished.

Akabzaa, T.M., Banoeng-Yakubo, B. K. Seyire, J. S. (2007). Impact of mining activities on water resources in the vicinity of the Obuasi mine. *West Afr. J. Appl. Ecol.* 11, 23–34

Aragon, F. M. & Rud, J. P. (2015). Polluting industries and agricultural productivity: evidence from ining in Ghana. *The Economic Journal, Volume 126, Issue 597, pages 1980–2011.*

Aryeetey, E, Bafour, O. & Twerefou, D. K. (2007). Impact of mining sector reforms on output, employment and incomes in Ghana, 1980-2002. Technical Publication 75, *Institute of Statistical, Social and Economic Research* (ISSER)

Ayensu, E. S. (1998). Ashanti Gold: The African legacy of the world's most precious metal. London

Banchirigah, S. M. & Hilson, G. (2010). De-Agrarianization, re-Agrarianization and local economic development: Re-orientating livelihoods in African artisanal mining communities. *Policy Sciences* 43(2): 157–180

Bhattarai, K.P. (2005). Livelihood strategies of squatter households in an urban environment: A case study of Kathmandu Metropolitan City, Nepal. University of Bergen, Bergen Norway

Botchway, F N N., (2015) Pre-colonial methods of gold mining and environmental protection in Ghana, in *Journal of Energy and Natural Resources Law* vol 13 (4): 299-311

Brennan, G. & Buchanan, J. M. (1980). *The power to tax: Analytic foundations of a fiscal constitution.* Cambridge University Press

Bryman, A. (2012). *Social research methods* (4rd Ed.). Oxford: Oxford University Press

Carney, D. (1998). Implementing the sustainable rural livelihood approach, In Carney, D (ed), *Sustainable rural livelihoods: What contributions can we make?* Department for International Development (DFID), London pp 3-23, 1998.

Chambers, R. & Conway, G. R. (1991). Sustainable rural livelihoods: Practical concepts for the 21st century. *IDS Discussion Paper 296*, Institute for Development Studies, Brighton.

Department for International Development (1999). Sustainable livelihoods guidance Sheets. DFID, UK.

Fanon, F. (1963). The Wretched of the Earth. New York: The Grove Press

Franco, I, B. & Ali, S. (2016). Decentralization, corporate community development and resource governance: A comparative analysis of two mining regions in Colombia. *The Extractive Industries and Society*, pp 1-9. http://dx.doi.org/10.1016/j.exis.2016.12.00

Gray, D. E. (2014). *Doing research in the real world* (3rd Ed.). London: Sage Publication

Hilson, G. & Garforth, C. J. (2012). Agricultural poverty and the expansion of artisanal mining: Case studies from West Africa. Population Research and Policy Review 31(3): 435–464.

Hilson, G. & Garforth, C. J. (2013). Everyone now is concentrating on the mining: Drivers and implications of changing agrarian patterns in the eastern region of Ghana. *The Journal of Development Studies* 49 (3): 348–362.

Hilson, G. & van Bockstael, S. (2012). Poverty and livelihood diversification in rural Liberia: Exploring the linkages between artisanal diamond mining and smallholder rice production. *The Journal of Development Studies* 48 (3) 416–431.

Hilson, G. (2008). Fair trade gold: Antecedents, prospects and challenges. *Geoforum* 39(1): 386–400.

Hilson, G. (2011). A Conflict of interest? A critical examination of artisanal/large-scale miner relations in Sub-Saharan Africa, *In New Directions in Resource Investment and African Development* (ed. F. Botchway), Edward Elgar, London

Hilson, G. (2014). Constructing ethical mineral production schemes: The case of Nyala Ruby. *Development and Change* 45(1): 53–78.

Hilson, G. (2016). *Artisanal and small-scale mining and agriculture exploring their links in rural sub-Saharan Africa.* London: IIED issue paper.

Hilson, G. Van Bockstael, S. (2011). Diamond mining, rice farming and a 'Maggi Cube': A viable poverty alleviation strategy in rural Liberia? *Journal of International Development* 23(8): 1042–1053.

Hilson, G., & Potter, C. (2005). Structural adjustment and subsistence industry: artisanal gold mining in Ghana. Development and Change 36(1): 103–131.

Hilson, G., Amankwah, R., & Ofori, G. (2013). Going for gold: Transitional livelihoods in Northern Ghana. *The Journal of Modern African Studies* 51(1): 109–137.

Hilson, G., Hilson, A. & Adu-Darko, E. (2014). Chinese participation in Ghana's informal Gold Mining economy: Drivers, implications and clarifications. *Journal of Rural Studies* 34: 292–302

Kesse, G. O. (1980). *Mineral and rock resources of Ghana.* Rotterdam: A.A. Balkema

Labonne, B. & Gilman, J. (1999). Towards building sustainable livelihoods in the artisanal mining communities. Tripartite Meeting on Social and Labour Issues in Small-scale mines, *ILO, Geneva,* 17-21 May 1999

Larmer, M., (2016). *At the crossroad: mining and political change on the on the Katangese-Zambian Copperbelt*

Latour, B. (2005) Reassembling the Social: An Introduction to Actor Network Theory. Oxford: Oxford University Press

Marshall, F., Ashmore, M. & Hinchcliffe, F. (1997). A hidden threat to food production: Air pollution and agriculture in the Developing World. Gatekeeper Series SA73, *International Institute for Environment and Development* (IIED)

Matambalya, F. A. S. T. *et al.*, (2015). Leveraging African-European Union cooperation for Africa's industrialisation: An introduction, in Matamalya F A S T, ed, *African industrial development and European Union Cooperation: Prospects for a reengineered partnership.* London and New York: Routledge

Mensah, S. O & Okyere, S. A. (2014). Mining, environment and community conflicts: A study of company-community conflicts

211

over gold mining in the Obuasi Municipality of Ghana. *Journal of Sustainable Development Studies,* Volume 5, Number 1: 64-99

Menz, F. C. & Seip, H. M. (2004). Acid rain in Europe and the United States: An update. *Environmental Science & Policy,* 7 (4), 253–265

Minerals Commission, (2010). An Overview of Ghana's artisanal and small scale mining (ASM) sector, Accra, Ghana.

Mining Journal, (2010). Ghana, a supplementary to the mining journal. Special publication Ghana. Aspermont UK, (March)

Obiri, S., Dodoo, D.K., Essumang, D. K., Okai-Sam, F., Adjorlolo, G. (2006). Cancer and non-cancer human risk from eating cassava grown in some mining communities in Ghana. *Environ. Monit. Assess, 3 (2): 31-51*

Ofosu-Mensa, E. A., (2011) Gold mining and the socio-economic development of Obuasi in Adanse, in *African Journal of History and Culture* vol 3 (4): 54-64

Ofosu-Mensah, E. A. (2011). Gold mining and the socio-economic development of Obuasi in Adanse. *African Journal of History and Culture* Vol. 3(4), pp. 54-64

Ofosu-Mensah, E. A. et al., (2011) Historical overview of traditional and modern gold mining in Ghana, *International Research Journal of Library, Information and Archival Studies* vol (1): 6-22

Ontoyin, J. & Agyemang, I. (2014). Environmental and rural livelihoods implications of small scale gold mining in Talensi-Nabdam District in the Northern Ghana. *Journal of Geography and Regional Planning, 7(8) 150-159*

Salomons, W. (1995). Environmental impact of metals derived from mining activities: Processes, predictions, prevention. *Journal of Geochemical Exploration,* 52 (1), 5–23

Sanders, K., (2008) Sustainable trade in pre-colonial Asante, Senior honors thesis, paper 188 Eastern Michigan University

Sarris, A., & Shams, H. (1991). *Ghana under structural adjustment: The impact on agriculture and the rural poor.* New York University Press, New York.

Sen, A. (1981). Poverty and fairness: An essay on entitlement and families. Oxford: Clarendon press

Sen, A. (1984). Resources, values and development. Oxford: Basil Blackwell

Sen, A. (1987). The standard of living, the Tanner lectures, Clare Hall, Cambridge 1985. Cambridge: University Press Cambridge

Smith, M. (2011). Against Ecological Sovereignty: Ethics, Biopolitics and Saving the Natural World. Minneapolis: University of Minnesota Press

Trades Union Congress of Ghana. (2007). Assessment of the 2007 budget statement and economic policy of the Government of Ghana. *The Ghanaian Worker*, 32, 10-11.

U.S. Environmental Protection Agency. (2012) Acid rain. Accessed from the Website: http://www.epa.gov/acidrain/effects/forests.html, on January 14 2017

United Nations Economic and Social Council (2003). Economic Commission for Africa, Third meeting of the committee on sustainable development, 7-10 October 2003, Addis Ababa, Ethiopia, reports on selected themes in natural resources development in Africa: artisanal and small-scale mining and technology challenges in Africa

Vital Statistics. (1998). Mining in Africa. *Drillbits and Tailings*, 21, 8.

Wassa Association of Communities Affected by Mining, (2013). Mining is destroying livelihoods in Ghana [online] available at: www.wacamgh.org [Accessed 11 March 2013]

Whiteman, G. & Mamen, K. (2002). Examining justice and conflict between mining companies and indigenous peoples: Cerro Colorado and the Ngabe-Bugle in Panama, *Journal of Business and Management,* 8(3), pp. 293–329

World Commission on Environment and Development (1987). Food 2000, Global policies for sustainable agriculture, A report on the advisory panel on Food Security, Agriculture, Forestry and Environment to the World Commission on Environment and Development. London: Zed Book Limited

Chapter Seven

Re-thinking Mining in Embattled Africa: A Calculative Sociological Logic

Oliver Mtapuri

Introduction

The African continent is endowed with a vibrant and massive natural resource base, mainly in the form of minerals. These include gold, diamonds, platinum, iron ore, copper, oil, natural gas, coal, and asbestos, to name but a few. Because of the vastness of these minerals, the extractive sector is one of the most rewarding and exploitative industries through which equally massive and catalytic social and economic development should be derived but which has also caused untold vulnerability and exploitation of many communities without the resilience that it promises. The mining industry in Africa has the potential to bring about revolutionary and significant economic growth, which is pro-community if the moral logics and technologies of distribution and re-distribution were just and equally pro-community, a community of people with a common destiny and shared aspirations. However, many opportunities have been missed due to rampant, protracted, well-organized transnational theft of the continent's mineral wealth. A number of African countries have sought to build their economies on the back of mineral extraction. Examples include South Africa, Botswana, Nigeria, Ghana, Zambia, Zimbabwe and the oil rich North African Arab states. South Africa arguably has one of Africa's biggest extractive industries and its massive gold, diamond and platinum outputs make the nation a mining giant. Ghana also has a vibrant mining sector and ranks second to South Africa in gold production on the continent (Akabzaa & Darimani, 2001: 4). Besides gold, Mate (2002) identified minerals such as bauxite, diamond and manganese as being available in large quantities in Ghana and these have also played a pivotal role in generating foreign currency for the country's economy.

In East Africa, Tanzania has an abundant natural resource base, mainly anchored on high value minerals such as gold and diamonds as well as gypsum, cobalt, natural gas, phosphate, iron ore, coal, nickel and tanzanite (Kitula, 2004). In Southern Africa, Botswana has substantially improved its economic performance due to the extraction of diamonds. In Zambia, copper extraction has been the mainstay of the economy for many decades. Zimbabwe reaped decent gains from mining, which saw much economic and infrastructural development, especially during the early years of independence, until the economic meltdown of the early 2000s.

In its simplest terms, mining is the extraction of minerals from the earth's crust. For Encarta (2005) it is the selective recovery of different minerals and materials, besides the recently formed organic materials from the earth's crust. Mining is an economic activity upon which many economies in both the developing and developed worlds heavily depend. In Africa, it is credited for making a tangible contribution and playing a pivotal role in socioeconomic development, especially in South Africa, Ghana, Botswana, Nigeria, Zambia, Libya and Zimbabwe, among others. Returns on the extraction and export of minerals such as gold, diamonds, coal, copper, oil, platinum, bauxite, and manganese and iron ore have boosted economic development in many of these nations. South Africa, Democratic Republic of Congo and Ghana are ranked among the major producers of valuable minerals in Africa while the top diamond producers include South Africa, Botswana, Ghana, and Sierra Leone with South Africa alongside Zimbabwe ranked among the top platinum producers. Libya, Nigeria and most of North Africa are oil rich and this strong mineral base is partly credited for spurring economic development and growth in these nations. The following section briefly summarises how mining has made variegated contributions to socioeconomic development in Africa.

Mining has driven Africa's quest to achieve economic growth since mineral extraction is regarded as one of the major drivers of a nation's development. Besides economic growth, mining is also expected to play an important role in efforts to alleviate poverty.

Poverty is a widespread problem whose effects are felt in every corner of the continent. It is as a result of these imperatives that mineral extraction is practised extensively at all levels, attracting a variety of actors that include individual or small groups of informal/artisanal miners, small scale miners, and governments as well as international mining monopolies that are mainly involved in large scale extraction. Among these groups are enclaves of winners and losers. Mining operations are a common sight in most African states, as miners scramble for every available natural resource, from river sand, to quarry stone and precious stones such as diamonds and gold in order to merely survive, or make a fortune through looting, for those who loot. It is therefore critical that mining systems, processes, mechanisms and governance of mining must ensure citizens protection. Citizen protection means that their mining assets are safe and that the risk of foreign expropriation is minimised as a calculative sociological logic. Political turmoil and instability also represent risk. Within the context of the calculative sociological logic is the concept of mining sovereignty. The logics of mining sovereignty dictate that the benefits of mining should accrue to the rightful owners of the mineral resources – the citizenry. Mining sovereignty, therefore, bestows mining's first/supreme rights to citizens to determine how they mine, what they mine and when they mine, where they mine, why they mine, who mines and who does not mine and how much they mine within the culturally accepted norms of that society; the right to beneficiate or not to beneficiate, how to sell and to whom to sell and trade while engaging in environmentally friendly and sustainable mining practices with the capability and capacity to determine the terms of trade for community self-reliance and community self-aggrandisement. This is founded on the basis that precarious mining, as practised by subalterns and precariats, cannot compete with organised transnational corporations who exploit human and material resources by denuding and stripping them and leaving little room for renewal through the use of high technology machinery and equipment and little or no hope to plough back.

Because of the importance of mining to communities, a counter narrative is required on the kind of freedom and liberation that enables current and future generations to benefit from those resources with impunity for themselves and their posterity in order to ignite a new form of accumulation which I call emancipatory accumulation by re-possession. Emancipatory accumulation by re-possession is characterised by the accumulation of assets, mineral wealth, biodiversity, and flora and fauna for the benefit of indigenous communities. Repossession means taking back what belongs to the sons and daughters of the soil by all means possible led by an indigenous intelligentsia with community interests at heart in an organic process of indigenisation. It was during the colonial times when their possessions were forcefully confiscated and seized with no compensation. The land, the flora and fauna and the creatures that crept on them, the sheep, the goats, cows, the ducks, their wildlife and all livestock and harvests were all appropriated by colonists with unprecedented brute force and ruthlessness. When the indigenous communities tried to reclaim what belonged to them, they were labelled thieves for their harvests, livestock and land; and poachers for their wildlife - in their own lands. The changed landscape was reinforced by the proclamation of laws and regulations that sanctified property rights to the extent that indigenous communities were stripped of their rights to their property and all that belonged to them to induce total alienation. Those rights were transferred to the colonists and their children. Therefore, repossession without compensation and no regrets becomes imperative in the interest of social and emancipatory justice. The next section provides the various benefits derived from mineral extraction which must accrue to indigenous communities, with examples from across Africa.

The "Celebrated" Side of Mining and the winners

One of the foremost and most obvious contributions of mining to African economies is employment creation. Where mining operations are established there is bound to be job creation, not only for those directly involved in extraction but those in downstream and upstream firms which either feed the mining industry with inputs or absorb some of its outputs in their operations. Gualnam (2008: 2) notes that mining brings about the 'promises of wealth and jobs'.

Formal employment is ranked among the most sustainable livelihoods in many economies because of the several benefits it offers as well as the security normally associated with formal jobs barring the exploitation and slave conditions that some miners are subjected to. Poverty levels are generally lower in households whose members are gainfully employed. Thus, jobs created by the extraction industry are good news to many, especially when returns and wages from this activity are used to address colonially generated poverties and inequalities.

Like the manufacturing sector, the mining industry has a diverse workforce, from unskilled, to semi-skilled, skilled and highly skilled jobs that are usually life sustaining. The Associated Mineworkers of Zimbabwe (AMZ) quoted in Saunders (2008) noted that, at its peak in 1995, the mining sector employed at least 83,000 workers. However, as a result of the national economic slowdown, this fell to less than 50,000 in 1999. Hawkins (2009) observes that besides formal jobs, many other people survive through informal mining jobs and activities. Thus, in an economy where a significant number of people rely on employment for livelihoods, mining is beneficial for employment creation. Jul-Larsen (2006) contends that gold mining firms have played an instrumental role in employment creation in Mali, while Kitula (2004) noted that a significant number of people worked in mining and mining-related employment in Tanzania. Jul-Larsen (2006) noted that by the end of the 20th century, an increasing number of people were engaged in informal mineral extraction in what is known as artisanal mining activities; this is common in Mali, Benin (Grätz, 2002), Burkina Faso (Werthmann, 2003), Ghana, Niger, Guinea (Keita, 2001) and Zimbabwe.

Other than employment creation, mining is also instrumental in infrastructural development. Some companies run by people with a conscience invest in improving the living conditions and welfare of their staff. This benefits local communities and the nation at large. Infrastructural development includes the construction of roads, schools, health centres, dams and bridges, among others. The Centre for Research and Development (2014: 43) in Zimbabwe noted that companies in Bikita have electrified schools in the areas surrounding their mines. Others have constructed roads and bridges in the areas in which they operate while some build houses for their employees. Zimplats, a company operating in the Ngezi area in Chegutu District, has been applauded for constructing a state-of-the-art road linking Selous with some of the remote parts of Mhondoro District and building more than 1, 000 housing units (*The Sunday Mail,* 5 April 2011), while SMM Holdings and Mimosa Mines in Zvishavane also constructed thousands of houses for their employees. Workers will own their homes after serving the company for a set number of years (Sustainability Reports, 2011).

Mining companies have also built clinics and hospitals. While these primarily cater for staff, some extend their services to the wider community. Hwange Colliery Company owns a state-of-the-art hospital, the largest in the Matebeleland region outside Bulawayo that is the major referral health centre in Matebeleland North Province (Hwange Colliery Company Limited, n.d). Mining companies also promote education across the country. Mbada Diamonds, a company extracting diamonds in Zimbabwe's Manicaland Province constructed a school in Zvimba District, Mashonaland West Province, although this was criticised by some that argued that the school should have been built in the area where the company operates. Falcon Gold runs a high school in Matebeleland South Province and other mines such as Renco Mine (Masvingo Province), Connemara Mine, Rio Tinto, Redcliff (Midlands Province), Arcturus Mine (Mashonaland Central) and Bikita Minerals (Masvingo) operate schools. Mining company ZIMASCO owns a number of schools in Mutorashanga.

Mining companies also promote social activities such as sports, which are an important aspect of youth development. Between 2010 and 2014, Mbada Diamonds sponsored Zimbabwe's richest cup in the Premier Soccer League, the Mbada Diamonds Cup (Mbada diamonds, n.d), and soccer clubs such as How Mine FC, Shabani Mine FC, FC Platinum, Ngezi Platinum and Hwange FC among others are sponsored by such companies. Some of these clubs have constructed stadiums which are also used for socioeconomic activities. Thus, in addition to youth talent identification and development, jobs have been created outside the mining sector.

In Zimbabwe, mining has overtaken agriculture as the country's largest foreign currency earner (*The Herald,* 26 September 2013). The mining industry contributes up to 16.9 per cent of Zimbabwe's GDP and accounts for at least 50 per cent of foreign currency earnings, making it the largest contributor to the national economy. Coal mining at Hwange boosted energy generation in the country while other minerals such as gold, asbestos, lithium, platinum and diamonds record high exports which generate foreign currency and strengthen the national economy. While minerals such as coal, nickel chrome, diamonds and platinum are important, gold is the mainstay of the mining sector with a contribution of about 40 per cent to the total mineral output (Dreschler, 2001).

In 1999, mining contributed about 6,5 per cent of South Africa's GDP and 33,5 per cent of total export revenues and attracted significant foreign direct investment (FDI) after the advent of democracy in 1994 (Gaven et al., 2001). This boosted economic growth and job creation. Today, the South African economy is acknowledged as a giant, which can be partly credited to its rich mining sector. FDI also promotes international trade, which is a key aspect of development. Zimbabwe has also attracted FDI in mining, including Anjin, a diamond mining company. Relations between Zimbabwe and China have also improved thanks to the mining industry (*The Herald,* 14 March 2014). In West Africa, Ghana's mineral wealth has been a major foreign exchange earner (Mate, 2002: 3). Akabzaa and Darimani (2001: 4) noted that in 1999 the mining sector attracted at least US$3 billion in FDI which accounted for 30 per cent of the economy's foreign exchange.

Jul-Larsen et al. (2006) noted that the growth of Mali's mining industry attracted investment from foreign mining companies. They cited three key foreign players, South Africa's Anglogold and Randgold Resources and Canadian company Iamgold that hold significant shares in at least one of Mali's four major gold mining firms. They added that gold mining made a contribution of between 40 and 67 per cent of Mali's exports between 1998 and 2003 which, according to EIU (2004) was an average US$383 million per year. Mining's contribution to the country's GDP increased from six per cent in 1998 to 14 per cent in 2002. Botswana has a long history of

221

mining that is responsible for around 60 per cent of GDP (Isaksen et al., 2004; Lange and Musonda, 2005). In Ghana, the sector plays a vital role in economic development. In the year 2000, minerals accounted for 38.96 per cent of total exports, contributing 41 per cent of the economy's foreign exchange, and making it the highest foreign currency earner (ISSER, 2001). Besides being a leading forex earner, mining also encourages innovation and attracts new technology as host nations strive to maximise production.

The "Other", Ugly Side of Mining and the Losers

While mineral extraction can bring significant benefits to communities and economies, the mining industry has been criticised by academics and development practitioners from various disciplines and sectors. Rhett (2006) noted that while mineral extraction has become an important industry in many countries as they seek to address their development challenges, exploitation of these resources is often destructive as it damages the ecosystem and creates problems for people living in the vicinity of mining operations. Furthermore, mine workers are at risk of contracting silicosis and tuberculosis (TB). With reference to Ghana, Awudi (2002: 65) argues that, 'despite the positive indicators, the role of the mining industry in economic development is suspect... despite the over U$2 billion Foreign Direct Investment (FDI) in mineral exploration and mine development during the last decade indicating over 56 per cent of total FDI flows to the country, (with the attendant increase in mineral exports) the sector is yet to make any meaningful impact on the country's overall economy'. Awudi further noted that the gains derived from the sector come at huge health, social and environmental costs to nearby communities, (to which I add psychological costs) and that there has been on-going public outcry against companies mining in Ghana (Awudi, 2002). Such concerns are common in most mining operations across Africa.

Mining is known for its disruptive impact, especially on host and surrounding communities. Kitula (2004) noted that most mining operations produce large quantities of waste material which are often inappropriately dumped, causing environmental problems. Akabzaa

(2000) notes that mining activities follow a number of stages, all of which are potentially harmful to the environment, society, cultural heritage and the health and safety of those involved in extraction as well as communities surrounding the mining sites. Kitula (2004) noted that the social impacts of mining include communities being displaced from their ancestral homelands, the marginalisation of host areas and oppression of local low-income citizens. Displacement is engineered to enable the theft of minerals in a paradigm of shameless theft, brutality, exploitation and plunder. The harm done to the environment is colossal as transnationals move on in search of new greenfields of opportunity for more robbery and exploitation in cahoots with the 'people's Governments – African Governments'. In many ways, African Governments by their naivety or corruption are setting back the people's emancipation in defiance of a calculative sociological logic of distribution and re-distribution to indigenous communities for the attainment of mining sovereignty as means to an end. The means are repossession without compensation and no regrets followed by distribution and equitable redistribution; the end being mining sovereignty. The modalities repose and rest with the indigenous communities as acts of the revalorisation of their worth, wealth, capacity, capabilities, rights, freedoms and knowledge. African Governments, through their actions, can either delay or facilitate the transition to mining sovereignty. Their actions and/or inactions with regard to the environment, also impact either positively or negatively the pursuit and realisation of mining sovereignty.

Mining, thus, has significant effects on the environment and/or the social fabric of society, especially in the absence of proper management (World Bank & International Finance Corporation, 2002: 2). Kapelus (2001: 1) went further to argue that many host communities become poorer as a result of restricted access to resources, especially when mining ventures fail. Reed & Miranda (2007: 15) contend that, 'to date, mining has a poor record in terms of its contribution to sustainable development, with few communities receiving significant benefit and mining sites experiencing lasting negative ramifications'. The corpses of buildings, disused mines and deep dump sites of waste and chemicals that penetrate the earth's surface are some of the ramifications of mining. Many miners will never own even a minute piece of the gold, diamonds and other precious minerals they mine under very dangerous conditions both on the surface and underground. Mines represent impersonal institutions with a total disconnect from humanity in the name of profit instead of uplifting communities' standards of living. This calls for a new discourse of mining which benefits those who work on the mines, and imparts new skills, knowledge and attitudes and empowers for the betterment of all indigenous communities as an emancipatory and calculative sociological logic. Eggert (2001) notes that most mineral-dependent nations are ranked among the poorest and worst performing economies in the world; this assertion resonates with the resource curse. Hawkins' (2009:1) account of the resource curse maintains that 'export-driven natural resource sectors such as oil, gas, minerals, precious metals and gemstones – generate substantial revenues both for the state and foreign-owned multinational businesses, yet these do not translate into broad-based economic development benefiting all sectors of the population and especially the poor'. In the same vein, Bebbington et al. (2008: 890) state that nations with rich natural resources tend to be over-dependant on mineral extraction and often fail to develop other sectors, leading to development problems as the mining sector fails to sustain the economy as a whole. Most large scale mining operations in developing countries are monopolised by Transnational Companies (TNCs) which contribute to the resource curse as many do not prioritise the development and welfare of host communities. Instead, their priority is making as much profit as possible. The *Southern Eye* Newspaper (15 December 2013) noted that Chinese mining firms are causing serious damage to the environment in Zimbabwe's Matebeleland South Province, yet are not benefiting local communities in any significant way In Nigeria, Jike (2004: 686) argued that 'part of the development enigma is orchestrated by the exploitative tendencies of multinational oil companies that have plundered fossil fuels and thereby truncated the sustainability of the indigenous environments.' The author added that such 'warped development initiatives roundly undermine the existential base of the Niger Delta people.' As such, the discourse I propose is one of a resource dividend rather than a resource curse – a blessing in Christian jargon – to constitute a mineral blessing. The edifice of mining should be configured in such a way as to benefit indigenous communities scaffolding on prudent laws and regulations promulgated by real people's governments if those Governments support their people in the quest for mining sovereignty. It behoves upon real people's Governments to ensure citizen protection and access to mining information, tools, techniques, equipment, technologies and mining markets to indigenous communities within the context of mining sovereignty.

Akabzaa and Darimani (2001: 34) raised a concern that communities which host mining activities 'have been victims of air and water pollution as well as other forms of environmental degradation resulting from mining operations.' Gualnam (2008: 1) also noted that while it may be true that most economies need to extract their mineral resources and use the proceeds to satisfy their basic needs, continuous exploitation of these resources destroys the livelihoods and environments of indigenous communities and has been identified as one of the major causes of civil unrest and wars, widespread human right abuses, poisoning of people and environments, and vegetation degradation in many communities and countries – all in the name of profit. Under such circumstances profit becomes a dirty word.

The Declaration of Principles on the Rights of Indigenous Peoples, Numeral 4 (cited in Warden- Fernandez, 2001: 2) states that, 'Indigenous Nations and Peoples are entitled to the permanent enjoyment of their aboriginal ancestral historical territories. This includes air space, surface and subsurface rights, inland and coastal waters, sea ice, renewable and non-renewable resources, and the economies based on these resources.' Besides these rights, Mate (2002: 3) asserts that in areas where mining is carried out, indigenous communities and peoples 'have been the least regarded of the actors and have historically been neglected in policy and other discussions relating to many development issues such as mineral development.' McMahon (2000 in Mate, 2002: 3) adds that 'the negotiations and discussions have been primarily between governments and companies and to the neglect of those whose lives and livelihoods are impacted directly and, usually, adversely by mineral operations.' This has sparked protest by communities to fight for recognition as they assert the right to be consulted in decision making. Akabzaa (2000 cited in Mate, 2002: 4) observes that it is unfortunate that such concerns fall on deaf ears as governments regard protesting communities as 'obstacles to foreign investment' and in most cases responded violently, resulting in various human right abuses. It is an indictment that such governments fight their own people in the name of foreign investment and looting. A case in point is the Marikana. In the Marikana case, 34 mineworkers were killed, 78 wounded and about 250 people arrested when police fired on the mineworkers who were demanding a wage increase from their employer Lonmin (SAHO, 2013). Lonmin is a private platinum mining company with a strong colonial history of mining in the sub-region and an equally strong colonial affiliation to London as the company name insinuates. In this case, Government, in the name of law and order, fired on citizens – the real owners of the mineral wealth beneath the soil of the country in terms of the Freedom Charter adopted by the Congress of the People in 1955 - on behalf of business in a labour dispute which is ordinarily settled through negotiation, mediation, arbitration and the courts.

Mining and the Environment

As noted earlier, if not properly planned, mining can have significant negative impacts. This section examines its environmental impacts. Mining involves a number of stages including prospecting, exploration, mine development and preparation, extraction and treatment/processing. Each stage has profound environmental impacts (Gualnam, 2008).

Purification of minerals like gold requires the use of chemicals which are dangerous to human and animal health. On disposal, waste chemical residue finds its way into water reservoirs, contaminating the water as well as the land. Mercury is an example of these highly toxic chemicals. It is very harmful to animals, humans and aquatic life through bio-accumulation in the food chain (Tunhuma, 2006). Mercury is poisonous when inhaled or washed into water bodies

226

(UNDP 2005). When inhaled or when it comes in contact with the skin, it can cause lung cancer and skin diseases and if it is washed away during a process known as amalgamation, it settles onto the surrounding environment where it is absorbed and processed by a variety of living organisms. The UNDP (2005:57) noted that the amalgamation process changes mercury into a highly toxic substance and that 'the process transforms elemental mercury into methyl mercury. Methyl mercury is one of the most toxic organic compounds and a powerful neurotoxin that works its way up the food chain through bioaccumulation'. This not only poses a hazard to human and animal life but also destroys the soil and aquatic life and disrupts livelihoods, especially among those who depend on farming and fishing. Gualnam (2008) raised the challenge of mining waste and highlighted that on a larger scale, the environmental impacts of mining manifest when chemicals such as sulphur dioxide released from mines cause acid rain. Carbon dioxide and methane released from burning fossil fuels during mining results in the formation of greenhouse gases which in turn may result in climate change. Besides air and land pollution, noise pollution is caused by machinery and through extraction activities such as blasting (Gualnam, 2008: 2). Blasting can damage miners' eardrums and condemn them to a post-mining life with impaired hearing.

In Zimbabwe, small scale artisanal mining in Umzingwane has resulted in serious degradation of the natural environment (Phiri, 2011). Soil erosion has reached serious proportions and now requires adequate management (FAO, 2004). The same is true for mining in Chiyadzwa, Penhalonga and Chimanimani (CRD, 2014) and in Bindura, Shamva, Kwekwe, Gweru and surroundings, Gokwe, Bikita, and Mutoko (Manyunga, 2012) and elsewhere. Environmentalists attribute climate change and desert-like weather which includes prolonged dry spells on the African continent to human activities, including mining.

In tropical areas where mining is rampant, the World Rainforest Movement (WRM, 2004), noted that it is a major cause of deforestation and forest degradation. Surface mining poses a serious threat to Ghana's remaining forest resources and to the rich biodiversity of its tropical rainforest, reflecting the dialectics and

227

conflicts that occur between sustainable forest management and mining. Besides the threat to biological diversity, the WRM (2004) argues that the removal of the forest cover is swiftly drying up water sources and reservoirs, leading to water shortages and endangering animal and plant aquatic species. Communities in the tropical forest areas of Africa complained to the WRM that snails, mushrooms, and medicinal herbs among others are no longer as abundant as they used to be and stated that this was partly due to mining activities (World Rainforest Movement, 2004; Awudi, 2002). This resonates with the concern that large-scale mining activities generally reduce vegetation to levels that are destructive to biological diversity (Akabzaa & Darimani, 2001: 47). In Mongolia, the World Bank (2006: 1-2) noted deteriorating levels of water quality emanating from water pollution, waste rock piles, mercury contamination and tailings repositories as well as air pollution, showing the ugly effects of mining on host communities.

In Zimbabwe, the drying up and siltation of dams and rivers in Umzingwane, Matebeleland South Province has been attributed to small scale mining in areas around the district (ZINWA, 2009). The effect on the storage capacity of dams has already been profound, with Bulawayo being the worst hit by water shortages (Phiri, 2011). In 2011, Bulawayo City's water consumption stood at an average of $134,000m^3$ to $140,000m^3$ of which 58 per cent came from the Umzingwane catchment area (Bulawayo City Council, 2011). Siltation of water bodies in Umzingwane as a result of mining and related activities has reduced the amount of water available to Bulawayo and other urban centres in Zimbabwe. Elsewhere in Manicaland, the CRD (2014: 28) noted that alluvial mining has resulted in siltation of the Mutare and Odzi Rivers while in Mashonaland Central province, EMA instructed mining companies to stop alluvial mining near and along the Mazowe River citing high levels of siltation. Chazovachii and Musingarimi (2013) note that Runde River has suffered a similar fate.

Besides drying up water sources, depletion of ground and surface water is also common in mining areas. Shoko (2005) argues that because mines require large volumes of water, mining operations are located close to water sources or at the source. Gold mining and refining requires large volumes of water and therefore imposes much strain on this resource. Small scale artisanal mining in the Amazon Basin in Latin America (Shoko, 2005) has caused water pollution and depletion of both surface and natural underground sources.

Furthermore, numerous health problems, including malaria, tuberculosis (TB), conjunctivitis, and skin diseases are believed to be directly or indirectly attributable to mining activities (World Rainforest Movement, 2004: 43-44; Awudi, 2002). Miners are also at risk of contracting and spreading diseases such as HIV/AIDS and other transmittable infections (Rhett, 2006). *The Zimbabwean* (25 July 2011) claimed that the mining industry fosters activities like prostitution which is directly linked to the spread of HIV and other STIs. The National Aids Council (NAC) also noted that HIV/AIDS prevalence rates were high in mining areas and towns such as Zvishavane, Hwange and Bindura in Zimbabwe (NAC, 2006). Shoko (2005) suggested that the rapid establishment of settlements in newly discovered gold and gemstone areas result in the social ills associated with urbanization. These include robbery, theft, prostitution, and high levels of pollution, among others.

Mining and Society

While much of the earlier focus was on effects of mining on the environment, its social impact has received increasing attention of late. While mining can be of vital economic importance as it facilitates industrialization and promises wealth and jobs (Gualnam, 2008), it can also be a source of social discontent, civil unrest and high social costs (Gualnam, 2008). The social cost of mining is intertwined with cultural and environmental issues. There can be no gainsaying that mining appropriates land that belongs to host communities; negatively impacts health; interferes in and compromises social relationships; destroys and disrupts community subsistence and life; causes social disintegration due to radical and abrupt changes in regional cultures; displaces current or future local economic activities; and is characterised by hazardous and unhealthy working conditions (Gualnam, 2008).

Awudi (2002: 7) noted that in most mining communities, 'the degradation of large tracts of land by the large-scale surface mines constitutes a major threat to agriculture in the communities and their economic survival.' Akabzaa (2009: 38) also noted that 'mining companies are annexing vast lands in their operational areas and depriving communities of their chief source of livelihood'. Most rural people depend on farming for survival. In Zimbabwe, the discovery of the Chiyadzwa diamond fields in 2005/06 and eventual extraction resulted in forced displacement of local communities from their ancestral lands and resettlement elsewhere (Chimonyo et al., 2014: 13). Mwandayi (2011) notes that the Shona people are culturally attached to their ancestral land and relocation can only be done on the basis of culturally acceptable reasons, something that mining induced displacements do not respect. Furthermore, these communities lost rich agricultural land upon which their livelihoods depended, compromising their food security and exposing them to food shortages. Relocations also disrupted education, and cultural linkages, networks and practices. It is of grave concern that five years after the evictions, victims have not received any meaningful compensation despite their well-documented losses (Chimonyo et al., 2014; CRD, 2014). A number of authors have identified the impact of displacements. Akabzaa & Darimani (2001), the WRM (2004), Gualnam (2008), Shoko (2005), and NAC (2006) among many others have cited an increase in social problems such as 'prostitution, drug and alcohol abuse, gambling, incest, inadequate housing, youth unemployment, family disorganization' and dislocation and increasing rates of school dropout.

In more extreme cases, mining has caused conflict between government and mining companies, and local communities over control of minerals. While laws prohibit unlicensed individuals from accessing minerals, local communities feel entitled to the resources within their localities – their birth right had it not been for government. Denial of access can lead to violent clashes with the authorities. Akabzaa remarked that 'the growing incidence of conflict between mining communities and their chiefs on one hand, and the mining companies on the other hand, echoes the growing concerns about the effects of the mining sector on the population' (Akabzaa,

2000 cited in Akabzaa, 2009). Operation '*CHIKOROKOZA CHAPERA*' (An end to panning) during which illegal miners were violently driven out of Chiyadzwa diamond fields in Zimbabwe is a perfect example of how conflicts can arise as a result of mining. After initially facing resistance from illegal miners, government deployed the armed forces (Chimonyo, 2014; CRD, 2014). In South Africa, 34 miners were shot dead at Lonmin Mine in Marikana while demonstrating against poor remuneration in 2012 (*Mail & Guardian*, 21 August 2012) as earlier mentioned. This is a clear demonstration of mining companies and governments' exploitation of workers and their families in pursuit of profit. It is for this reason that some commentators describe minerals as a curse and a source of conflict.

After the acquisition of the land and mineral fields in Chiyadzwa, local communities continue to face harassment at the hands of state security forces and mine guards, and many are persecuted for petty crimes such as trespassing (CRD, 2014). Hawkins (2009:15) noted that towards the end of 2008, there were numerous media reports of police and military action against illegal miners, resulting in an unknown number of fatalities. This prompted the imposition of trade sanctions on the Zimbabwe Mining Development Corporation (ZMDC) (a government mining company) by the European Union and the Kimberly Process labelled Chiyadzwa diamonds as blood diamonds that cannot be sold on the world markets (Hawkins, 2009). This was subsequently lifted after protests by the Government of Zimbabwe. Thus, mineral extraction can be a source of conflict (Bebbington et al., 2008). The United Nations (2006) noted that most wars fought in Africa and across the world are related to control of natural resources. Governments can also abuse mining gains to supress their people; Bryant and Bailey (1997: 40) pointed out that 'power can be used to control people's access to a diversity of environmental resources such as land, minerals, water and forest, control over the environment of others through control over societal priorities of environmental projects hence the marginalization of vulnerable groups who are often left with a plethora of problems.' In Zimbabwe, allegations are rife that the ZANU (PF) government used Chiyadzwa diamonds to finance the June 2008 presidential elections runoff (Hawkins, 2009). Opposition parties, civil society and private media believe that this campaign was bankrolled by diamond monies.

The closure of mines usually results in the creation of ghost towns or settlements. In areas where no other economic activities are viable, the mine and its infrastructure are usually abandoned. It is used as hiding places by criminals and can also harbour dangerous wild animals which are a threat to humans and livestock. Abandoned ghost towns can be havens for prostitution as some locals seek alternatives livelihoods after the closure of the mine. *The News Day* (11 May 2012) reported that Mhangura is now a ghost town which has been transformed into a hive of illegal activities. Other abandoned mines that have turned into ghost towns in Zimbabwe include Kamativi and Mashava.

Summarising the impacts of mining, Abdus-Saleque (2008, 25) noted that all the stages of mining, from preparation to processing, result in:

> deforestation of the land and elimination of vegetation which affects the habitats of hundreds of endemic species, causes soil erosion and silting of the land, reduction of water table, contamination of the air, water and the land by chemicals such as cyanides, concentrated acids and alkaline compounds and air pollution caused by dust, gases and toxic vapour which can have diverse effects on the environment and health and social life of the local communities (Abdus-Saleque, 2008, 25).

While a number of benefits can be derived from mining, its destructive effects on the environment and society cannot escape interrogation.

Conclusion

In conclusion, this chapter described the contradictory tapestry of mining necessitating a re-think of it. On the one hand, it has the potential to create jobs, produce minerals which earn foreign currency, and promote investment in infrastructure and skills. On the other, it can pit governments and multinational companies against citizens and produce conflict and sorrow. The miners that unearth precious minerals are totally alienated from the product. Mining thus creates winners and losers – the former in miniscule numbers and the latter in their multitudes.

Mining sovereignty behoves real Governments to ensure mining systems and processes are pro-indigenous communities. It enlists real Governments to work with communities and not against them, in a calculative sociological logic to advance the notion of emancipatory accumulation by re-possession which is deliberate, real Government supported accumulation of mineral wealth and assets for the benefit of indigenous communities for the attainment of mining sovereignty as an end in itself. A precondition for the achievement of mining sovereignty, is the re-configuration of the edifice of mining through the promulgation of laws and regulations which are pro-indigenous communities that give these communities the decision-making prerogative to determine what is mined, where it is mined, who should mine, how much should be mined, what to beneficiate and what to sell or trade and to whom to sell, how much to keep and what to dispose of, access to mining information, logics and technologies and markets within the sustainable and culturally acceptable norms of the community and in the name of and for the sake of the realisation of mining sovereignty.

References

Abdus-Saleque, K. (2008). Social and Environmental Impacts of Mining-Australian Lessons on Mitigation. Available at http://phulbariproject. wordpress. com/2008/10/28/% E2, 80. Accessed 15 December 2016.

Akabzaa, T. (2000). 'Mining Boom: Health Service Report of Wassa-West District, Tarkwa', *Africa Agenda, No. 1.15.*

Akabzaa, T. (2009). 'Mining in Ghana: implications for national economic development and poverty reduction'. *Mining in Africa: Regulation and Development*, 25-65.

Akabzaa, T. and Darimani, A. (2001) 'Impact of mining sector investment in Ghana: A study of the Tarkwa mining region'. *Third World Network.*

Awudi, G.B. (2002). 'The role of foreign direct investment (FDI) in the mining sector of Ghana and the environment'. *Conference on Foreign Direct Investment and the Environment, OECD, Paris.*

Bebbington, A., Hinojosa, L., Bebbington, D.H., Burneo, M.L. and Warnaars, X. (2008). 'Contention and ambiguity: Mining and the possibilities of development'. *Development and Change, 39*(6), 887-914.

Chazovachii, B. and Musingarimi, A. (2013). 'Gold Panning and Runde River Course Morphology in Mwenezi: A Quest for a Sound Catchment Management and Sustainable Development', *Global Advanced Research Journal of Social Science,* 2(5).

Centre for Research and Development Zimbabwe. (2014). *Raising the Community Voice in the Extractive Sector: Challenges and future prospects of the mining sector in Zimbabwe,* Mutare: Centre for Research and Development Zimbabwe.

Chimonyo, G.R., Mungure, S. and Scott, P.D. (2011). *The Social, Economic and Environmental Implications of Diamond Mining in Chiadzwa.* Mutare: Centre for Research and Development.

Davies, N. (2015). The savage truth behind the Marikana massacre. *The Mail & Guardian*
22 May 2015, http://mg.co.za/article/2015-05-21-the-savage-truth-behind-the-marikana-massacre Accessed 20 Jan 2017.

Eggert, R.G. (2001). Mining and economic sustainability: national economies and local communities. *A Study Prepared for the Mining, Minerals, and Sustainable Development Project,* Colorado School of Mines.

Hawkins, T. (2009). The Mining Sector in Zimbabwe and its Potential Contribution to Recovery, *United Nations Development Programme Comprehensive Economic Recovery in Zimbabwe Working Paper Series Working Paper 1:* Harare: UNDP.

Hwange Colliery Company Limited, (n.d) Social Responsibility. Available at
http://www.hwangecolliery.net/index.php?option=com_content&view=article&id=7:social Accessed 23 December 2016

Jike, V.T. (2004). 'Environmental degradation, social disequilibrium, and the dilemma of sustainable development in the Niger-Delta of Nigeria', *Journal of Black Studies, 34*(5), 686-701.

Jul-Larsen, E., Kassibo, B., Lange, S. and Samset, I. (2006) *Socio-Economic Effects of Gold Mining in Mali. A Study of the Sadiola and Morila Mining Operations.* Bergen: Chr. Michelsen Institute.

Kitula, A.G.N. (2004). 'The environmental and socio-economic impacts of mining on local livelihoods in Tanzania: A case study of Geita District'. *Journal of cleaner production, 14*(3), 405-414.

Manyunga, A. (2012). 'An Investigation into the Effects of Black Granite Mining on Environmental Degradation and Community Livelihood Strategies in Mutoko: The Case of Ward 7 and 8 (2000 – 2010)', unpublished MSc. Thesis, National University of Science and Technology

Mate, K. (2002). 'Communities, civil society organisations and the management of the mineral wealth'. *London: International Institute for Environment and Development (IIED) No, 16.*

McMohan, G. and Remy, F. (2001). 'Large Mines and the Community: Socioeconomic and Environmental Effects in Latin America'. *Canada and Spain, IDRC, Ottawa, 4-7.*

Mbada Diamonds. (n.d). Harnessing Diamonds for the people. Accessed on 20 December 2016, Available at http://thedirectory.co.zw/company.cfm?companyid=7566

Miththapala, S. (2008). *Coral reefs, Coastal ecosystems series (1).* IUCN: Ecosystems and Livelihoods Group.

Mwandayi, C. (2011). Death and After-life in the eyes of the Shona: Dialogue with Shona customs with the quest for authentic inculturation. *Bamberg: UBP.*

Phiri, S. (2011). 'Impact of Artisanal Small Scale Gold Mining in Umzingwane District (Zimbabwe), a Potential for Ecological Disaster', Unpublished MSc. Thesis, University of the Free State.

Reed, E. and Miranda, M. (2007). 'Assessment of the mining sector and infrastructure development in the Congo Basin region'. *Washington DC, USA: World Wildlife Fund, Macroeconomics for Sustainable Development Program Office,* p.27.

Rhett, B.A. (2006). Environmental impact of mining in the rainforest. *Mongabay. com/ Place Out of Time: Tropical Rainforests and the Perils They Face.* Accessed at http://rainforests.mongabay.com/0808.html 23 Jan 2017.

SAHO, (2013). 'Marikana Massacre 16 August 2012'. Available at http://www.sahistory.org.za/article/marikana-massacre-16-august-2012 (Accessed on 13 March 2017)

Same, A.T. (2008). *Mineral-rich countries and Dutch Disease: Understanding the macroeconomic implications of windfalls and the development prospects the case of Equatorial Guinea* (Vol. 4595), Washington DC: World Bank Publications.

Shoko, D. S.M. (2002). 'Small scale mining and alluvial gold panning within the Zambezi Basin': Paper presented at the 9th Conference of International Association for the Study of Common property held in Victoria Falls in June 2002, Victoria Falls, Zimbabwe.

Tunhuma, N. M. (2007). Environmental impact assessment of small-scale resource exploitation: a case of Zhulube catchment, Limpopo basin, Zimbabwe. PhD Thesis, Unesco-IHE

Warden-Fernandez, J. (2001). 'Indigenous communities and mineral development'. *Mining, Minerals, and Sustainable Development, 59*, 1-30.

Werthmann, K. (2003). 'The president of the gold diggers: sources of power in a gold mine in Burkina Faso'. *Ethnos, 68*(1), 95-111.

World Bank and International Finance Corporation. (2002). 'Treasure or trouble? Mining in developing countries'. Washington DC: World Bank and International Finance Corporation.

World Rainforest Movement. (2004) 'Mining: Social and Environmental Impacts'. Montevideo: World Rainforests Movement.

The News Day (11 May 2012). 'Former Mining Towns turn into Ghost towns' Available at https://www.newsday.co.zw/2012/05/11/2012-05-11-former-mining-centres-turn-into-ghost-towns/ Accessed on 20 Jan 2017.

Chapter Eight

Towards a Pan-Africanist Mining Regulatory Framework for Africa: Drawing Lessons from the Pre-colonial Customary Law Based Mining Practices

Tapiwa V Warikandwa & Ndatega V Asheela

> *Black economic empowerment programmes ... have often seen the indigenous people who were previously and who remain largely excluded from the economic mainstream going into a state of euphoria based on the genuine belief that such programmes are an effective panacea for their existential socio-economic challenges* (Warikandwa & Osode 2017).

Introduction

Mining activities in pre-colonial Africa were mainly regulated through uncodified customary law formulated from community-based value systems and moral principles (Botchway 1995). The community-based value systems and moral principles placed emphasis on State resources benefiting the natives through value addition on minerals and subsequent barter trade with other States, including Western nations (Pritchard & Fortes 1940). At the core of the community-based value systems was the concept of "humaneness" now popularly known as Ubuntu (Cornell 2014). In pre-colonial Africa, the concept of Ubuntu dictated that the extraction of natural resources had to be pursued in a manner that did not prejudice the best interests of human inhabitants of societies from which such mineral resources were extracted (Hammel *et al* 2000). It was evident that the extraction of mineral resources, under the customary law regime, had to benefit the owners of the mineral resources who in this case were the indigenous Africans (Downey *et al* 2010). Further, the existent customary laws regulating mining activities were implemented in such a manner that ensured that mining practices would not compromise the environment inhabited by African people as a mechanism of avoiding putting the human life at health risk (Sarbah 1966; Ollennu 1985).

Customary law regulated mining practices ensured that mineral resources benefited communities from which the natural resources were extracted (Botchway 1995; Murombo 2013). In principle, pre-colonial African societies employed a Pan-Africanist approach to mining practices (Hammel *et al* 2000). Proceeds from the mining process were exploited for the greater good of the society. The African mining societies were socialist by nature and placed emphasis on equality amongst its members as opposed to individualism, which informs the contemporary capitalist driven institutions (Kahn 2013). As such, it is plausible to contend that pre-colonial African societies were an anti-thesis of the contemporary societies driven by the new world order agenda in which resources are owned by the States, per se, yet exploited by multinational corporations in the best interests of such companies' countries of origin (Marshall 2012; Kah 1992). The celebrated yet development African unfriendly free market policies which prohibit trade barriers are now the order of the day in the globalised world. The anarchy of the colonial era has been replaced by the order in chaos of the new world regime (Acharya 1998).

It is therefore regrettable that the customary law regulated, traditional community-centred mining practices were supplanted and replaced by arguably "exploitative" neo-liberal, free market-based mining regulatory frameworks which focus on the natural resources benefiting foreign investors with little accruing to communities from which such resources have been mined. The argument has often been that African countries cannot do without the capital injection from Western investors as mining is a capital intensive business venture (Samuel 2013; Eggert 2002; Davis & Tilton 2002). However, Burkina Faso under the leadership of the robust Pan-African president, Thomas Sankara, proved that African countries can become independent of traditional lending institutions such as the International Monetary Fund (IMF) and World Bank (WB) and run their economies through positively exploiting their mineral resources in the best interest of their people (Mhango 2016).

If African countries cannot do away with capital injections from foreign investors then it has to be questioned why pre-colonial African mining States were able to mine and trade in the products from the mining sector without so much concern of the so-called intensive capital investments (McCandless & Karbo 2011). So efficient were the indigenous mining practices that the colonialists forcibly took over the lucrative African run mining business ventures (Goucher *et al* 1998). Africans were well aware of the importance of mining as well as the relevant trade markets and always sought to maximise from the proceeds of trade in their precious natural resources (Hammel *et al* 2000). This forced colonialists to repudiate the customary laws which regulated the lucrative mining practices in Africa. As a result, customary law which regulated community centred mining activities was relegated and replaced by the so-called "civilised" Western oriented and exploitative mining law regime, through the process of colonisation (Botchway 1995). Colonisation infringed upon the steady growth of customary mining law. The colonialists disregarded customary law and made significant conscious efforts to repudiate the importance of the former. Through force, the colonists took over existing mining sites which belonged to indigenous Africans who were fully cognisant of the importance of mined natural resources to their quest for development. In essence, the indigenous Africans' absolute property rights to mines were supplanted by the colonists who then imposed their foreign legal systems as a means of legitimising their ill-gotten mining rights.

Generations of colonialists' heirs have since benefited from the now "dignified robbery" or "economic violence" emanating from the colonial era (Laura 2004; Collins 2006; Connell 2006; Cooper 2005; Nhemachena 2017). This approach has caused the impoverishing of African States and their people as raw materials from mining are continually extracted and sent to Western countries for value addition. African States often have to buy finished products whose raw materials are obtained from their territories, with proceeds from mining benefiting foreign investors and not African natives (Rodney 1972). The ruthless, yet celebrated free market policies and regulatory frameworks, which are often regarded as a panacea to Africa's economic woes by some African scholars (Zongwe 2016) must now be abolished and replaced with a Pan-African centred mining regulatory framework. Lessons in this regard should be drawn from the Pan-African Investment Code (PAIC) which aims at ensuring that African countries benefit from the exploitation and trade in their mineral resources (Draft Pan-African Investment Code 2016).

However, before a new Pan-African mining law regime is adopted, it must be established as to what form such regulatory framework should adopt. With the prevalence of incidences detailing State capture and corruption in African governments, anything that is indigenous in form must not be construed and interpreted as constituting Pan-Africanism. There is the emergence of the elitist class of Africans who consider themselves as Pan-Africanists yet they are just but a front of the same colonialist regimes which have impoverished Africa (M'buyinga 1982; Shivji 2006). This group of Africans, amongst which are the so-called African liberators, can also be branded as the "African Gestapo" who like the ruthless Gestapo under Hitler cared less about the concerns of the ordinary person but were concerned more about party politics and obsession with power. This book chapter will draw lessons from the uncodified pre-colonial African mining regulatory systems (customary law regulating mining) to ascertain the ideal construction of the envisaged Pan-Africanist mining regulatory framework. An appraisal of the pre-colonial, colonial and post-colonial mining regulatory frameworks will provide a plausible reflection of the envisaged Pan-African mining legal framework.

Why adopt a Pan-Africanist regulatory framework for Africa's mining sectors?

Contemporary mining practices informed by neo-liberal economic policies have often been fixated on business principles that frustrate human capital and sustainable development in Africa (Warikandwa & Osode 2014; Monbiot 2016; Haque 1999). A case in point is the disastrous effects of the Economic Structural Adjustment Programmes which sent economies in Southern Africa into a meltdown and the Washington Consensus which compromised the economic viability of South American countries (Mlambo 1997; Mlambo & Pangeti 2001). Emphasis has often been placed on profit maximisation with little or no regard being placed on the welfare of those that "slave" in hazardous conditions to extract the minerals used to generate the massive profits that accrue from such processes. This book chapter undertakes a critical historical analysis of the pre-colonial mining practices and compares them with those prevailing in the post-colonial era. The objective of this analysis is to curb the rate of occurrence of exploitative business practices in Africa's mining sectors, similar to those that prompted the labour unrest which led to the Marikana tragedy in South Africa. Such atrocities should naturally not occur in the so-called human rights driven era; an era in which African mine workers are strangely being constantly subjected to harsh working conditions on the basis of capitalism as informed by the game theory (Mekonnen 2015). A paradigm shift will be advocated for in this book chapter through proposals aiming at adopting an Ubuntu driven Pan-Africanist mining regulatory agenda. Such an agenda, similar to the one envisaged by the Pan-African Investment Code, will be formulated from the lessons drawn from mining practices employed in pre-colonial African States which sought to benefit all members of the society and not a few well connected individuals and their foreign actors as is the practice in today's world. It is hoped that such an approach will be used to create a balance between people oriented mining practices and contemporary free-market driven mining practices. It is not the main thrust of this work to entirely dismiss foreign capital investment in Africa's capital intensive mining sector but to call for a paradigm shift which recognises mining activities informed by African value systems.

It would be unscientific for African leaders to continue with a trajectory that perpetuates poverty in Africa and sustains development in the Western and Asian countries. In 2009, the European Union (EU) Parliament pointed out that Europe was in short supply of mineral resources which were important to sustaining their economies and/or markets (Szczepanski 2012). From a research conducted and published in the 2009 EU Legal Brief, the revenue from the mining sector was valued at € 72 000 million (*ibid*). Labour productivity per person in the oil and gas sector was pegged at €569 000 per year (*ibid*). This is evidence that the mining sector is lucrative and has the potential to ensure that Africa realises its industrialisation dreams (Morris & Fessehaie 2014). After all, mineral resources from Africa were used to realise industrialisation for the West and to sustain such industrialisation levels. Mineral rich countries such as the Democratic Republic of Congo, Congo Brazzaville, Ghana and indeed many other African States have fallen victim to the neo-liberal expansionist economic policies and have seen their economies grow at insignificant rates. The mineral resources which were supposed to be their competitive advantage are now being exploited for the benefit of Western and Asian countries and not the social and economic development of Africa. This approach has to radically change hence the call for the Pan-Africanist mining law regulatory regime. There are so many benefits which can accrue from mining activities in Africa, and in particular a Pan-African approach to mining. Some of the benefits are highlighted below.

Mining in Africa has socio-economic benefits

A people centred Pan-African mining law regulatory regime is likely to translate to socio-economic benefits for indigenous Africans (African Union 2009). Africa is home to leading African resources as illustrated in the table below.

Table 1: Some of Africa's Leading Mineral Resources

Mineral	Production	Rank	Reserves	Rank
Platinum Group Metals	54%	1	60+%	1
Phosphate	27%	1	66%	1
Gold	20%	1	42%	1
Chromium	40%	1	44%	1
Manganese	28%	2	82%	1
Vanadium	51%	1	95%	1
Cobalt	18%	1	55+%	1
Diamonds	78%	1	88%	1
Aluminium	4%	7	45%	1

Source: African Union 2009

The commodity price trends of some of the minerals listed in Table 1 are reflected in Figure 1 below.

Figure 1: Global Commodity Price Trends (2016)

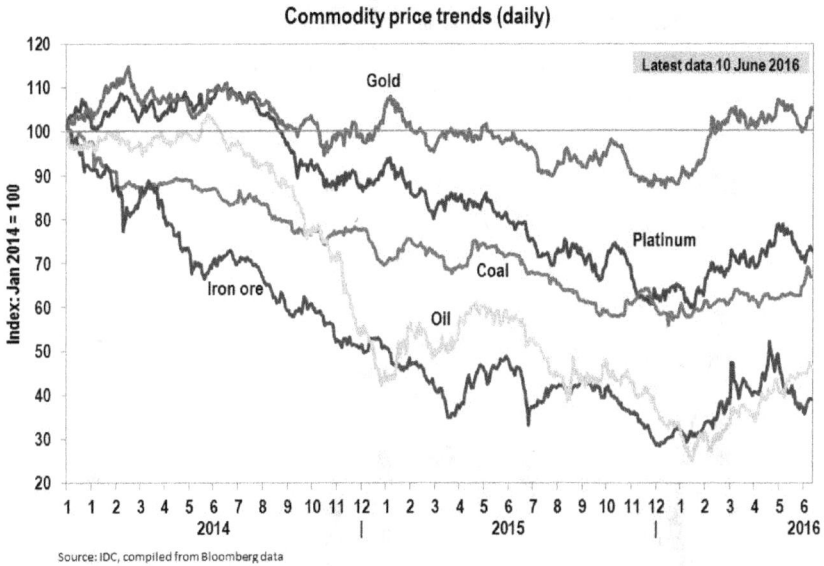

Source: IDC, compiled from Bloomberg data

In the contemporary world, the exploration and development of mineral wealth is considered as a good source of national revenue through the provision of various forms of taxation such as company tax, income tax and royalties (Pricewaterhouse Coopers 2012). It is also a plausible source of employment for the citizens of Africa. However a caution must be entered here as mining operations tend to be capital intensive. This is especially the case in the oil and gas sub-sectors. It is interesting to observe that in the pre-colonial era, mining operations were community based and were thus not capital intensive but labour intensive. Labour was not in short supply as communities worked together to increase productivity.

Mining has also been regarded as a mechanism to attract foreign investment into African economies. In the pre-colonial era, emphasis was placed on value addition to raw materials obtained from the mining process. The shrewd and productive African miners knew the value of their minerals such as gold, iron and diamonds and opted to trade in them with the Portuguese, Indians and Swahili Arabs. As such, they needed no foreign investors but trade partners. The scale of the mining practices was sufficient to sustain the economies of such States. It is evident that mining influences trends in global growth. Developing countries rely on mineral resources to sustain their economies (Mayundo 2016; World Bank 2014). Developing countries, such as African countries, are in the main resource rich and will realise an economic growth of around 4.7% per annum up until 2020 as reflected in Figure 2 below.

Figure 2: Trends in Global Growth

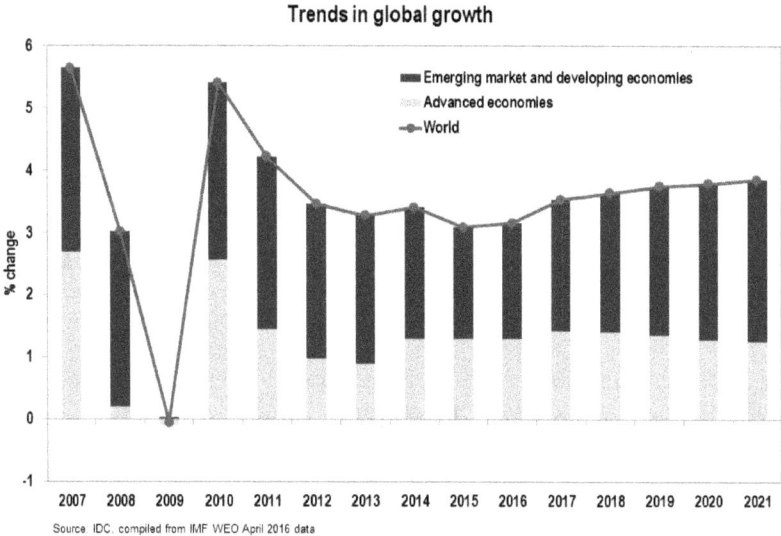

Trends in global growth

Source IDC. compiled from IMF WEO April 2016 data

In the globalisation era, mining practices have also been regarded as a tool to release mining technology transfer into the country through the training of nationals. However, it is interesting to note that during the pre-colonial era, though the mining practices in African societies were not at the level that they are in the contemporary era, they employed sophisticated mining practices which were even adopted by the colonialists when they forcibly took over the mining activities of the indigenous people. It is without doubt that such technologies could have developed with time and increased productivity to commercial levels. After all, the minerals extracted during the pre-colonial era were sufficient to sustain trade

244

with the Portuguese, Swahili Arabs, and Indians amongst other traders.

In recent times, African countries such as South Africa, Zimbabwe, Zambia, Botswana, and Namibia have realised the need to develop indigenous people's participation in the mining sector through Black Economic Empowerment (BEE) schemes. South Africa adopted BEE legislation to ensure that the previously disadvantaged South Africans increase their participation in the economic mainstream (Broad-Based Black Economic Empowerment Act, No. 53 of 2003; Broad-Based Black Economic Empowerment Amendment Act No. 46 of 2013). The mining sector is a key component of any country's economic mainstream. Zimbabwe adopted the "controversial" Indigenisation and Economic Empowerment Act [Chapter 14:33] and the accompanying regulations. The Act and the regulations made provision for foreign owned companies to cede 51 percent equity share ownership to indigenous Zimbabweans (Warikandwa & Osode 2017). Further, the regulations made provision for Community Share Ownership Schemes from which mining companies had to contribute United States $10 million towards community development programmes. Zambia nationalised its copper mines (*ibid*). Botswana increased State ownership of its diamond mines, and Namibia has recently introduced the New Equitable Economic Empowerment Framework to augment the 2002 Minerals Policy in so far as socio-economic development is concerned. The pre-colonial mining sector was controlled by indigenous Africans through Kings and Chiefs (Ayittey 2011). The Kings and Chiefs directed mining operations in the best interests of the community. Mining activities were conducted in pursuit of the best interests of the people and the environment. Emphasis in this regard was on improving the general welfare of people in the society and not a few individuals.

The mining industry is a major source of foreign exchange for the countries. This was also partly the case in the pre-colonial era. It was partly the case in the sense that indigenous Africans traded in their mineral resources in two primary ways. Firstly, they traded in goods for goods (barter trade). In this case, indigenous Africans would trade their iron and gold products for products that they did not produce such as sugar and clothing. Trading posts such as the Zumbo, Sena, Tete amongst others, became popular for trade activities between shrewd indigenous African traders and the Portuguese, Swahili Arabs, Indians and the British, amongst others. The second approach to trade related to indigenous Africans trading their gold for cash. This approach was informed by the indigenous Africans' realisation that they could shrewdly bargain for more cash yet parting with little gold.

The pre-colonial era: A customary law approach to mining regulation

Customary law refers to "rules of law which by custom are applicable to particular communities" in Africa (Blanstein and Flanz, 1993). Customary law was used to regulate mining in Africa. Customs, traditions and practices of African people in countries such as Ghana, Zimbabwe and South Africa were used to regulate the extraction of mineral resources in definable areas. Customary law regulating mining was of importance because it constituted practices which had assumed, "...definite juridical characteristics such as obligatory consequences" and therefore are accorded recognition as a body of law (Hart, 1994; Allot, 1970). Customary law in Africa is now recognised in many jurisdictions as a body of law that contains enforceable legal rules. However its application is subject to its conformity with national constitutions, most of which are now modelled along the western "civilised" legal systems and their norms and values. Customary law's application was useful for a number of reasons as will be discussed in this section.

Customary law regulating mining practices in pre-colonial Africa was important because it ensured the conservation of water and sought to avoid the contamination of water sources and/or bodies due to pollutants emanating from mining practices (Ofori, 1977: 11). Ofori points out that customary law regulating mining provided that, "...water in its natural form such as rivers, lakes, ponds, and the sea, was largely public property and no individual could claim exclusive ownership and use even if he or she had riparian rights" (Ofori, 1977). However, miners could obtain permission from village chiefs

246

and elders to divert water from a public river onto their private land for purposes of washing mineral ores.

The diversion of water for purposes of washing mineral ores was not without restrictions. Diversion of water was subject to actual restraints on the quantity of water a miner needed for a specific mining operation such as washing of the mineral ore (Botchway 1995). Emphasis was placed on the collective sharing of resources by communities hence a miner could get water for a specific purpose and to the extent that a water body could meet the quantities of water demanded by the user, in this case the miner. In principle, the miner's right of access to the water needed was subject to the legitimate interests of other members of the community (Botchway 1995). Adequate supplies of water had to be reserved for other members of the community, in a clean state. The need to keep water in a clean state meant that there were further restrictions on the miners in terms of customary law with regards to the type of instruments they would use to fetch water from the designated water source. The use of metal objects to extract water for use in the mining process was prohibited. Only calabashes and earthenware were regarded as permissible instruments to use in the process of extracting water from its original source. The approach to the use of water sources for mining purposes differs significantly from that employed in the colonial and post-colonial capitalist eras. Emphasis in the colonial and post-colonial eras shifted from concern over the environment to profiteering. The capitalist driven colonial and post-colonial eras have seen environmental laws being passed yet more harm to water sources being realised. Emphasis has now been placed on processes such as rehabilitation with little or no positive outcomes being realised as compared to the pre-colonial era. Worse still, the large scale mining that has characterised mining in the colonial and post-colonial eras has made the contamination of water sources to reach levels of great concern (Koku & Singh 2005).

For one to acquire land for mining, under customary law, express authorisation of the chief or the family head and village elders had to be granted before any mining activities could be undertaken (Ollenu, 1985; Sarbah 1966; Richardson 1993; Garrard 1980). In pre-colonial mining activities, in Africa, the chief would determine where mining

247

would take place. Mining fields were allocated far from villages. The Ubuntu principle which is so often rejected as a legal principle in the post-colonial legal era informed mining practices in pre-colonial Africa. Emphasis was placed on the welfare of the people to such an extent that, "the habitation of people and their sacred sites were not forsaken in favour of gold mining" (Botchway 1995). Restrictions were imposed to prospective miners concerning the depths of, "…pits, royalties to the chief, mining seasons, and days when no mining was done …" (Garrard 1980: 12). In some African communities, mining was done in two or three months of the year (Botchway 1995). Most significantly Botchway pointed out that it was a customary law obligation for every miner:

> … to give a third of the ore or gold he or she obtained to the chief of the area. Even though this was more in the nature of royalty paid by the miner for mining the resource controlled by that chief, it had an environmental implication. In the first place the high royalty had the potential to speed up the rate of mining of the resource. At the same time, it was one of the means available to the chief for assessing the value of the designated minefield(s). If a pit or field could not yield sufficient quantity of gold, it was abandoned for a new one. This, in a way, helped avoid digging too deeply. At the same time it must have contributed to the mushrooming of pits in the mining areas and their consequent threat to life (Botchway 1995: 299).

The one third levied on royalties was much more significant if compared to the lower royalty levies imposed by contemporary resource rich Africa States such as Namibia. Namibia imposes a 2.5 % royalty levy. The customary law rules regulating mining activities in Africa were stringently enforced (Garrard 1980). Communities internalised the customary law rules regarding their environment and their lifestyles. To them, mining at the expense of the environment was a direct affront to their socio-economic interests. As such they had to internalise the customary rules in a utilitarian manner (Brunn-Otto 1976). They were willing to sacrifice "happiness" today for the greater good of the majority tomorrow.

Politically, African communities had, "well-organised and well-ordered political structures" (Evans *et al* 1940; Manoukian 1950). Apart from granting mining rights, the political head of a mining community exercised control over the nature and extent of mining that the miners fulfilled their customary law obligations. Sadly in the contemporary era, such a stringent approach to regulating the mining sector would be deemed as not being investor friendly. Concepts such as the ease of doing business index have been introduced by the WB to advance the interests of western investors in the quest to maximise profits in the mining exploration and extraction processes (Fraser & Larmer 2010). Rigid regulation is regarded as a mechanism of scaring away investors. African countries in the post-colonial era are said to be in a desperate need of foreign investors to such an extent that they have to lower their regulatory standards to attract investors. The end result has been economic rationalisation of the realisation of little or no beneficiation for the indigenous people and obscene profits being ripped by foreign investors. The general and intellectually bankrupt argument from some African leaders, Western scholars, Western oriented African trained scholars and Western trained African scholars is that half a loaf is better than nothing. Pre-colonial Africans had scales to weigh minerals which they traded [in Feiras] in the eastern part of Zimbabwe. This was indicative of the fact that Africans were not willing to be cheated by the Portuguese traders. Sadly, postcolonial Africans including "educated" ones have thrown their scales to the wind.

Religious institutions were also used as tools for ensuring compliance with customary rules regulating mining. In pre-colonial African systems, the line between political and religious authority was indistinct (Evans *et al* 1940). Political leaders carried out significant religious functions (*ibid*). As such religious leaders were to a larger extent the custodians of rules of morality and custom. Failure by miners to adhere to the customary rules would translate to a misfortune punishable by the deity (Owusu-Nimoh 1977). However, colonialism and post-colonial business practices and ideologies came and eviscerated the customary rules governing mining activities as a mechanism for maximising production and robbing the Africans off their valuable mineral resources.

It remains clear though that pre-colonial Africa had a thriving mining industry which was regulated by customary law and was Ubuntu centred. For example, iron products thrived despite competition from European products. In Yatenga, in the modern day Burkina Faso, there were 1500 smelting furnaces in 1904 (Botchway 1995). West and Southern Africa were also the major exporters of gold to the world (*ibid*). Major copper producing areas were sites of indigenous production for years (*ibid*).

Colonial era: Using colonisation as a tool to supplant customary mining laws

Colonialists from the West discovered the abundant mineral wealth which was in Africa. Instead of negotiating for access to minerals or trading with the Africans for mineral wealth, the Westerners used force or violence to take over what was by right not theirs. This came through the process of colonisation; a zero-sum game for Africa in which the West gained "everything" and Africa lost "everything". Colonisation, a game theory tactic, was in part informed by the growth in demand for minerals during the industrial revolution period. The manner of colonisation was such that the colonialists took over the mines and mining processing industries located in exactly the same places as pre-colonial mines used to be. Globe and Phoenix gold mines in Zimbabwe, Ashante goldfields in Ghana, copper mines in Phalaborwa, Musina and the Copperbelt in Zambia were built on sites of ancient mines. The colonialists also used exactly the same technologies employed by pre-colonial ancient miners. Western prospectors exploring for places to mine followed the examples left by displaced indigenous African miners.

Africa's mining past forms an important component of the continent's rich heritage. It provides contemporary generations with ways through which solutions can be obtained to address contemporary socio-economic problems. It is not in doubt that indigenous Africans were treated by colonists as "things" without legal entitlements or any recognised legal system. Africa had a customary law based legal system which was not static. This legal system was undergoing transformation through modifications and

250

innovations driven by its originators. However, the Western driven quick search for mineral resources interfered with the steady development of the customary law regulating mining in Africa. The colonialists regarded themselves exempt from the customary law of the indigenous Africans and sought to quickly repudiate it. Surprisingly, the same colonialists imposed their own taxations and flawed property laws on the indigenous persons whom they had robbed of their entitlements to the land on which the lucrative minerals could be found. This leaves one to question whether unlawfully obtained "rights" can be regarded as enforceable.

It is important to note that during the colonial era, the right to minerals fell within the ambit of property law (Badenhorst 2010). Mineral rights could be severed from the title to the land. Severance of the mineral rights from the surface rights enabled third parties to become holders of the mineral rights (Badenhorst 2011). The right to minerals could thus exist separately from the ownership of land once the right had been severed (Badenhorst 2006). In terms of the common law principle of *cuius est solum eius est usque ad coelum et ad inferos* the owner of land is the owner not only of the surface but of everything above and below it. Ownership of minerals therefore had to be passed from the landowners to the mineral rights holders (Badenhorst 2010). Therefore, for the West to avoid negotiating for mineral rights, which were and are indeed valuable assets, they simply had to use force and become the "legitimate" yet very illegitimate "owners" of the land on which minerals could be obtained. It is also interesting to note that, had the land reform process taken place during this common law dispensation, the land owners (indigenous Africans) would become the owners of the minerals and would therefore exercise the right to transfer the mineral rights to "investors". Direct benefit would therefore go to the land owners. In principle, the customary law system which prevailed in the pre-colonial era would thus be realised using this approach.

However, the colonialist's capitalist approach left no room for indigenous ownership of land as property (Li 2010). If at all land ownership had to be realised by Africans, it would be on unproductive mineral barren and unfertile land. If minerals were discovered on a piece of land allocated to an African, such party

251

would be relocated to a mineral barren and unfertile land to allow the colonialists to exploit the minerals. Such laws were regarded as being just yet they were not. They were simply immoral laws. Dworkin whilst advancing his legal interpretivism view argued that, "…law is not entirely based on social facts, but includes the morally best justification for the institutional facts and practices that we intuitively regard as legal" (Dworkin 1965). From Dworkin's argument, it is plausible to contend that it is improbable for one to know the legitimacy of a legal system in force without the substantive knowledge of the moral truths about the justifications for the practices in a society. Colonialism was implemented to supplant African's customary values and natural resources. Protagonists of the "exclusive legal positivism" school of thought have tried to undermine the link between law and morality by arguing that the legal validity of a norm can never depend on its moral correctness. Using this construction, colonial laws which were used to usurp mineral wealth from Africans and suppress them would be regarded as being legitimate. However, the "inclusive legal positivism" school of thought dismisses the notion that law and morality are not linked. The school of thought advances the plausible view that moral considerations may determine the legal validity of a norm. Joseph Raz in supporting the connection between law and morality pointed out that, it is a necessary truth that there are vices that a legal system cannot possibly have (for example, the law cannot be seen to promote rape or murder) (Raz 1985). As such, the law cannot be seen to justify the "theft" of African minerals and/or wealth and legitimise such a process through law. This is exactly what the process of colonialism achieved and has been the case in the post-colonial era. Law and morality overlap (Wilkins 1996). Failure to do so will promote social upheaval, anarchy and a society underlined by order in chaos. The recent land grabs and violent seizure of western "owned" business interests in Zimbabwe is a case in point (Moyo 1995; Chitiyo 2000). Similar threats to grab land are being made by desperate previously disadvantaged indigenous Africans in South Africa and Namibia. This serves as reason why a Pan-Africanist approach to regulating the mining industry in Africa is proposed in this work. The law must be seen to empower and not coerce people into a social order in which they do not approve of yet are compelled to adhere to (Schauer 2015; Hart 1957; Hart 1961). Sadly, as Austin pointed out, the law is the command of the sovereign (Austin 1885; Austin 1995; Yankah 2008). The sovereign has to be obeyed but such sovereign does not obey any legal system or anyone (Austin 1832; Bentham 1776). The sovereign is the "unobeying obeyed". This sovereign refers to the Western countries. If human rights were introduced in the Universal Declaration of Human Rights and many other international instruments such as the International Covenant on Civil and Political Rights, International Covenant on Economic Social and Cultural Rights, and the African Charter on Human and People's Rights, why do the colonialists see no evil in their "theft" of African minerals yet through institutions such as the International Criminal Court they are eager to prosecute African leaders who infringe upon the rights of African people? This is the hypocrisy of Western civilisation.

Can unlawfully obtained property rights be enforceable?

Indigenous mines in Africa were taken over as if they were not previously owned and not anybody's property (*res nullius*). Negotiated political settlements downplayed the seriousness of the "theft" of property rights of indigenous Africans to their land and minerals. The net implication of this violent seizure of indigenous African people's land and minerals was irregularly "legitimised" by the colonists' brazen act of granting themselves ownerships rights to the land containing the valuable minerals. In this regard, the legitimacy of such ownership rights is subject to question. Can one acquire and maintain ownership rights to property that such legal subject has stolen? The law as it currently stands does not protect interests to property which has otherwise been unlawfully obtained (Mostert & Pope 2010).

Western jurisdictions such as the United Kingdom (England, Wales and Scotland), Northern Ireland, and the United States of America all concur that it is a criminal offence to possess property or a thing or any proceeds of any property or thing knowing that all or part of the property or thing or of the proceeds was obtained by or indirectly from a punishable offence. In so far as the African minerals are concerned, both those that stole the land from the indigenous Africans and the successors in title are equally liable for the same offence. Possession of stolen goods is an offence as much as the act of wantonly and forcibly taking another person's property without their consent is a criminal offence.

For one to possess a thing or goods, such party must have the intention to possess (*animus possidendi*) (Mostert & Pope 2010). The colonialists had the intention to unlawfully and forcibly possess indigenous Africans' mines and mineral resources. Such intention can be inferred from the end product of their malicious desire to usurp Africans of their mineral resources which culminated in the process of colonisation. For possession to be legitimate, it should have been acquired by consent. The use of force does not entail consent. The process of colonisation was a violent process akin to animism which regards Africans as lesser beings in the order of animals whose entitlements were subject to the whims and caprices of the colonialists.

Possession can still be acquired without consent and still be legal if one takes possession of what has never been owned before (Mostert & Pope 2010). However, this is not the case with African mines. As already indicated the colonialists took over the sites and mining technologies used by indigenous Africans. This in itself is a theft of property with regards to a perceptible and immovable thing (the mines), the movable things (the minerals) and intellectual property (mining technologies used by indigenous Africans). Possession without consent can also be acquired if the owner loses the property and does not intend to own it again. This construction would have applied if indigenous Africans had abandoned the mining sites for reasons best known to themselves. However, scholarly evidence suggests that the ownership of the mines was lost due to the forcible and violent colonisation process at the hands of the West (Botchway 1995). Transfer of property rights is another recognisable form of giving rise to possession. Taking a thing from another person without their consent also gives rise to possession. However, possession acquired without consent is a property right which the law protects. It gives rise to a right of possession which is enforceable against everyone except those with a better right to possession. As

254

such indigenous Africans had a better right to possession to their land which contained rich mineral resources. To legitimise the "theft" of African land and mineral resources, through laws such as the draconian Natives Land Act No. 27 of 1913 and the Group Areas Act No. 41 of 1950 were passed. Indigenous Africans were relegated to economically deprived land without the valuable minerals which had earlier been the source of their trade with Swahili Arabs, Portuguese, Indians and the Westerners using the "law". As such, the colonialists used a combination of violent force and law fare to strip the Africans of their rights to the use and enjoyment of the property and realise the fruits thereof.

The theft of the land and minerals resources and the subsequent '"legitimisation" of the flawed process through laws crafted in favour of the colonialists and prejudicial to the Africans implies that there is a legitimate case of unjust enrichment in favour of the Africans. Remedies for unjustified enrichment apply when a person (colonialists) other than the owner (indigenous Africans) receives benefit at the expense of the owner. The owner may institute an action (*condition sine causa*) against the one who has benefited, without cause, from the possession of his property, when the benefit ought to have accrued to him. To succeed in the claim of unjust enrichment, Africans must prove that:

1.   They have been impoverished by the deeds of the West, in the sense that what should have accrued to them has not;
2.   The West has been enriched at Africa's expense;
3.   The financial shift was without a legal basis (*sine causa*); and
4.   The West acted *mala fide* (in bad faith).

The prior outlined requirements for unjust enrichment can be easily satisfied in so far as African countries' loss to the West is concerned.

The post-colonial era: A change in the regulatory regime regarding acquisition of mineral rights

The regulatory regime informing the acquisition, use and disposal of mineral rights was changed from the common-law based principles of property law to a legal regime in which the State controls the mineral resources of a country (Mostert & Pope 2010). Under common law, a mineral right comprised entitlements to enter land, to prospect and to mine upon the land and to remove minerals, along with all ancillary rights which enabled the extraction of minerals. The post-colonial mineral-law dispensation thus introduced a system of State custodianship of minerals as the basis for regulatory control over minerals and mining. The only way to acquire new minerals and mining rights was to obtain them from the State. This was a significant departure from the common law position of the land owner being the owner of the minerals. As such colonialists who had illegally acquired mineral and mining rights now acquired their mineral rights from African governments. However, this change must be understood in the context of Roscoe Pound's preference of sociological jurisprudence as opposed to "mechanical jurisprudence". Pound believed that common law should develop slowly and should follow changes in society (Pound 1959). He was of the view that areas such as commercial law and property law benefitted from the slow development of common law as opposed to practical alteration. Pound distrusted statutes and believed that the radical change of the law could bring unexpected and undesirable results in the distant future. For Pound, the legal system worked best when the law followed society. Any attempt to make society follow the law was futile. The post-colonial era has thus been characterised by African countries such as Zimbabwe, South Africa and Namibia's resistance of colonial legal regimes which relegated indigenous Africans to impoverishment. They have considered State custodianship of mineral resources as the basis for redistributing wealth to the poor.

At the root of the new approach of State ownership of mineral and mining rights has been the United Nations (UN) General Assembly Resolution 1803 (XVII) on the "Permanent Sovereignty over Natural Resources" adopted on the 14th of December 1962. The resolution emanated from the UN General Assembly's focus on; 1) the promotion and financing of economic development in under-developed countries and, 2) in connection with the right of peoples to self-determination in the draft international covenants on human rights.

In 1952, the General Assembly requested the Commission on Human Rights to prepare recommendations concerning international respect for the right of peoples to self-determination. The Commission on Human Rights recommended the establishment of a commission to conduct a full survey of the right of peoples and nations to permanent sovereignty over their natural wealth and resources, having noted that this right formed a "basic constituent of the right to self-determination". In accordance with this recommendation, the General Assembly established the UN Commission on Permanent Sovereignty over Natural Resources on 12 December 1958 under Resolution 1314 (XIII). In 1961, the UN Commission on Permanent Sovereignty over Natural Resources adopted a draft resolution outlining principles concerning permanent sovereignty over natural resources. Following consideration of this draft Resolution by the Economic and Social Council and the Second Committee of the General Assembly, the General Assembly adopted Resolution 1803 (XVII).

Resolution 1803 (XVII) provides that States and international organisations shall strictly and conscientiously respect the sovereignty of peoples and nations over their natural wealth and resources in accordance with the Charter of the UN and the principles contained in the resolution. These principles are set out in eight articles concerning, inter alia, the exploration, development and disposition of natural resources, nationalisation and expropriation, foreign investment, the sharing of profits, amongst other issues.

The principle of permanent sovereignty over wealth and natural resources has now evolved into an important international legal principle governing the ownership, control and development and exploitation of the wealth and natural resources of states especially of developing countries (*De Sanchez v Banco Central de Nicaragua* 770 F.2d 1385 US Court of Appeals 5th Circuit September 19 1985 at paragraph 17 and *AMCO v Republic of Indonesia (Merits)* 1992 89 ILR 368 at paragraphs 405 and 466). The principle of permanent sovereignty over wealth and natural resources of states is the foundation principle of the economic self-determination of the newly emerging independent States in Africa, Asia and the Pacific. It emerged as a counterpoint to the exploitation of the wealth and natural resources of these States by companies based in the metropolitan colonial powers which exercised hegemony over these territories. It was a direct challenge or response to the economic/business privileges monopolised by the colonial companies in the various colonised territories under the regime of traditional concessions which were granted to them with extremely favourable terms such as the actual ownership of the natural resources of the territories in which they operated. These concessions were usually for long periods sometimes extending to periods of over 60 years.

Resolution 1803 (XVII) substantially elaborated on the principle of Permanent Sovereignty over Natural Resources to include the following matters:

i.   The right of host States to admit multinational corporations into their economies and grant them permits to develop their natural resources subject to the legislative/ regulatory framework of the host state;

ii.   The right of host States to revise inequitable concession agreements which were granted to multinational corporations during the colonial period usually by the metropolitan/ colonial power; Many of these concession agreements with respect to the natural resources of colonised territories were of long periods ranging from 30 to 60 years; under such agreements, the companies owned their minerals/petroleum which they mined and were free to dispose of them the way they deemed fit. These colonial concessions also covered vast tracts of territory over which they exercised unrestricted jurisdiction; the concessionaires paid minimal tax to the colonial government which could have used such tax revenue for the infrastructural development of the colony.

Resolution 1803 also stated the right of host States to expropriate/nationalise their mineral resources which were under foreign control subject to the payment of "appropriate" compensation. The standard of "appropriate" compensation, for the first time, stated a standard of compensation different from the traditional standard formulated by the United States Secretary of State, Mr Cordhell Hull in 1938 which required that the compensation payable should be prompt, adequate and effective. The question to be raised though is; can one who unlawfully acquires ownership over mineral and mining rights claim for compensation for the loss of something that they were not entitled to in the first place? It is clear that asking African countries to compensate parties that unjustly exploited their mineral resources to the detriment of African people is an attempt to realise "order out of chaos" a feature of the New World Order Agenda. How can justice be realised through economic violence? Why should the oppressed compensate the oppressor? Africa has been plundered by the West through actual and structural violence. It is an insult to every African to have the African governments pay for expropriation. Even if there is an ill-advised intention to pay foreign companies for expropriation, where would the African governments get the money from when actual and structural violence impoverished these countries and their inhabitants? Colonisation, economic adjustment programmes and State capture have betrayed legitimate attempts for African countries to industrialise. There is no way the poor African countries can compensate the Western companies hence Western control of the mining sector is likely to perpetuate.

The principle of Permanent Sovereignty over Natural Resources was further elaborated upon and incorporated into the UN General Assembly document entitled the Charter of Economic Rights and Duties of States in 1974. The Charter was adopted by a large majority of the member states of the UN. Other important international instruments into which the principle has been incorporated include the International Covenant on Economic, Social and Cultural Rights (ICESCR). Article 1 of the ICESCR provides that:

All peoples may, for their own ends, dispose of their natural wealth and resources without prejudice to any obligations arising out of international economic co-operation, based upon the principle of mutual benefit, and international law. In no case may a people be deprived of its own means of subsistence.

The ICESCR provisions are stated verbatim in Article 1 (2) of the International Covenant on Civil and Political Rights. Regionally, the principle has also been incorporated into the African Charter on Human and Peoples Rights (ACHPR), which is the foremost African human rights instrument. Article 21 of the ACHPR provides as follows:

1.   All peoples shall freely dispose of their wealth and natural resources. This right shall be exercised in the exclusive interest of the people. In no case shall a people be deprived of it.

2.   In case of spoliation the dispossessed people shall have the right to the lawful recovery of its property as well as to an adequate compensation.

3.   The free-disposal of wealth and natural resources shall be exercised without prejudice to the obligation of promoting international economic cooperation based on mutual respect, equitable exchange and the principles of international law.

4.   State parties to the present Charter shall individually and collectively exercise the right to free disposal of their wealth and natural resources with a view to strengthening African unity and solidarity.

5.   State parties to the present Charter shall undertake to eliminate all forms of foreign exploitation particularly that practiced by international monopolies so as to enable their peoples to fully benefit from the advantages derived from their natural resources."

The SADC Protocol on mining has also placed significance on the need for governments to ensure that the exploration and exploitation of mineral resources benefits indigenous Africans in their respective communities.

In view of the above stated Zimbabwe, South Africa and Namibia have embarked on indigenisation programmes aimed at ensuring that indigenous people who were previously and are still excluded from the economic mainstream start benefiting from the exploitation of their mineral resources, currently monopolised by foreign owned companies.

Zimbabwe

Zimbabwe has a Mines and Minerals Act [Chapter 21:05]. There are a number of regulations accompanying the Act. However, it is clear from the wording of the Act that the mineral resources in Zimbabwe are vested in the President. This provision is arguably consistent with the permanent sovereignty of natural resources if it is assumed that the President exercises the rights of ownership of the mineral resources on behalf of the State. However, regardless of the existence of this piece of legislation, the government of Zimbabwe realised that more had to be done to ensure that the mineral resources of the State benefit the previously disadvantaged Zimbabweans (Warikandwa & Osode 2017). The Zimbabwean Indigenisation and Economic Empowerment Act (IEEA) [Chapter 14:33] of 2007 was thus passed into law to ensure that foreign companies contribute to the development of the country and the communities in which they extracted mineral resources from. Section 2(1)(b) of the IEEA provides that:

> ...'indigenous Zimbabwean' means any person who, before the 18th April, 1980, was disadvantaged by unfair discrimination on the grounds of his or her race, and any descendant of such person, and includes any company, association, syndicate or partnership of which indigenous Zimbabweans form the majority of the members or hold the controlling interest.

Section 2(1)(b) of the IEEA must be read together with section 14 and section 20(1)(c) of the Zimbabwean Constitution Act 20 of 2013. However, since the passing into law of the IEEA, Zimbabwe's economy has plummeted to an all-time low leading to the abandonment of the country's currency, the Zimbabwean dollar and its replacement with the United States dollar. The country's economic demise has been attributed to a combination of factors which include exploitation of the country's natural resources by Western and Asian companies with little or no revenue being registered (Warikandwa & Osode 2016). Most of the returns from the country's vibrant diamond mining sector have mysteriously disappeared. A case in point is the disappearance of 15 billion United

States dollars worth of revenue which had been obtained from the Marange diamond fields mainly run by the Chinese companies. This implies that mal-governance emanating from State capture is also a chronic challenge facing the exploiting of mineral resources in Africa. The indigenisation laws have also been drafted in a manner which benefits the African elites and not the intended beneficiaries who in this case are the previously disadvantaged Zimbabweans. Such an approach provides legitimate basis for the adoption of a Pan-African legislative regulatory framework for the mining sector.

South Africa

South Africa has a raft of pieces of legislation which regulate the country's mining sector. Key amongst these instruments is the Minerals and Petroleum Resources Development Act, No. 28 of 2002. The Act seeks to promote mineral development including urban renewal, rural development and black economic empowerment. Section 29 of the Act requires that holders of mining rights must report their level of compliance with the Broad-Based Socio-Economic Empowerment Charter for the South African Mining Industry as contemplated in section 28(2)(c). However, as the case was with Zimbabwe, the pace of economic empowerment of previously disadvantaged people through the mining laws of South Africa has been too slow. Only the well-connected African elites have benefited from the black economic empowerment programme. As such, South Africa has come up with a raft of pieces of legislation to strengthen their resolve to promote interests of indigenous people. These include the Broad-Based Black Economic Empowerment Act (B-BBEEA) 53 of 2003, the 2013 Black Economic Empowerment Amendment Act which regulates business fronting, the use of scorecards which offer incentives to companies which increase black representation in the managerial levels of companies, the Promotion and Protection of Investment Act 22 of 2015, and the Preferential Procurement Policy Framework Act No. 97 of 2000 which are all pro-indigenisation.

Section 1 of the B-BBEEA 53 of 2003 provides that: "'black people' is a generic term which means African, Coloureds and Indians". In the same section of the B-BBEEA, it further provides

262

that "broad-based economic empowerment" means the economic empowerment of all black people including women, workers, youth, people with disabilities and people living in rural areas through diverse but integrated socio-economic strategies..."

South Africa also has in place the King Reports on Corporate Governance and Corporate Social Responsibility. The King reports contain and institutionalise South Africa's celebrated corporate governance rules. Though not equivalent to official legal documents the King reports are regarded as fundamental good corporate governance guidelines. Their adoption has been greatly welcomed in South Africa's business domain. The key objectives of the King Reports are briefly outlined as follows:

1.   King I Report: In 1994, the King Committee on corporate governance issued the first report, King I, aimed at promoting corporate governance and adequate standards for the board of directors of listed companies, financial institutions and some public enterprises. While encouraging good governance practices, the report also emphasized the need for corporations to be socially responsible in the areas and communities in which they operate.

2.   King II Report: In 2002, the King II report on corporate governance was published. More or less at the same time, the Johannesburg Stock Exchange requested listed companies to comply with the King Report or otherwise justify why they were not adhering to the norm. The King II Report clearly established and explained the seven good corporate governance elements that any corporation adopting the report should pay attention to: discipline, transparency, fairness, social responsibility, independence, accountability and responsibility.

3.   King III Report: The third Report on corporate governance in South Africa (King III) became necessary because of the anticipated South African Companies Act No. 71 of 2008 and changes in international governance trends. The King III Report became effective in March 2010. As compared to the previous versions (King I and King II), the King III report focuses on sustainability and risk issues, while continuing to highlight the importance for companies to respond to all stakeholders. The topics covered in the King III report

are: ethical leadership and corporate citizenship, boards and directors, audit committees, the governance of risk, the governance of information technology, compliance with laws, rules, codes and standards, internal audit, governing stakeholder relationships and integrated reporting and disclosure. The companies must report annually on how they:

i.   ... both positively and negatively affected the economic life of the community in which they operated during the year under review; and

ii.   ... Intend to enhance those positive aspects and eradicate or ameliorate the negative aspects on the economic life of the community in which they will operate in the year ahead.

All the policies and laws relating to indigenisation in the three countries referred to have adopted a "comply or else approach".

However, pessimists refer to the implementation of the Sarbanes-Oxley Act of 2002 (SOX) ([Pub.L. 107-204, 116 Statute 745] enacted on 30 July 2002) as a warning to African countries not to dare follow the plausible indigenisation approach. Through the Sarbanes-Oxley Act, the United States of America used the "comply or else" statutory regime to corporate governance a policy approach which produced negative effects on business. Professor Ribstein of Illinois Law School said at the time:

It is unlikely that hasty, crash-induced regulation like SOX can be far sighted enough to protect against future problems, particularly in light of the debatable efficiency of SOX's response to current market problems. Even the best regulators might err and enact regulation that is so strong that it stifles innovation and entrepreneurial activity. And once set in motion, regulation is almost impossible to eliminate...

However, it must be observed that the determined efforts by the African countries to adopt their Pan-Africanist approach to economic development will not be easy. An example of the problems posed by the BEE driven policies and legislation is that in 2014 South Africa's Foreign Direct Investment (FDI) declined and has largely remained in the negative. The volatile global economic patterns have been blamed for this development but evidence points to the problem lying in external investment flows exceeding internal investment flows by a significant amount estimated at R13 billion.

This pattern has been informed by the aggressive indigenisation policies which have reportedly threatened investor security. The negative FDI trends continued into 2015, with first quarter figures of the year showing that, "inward directed FDI declined by R22 billion due to foreign investors withdrawing capital injection from South African markets." Further, South Africa's credit rating was downgraded by Moody's to a level just one rank above the "junk economy" status. The 2015 AT Kearney Foreign Direct Investment Confidence Index which lists the world's 25 most business friendly destinations also saw South Africa dropping out of the group of the world's 25 most attractive investment destinations. The latest developments must be viewed from the perspective that in 2012, South Africa was ranked 11th, fell to 15th in 2013 and rose to 13th in 2014.

As has been the case with Zimbabwe, South Africa has faced challenges with the countries' African elites benefiting at the expense of the previously disadvantaged South Africans. State capture has also been a chronic challenge with the controversial Gupta Gate scandal being a case in point. Mal-governance by President Jacob Zuma's African National congress led government has been another Achilles heel to the indigenisation programme in South Africa.

To their credit, South Africa is still working on pieces of legislation to ensure that the mining sector benefits all South Africans. As at the time of drafting this book chapter, South Africa had tabled before parliament the African Exploration Mining and Finance Corporation Draft Bill of 2015. The Bill seeks to provide for the establishment of the African Exploration Mining and Finance Corporation as a State owned mining company to be known as the African Exploration Mining and Finance Corporation SOC Limited. The approach here is consistent with that of the permanent sovereignty of natural resources. The valiant efforts being made by South Africa in regulating its mining sector, in the best interests of ordinary South Africans, could inform the drafting of the Pan-African mining laws as envisaged in this work.

Namibia

The Namibia Minerals Policy of 2002 recognises the importance of the mining industry to the socio-economic development of Namibia. Further, Article 23 of the Namibian Constitution prohibits discrimination, except under an Act of parliament expressly providing for the advancement of persons who have been socially, economically or educationally disadvantaged by past discriminatory laws. In December 2010, the Namibian Chamber of Mines officially presented its proposal on empowerment in the form of a draft "Mining Charter for Sustainable Broad Based Transformation" to the Prime Minister and the Minister of Mines and Energy. This Charter endeavours to address the following issues:

i.   Ownership: (all mining, development and exploration companies would have to make a minimum of 5% and a maximum of 25% equity available exclusively to historically disadvantaged Namibian investors by the year 2015);

ii.   Education and skills: (mining companies to invest a percentage of their annual payrolls in developing skills of historically disadvantaged employees – from 3% in the year 2011 to 5% in the year 2015); and

iii.   Affirmative Action: (historically disadvantaged Namibians to be represented at all levels of management over 10 years, from 20 percent in the year 2012 to 60 percent in the year 2020.

The Cabinet of the Republic of Namibia, towards the end of the year 2011, adopted the New Equitable Economic Framework (NEEEF). Legislation is envisaged to be implemented as per NEEEF. The NEEEF does not have the force of law but is a policy framework. It will be based on voluntary business practice but the Government of Namibia would use all the legitimate market mechanisms at its disposal, in the form of procurement programmes and licensing regimes, to promote transformation and empowerment.

The objectives of this policy are to be achieved through five empowerment pillars. In order to be recognised as compliant with

NEEEF, a business would have to achieve 50 of a total of 100 points made up of 20 points per empowerment pillar. A minimum of 10 points on each of the three pillars of ownership, management control, and employment equity, and human resources and skills development would be mandatory. The five pillars are:

i.   Ownership;
ii.   Management control and employment equity;
iii.   Human resources and skills development;
iv.   Entrepreneurship development; and
v.   Community investment.

The NEEEF mirrors South Africa's Preferential Procurement Policy Framework Act (PPPFA) 97 of 2000 which prohibits discrimination on the basis of race, gender amongst other issues in awarding tenders. There were three conclusions drawn at the time the NEEEF was adopted. These are:

1.   NEEEF is a policy and no more. There are some companies that produce NEEEF scorecards because they feel it is a competitive advantage. But without some pressure from the government nothing is going to happen.

2.   A transformation policy that must apply to the whole economy needs something like preferential procurement to make it work. NEEEF assumes that government procurement will force companies to comply but all that will happen under these circumstances is that a handful of compliant companies will become agents for those that do not. And it will only be those few that do comply.

3.   There is no comprehensive definition of a Previously Disadvantaged Namibian yet (Janisch 2014).

In 2016, Namibia tabled before parliament the New Equitable Economic Empowerment Bill (NEEEB). Article 23(2) of this Bill provides that the Namibian parliament should directly and indirectly enact legislation providing for the advancement of socially, economically or educationally disadvantaged Namibians. As part of this initiative, foreign companies are to cede 25% of their equity share ownership to local Namibians. Sectors which have to comply with this requirement include the mining sector. Namibia also passed the Namibia Invest Protection Act in 2016 to achieve similar objectives of increasing the participation of previously disadvantaged Namibians into the economic mainstream. This reasoning appears to be premised on the values set in the African Charter on Human and People's Rights, which advance a need to recognise the right to the free disposition of wealth and natural resources, in the best interests of indigenous people (Warikandwa & Ndatega 2016). Sadly, like Zimbabwe and South Africa, the moment Namibia tabled the NEEEB for discussion before parliament, FITCH, an international economic outlook rating agency gave a negative economic outlook to Namibia. It is difficult in this case to ignore the West's hand in this negative rating.

On the whole, it is not surprising to realise that as justification for indigenisation in Zimbabwe, South Africa and Namibia there is an ideology that land and mineral resources are there to solely benefit indigenous people and not multinational corporations. A distributive justice agenda is being pursued by African countries albeit with significant difficulties as the West are not ready to relinquish the benefits accruing to them from Africa's minerals.

Characteristics of mining in post-colonial Africa

Mining activities are widely expected to generate revenue, provide employment opportunities to Africans and translate to the development of the communities in which mining takes place. However, as the mining practices of Lonmin in Marikana, South Africa and the Chinese companies in most African countries have suggested, the mining sector brings sadness to many an African (Warikandwa & Osode 2016; Warikandwa 2013). Some potential drawbacks of the mining industry are as follows:

The occurrence of the resource curse

The mining industry potentially has a number of drawbacks which mineral rich countries must be alerted to. The "resource curse" refers to the situation where the discovery of minerals or petroleum resources by a country usually a developing country results in a marked or substantial economic dependency on only or mainly the proceeds of that particular resource to the total neglect of all other industries.

An example of this phenomenon in Africa is the Federal Republic of Nigeria where the discovery and development of the petroleum industry in the 1960s-1970s has resulted in the dramatic shift away from other economically productive activities such as agriculture. Before the discovery of petroleum, the country was well known as a world exporter of groundnuts from Northern Nigeria ("the Kano pyramids"), cocoa from Western Nigeria and palm oil from Eastern Nigeria. For over three decades, all these agricultural industries have become inactive as the focus has shifted to petroleum.

An important aspect of the resource curse is that the proceeds of the natural resources are not utilised to develop other alternative sources of national income to safeguard the country against the future when these resources cease to exist. In Africa other potential victims of the resource curse are Angola, Gabon and Equatorial Guinea. Again foreign investors exploit the mineral resources and externalise their gains hence the "resource curse" perpetuates.

Corruption

Another potential drawback is the phenomenon of corruption which may become endemic in an African country endowed with mineral resources. Most foreign companies aiming to avoid the indigenisation laws have bribed corrupt African elites to circumvent laws aimed at advancing the best interests of previously disadvantaged Africans (Warikandwa & Osode 2017). Examples of countries in which there is chronic corruption in the mining sector include The Federal Republic of Nigeria, Angola, Cameroon, South Africa, Zimbabwe and Equatorial Guinea. In these countries, there is no transparency or accountability of the national income receipts from the mineral resources of the country and also the expenditure patterns of such proceeds. Corruption has been informed by practices of State capture. This practice entails that the State in Africa does not act in the best interests of the ordinary African citizens but holds African wealth on behalf of foreign super powers in exchange for maintaining power (Skalr 1979). This thus implies that the principle of State ownership of mineral resources is compromised as the benefits do not accrue to the masses but to corrupt African elites and their western or Asian handlers.

Threat of environmental degradation

A Globally well-known case is the Niger Delta region of the Federal Republic of Nigeria where the discovery and development of petroleum and gas has resulted in the pollution and destruction of the environment of the oil producing communities. Their previously fertile and productive lands have become unproductive due to oil spills arising from oil producing activities and oil pipe bursts. It is interesting to note that the companies mining for oil in Nigeria are Western companies such as Shell. The fishing industry has ground to a halt due to the pollution of the rivers and creeks of the area and also the sea. The environment has been polluted by the unregulated flaring of associated gas.

Unemployment especially among the youth and social unrest

Again, the Niger Delta region of Nigeria is a perfect example of this phenomenon. The economic neglect of this part of the country, the environmental degradation have all combined to spawn social unrest over the years leading to violent attacks on the multinational oil companies and their workers resulting sometimes in the taking of hostages and the disruption of oil production and its export.

Recommendations

The mining industry has potential socio-economic benefits that can accrue to African countries and their previously disadvantaged citizens. It is a source of national revenue through the provision of various forms of taxation such as royalties, company tax, and income tax. It is also a source of employment for African citizens. In principle, the mining sector is a tool for realising economic and human capital development for Africa. Lessons from the precolonial states' mining practices which were regulated by customary law indicate that the mining industry was regulated in the best interests of indigenous people. The customary law rules regulating mining activities recognised Ubuntu as a central moral value to a Pan-Africanist mining approach in Africa. Emphasis was placed on the benefits that the mined resources had on the communities in which they were extracted and not just profiteering. Colonisation and post-colonial neoliberal economic policies and laws derailed the development of the people centred customary law regulating mining in Africa. The end result is that African communities have been impoverished yet mining companies continue to make obscene profits at the expense of indigenes' welfare and developmental interests. To that end, a Pan-African oriented legal framework must be developed to replace the capitalist laws which are not concerned with the developmental interests of Africans. The following is thus recommended:

1.   So much emphasis has been placed on the role that foreign direct investment plays in sustaining African economies. However, it is evident as indicated in the historical analysis of mining practices regulation in Africa as conducted in this book chapter that foreign companies are part of Africa's problem as they are a Western economic and political expansionist agenda. If Africa has to develop, it has to grow its infant industries a development which might require a closed markets approach. China has adopted a closed markets approach and recently adopted an open market approach not as a consumer but producer and foreign investor. This approach has seen China's economy grow significantly as well as realising a marked improvement in human capital investment and the welfare of its people. To that end, a people centred harmonised Pan-African mining regulatory framework must be adopted for Africa. Uniformity in the application of the envisaged Pan-African mining regulations will deter foreign investors from advancing the "beggar thy neighbour" construction as African countries will have uniform rules on mining. Investors will therefore not have the latitude to force the lowering of regulatory standards in selected jurisdictions so as to get business opportunities.

As opposed to the pre-colonial mining regulatory regime which was uniform in most African States, the divide and rule element ushered in by colonisation has led to a differential application of standards under the auspices of individual African countries' "sovereignty". This so called concept of sovereignty has led to African States divorcing from each other economically and undermining the spirit of Ubuntu, to their detriment. At the end, the colonisers have benefited from divided African countries' African resources at the expense of the needy Africans.

Therefore, the Pan-Africanist regulatory framework envisaged must focus on maximising the benefits obtained by Africans from the mining industry. For the purposes of this book chapter, such a Pan-African regulatory framework should be modelled along what, for the purposes of this work, shall be called the Sankara Pan-Africanism. Thomas Sankara was a former Burkina Faso president who lived a modest life on a salary of 400 United States dollars. He increased productivity in so far as local products and a development which subsequently resulted in export growth. From this approach Sankara was able to settle all the debts owed by the country to the international lending institutions (the IMF/World Bank). Such realisation of economic autonomy is what most African countries should aspire for. Africans should resist elitist Pan-Africanism driven by African leaders who think everyone is indebted to them simply because they led their countries to independence. As such they create a circle of bootlickers and promote the politics of patronage. This elitist group of an emerging class of African bourgeoisie has long lost touch with the legitimate concerns of the majority of Africans most of whom are poor. They brazenly regard allegiance to corrupt ruling organisations as the alpha and omega of decent citizenry. This cabal of sybarites and their sycophants is not only lethally dangerous to self but poses significant socio-economic harm to ordinary Africans. The group considers itself as a footstool to the "economic emancipation" of previously and still disadvantaged Africans. It considers itself indispensable and cuts across as a group of overfed as well as gluttonous individuals who are exceedingly corrupt. Shockingly, this dangerous group erroneously brands itself as the legitimate symbol of Pan-Africanism. It maintains dangerous liaisons with former colonial masters and new African imperialists such as China and will do anything to remain in power (Warikandwa & Osode 2016; Warikandwa *et al* 2017). They carelessly flaunt their ill-gotten wealth in the eyes of the grieving poor Africans. Such is not Pan-Africanism as it is Ubuntu bankrupt.

As such, indigenisation laws passed under the leadership of these false Pan-Africanists mean no more than instruments to reward their close friends as a means of remaining in power (Warikandwa & Osode 2017). In most instances such leaders hold power on behalf of their foreign handlers hence the concept of state capture. Such type of cronyism perpetuates capitalism and/neoliberalist business practices which have greatly harmed the African continent. As such, an Ubuntu driven Sankaraist type of Pan-Africanism mining regulation is required as a basis of serving the best interests of the ordinary previously disadvantaged and still disadvantaged Africans. Distributive justice will be realised in this manner. Such Pan-African mining legislation must incorporate the following:

a) A mandatory Corporate Social Responsibility clause;

b) A mandatory value addition clause on all minerals mined in Africa. No raw materials must be externalised before value is added. Only finished mining products must be traded in;

c) A mandatory clause on rehabilitation of mines;

d) A mandatory clause on human capital investment through skills transfer; and

e) A mandatory employee share ownership clause.

The rationale of the above outlined proposals is that there can be no true empowerment without ownership of the means of production. The Western imposed templates on mining regulation must be resisted as far as is possible. The difference between wealth and poverty lies in value addition. If the neoliberal economic order is not challenged, poverty will be exacerbated in Africa. The neoliberal economic order template does not have distributive justice as a fundamental objective (Warikandwa & Osode 2014; Warikandwa 2013).

2. The Pan-African mining regulatory framework must be preceded by the drafting of a Pan-African Mining Code. The code

273

which should be drafted along the lines of the Pan-African Investment Code must oblige foreign investors to contribute significantly to the development of African countries from which they exploit natural resources. African mineral resources have been exploited to generate the necessary capital needed to realise the industrialisation of the West and as well as sustaining it in the contemporary globalised world. Interestingly, the global agenda promotes the equal sharing of resources and free market policies. Such equal sharing of resources is driven by a few elites who own the world's wealth at the expense of the poor. This has become the feature of the new world order in which order is realised in a chaotic environment. Mother Africa should resist this Hegelian approach and adopt policies which serve the best interests of her people.

Conclusion

African countries are resource rich yet the continent is ravished with poverty. Most African countries are characterised by the interference of the West and Asia in their affairs all in the name of African mineral resources. Laws have been formulated in the colonial and post-colonial era to perpetuate the plunder of African resources by Western investors "for a song". Colonial common law property regulations were formulated after the forcible grabbing of African land. At the time of colonisation, mineral rights were linked to property ownership. The settler owners of the forcibly taken African land became the owners of the minerals. In the post-colonial era, the regulatory regime had to be changed. The state, and not the land owners, became the property owners. This change in regulation was particularly interesting as most African States never represent the best interests of their people but those of their foreign handlers. With a lot of corruption in the mineral resource sectors of Africa, state capture has become common. The foreign investors thus maintain their stranglehold on African resources through their African puppets who in most instances are senior government officials, including heads of state. For this reason this book chapter has made a case for the need to draft harmonised Pan-African mining laws which should aim at realising development for Africa and human capital development. Lessons can be drawn from the African customary rules used to regulate the mining sector in the pre-colonial era. The customary laws were people centred and focused on preserving the environment. Africans should realise that they have their fate in their hands and should invest wisely in the mineral resources which are non-renewable. Wise investments and laws should be adopted in the best interests of the future generations. A Pan-African regulatory framework for the mining sector is thus a plausible starting point.

Bibliography

Achraya, A., (1998). "Beyond Anarchy? Third World Instability and International Order after the Cold war" in Stephanie G. Neuman (ed) *International Relations and International order after the Cold War*, St. Amrtin's Press, pp. 159-211.

African Union (2009). "Africa Mining Vision" February 2009 available at http://www.africaminingvision.org/amv_resources/AMV/Africa_Mining_Vision_English.pdf (accessed 17 March 2017).

Allott, A. N., (1970). *New Essays in African Law*, (Butterworths, London), pp 9-13 and 145-181.

Austin, J., (1885). *Lectures on Jurisprudence*. Ed. R. Campbell. John Murray: London (1st ed. 1832).

Ayittey, G. B. N., (2011). "Indigenous African Free-Market Liberalism" August 24, 2011 available at https://fee.org/articles/indigenous-african-free-market-liberalism/ (accessed 17 March 2017).

Badenhorst, P. J., (2011). "Conflict Resolution between Owners of Land and Holders of Rights to Minerals: A Lopsided Triangle?" *Journal of South African Law* volume 30, pp. 328.

Badenhorst, P. J., (2006). "Mineral Law and the Doctrine of Rights: A Microscope of Magnification" *OBITER*, pp 539-553.

Badenhorst, P. J., (2010). "Right of Access to Land for Mining Purposes: on Terra Firma at Last?" *THRHR*, pp 318-328.

Blanstein, A. and Flanz, G., (eds), (1993). *Constitutions of the Countries of the World A series of updated texts, constitutional chronologies and Annotated Bibliographies*, Oceana publications, New York.

Botchway, F. N. N., (1995). "Pre-colonial Methods of Gold Mining and Environmental Protection in Ghana," *Journal of Energy and Natural Resources Law* volume 13, pp. 299-311.

Brun-Otto, B., (1976). *The Politics and Sociology of African Legal Development*, Alfred Metzner Verlag GmbH, Frankfurt am Maine, pp 91-194.

Chitiyo, T. K., (2000). "Land violence and compensation" *Track Two: Constructive Approaches to Community and Political Conflict*, volume 9(1) available at http://journals.co.za/docserver/fulltext/track2/9/1/track2_v9_n1_a1.pdf?expires=1489745232&id=id&accname=guest&checksum=14B61C4D62CAEF62FBF49FD9392C1B58 (accessed 17 March 2017).

Chrisman, L., (2004). "Du Bois in Transnational Perspective: The Loud Silencing of Black South Africa," *Current Writing*. Volume 16, pp 18-30.

Collins, P., (2006). "The Racial Threat," *The British Journal of Sociology*, volume 57(2), pp 206-208.

Connell, L., (2006). "Business as usual: The Image of the Corporation in the Cultures of Globalisation" in Stan Smith (ed) *Globalisation and its Discontents* Cambridge: D.S. Brewer.

Cooper, F., (2005). *Colonisation in Question: Theory, Knowledge, History*, University of California Press: Berkeley, Los Angeles and London.

Cornell, D., (2014). *Law and Revolution in South Africa: Ubuntu, Dignity, and the struggle for Constitutional Transformation*, New York: Fordham University Press 2014.

Davis, GA and Tilton, JE (2002). "Should Developing Countries Renounce Mining? A Perspective on the Debate" Available: http://citeseerx.ist.psu.edu/viewdoc/versions?doi=10.1.1.468.8759 Executive Summary (accessed 17 March 2017).

Downey, L., Bonds, E., and Clark, K., (2010). "Natural Resource Extraction, Armed Violence, and Environmental Degradation" *PMC* volume 23(4), pp 417-445.

Draft Pan-African Investment Code, 26 March 2016, AU/STC/FMEPI/EXP/18 (II).

Dworkin, R., (1965). "The elusive morality of law" *Vanderbilt Law Review* volume 10, pp. 631-639.

Eggert, R. G., (2002). Mining and Economic Sustainability: National Economies and Local Communities. Project of the International Institute for Environment and Development (IIED). Division of Economics and Business, Colorado School of Mines, US.

Fraser, A. and Larmer, M., (ed) (2010). *Zambia, Mining, and Neoliberalism: Boom and bust on the globalised copperbelt* Palgrave Macmillan: New York, pp. 1-85.

Garrard, T., (1980). *Akan Weights and the Gold Trade*, Longman Group Ltd: London, p 12.

Goucher, C., LeGuin, C., and Walton, L., (1998). *In the Balance: Themes in Global History*, Boston: McGraw-Hill, chapter 17.

Hammel, A., White, C., Pfeiffer S and Miller, D., (2000). "Pre-colonial mining in Southern Africa" *The Journal of The South African Institute of Mining and Metallurgy* volume 100(1) pp. 49-56.

Haque, S. M., (1999). "The Fate of Sustainable Development under Neo-liberal regimes in developing countries" *International Political Science Review* volume 20(2), pp 197-218.

Hart, H. L. A., (1957). "Positivism and the Separation of Law and Morals", *Harvard Law Review* volume 71, pp 593-629.

Hart, H. L. A., (1961). *The Concept of Law* Oxford University Press: Oxford.

Hart, H. L. A., (1994). *The Concept of Law*, Oxford Clarendon Press: New York, pp 3-102.

J. Austin., (1995). *The Province of Jurisprudence* Determined. Ed. W. Rumble. Cambridge University Press: Cambridge, originally Published in 1832.

Janisch, P., (2014). "New Equitable Economic Empowerment Framework (NEEEF)" May 20, 2014 available at http://bbbee.typepad.com/paul_janisch/new-equitable-economic-empowerment-framework-neeef/ (17 March 2017).

Kah, G. H., (1992). *En Route to Global Occupation,* Huntington House Publishers, pp. 8-23.

Kahn, M., (2013). "Natural Resources, nationalisation, and nationalisation" *Journal of the Southern African Institute of Mining and Metallurgy*, volume 113(1), pp 3-9.

Koku, J. E. and Sigh, N., (2005). "Mining Policy, Water Conflicts and Corporate Social Responsibility in Ghana: Perspectives from the Wassa West District" Paper presented at the 4th International Water History Association Conference: "Water and Civilisation", Paris, France, 1-4 December 2005.

Li, T. M., (2010). "Indigeneity, Capitalism, and the Management of Dispossession" *Current Anthropology,* volume 51(3) pp 385-414.

M'buyinga, E., (1965). *Pan Africanism or Neo-Colonialism? The Bankruptcy of the O.A.U* Zed Press: Cameroon.

Manoukian, M., (1950). *Akan and Ga-Adangme Peoples, International African Institute, London,* p 35-46 and 81-84.

Marshall, A., (2012). "The Global Political Awakening and the New World Order" available at http://projectavalon.net/forum4/showthread.php?42859-The-Global-Political-Awakening-and-the-New-World-Order (accessed 15 March 2017).

Mayundo, K. J. (2016). "Economic Growth, Natural Mineral Resources and Education in Developing countries" Applied Economic Theses available at http://digitalcommons.buffalostate.edu/economics_theses/17 (17 March 2017).

McCandless, E. and Karbo, T., (2011). *Peace, Conflict, and Development in Africa: A Reader*, University of Peace, Switzerland, pp. 51-100.

Mekonnen, A., (2015). *The West and China: Civilization without Justice,* Wipf & Stock Publishers: Eugene, Oregon, pp 37-358.

Mhango, N. N. (2016). *Africa's Best & Worst Presidents: How Neocolonisation & Imperialism Maintained Venal Rules in Africa.* Langaa Research & Publishing Common Initiative Group: Mankon, Bamenda, p 160.

Mlambo, A. S. and Pangeti, E. (2001). "Globalisation, Structural Adjustment and the Social Dimensions Dilemma in Zimbabwe, 1990-1999", in Taye Assefa *et al* (eds.), Globalisation, Democracy and Development in Africa: Challenges and Prospects, Addis Ababa: OSSREA, pp. 163-178.

Mlambo, A. S., (1997). *The Economic Structural Adjustment Programme: The case of Zimbabwe, 1990-1995* University of Zimbabwe Publications.

Monbiot, G. (2016). *How did we get into this mess?: Politics, Equality, Nature* Verso: London.

Morris, M. and Fessehaie, J., (2014). "The industrialisation challenge for Africa: Towards a commodities based industrialisation path" *Journal of African Trade* volume 1(1), pp. 25-36.

Mostert, H. and Pope, A. (2010). *The Principles of Property Law in South Africa*, Oxford University Press: Cape Town.

Moyo, S., (1995). *The Land Question in Zimbabwe*, SAPES Books: Harare, Zimbabwe.

Murombo, T., (2010). "Regulating Mining in South Africa and Zimbabwe: Communities, the Environment and Perpetual Exploitation" *Law, Environment and Development*, volume 9(1), pp 31-49.

Nhemachena, A., (2017). *Relationality and Resilience in a not so Relational World? Knowledge, Chivanhu and (De-) Coloniality in 21st Century Conflict-Torn Zimbabwe*, Langaa Research & Publishing Common Initiative Group: Mankon, Bamenda.

Ofori-Boateng, J. (1977). "Ghana's water laws", *In 9 Review of Ghana Law*, pp 11-14.

Ollennu, N. A. (1985). *Ollennu's Principles of Customary Land Law*, University Press: Birmingham, pp 4-86.

Owusu-Nimoh, M., (1977). *Rivers in Ghana*, Ghana Publishing Corp, Accra, pp 8, 52-53.

Pound, R (1959), *Jurisprudence*, West Publishing: St Paul Minnesota.

Pricewaterhouse Coopers (2012). "Corporate income taxes, mining royalties and other mining taxes: A summary of rates and rules in selected countries" available at https://www.pwc.com/gx/en/energy-utilities-mining/publications/pdf/pwc-gx-miining-taxes-and-royalties.pdf (accessed 17 March 2017).

Pritchard, E. and Fortes, M., (eds), (1940). *African Political Systems,* Oxford University Press, London, pp 1-21.

Raz, J. (1985). "Authority, Law and Morality" *The Monist* volume 68(3), pp.295-324.

Richardson, B., (1993). "Environmental Management in Uganda: The Importance of Property Law and Local Government in Wetlands Conservation," *Journal of African Law*, 1993 volume 37 No 2), p 114.

Rodney, W., (1972). *How Europe Underdeveloped Africa*, Bogle L'Ouverture Publications: Britain, pp 31-203.

Samuel, C., (2013). "The Dark Side of Foreign Direct Investment: A South African Perspective" Economic Diplomacy Programme Occasional Paper No 167, December 2013 pp. 5-19.

Sarbah, M., (1966). *Fanti Customary Law*, Frank and Cass: London, pp 72-75.

Schauer, F., (2015). *The Force of Law*, Harvard University Press: Cambridge, MA.

Shivji, IG (2006), "Pan-Africanism or Imperialism? Unity and struggle towards a New Democratic Africa" *African Sociological Review* volume 10(1), pp. 208-220.

Sklar, R. L., (1979). "The Nature of Class Domination in Africa" *Journal of Modern African Studies,* volume 17(4), pp 531-552.

Szczepanski, M., (2012). "Mining in the EU: Regulation and the way forward" Library Briefing, Library of the European Parliament, 19 December 2012, pp 1-6.

Warikandwa, T. V. (2013). "Linking Trade to Core Labour Standards to Limit Labour Unrest: A South African Perspective" *Transformer, volume* 19(1), p 31.

Warikandwa, T. V. and Asheela, N. V., (2016). "Economic Transformation and Investment Security in Namibia: An Appraisal of the National Equitable Economic Empowerment Framework Bill" *University of Namibia Law Review,* volume 3(1), p 53.

Warikandwa, T. V. and Osode, P. C., (2014). "Legal Theoretical Perspectives and their Potential Ramifications for Proposals to Incorporate a Social Clause into the Legal Framework of the World Trade Organisation" *Speculum Juris*, volume 28(2), p 41.

Warikandwa, T. V. and Osode, P. C., (2016). "Chinese Companies' Trade Practices and Core Labour Standards: A South African, Zambian and Zimbabwean Perspective" *African Nazarene University Law Journal (Published by JUTA),* volume 4(1) p 102.

Warikandwa, T. V. and Osode, P. C., (2017). "Regulating against business 'fronting' to advance black economic empowerment in Zimbabwe: Lessons from South Africa" *Potchefstroom Electronic Law Journal,* volume 20, pp 1-43.

Warikandwa, T. V. Nhemachena, A. and Mpofu, N., (2017). "Double Victimisation? Law, Decoloniality and Research Ethics in post-colonial Africa", *Africology: The Journal of Pan African Studies* volume 10(2), (forthcoming April 2017).

Wilkins, D. B., (1996). "In defence of law and morality: Why lawyers should have a prima facie duty to obey the law" *William and Mary Law Review* volume 38 pp. 269-295.

World Bank (2014). "Minerals can boost well-being in developing countries" June 18, 2014 available at http://www.worldbank.org/en/news/feature/2014/06/18/minerals-can-boost-well-being-in-developing-countries (accessed 17 March 2017).

Yankah, E. N., (2008). "The Force of Law: The Role of Coercion in Legal Norms" *Richmond Law Review* volume 42 pp. 1195-1255.

Zongwe, D. P., (2016). "Natural Resources for National Reconstruction: A New Generation of Investment Contracts" Society of International Economic Law, Fifth Biennial Global Conference, Working Paper No. 2016/28.

LAW

United Nations Instruments

United Nations (UN) General Assembly Resolution 1803 (XVII) on the "Permanent Sovereignty over Natural Resources" adopted on the 14th of December 1962.

International Covenant on Economic, Social and Cultural Rights, Adopted and opened for signature, ratification and accession by General Assembly resolution 2200A (XXI) of 16 December *1966* and entered into force 3 January 1976.

African Charter on Human and People's Rights adopted 27 June 1981 and entered into force on 21 October 1986.

281

Zimbabwe

Zimbabwean Constitution Act 20 of 2013

Zimbabwean Indigenisation and Economic Empowerment Act (IEEA) [Chapter 14:33] of 2007

Mines and Minerals Act [Chapter 21:05]

South Africa

Natives Land Act No. 27 of 1913

Group Areas Act No. 41 of 1950

Minerals and Petroleum Resources Development Act, No. 28 of 2002.

Broad-Based Black Economic Empowerment Act (B-BBEEA) 53 of 2003

Broad-Based Black Economic Empowerment Amendment Act 46 of 2013

Promotion and Protection of Investment Act 22 of 2015

Preferential Procurement Policy Framework Act No. 97 of 2000

South African Companies Act No. 71 of 2008

African Exploration Mining and Finance Corporation Draft Bill of 2015.

Namibia

Namibia Minerals Policy of 2002.

Namibian Constitution Act 1 of 1990.

Namibia Investment Promotion Act 9 of 2016.

New Equitable Economic Empowerment Bill 2015.

United Kingdom

Sarbanes-Oxley Act of 2002 (SOX) ([Pub.L. 107-204, 116 Statute 745] enacted on 30 July 2002)

Chapter Nine

Towards the Promotion of Corporate Social Responsibility and the Adequacy of Mining Laws in Zimbabwe

Howard Chitimira & Moment Tembo

Introduction

Although no clear mining policies were available, mining has been crucially important to Zimbabwe's economic growth since the 17th century, especially, during the reign of the Mhunumutapa kingdom (Hollaway 1997: 27-28). This *status quo* continued between 1890 and 1914 despite the fact that it was impeded by colonial invasions of the country by white settlers who were largely sponsored by Cecil Rhodes during the same period. Nonetheless, the mining sector has remained key to the overall economic empowerment and development of the Gross Domestic Product (GDP) of Zimbabwe to date (Chindori-Chininga 2012: 8-9; Murombo 2016: 230–263). This follows, *inter alia*, the fact that a variety of minerals such as gold, silver, diamonds, nickel, copper, uranium and platinum are found in the Great Dyke and many other parts of Zimbabwe (Hollaway 1997: 27; Gwimbia and Nhamo 2016: 10-21). Nonetheless, the overall contribution of the mining sector to the GDP of Zimbabwe has been severely and consistently impeded by negative factors such as corruption, inadequate mining laws and the lack of adequate corporate social responsibility (CSR) policies to empower the ordinary people in affected communities, towns and cities to date (Murombo 2010: 570-588; Murombo 2013: 33-49; Chindori-Chininga 2012: 7-22; Saurombe 2014: 7-14). Accordingly, this has adversely affected the social and economic development benefits that are usually brought by the mining sector in Zimbabwe (Nyamunda and Mukwambo 2012:145-166). Given this background, this article investigates the adequacy of the mining regulatory framework in Zimbabwe. To this end, the regulatory flaws and other related constitutional challenges associated with the Zimbabwean mining sector are isolated and discussed. This is done to explore the adequacy of the provisions of relevant legislation such as the Environmental Management Act 13 of 2002 [Chapter 20:27] (Environmental Management Act), the Mines and Minerals Act 1135 of 1975 [Chapter 21:05] (Mines and Minerals Act) and the Indigenisation and Economic Empowerment Act 14 of 2007 [Chapter 14:33] (Indigenisation and Economic Empowerment Act) in relation to the combating of corruption and the promotion of sustainable CSR policies amongst the mining companies in Zimbabwe.

Mining and CSR policies in Zimbabwe prior to 1980

CSR has several definitions and can mean different things to different people. For instance, CSR could include those initiatives that are employed by various organisations or companies to assess and take an active role in the protection of the environment and well-being of the communities in which they conduct their businesses (Hopkins 2007: 15-43; Griffiths, in Hancock (ed) 2004: pvi). Moreover, it is submitted that CSR occurs when all the stakeholders of the company are treated equally, fairly and responsibly in accordance with the relevant laws and societal values (Hopkins 2007: 38). According to the International Organisation of Employers (IOE), CSR policies are those measures that are voluntarily employed by companies to address social and environmental concerns in their business operations and in their interaction with their stakeholders (International Organisation of Employers 2003: 21 March 2003, Geneva). Similarly, the European Union (EU) defines CSR as a concept that enables all companies to integrate social and environmental concerns in their business operations and interactions with their stakeholders on a voluntary basis (EU White Paper, July 2002; Hopkins 2007: 25-26). Thus, CSR is primarily concerned with the manner in which a company's business activities are executed in order to minimise systemic risks to all its relevant stakeholders in various markets. The International Labour Organisation World Commission on the Social Dimension of Globalization defines CSR as the voluntary initiatives that companies or organisations undertake over and above their legal obligations (Hopkins 2007: 26). Nigel Griffiths submits that CSR involves the manner in which companies take account of their economic, social and environmental works during their operations in order to maximize the benefits and minimize the losses in respect thereof (Hopkins 2007: 24). Thus, in accordance with the various definitions stated above, CSR policies of all mining companies must be community oriented in order to provide adequate environmental and socio-economic benefits to such communities. Be that as it may, no such policies were available in Zimbabwe prior to 1980.

In other words, mining commenced as early as the 15th century in Zimbabwe and during this era, mining activities for minerals such as gold and iron were generally executed at a small-scale by unregulated and unskilled people (Hollaway 1997: 27; Kaseke, Chaminuka and Musingafi 2015: 90-92). These mining activities were merely executed for profit and territorial gain without adopting any CSR policies. It is submitted that the situation improved and mining activities were modernized a bit in the 20th century with the establishment of over 4000 gold mining centres by the British South Africa Company (BSAC) (Viewing 1984: 21-51; Hollaway 1997: 28). The colonial era between 1890 and 1980 culminated into various illegal and/or unlicensed extractions of several minerals such as gold, coal, copper, asbestos, iron and chrome by the white minority government without adopting CSR policies to adequately benefit the local communities that were affected by such mining activities. Put differently, the mining sector was mainly beneficial to the white minority communities. This suggests that the majority of the black communities were negatively affected by mining activities which simply exploited their minerals without improving their social, economic and infrastructural development (Kaseke, Chaminuka and Musingafi 2015: 90-92). Moreover, prior to 1980, no adequate CSR mining policy was adopted by the colonial government. Thus, the pre-independence mining policy was largely motivated by greed, exploitation and illicit desire to grab all the minerals that were economically viable to mine. This colonial mining policy vested all mining titles and minerals in the state. The state was empowered to sell, cede or give such rights to other persons such prospectors and mining companies from time to time (Hollaway 1997: 28).

Mining and CSR policies in Zimbabwe subsequent to 1980

The demise of the colonial regime did not automatically translate into the adoption of sound and robust CSR mining policies by both the government and other relevant stakeholders in Zimbabwe. For instance, illegal and unlicensed mining was and still is, occurring in many parts of Zimbabwe, especially, in small towns like Kwekwe, Kadoma and Gwanda (Bhebhe, Kunguma, Jordaan and Majonga 2013: 70-76; Maponga and Ngorima 2003: 147–157). This resulted in the slow growth of the mining sector and its contribution to the GDP of Zimbabwe, particularly during the period between 1980 and 1985. Consequently, minerals and other related commodity prices were severely reduced and most mining companies incurred huge losses. Accordingly, the infrastructural and socio-economic benefits of most communities that relied on mining activities were also negatively affected. This negative status *quo* was exacerbated by the lack of robust CSR mining policies on the part of the government and the mining companies during the same period (Kaseke, Chaminuka and Musingafi 2015: 90).

Notwithstanding the government's efforts to empower and encourage local Zimbabwean people to actively participate in the available economic opportunities and activities, no provision in the Indigenisation and Economic Empowerment Act deals expressly with the adoption of CSR policies for mining companies (see ss 3-6 read with ss 12-16). This Act simply obliges the government to adopt relevant regulations and/or other measures to ensure that at least fifty-one per cent of the shares of every public company and any other business is owned, acquired or controlled by indigenous Zimbabwean people (s 3(1) and (2) of the Indigenisation and Economic Empowerment Act). The objectives of the Indigenisation and Economic Empowerment Act are merely aimed at empowering indigenous women, young persons and disabled persons (s 3(3)). Precisely, the Indigenisation and Economic Empowerment Act's indigenisation policy is not directly or indirectly targeted at

286

encouraging companies and related stakeholders to have sound CSR mining policies. In other words, the indigenisation policy is largely aimed at revamping black economic empowerment and/or related affirmative action policies and as such, it does not necessarily relate to CSR mining policies (s 3(3) of the Indigenisation and Economic Empowerment Act). Similarly, although miners are obliged to make certain payments to local authorities under the Mines and Minerals Act (s 255), this Act does not have any provision that directly deals with the CSR mining policies in respect of such miners and other related persons. Moreover, although the Environmental Management Act provides for the establishment of the environment fund (ss 48-55), its provisions do not expressly give effect to CSR mining policies in respect of mining companies.

Despite the flaws stated above, the end of the colonial regime brought several positive legislative and related policies to the Zimbabwean mining sector (Kaseke, Chaminuka and Musingafi 2015: 90; Muza and Magadi 2014: 82-92). For instance, colonial mining policies that were merely based on greed and exploitation of minerals were outlawed. Furthermore, several efforts were made by the government to enact the relevant legislation to improve the regulation of mining operations in all the Zimbabwean communities. The government adopted a number of policies to regulate different minerals. Put differently, the government adopted policies on how the mining activities for gold, silver, uranium, copper and other minerals that were recently discovered such as diamonds should be regulated (Dhliwayo and Mtisi 2012: 1-2, for related discussion on the government's Diamond Policy).

The adequacy of the Zimbabwean mining regulatory framework subsequent to 1980

Policy makers have drafted and enacted several statutes and regulations in a bid to enhance the regulation of mining in Zimbabwe since 1980 to date. Such legislation includes the Mines and Minerals Act, the Indigenisation and Economic Empowerment Act and the Environmental Management Act (see related discussion in paragraph C above). The Mines and Minerals Act is the principal law regulating

287

the mining industry in Zimbabwe. This Act outlines the administration of all mining activities in Zimbabwe (ss 341-367 of the Mines and Minerals Act). Such mining activities are directly administered by the Ministry of Mines and Mining Development (ss 341-342 of the Mines and Minerals Act). The Minister of Mines and Mining Development oversees all mining activities through Mining Commissioners who are appointed for the administration of such activities in various districts (ss 343-361 of the Mines and Minerals Act). The Mines and Minerals Act does not clearly state the person who appoints such Commissioners. Nonetheless, one could assume that all Mining Commissioners are appointed by the Minister of Mines and Mining Development in accordance with the Mines and Minerals Act. All Mining Commissioners play a pivotal role in the day to day running of mining activities across all the mining districts of Zimbabwe. For instance, they are empowered to issue or amend summons and commence proceedings in respect of all mining-related offences in Zimbabwe (s 347 of the Mines and Minerals Act). Mining Commissioners are also empowered to hear complaints, grant writs of execution and injunctions against the offenders (s 348-366 of the Mines and Minerals Act). Despite this, the Minister usually acts on the advice of the Mining Affairs Board (instead of Mining Commissioners), particularly in respect of more serious matters involving mining activities (ss 6-13 of the Mines and Minerals Act).

The Mines and Minerals Act commendably enumerates a number of mining rights that are available to all the relevant persons (ss 20-62). For instance, reservations, pegging and prospecting licences may be granted to any person who is at least 18 years old and permanently resident in Zimbabwe after the payment of the appropriate prescribed fee (ss 20-134 of the Mines and Minerals Act). A prospecting licence is generally valid for about 2 years (s 23 of the Mines and Minerals Act). There are usually two types of prospecting licences, namely, the Ordinary Prospecting Licence and the Special Prospecting Licence. A holder of any of these licences is empowered with the right to search for minerals and peg claims in respect thereof. Nonetheless, the Mines and Minerals Act provides very minimal penalties against the perpetrators of mining-related offences. Most of such penalties merely include prescribed fines or imprisonment for a period that ranges between three months and one year or both such fine and imprisonment (ss 368-391 of the Mines and Minerals Act). These relatively less deterrent penalties could have encouraged unscrupulous persons to frequently engage in corruption and other prohibited illicit mining activities to the detriment of the local communities, the state and the economy at large. Furthermore, the vesting of all minerals in the president and not in the state is probably one of the biggest flaws of the Mines and Minerals Act (see s 2). In other words, the dominium in and the right of searching and mining for, and disposing of all minerals, mineral oils and natural gases should have been vested in the state and not the president. This could have promoted transparency and more accountability on the part of the president and other members of the executive (Murombo 2016: 230–263).

In most instances, the right to mine under the Mines and Minerals Act takes precedence over the usufructuary rights of communal land owners. Thus, the provisions of the Mines and Minerals Act will prevail over those of the Communal Land Act 20 of 1982 [Chapter 20:04] (Communal Land Act), in respect of acquiring land for mining activities. This could have been influenced by the fact that the Communal Land Act does not provide security of tenure for communal land (ss 3-11). Consequently, a majority of communal land owners living in rural areas are sometimes forcibly displaced from their land by the government in favour of mining activities in accordance with the Mines and Minerals Act. The recent Chiadzwa communal land displacements are a case in point. Such displacements by mining companies or the state also give rise to severe environmental degradation and socio-economic challenges on the part of communal land owners in most rural areas (Centre for Research and Development 2014: 5; Rajah, Dino and Jerie 2012: 408-414). These challenges are worsened by the lack of a clear and robust CSR mining policy in the Mines and Minerals Act (see related comments in paragraph C above). Put differently, despite the fact that miners are required to make certain payments to local authorities under the Mines and Minerals Act (s 255; see related comments in paragraph C above), this Act does not clearly state the amounts, purpose and/or reason for such payments. This obscurity could have

289

encouraged mining companies, government officials and other related stakeholders to avoid making such payments to the affected communities and to engage in corrupt mining activities.

As stated earlier, the Indigenisation and Economic Empowerment Act was mainly enacted to promote the government's black economic policies and affirmative action policies for indigenous Zimbabweans (s 3; related remarks in paragraph C above). In this regard, it is crucial to note that an indigenous Zimbabwean includes any person who, before 18 April 1980, was disadvantaged by unfair discrimination on the grounds of his or her race and any descendant of such person. An indigenous Zimbabwean further includes any company, association, syndicate or partnership of which indigenous Zimbabweans form the majority of the members or hold the controlling interest (s 2(1) of the Indigenisation and Economic Empowerment Act; Dhliwayo 2014: 2-41). Put differently, the Indigenisation and Economic Empowerment Act is mainly targeted at empowering vulnerable and marginalised persons such as women, youth and disabled persons who were previously overlooked by the government and other relevant stakeholders in their economic activities (s 3(3)). This Act defines 'empowerment' as the creation of an environment which enhances the performance of the economic activities of indigenous Zimbabweans into which they would have been introduced or involved through indigenisation (s 2(1)). The duty to create that environment is correctly placed on the government. Indigenisation is defined as a deliberate involvement of indigenous Zimbabweans in the economic activities of the country which they previously had no access to, in order to ensure the equitable ownership of that country's resources (s 2(1) of the Indigenisation and Economic Empowerment Act; Murombo 2010: 570-588). Such resources include minerals and/or mining rights in respect of such minerals. Nonetheless, apart from merely stating that external investors are obliged to cede fifty-one per cent of their company shares to indigenous Zimbabwean people (s 3(1) and (2)), the Indigenisation and Economic Empowerment Act does not clearly provide CSR related mining policies or relevant measures that could be employed by the relevant stakeholders to promote socio-economic development projects in the affected communities (Dhliwayo 2014: 2-41).

The Environmental Management Act promotes sustainable management of natural resources and the protection of the environment in Zimbabwe (ss 4-10). This is aimed at the prevention of pollution and environmental degradation in all parts of Zimbabwe. In this regard, the Environmental Management Act established the National Environmental Council, the Environmental Management Agency and the Environment Management Board which are all directly involved in the management and enforcement of environmental rights in Zimbabwe (ss 7-33). The Act also established the Environment Fund which is, *inter alia*, aimed at making grants to local authorities and/or their appointed agents for the purpose of assisting needy persons for them to access natural resources without affecting the environment (s 52(b)). In the same vein, the Standards and Enforcement Committee is further established to enforce environmental quality standards across all towns, cities and communities of Zimbabwe (ss 56-86 of the Environmental Management Act). Moreover, like the Zimbabwe Constitution 20 of 2013 (Zimbabwe Constitution 2013, s 73(1)), the Environmental Management Act provides that every person has a right to a clean environment that is not harmful to their health and to have that environment protected for the benefit of present and future generations through reasonable legislative and other measures (see s 4(1); Madebwe 2015: 115-118). Be that as it may, apart from the Environment Fund (s 52(b)), the Environmental Management Act does not expressly deal with the regulation of mining activities. The Act also fails to expressly provide CSR related mining policies (Hawkins 2009: 1-53). Furthermore, the Act only provides minimal penalties against those who engage in environmental offences (ss 137-139; Madebwe 2015: 108-119).

Additionally, the Zimbabwe Mining Development Corporation Act 31 of 1982 [Chapter 21:08] as amended (Mining Development Corporation Act) was enacted. This Act, *inter alia*, established the Zimbabwe Mining Development Corporation (ZMDC). Over and above, the Mining Development Corporation Act outlines the functions, powers and duties of the ZMDC (ss 20-25). Apart from empowering the ZMDC to issue shares and engage in lawful commercial business activities, the Mining Development Corporation Act does not have any measures or policies for mining-related CSR activities (s 20(a) and (c)). The Act does not clearly indicate whether the ZMDC is also empowered to issue shares to both local and external companies on behalf of the state (ss 26-27 read with ss 20; 22-23 of the Mining Development Corporation Act).

The Base Minerals Export Control Act 4 of 1949 [Chapter 21:01] as amended (Base Minerals Act), also regulates the export of base minerals from Zimbabwe. The Act defines base minerals to include coal and all other minerals and mineral substances such as coke, slimes, concentrates, slags, tailings and valuable residues that contain base minerals (s 2). Nonetheless, base minerals do not include precious metals, precious stones, mineral oils and natural gases (s 2 of the Base Minerals Act). Likewise, the Minerals Marketing Corporation of Zimbabwe Act 2 of 1982 [Chapter 21:04] as amended regulates the marketing, export, sale and stockpiling of minerals and other related matters in Zimbabwe (ss 30-50). Moreover, the Chamber of Mines of Zimbabwe Incorporation (Private) Act 5 of 1939 [Chapter 21:02] as amended is mainly aimed at enhancing the promotion, encouragement, protection and fostering of the Zimbabwean mining industry (ss 3-10). All the stated statutes are administered by the Ministry of Mines and Mining Development. Despite this, none of these statutes adequately provides for the compulsory adoption of CSR related mining polices by mining companies and related stakeholders prior to the commencement of their business activities in Zimbabwe (Dhliwayo and Mtsi 2012: 15-26; 42-48; Mahonye and Mandishara 2015: 1-18). Moreover, all the stated legislation provides very minimal penalties for mining-related offences.

Other related mining-related legislation include the Explosives Act 9 of 1961 [Chapter 10:08] as amended (Explosives Act) which regulates the possession, purchase, acquisition, delivery, manufacture, storage, use, conveyance and handling of explosives in Zimbabwe (ss 3-11). All persons that use explosives to conduct their mining are obliged to comply with the Explosives Act. Additionally, the Pneumoconiosis Act 13 of 1971 [Chapter 15:08] as amended

(Pneumoconiosis Act), deals with the control and administration of persons employed in dusty occupations and other related conditions (ss 22-53). Such persons include miners and as such, all mining companies must comply with the provisions of the Pneumoconiosis Act to curb negligent-related health problems and hazardous conditions in the mining work-place. Similarly, the Factories and Works Act 20 of 1948 [Chapter 14:08] as amended (Factories and Works Act), regulates the registration and control of factories as well as their working conditions across all the Zimbabwean industries (ss 8-20). Thus, all mining companies and their related factories are obliged to register and comply with provisions of the Factories and Works Act to enhance the safety of their employees.

The Gold Trade Act 19 of 1940 [Chapter 21:03] as amended prohibits the possession of gold by unscrupulous and unauthorised persons (ss 3-12). This Act also regulates trade-related transactions involving gold between different persons in Zimbabwe (ss 3-22). Moreover, the Precious Stones Trade Act 8 of 1978 [Chapter 21:06] as amended (Precious Stones Trade Act), regulates the possession of, and dealings involving precious stones between different persons in Zimbabwe (ss 3-19). Consequently, illegal smuggling and illicit dealings involving precious minerals such as diamonds is expressly prohibited under the Precious Stones Trade Act. Any contravention in respect thereof will give rise to both civil and criminal penalties on the part of the offenders (ss 15 and 15A of the Precious Stones Trade Act). Over and above, the Forest Act 37 of 1949 [Chapter 19:05] amended (Forest Act) regulates the cutting and taking of timber for mining purposes and provides for the conservation of timber resources (ss 35-63). This is enforced through the Mining Timber Permit Board and compulsory afforestation of the land in communities that are affected by mining (ss 43-53 of the Forest Act). Accordingly, any reckless and unlawful deforestation for mining purposes will give rise to both civil and criminal penalties under the Forest Act (ss 78-82). The Water Act 31 of 1998 [Chapter 20:24] as amended (Water Act), regulates the granting of water use permits for commercial purposes (ss 32-60). This Act regulates the use of water when water is in short supply and the acquisition of servitudes in respect of water (ss 61-67; 69; 72-85). The Water Act outlaws water pollution in order to protect the environment from degradation and other related the challenges (s 118; also see Spiegel 2014: 541-570). Accordingly, any mining activities that contaminate water and/or illicit commercial use of water will result in criminal or civil liability on the part of the offenders under the Water Act. The Labour Act 16 of 1985 [Chapter 28:01] as amended (Labour Act) which regulates the employer-employee relationship in Zimbabwe (ss 4-22). The Act provides for the formation and termination the employer-employee relationship. It also enumerates various fundamental rights of employees in accordance with the International Labour Organisation (ILO) guidelines and other international best practices (ss 4-7). In light of this, it is submitted that all employees of mining companies must be adequately remunerated in terms of the Labour Act. Such employees must also receive adequate social security and relevant employee benefits in terms of the National Social Security Authority Act 12 of 1989 [Chapter 17:04] as amended (ss 3 and 3A). Despite these positive developments, none of the stated statutes expressly provide for the adoption CSR related mining polices by mining companies and other relevant stakeholders in the Zimbabwean mining sector. Various human rights abuses often occur to those employed in the mining sector as well as to those who reside in the areas affected by mining activities (Saurombe 2014: 7-14). The recent gross human rights violations and displacements of local villagers in Chiadzwa are a case in point (Nyamunda and Mukwambo 2012:145-166).

The lack of an adequate Diamond Policy presents a further challenge to the Zimbabwean mining regulatory framework. The government has also struggled to consistently implement this Diamond Policy. This status *quo* has been worsened by the lack of an adequate Diamond Act in Zimbabwe (Dhliwayo and Mtisi 2012: 1-2). In other words, despite the enactment of the Mines and Minerals Unit) Regulations of 2008 and the Minerals Marketing Corporation (Diamond Sales to Local Diamond Manufactures) Regulations of 2010, no rule, regulation or provision in the relevant mining laws adequately provide for the regulation of diamond mining rights and transactions in Zimbabwe (Nyamunda and Mukwambo 2012:145-166; Centre for Research and Development 2014: 5-25). Moreover, the regulation of mining rights as well as the marketing, trade and export of diamonds and other minerals has remained flawed since 1980 to date. For instance, the current laws do not adequately comply with all the relevant minimum requirements and standards of the Kimberley Process Certification Scheme (KPCS). This has caused illegal mining, smuggling and illicit trading of minerals in Zimbabwe to the detriment of its social and economic growth (Robb JR 2012: 658-668; Murombo 2010: 570-588 and Murombo 2016: 238-242).

Concluding Remarks

As indicated above, Zimbabwe has made considerable efforts to enact some relevant environmental and other related mining legislation prior to, and subsequent to 1980. For instance, key legislation such as the Mines and Minerals Act and the Environmental Management Act were enacted. Moreover, the government's efforts to enhance the protection of the environment and minerals were recently buttressed by the entrenchment of environmental rights in the Zimbabwe Constitution 2013 (s 73; see related remarks in paragraph D above). Nonetheless, the growth of the Zimbabwean mining sector has been consistently impeded by the enactment of inadequate mining laws, poor enforcement of such laws by the enforcement authorities, corruption and the lack of robust CSR related mining policies since 1980 to date. For instance, the people's right to clean, un-harmful and unpolluted environment is sometimes violated by the government through its mining activities without granting them adequate compensation and/or redress in respect thereof (Madebwe 2015: 115-116). Forced displacements, brutal attacks on informal diamond miners by the police and soldiers as well as other related gross human rights of villagers in Chiadzwa is a case in point (Dhliwayo and Mtisi 2012: 1-2; Spiegel 2014: 541-570; Nyamunda and Mukwambo 2012:145-166; Saurombe 2014: 7-14). In this regard, it is submitted that the Mines and Minerals Act and the Environmental Management Act should be amended to introduce adequate provisions on mining courts and environmental courts respectively. This could empower and encourage all aggrieved persons to seek and receive timeous redress in these specialised courts (Madebwe 2015: 114-116). In the same vein, the Mines and Minerals Act should be amended to introduce adequate provisions on CSR related mining policies that obliges the government, mining companies and other relevant stakeholders to have developmental programmes in all the areas and communities affected by mining activities. Such CSR related mining policies should also oblige mining companies, the government and other offenders to compensate those affected by their mining activities (Centre for Research and Development 2014: 10-26). Additionally, the Mines and Minerals Act, the Environmental Management Act and other related legislation should be amended to enact to introduce adequate penalties for mining and related environmental offences.

Government officials and all other unscrupulous persons who violate the mining and environmental laws should be tried in the relevant courts without impunity. This could combat corruption, environmental degradation and the looting of minerals as well as other natural resources in Zimbabwe. The same approach could also revamp the Zimbabwean mining sector which is currently marred by corruption and several scandals such as: (a) the controversial Zimplats mining company deal involving the National Indigenisation and Economic Empowerment Board (NIEEB) which is also known as the NIEEBGATE Scandal; (b) the six million bribery scam involving former ZMDC boss, Godwills Masimirembwa in 2013 (diamond gate scandal); (c) gross financial irregularities at Hwange coal Colliery Company limited; and (d) a flawed Essar deal which sought to allow a takeover of Ziscosteel by an Indian firm, Essar Africa Holdings (Centre for Research and Development 2014: 5). These and other related corrupt governance practices in the mining sector culminated into harmful mining practices that had huge environmental consequences and human rights violations to all the persons in affected areas (Centre for Research and Development 2014: 5). In this regard, it is submitted that the mining companies, government officials and related stakeholders must consistently comply with the Mines and Minerals Act and related instruments such as the Environmental Management (Control of Alluvial Mining) Regulations 2014, SI 92/2014 (Control of Alluvial Mining Regulations) which prohibits alluvial mining activities to be conducted within 200 meters from river banks and the use of mechanical equipment or motor-powered equipment to conduct such activities in a bid to combat floods and other harmful environmental consequences to the people (s 3 of the Control of Alluvial Mining Regulations).

Notwithstanding commendable efforts such as the introduction of the Diamond Policy, the Draft Mines and Minerals Amendment Bill 14 of 2007 and the Ministry of Mines and Mineral Development Draft Minerals Policy of 2013 which were generally aimed at promoting transparency and accountability in the Zimbabwean mining sector, more still needs to be done to ensure that these laws and policies are adequate and legally binding laws that are consistently enforced to promote transparency and accountability in all mining-related activities (Murombo 2016: 242-243; Chindori-Chininga 2012: 6-12). This lack of transparency and accountability has given birth to various dubious mining agreements between government officials and fraudulent and/or incompetent foreign mining companies in Marange (Chiadzwa) diamond fields since 2006 to date (Centre for Research and Development 2014: 6). Accordingly, it is submitted that the government and other relevant stakeholders should promote transparency and accountability in their mining activities in Chiadzwa to curb the on-going human rights violations and ensure that the companies involved adopt sound CSR related mining policies that benefits the people in Chiadzwa community. This follows the fact that the Zimunya-Marange Community Ownership Trust has reportedly not been granted any remittances from all the diamond mining activities since 2012 to date (Centre for Research and Development 2014: 9-10; 41-45). It is further submitted that Zimbabwe should ratify and transpose the Extractive Industries Transparency Initiative (EITI) proposals and policies through the Zimbabwe Mining Revenue Transparency Initiative (ZMRTI) into the relevant mining legislation to encourage accountability and transparency among all the relevant stakeholders (Centre for Research and Development 2014: 5; Dhliwayo and Mtsi 2012: 2; Murombo 2016: 242–263 and Murombo 2013: 37-39).

Bibliography

Literature

Bhebhe, D., Kunguma, O., Jordaan, A. and Majonga, H. (2013). 'A case study of the perceived socio-environmental problems caused by illegal gold mining in Gwanda district, Zimbabwe' *Disaster Advances* Vol.6, No.10.

Centre for Research and Development (2014). 'Raising the Community Voice in the Extractive Sector Challenges and future Prospects of the mining sector in Zimbabwe' *Centre for Research and Development Report Series.*

Chindori-Chininga, E. (2012). *First Report of the Portfolio Committee on Mines and Energy on Diamond Mining (with special reference to Marange Diamond Fields) 2009-2013 Presented to Parliament June 2013* (S.C.4, 2012).

Dhliwayo, M. (2014). 'A review of Zimbabwe's draft minerals policy' *Zimbabwe Environmental Law Association (ZELA) Publication Series.*

Dhliwayo, M. and Mtisi, S. (2012). 'Towards the development of a Diamond Act in Zimbabwe: Analysis of the legal and policy framework on diamonds and Zimbabwe's compliance with the Kimberley Process Certification Scheme (KPCS) minimum requirements' *Zimbabwe Environmental Law Association (ZELA) Publication Series.*

European Union White Paper, July 2002.

Griffiths, N. in Hancock, J. (ed) (2004). *Investing in CSR – A Guide to Best Practice, Business Planning and the UK's Leading Companies,* London and Sterling: Kogan, pvi.

Gwimbia, P. and Nhamo, G. (2016). 'Translating mitigation measures proposed in environmental impact statements into planning conditions: Promises and practices by multinational platinum mining firms along the Great Dyke of Zimbabwe' *Environmental Science & Policy*, Vol. 57.

Hawkins, T. (2009). 'The mining sector in Zimbabwe and its potential contribution to recovery' *United Nations Development Programme Comprehensive Economic Recovery in Zimbabwe Working Paper Series*, Working Paper 1

Hollaway, J. (1997). 'Mineral policy in Zimbabwe: Its evolution, achievements and challenges' *Resources Policy*, Vol. 23, No. 1/2.

Hopkins, M. (2007). *Corporate Social Responsibility and International Development: Is Business the Solution?* London, United Kingdom: Earthscan.

International Organisation of Employers 21 March 2003, Geneva.

Kaseke, K.E, Chaminuka, L. and Musingafi, M.C.C (2015). 'Mining and minerals revenue distribution in Zimbabwe: Learning from our surroundings and past mistakes' *Journal of Economics and Sustainable Development*, Vol.6, No.6.

Madebwe, T. (2015). 'Carving Out a Greater Role for Civil Litigation as an environmental law enforcement tool in Zimbabwe's 2013 Constitution' *Law, Environment and Development Journal*, Vol.11, No.2.

Mahonye, N. and Mandishara, L. (2015). 'Mechanism between mining sector and economic growth in Zimbabwe: Is it a resource curse?' *Economic Research Southern Africa (ERSA) Working Paper* 499.

Maponga, O. and Ngorima, C.F. (2003). 'Overcoming environmental problems in the gold panning sector through legislation and education: the Zimbabwean experience' *Journal of Cleaner Production*, Vol.11.

Murombo, T. (2010). 'Law and the indigenisation of mineral resources in Zimbabwe: Any equity for local communities?' *SAPL*, Vol. 25.

Murombo, T. (2013). 'Regulating mining in South Africa and Zimbabwe: Communities, the environment and perpetual exploitation' *Law, Environment and Development Journal*, Vol.9, No.1.

Murombo, T. (2016). 'The effectiveness of initiatives to promote good governance, accountability and transparency in the extractives sector in Zimbabwe' *Journal of African Law*, Vol. 60, No. 2.

Muza, C. and Magadi, I. (2014). 'Environmental Management accounting implementation in Zimbabwe mining sector' *IOSR Journal of Business and Management* Vol.16, No. 9(1).

Nyamunda, T. and Mukwambo, P. (2012). 'The state and the bloody diamond rush in Chiadzwa: Unpacking the contesting Interests in the development of illicit mining and trading, c.2006–2009' *Journal of Southern African Studies*, Vol. 38, No.1.

Rajah, N., Dino, R. and Jerie, S. (2012). 'Challenges in implementing an integrated environmental management approach in Zimbabwe' *Journal of Emerging Trends in Economics and Management Sciences*, Vol. 3, Vol. 4.

Robb JR, M.J. (2012). 'Diamond's wealth is forever: Comparing Zimbabwe's and Botswana's diamond mining laws reveals changes that Zimbabwe should implement' *Wisconsin International Law Journal* Vol. 29, No. 3.

Saurombe, PB. (2014). 'Legal perspectives on the regulation of trade in (conflict) diamonds in Zimbabwe by means of the Kimberley Process Regulation Scheme', unpublished LLM dissertation, North-West University.

Spiegel, S.J. (2014) 'Legacies of a nationwide crackdown in Zimbabwe: Operation Chikorokoza Chapera in gold mining communities' *Journal of Modern African Studies*, Vol. 52, No. 4.

Viewing, K. (1984). 'Mining and the development' *Chamber of Mines Journal,* Vol. 8, No. 2.

Legislation, Bills and related instruments

Base Minerals Export Control Act 4 of 1949 [Chapter 21:01] as amended.

Chamber of Mines of Zimbabwe Incorporation (Private) Act 5 of 1939 [Chapter 21:02] as amended.

Communal Land Act 20 of 1982 [Chapter 20:04].

Draft Mines and Minerals Amendment Bill 14 of 2007.

Environmental Management Act 13 of 2002 [Chapter 20:27] as amended.

Explosives Act 9 of 1961 [Chapter 10:08] as amended.

Factories and Works Act 20 of 1948 [Chapter 14:08] as amended.

Forest Act 37 of 1949 [Chapter 19:05] amended.

Gold Trade Act 19 of 1940 [Chapter 21:03] as amended.

Indigenisation and Economic Empowerment Act 14 of 2007 [Chapter 14:33].

Labour Act 16 of 1985 [Chapter 28:01] as amended.

Mines and Minerals Act 1135 of 1975 [Chapter 21:05].

Minerals Marketing Corporation of Zimbabwe Act 2 of 1982 [Chapter 21:04] as amended.

Ministry of Mines and Mineral Development Draft Minerals Policy of 2013.

National Social Security Authority Act 12 of 1989 [Chapter 17:04] as amended.

Pneumoconiosis Act 13 of 1971 [Chapter 15:08] as amended.

Precious Stones Trade Act 8 of 1978 [Chapter 21:06] as amended.

Water Act 31 of 1998 [Chapter 20:24] as amended.

Zimbabwe Mining Development Corporation Act 31 of 1982 [Chapter 21:08].

Chapter Ten

Political Governance and Resource Exploitation in Cameroon: Challenges and Prospects

Jean-Pierre Wome

Introduction

Cameroon lies in the central region of Africa with a geographic territory measuring a total surface area of 475, 442km^2 of which, 472, 710km^2 constitutes the total land mass and 2, 730km^2 is occupied by water. The country has a total population of 24, 229, 247 million people, of which, 49.9% constitutes the male population while 50.1% is made up of women (Cameroon population 2017). Cameroon borders six countries which are; Central African Republic, Chad, Equatorial Guinea, Gabon, Republic of the Congo and Nigeria (Cameroon population 2017). More often, Cameroon is referred to as "Africa in miniature" due to the fact that it exhibits all the major climates and vegetation of the continent, mountains, deserts, rain forests, savannah grasslands, ocean coastlands and diverse animal and plant species (Belle, 2016). The presence of a rich natural environment also provides a reservoir for natural resources which in turn become a source of livelihood for ordinary Cameroonians. These natural benefits have been stratified by the government to ensure proper monitoring and accountability for their mismanagement (Belle, 2016).

In this chapter, natural resource partitioning and exploitation by the Cameroonian Government in relation to speculated economic output will be discussed. Identification and classification of targeted mineral reserves within the country's geographical territory has been a subject of consideration from the birth of the independent State of Cameroon. However, colonial administration prevailed prior to this period and of course, it contributed significantly in developing formal administrative structures governing natural resource exploitation in the modern State of Cameroon (Geschiere, 1993 : 151). With the aid of the formal administrative structures, targeted mineral reserves have been identified and programmed for present and future exploitations. This discussion therefore focuses on the policies and political interplays affecting resource partitioning and exploitation in Cameroon. The goal is to identify the gaps in both politics and law through which resource exploitation in Cameroon have evolved to attain its present state.

Historical timeline

Natural resource exploitation and policy implementation in Cameroon can be traced from the early history prior to colonization. Before the 1900s era that witnessed colonial administration in Cameroon, natural resource management was a matter of community concern through the use of family law (Mengang, 1995). According to this policy, the chiefs were vested with administrative power over resource management in their respective communities. Such exercise of administrative authority imposed limits on sectors like hunting and forest exploitation to the extent that, strangers in certain local communities were not allowed to hunt or exploit the forest without permission from the chief. Anyone who contravened this policy faced community sanctions which in most cases were not clearly defined (Mengang, 1995). According to the law makers at the time, the policy facilitated the preservation of the natural environment and kept track of the animals and plants species, including related natural resources that inhabited forest governed by local authorities.

Even though the said customary policy lasted for a while with a handful of positive impingements, it recorded alongside negative feedbacks for which, the policy became more of a liability than an asset to the country as a whole. The policy invoked the indigenisation of natural resource exploitation to localized communities. Accordingly, such resources were considered properties belonging to the communities in which they find themselves and of course, their exploitations were limited to community membership (Ngang, 2015). The policy of resource indigenisation was strenuous not only to the government but as well, the majority of Cameroonians as a number of local communities had poor environmental setup with limited natural resources. It seems the country's natural resources were being exploited and enjoyed by a select few in contrast with the principles of equity and good conscience (Ngang, 2015). The government had poor control over these resources and inhabitants of areas experiencing short supply felt cheated as they could not explore related resources in neighbouring communities without authorization. Due to its discriminatory nature, the policy was challenged by appropriate judicial mechanisms for conflicting with the principles of natural justice and subsequently, it failed to gain legal enforcement.

In the realm of legal discourse, the provision of Section 27(1) of the Southern Cameroon High Court Law 1955 for example was instructive in this regard (Ngwafor, 2000: 1). It provided that;

> The High Court shall observe and enforce the observance of every native law and custom which is not repugnant to natural justice, equity and good conscience, nor incompatible with any law for the time being in force, and nothing in this law shall deprive any person of the benefit of any such native law or custom.

At the down of colonisation, the former administration of natural resources by local authorities was replaced by formal administrative structures. According to the new administrative set up, forest exploitation, including hunting and cutting down of trees was forbidden to both indigenes and strangers of every community. Also, administrative authority over the natural environment conferred upon chiefs was revoked (Kengaum et al. 2016: 4). This new dimensional approach created tension between the administration and community members on the established grounds that the latter's resources have been taken away by the State. The State however provided options for people to continue with such exploitations provided they were in possession of a special permit issued by the State (Kengaum et al. 2016: 4). To avoid the extinction of endangered species, protected areas and game reserves were created by colonial administrators for the benefit of generations yet unborn (McCall and Minang, 2005). One among others includes the Limbe Botanical

Garden created by the Germans after World War I. The Garden still exists and serves as an example of biodiversity in Cameroon.

After Cameroon's political independence of 1960, a number of protected areas free from operational exploitation were created (Kiye, 2015: 86). These reserves included among others, the Korup National Park, Waza Park and the Kalamaloe Park (Linder, 2008: 216). The colonial administrative policy was geared towards species and resource protection and thereby counteracting the pre-existing policy of resource indigenisation and subsequent exploitation by local communities.

During the French occupation of Cameroon, massive sensitisation campaigns addressing issues related to forest conservation and mineral resource exploitations were conducted. The message was, all natural resources belong to the state and persons requiring use of such resources were expected to apply for special permits (Thomas et al. 2004: 211). To actualise this vision, the said natural resources were placed under different ministries, including the Rural Development Secretariat, the Department of Tourism, the Ministry of Livestock, Fisheries, Animal Husbandry and the Ministry of Environment and Forestry (Mengang, 1995). Forest activities like hunting and timber exploitations were managed by the Ministry of Agriculture, while, the Department of Tourism took control over national parks. Wildlife became the responsibility of Animal Husbandry and Fisheries catered for by the Department of Livestock (Mengang, 1995). These formal administrative structures marked the transitions from the pre-colonial to the colonial and post-colonial systems governing natural resource exploitation in Cameroon.

The period prior to colonisation in Cameroon recorded community principles of natural resource exploitation directed towards protecting the natural environment. However, such principles were not documented hence; responsibility could not be invoked for their breach. Such actions were only regulated by customary procedures which in most instances contradicted the law (Ashley, 2005: 9). There was a need therefore to transform the system into legal machineries governed by administrative units. In that way, natural resources became the exclusive property of the State and were used when and where necessary for commercial purposes.

The interphase between the colonial and post-colonial era in Cameroon is marked by the institutionalisation of natural resources within the legal framework of the State. The country's forest and wildlife sector is in the Department of Agriculture and the Department of Tourism (Mengang, 1995). The two sectors have undergone profound institutional and legislative reforms such as the establishment of Cameroon Forest Policy, the creation of new forestry laws, wildlife and fisheries regulations and the development and applications of all the said forestry laws (Ashley, 2005: 9). These modifications characterised regulations governing the entire sector.

The country's forestry policies constitute one component of national strategy for the enhancement of economic activities. The classification of natural resources also includes mineral resources govern by the Ministry of Industrial Mines and Technological Development (MIMTD) (Djeumo, 2001). The ministry takes responsibility for the issuance of mineral exploitation licenses. Upon obtaining the mineral exploitation license, licensed companies engage in the mining of commodities like gold, diamond, clay and sapphire (mostly through artisanal mining operations). Also, the government of Cameroon has gone beyond domestic administrative frameworks to recognise and ratify relevant international, continental and sub-regional treaties regulating the natural environment. In doing so, the country domesticated the international jurisprudence on environmental conservation. These international instruments guide the policy framework of the country and also, they fostered the classification and accreditation of the country's natural resources for international commercialization (Mengang, 1995). Below is a list of international, continental and sub-regional instruments to which Cameroon is a party to.

International Conventions
-    Convention on International Trade in Wildlife and Endangered Species (Washington, 3 March 1973);
-    Convention on the Protection of Cultural and Natural Heritage (Paris, 23 November 1972);

- Montreal Protocol on the Control of Chlorofluorocarbons (CFCs) (Montreal, 16 April 1987);
- Convention on Climate Change (14 June 1992);
- Vienna Convention on the Protection of the Ozone Layer (Vienna, 22 March 1985);
- Convention on Biological Diversity (14 June 1992);
- Convention on Desertification (Paris, October 1994);
- Cooperation Agreement with International Non-Governmental Organizations (IUCN, WWF, ITTO).

Continental Conventions
- Convention on the Conservation of Culture and Natural Resources (Algeria, 1968);
- Bamako Convention on Waste Importation in Africa and Trans-border Movement and Management of Toxic Wastes (Bamako, 1994).

Sub-regional Conventions
- Accord on joint regulations of fauna and flora within Lake Chad;
- 1964 Accord creating the Lake Chad Basin Commission;
- Convention on Cooperation relating to the protection and Development of the Marine Environment and the Coastal Area of the West and Central Africa (Abidjan, 16 March 1981);
- Accord for Cooperation and Consultation among Central African States relating to Wildlife Conservation (Libreville, 16 April 1983);
- African Timber Organization (ATO).

The above mentioned international legislations form the legal framework that guides and directs Cameroon's national forestry policy. In the policy orientation scheme, protecting the natural environment is top on the government's agenda. The agenda has been fostered by the institution of administrative departments as stated in previous sections. Also, the government has improved the forestry policy by sensitising the local population on the importance of environmental preservation. Government has organized alternative activities capable of generating revenue, reduce human pressure on the environment and improve environmental awareness (Mengang, 1995).

The forestry policy objectives are aimed at establishing a permanent forest estate through which resources can be monitored in a quantitative and qualitative manner. By so doing, there can be proper management, conservation and further development of forest biodiversity (Schroth *et al.*2004). It promotes the renewal of resources through regeneration and reforestation with a view to improve the environment. Also, the policy revitalises the forestry sector by setting up an efficient institutional system involving all the parties concerned in the sector (Schroth *et al.* 2004).

Targeted reserves and potential resource capacity

Due to the protective legal frame provided by the government, natural resources have been preserved with significant deposits found in different parts of the country. An estimated 140 gold targets have been discovered and 17 diamond targets documented out of which, 9 are presently undergoing exploitation by the artisan industry (Cameroon Mining Guide, 2014). Additionally, about 26 small-scale mining sites exist, including significant diamond occurrences discovered along 700km border with Central African Republic. In terms of aluminium production, 6 bauxite deposits have been discovered including the Mini-Martap deposit of 1.116 billion tons capacity with 43% of aluminium and 1.8% of silica (Cameroon Mining Guide, 2014).

Up to 25 iron ore targeted deposits have also been discovered, including the Mbalam deposits containing reserves of 807 million tons of which 220 million tons are grade 60% iron ore and 587 million tons are grade 22%-38% iron ore (Cameroon Mining Guide, 2014). Some 3 million tons of alluvial titanium reserves have been found in the AknoHenji area with superior concentration along the sea coast to 0.2 million tons of cobalt metal accompanied by an appreciable tonnage of nickel and manganese (Cameroon Mining Guide, 2014). These analyses present a comprehensive summary of targeted reserves booked for prospective operations by national and international companies operating within the territory of Cameroon.

Resource exploitation and production output

The most significant mining commodity produced in Cameroon as recorded from 2011 is the siliceous volcanic ash (pozzolana) used for the production of hydraulic cement (Cameroon Mining Guide, 2014). The production of aluminium as a metal is favoured by the use of bauxite as its primary raw material obtained from Guinea. Whereas the country is known for its rich bauxite deposits, the mineral has remained unexploited due to low mining and production capacity in terms of available industrial machineries (Newman, 2012). Precious minerals, including gold and diamond are mined primarily through artisanal mining operations. These artisanship accounts for the production of 1.600 tons of gold, 10.000 carats of diamond and probably 1.000 carats of sapphire per annum (Cameroon Mining Guide, 2014).

In the year 2011, a mining company named Botswana Diamond Ltd. was awarded a 430km2 exploration license to explore specified areas. Before commencement, the company initiated a bulk sampling program to examine the diamond potential in its license and concluded that more than enough reserve was available for exploitation (Cameroon Mining Guide, 2014). According to Business Monitor International (BMI), Cameroon is expected to become a significant centre for iron ore production given that major mining related projects have gone operational and more still expected to kick start within the coming years (Cameroon Mining Guide, 2014). The company however lamented that due to the country's poor infrastructural development and road networks, such developmental projects could be hindered (Cameroon Mining Guide, 2014). The high deposit of iron ore is expected to attract foreign investments especially from Chinese investors whose interests are channelled towards securing stable and long term supplies of iron ore.

While it seem most companies have begun operations in the Cameroon's mineral resource sector, most of such minerals including bauxite, cobalt, gold, granite, iron ore, lignite, nickel and uranium have remained under-developed due to the above stated infrastructural deficiency (Legend Mining Ltd., 2010). Poor road network is also a call for concern for which potential bauxite reserves at the Mini-Martap and Ngaouanda deposits located in the remote northern parts of Cameroon have remained unexploited. These two deposits are expected to hold a combine resource base of about 1.100million tons of bauxite. These deposits are expected to provide bauxite to Cameroon's largest aluminium smelter at Edea (Legend Mining Ltd., 2010). The plant is owned by Aluminium du Cameroon (ALUCAM) which presently relies on bauxite imports from Guinea. Generally speaking, the country's anticipated natural resource output seems great yet, unexplored due to national incapacitation in relation to industrial development and the possibility of successful extraction of the said resources. It is needful therefore, to elaborate on the national capacity of specific resources and the prospects of their extraction to satisfy both national and international demands.

Prospective resource extractions in relation to national capacity

Iron Ore extraction

The International Mining and Infrastructural Corporation (IMIC) engage the Nkout mine in a deal worth $190 million. Preliminary economic assessment of resource exploitation reports that the project contains potential iron ore reserve of 700 million tons. The project however faced challenges due to Nkout location 330km from the deep-water near Kribi which is still under construction by the government of Cameroon (De Bruyn, 2010). Faced with such difficulties, the company has proposed building the necessary transportation facilities to actualize the project and begin production.

Another project under development by Cam Iron SA is the Mbalam Iron Ore with production capacity of 90% Sundance Resource and 10% local investors within Cameroon. Cam Ore is in possession of Exploration Permit No. 92 (EP92) and Exploration Permit No. 143 (EP143). By virtue of these permits, the company is legally authorized to explore an area of over 1.800km2 (Cameroon Mining Guide, 2014). The Company, Sundance Resources was set up to be managed by Chinese Hanlong. However, Chinese Hanlong could not secure funding due to its $1.9 billion deal failure in 2013 and thereby bringing the entire Mbalam Iron Ore project to a stalemate (Sundance Resources Ltd., 2010). Even though it was generally feared that the project has come to an end, Sundance Resources re-assured bringing the project online by 2018 regardless of the setbacks (Sundance Resources Ltd., 2010). These are some of the challenges that continuously obstruct the country's iron ore extraction which calls for government intervention.

Bauxite extraction

With regards to the extraction of bauxite, Hydromine, Dubai Aluminium Company in partnership with Hindalco industries have been re-designed as Cameroon Aluminium Limited (CAL) with the ambition to engage in the development of 8.5 million tons of bauxite per annum, mined at Ngaounda and Mini-Martap, and a 3 million tons per annum aluminium refinery (Cameroon Mining Guide, 2014). It is a bulk project divided into two phase. The first phase involved the setting up of a 4.25 million tons bauxite mine per annum and 1.5 million tons aluminium refinery per annum. Subsequently, both phases would be expanded to8.5 million tons bauxite per annum and 3 million tons aluminium refinery per annum as defined by the project's original roadmap (Cameroon Mining Guide, 2014). According to CAL, the project which is expected at its peak execution phase to create around 7, 000 direct jobs and approximately 6, 000-8, 000 indirect jobs is worth $4 million-$6 million. At the operational phase, it is expected to generate a direct employment rate of 1, 500-2, 000 jobs and an indirect employment rate of approximately 4, 000 jobs. These speculations can lead to significant economic benefits provided the bauxite extraction is sustained. CAL therefore counts on the government's support to make this project become a reality for the benefit of the country (Cameroon Mining Guide, 2014).

Cobalt, Nickel and Manganese extractions

The Toronto based Geovic Mining Corporation owns 60% of Geovic Cameroon while the National Investment Corporation of Cameroon controls the remaining 39.5%. Geovic Cameroon is in possession of an exploitation permit worth 1.250km2 of land harbouring seven large deposits of Cobalt, Nickel and Manganese.

Of these seven sites, Nkamouna and Mada have been prioritized as the most lucrative of all (Geovic Mining Corporation, 2010a). The company reported that the Nkamouna-Mada project holds the world's largest known primary Cobalt deposit and also credited with significant Nickel and Manganese deposits (Geovic Mining Corporation, 2010b). Nkamouna-Mada holds 68.1 million tons of reserves with content analysed to the value of 0.26% Cobalt, 0.65% Nickel and 1.48% Manganese says Geovic report. Furthermore, the two sites are in possession of 120.8 million tons of measured resources with 0.23% Cobalt content, 0.65% Nickel content and 1.35% Manganese content (Geovic Mining Corporation, 2010b).

It is important to note that, the Nkamouna-Mada deposit is worth just 22% of the total mineralized area within Geovic Mining permit boundary. The company speculates an average annual production output within the first eleven years of full production at 6.11 tons of Cobalt, 3.297 tons of Nickel and 62.800 tons of Manganese Carbonate (Geovic Mining Corporation, 2010b). Geovic reached a definitive agreement in July 2013 with China's Jiangxi Rare Netals Tungsten Holdings Group Company Ltd (JXTC). In this agreement, JXTC's intent to acquire 60.5% of the existing shares of Geovic Cameron pursuant to the execution of a share purchase agreement between JXTC and Geovic (Cameroon Mining Guide, 2014). Therefore Geovic remarked that JXTC's arrival paved the way towards construction and mineral extraction at the Nkamouna project. The foreign Company became the life line for the development of the Nkamouna project (Cameroon Mining Guide, 2014).

Uranium and Diamond extractions

Uranium exploration in the North and South West regions of Cameroon is done by Canada's Mega Uranium Ltd through its Nu Energy Corporation. As part of the program, the company in 2010 started a drilling function in the region over an area of 300m length but unfortunately, nothing of economic significance was realized. Thus the program was terminated in order to provide room for reassessment and re-evaluation (Mega Uranium Ltd., 2010). The Cameroon government in collaboration with the Korean State further established the Mobilong diamond mine which became the first industrial mine to commence production in 2013. The mine holds about 416 million carats of proven gem quality including industrial diamond reserves evaluated at an annual production rate of about 800.000 carats (Musa, Tansa, 2010).

It is important to note that Cameroon was approved by the Kimberly Process (KP) Diamond Certification initiative in August 2012. The aim of the KP was and still is to control the trade of conflict diamonds (Cameroon Mining Guide, 2014). In essence, the initiative ensured that the country's diamond production can be sold in the international market where certified diamonds are sold. The certification guaranteed the commercialization of Cameroons natural resources for economic development (Cameroon Mining Guide, 2014). The above discuss so far enumerates how such resources have been monitored, preserved and managed for national interest. How beneficial have such resources been to the people of Cameroon will constitute our next point of discourse.

The call for reformative governance towards economic enhancement

From the brief summary discussed above, it is evident that Cameroon has the potential to become one of the fastest growing nations in sub-Saharan Africa. It is empowered with substantial resource base petroleum, forests, mineral deposits, a productive agricultural base and sufficiently skilled human resources (Amin, 2008: 126). It is also one among the few states in Africa that has not received any serious political turbulence. Unfortunately, such an advantage has not been transformed into economic progress. Instead, the country witnessed an economic down trend in the past decades, the result of which, it was listed among the few African countries under observation for having reached the heavily indebted poor countries initiative completion point (Sikod and Teke, 2012). Before 1986, Cameroons economic growth was seemingly strong due to the production and exportation of natural resources and later on the expansion of the petroleum sector. Notwithstanding, petroleum revenues dropped around 1986 owing to the coincidental reduction in monetary values and numerical decline of exploitable sites. At the same time, the terms of trade for crop exports declined. The slowing down of the economy brought to the fore serious structural and mismanagement issues (Njikam, 2003).

Supported by the World Bank and the International Monetary Fund (IMF), the government embarked on a series of economic reform programs that begun around the 1980s. By 1993, no significant improvements were apparent. The economy had deteriorated significantly: continuous public finance deficits emerged as falling revenues were not matched by spending costs (Sikod and Teke, 2012). Also, the growing economic decline was accompanied by increasing poverty levels. The government decided to take the harsh, but unfortunate measure of slashing nominal civil service salaries by over 60% in 1993. This was accompanied by a 50% devaluation of the CFA francs as used in the franc zone in 1994.

Despite all these measures, Cameroon was still caught in the horns of a dilemma for obvious reasons: (a) issues relating to administrative governance were not acknowledged in the measures; (b) the government failed to meet the conditions of the first four IMF programmes or implemented some of the measures late; and (c) slashing civil servants' salaries led to rampant rent seeking, as the civil servants tried to maintain consumption at the same degree as before the wage cuts and devaluation (Sikod and Teke, 2012). Workers were also generally demoralized and no longer productive. The situation deteriorated as the debts (external and internal) accumulated even after the country had rescheduled its loans a number of times. Eventually Cameroon qualified as a Heavily Indebted Poor Country (HIPC), and was enlisted to benefit from the HIPC forgiveness program in 2006. Appended to the economic situation was the rising depravity in the public sector, political repression and limited liberties (Sikod and Teke, 2012). In 1998 and 1999 Transparency International classified Cameroon as the most corrupt nation in the World. From 1976 to 2006, Freedom House classified Cameroon as a country that was not free, based on its political right and civil liberty indices. These two organizations underscored the issues of bad governance in the state (Sikod and Teke, 2012).

Pressure from international donors and civil society organizations led the government to acknowledge that without tackling the governance issues along with implementing the structural adjustment measures, no positive outcome could be anticipated (Amin, 2008: 126). In 1992, the American Embassy stated that while Cameroon's long-run growth potential was great, "it will take political and economic liberalization to be realized, greater transparency and accountability in government, an independent judicial system, and improved definition and enforcement of contracts and property rights" (Sikod and Teke, 2012). It is now fairly well recognized that since economic management is hampered by a lack of transparency and political accountability rooted in a still incompletely democratized political system, further democratization would facilitate recovery.

In 1998, the government reluctantly adopted a National Governance Program, with a commission to oppose corruption, ensure the rights and liberties of the citizens, etc. In his State of the Nations' address for the year 2005/2006, the President of Cameroon admitted that governance was at the core of the challenges facing the country (Sikod and Teke, 2012). He intimated that the main ground of the mitigated economic growth Cameroon was facing was inertia, and had perverted the Cameroonian bureaucracy. It was not the lack of resources, human or financial attributes as perceived by many. Hence, he acknowledged in 2006 that without fighting corruption, the nation was unlikely to enjoy the economic growth needed to alleviate the poverty level (Sikod and Teke, 2012). A number of studies on Cameroon have concentrated on examining socio-economic factors affecting economic performance, with very little emphasis on the institutional and administrative dimensions vis-à-vis, the role of good governance. This write up has been design to address these challenges with the view to identify and discuss the historic gaps in Cameroons political History.

An overview of Cameroon's political history

Historically, Cameroon was a German protectorate territory from 1884. The territory under German administration also included the British Northern Cameroon which became part of Nigeria in the plebiscite of 1961 (Ngoh, 1979). German Kamerun was later divided into British and French Cameroons in 1916 with slight modifications in the administrative structure achieved by virtue of the Milner-Simon Agreement of 10 July 1919 (Geschiere, 1993: 155). The British Cameroon which was a combination of the Northern and Southern Cameroons comprised one fifth while French Cameroon constituted four fifths of the entire territory. They were considered Class B Mandated Territories of the League of Nations until 1946 when they became United Nations Trust Territories. Both the British and French Cameroon had separate legal and political entities with different administrative systems designed to eradicate subsequent endeavours of reunification (Ngoh, 1979).

At the close of World War II (WW II), Article 76 (b) of the Charter of the United Nations (UN) out rightly called for the British and French to administer their respective spheres of Cameroon towards self-government. Accordingly, it called on the administrative authorities;

To promote the political, economic, social and educational advancement of the inhabitants of the Trust Territories and their progressive development towards self-government or independence as may be appropriate to the particular circumstances of each territory and its peoples and the freely expressed wishes of the peoples concern...

Before the London Constitutional Conferences held in the years 1957 and 1958, three political options regarding independence had emerged for British Southern Cameroons. In their order of priority, the first option was independence as a separate political entity while, the second was independence in association with Nigeria and the last option was independence by reuniting with French Cameroun. The three options persisted for a while with the most popular being independence as a separate political entity (Ngoh, 1979).

However, the UN General Assembly resolution 1352 (xiv) on British Cameroons Plebiscite of 1961 eliminated the possibility of separate independence for Southern Cameroons which of course cancelled the first and most popular option available for Southern Cameroons Independence. The denial of the right to independence as a separate entity was achieved with thanks giving to the British who tactfully block every chance of the Southern Cameroonians voting for independence as a separate entity (Ayim, 2010: 66). In her view, the territory of Southern Cameroon was fragmented and not viable economically to survive without depending on Nigeria or the Republic of Cameroon. This opinion gained popular recognition and the option for Southern Cameroons independence as a separate political entity was ruled out in the Mamfe All Party Conference of August 1959 (Ayim, 2010: 66). Hence, two options were left for Southern Cameroonians to decide. They had the option to either gain independence by joining the independent Federation of Nigeria or by joining the independent Republic of Cameroon.

This novel position was not appreciated by the majority of Southern Cameroonians and therefore, John Ngu Foncha was asked to lead a delegation to London in November 1960 to include the option of independence as a separate political entity. Despite the efforts made, the option was not granted. However, Principles VII and VIII of UN General Assembly Resolution 1541(XV) provided for Southern Cameroons independence either through association or integration. The principles emphasized that the union "should be on the basis of complete equality between the peoples of the erstwhile Non-Self-Governing Territory and those of the independent country with which it is integrated. The peoples of both territories should have equal status and rights". It was through this contractual understanding that British Southern Cameroons were convinced to vote for unification with the French Cameroun on the 11th of February 1961 while British Northern Cameroon voted to join the Federal Republic of Nigeria (Nfor, 2016: 176).

The Foumban Constitutional Conference of 17th–21st July 1961 came to a broad consensus on what the union between the two Cameroons was going to look like. The Agreement was legalized by the Yaoundé Tripartite Conference of 2nd–7th August 1961 (Chiabi, 1997). Whereas significant progress was made in the realm of legal reforms, the inclusion of these laws into the draft 1961 constitution was never brought to the attention of the Southern Cameroons House of Chiefs (SCHC) and the Southern Cameroons House of Assembly (SCHA) for deliberations and approval as stipulated by the

UN principles on equality through which the union became a reality. More so, the Agreement was signed by the president of the Republic of Cameroon, Ahmadou Ahidjo on the 1st of September 1961 when the Federal Republic of Cameroon had not yet come into existence (Emeh, 2017). Ironically, the president exercised executive power under the administrative authority of the Republic of Cameroon to affect the governance of the Federal Republic of Cameroon which was yet to come into being. Whatever the case may be, the fact remains! The two territories came together in this union as a Federation of East Cameroon and West Cameroon (Cameroon Constitution, 1961: Article 1(1)).

While the West Cameroonians struggle to deal with the political dispensation regarded as imposed upon them by circumstances beyond control, the president proposed a new constitution to convert the Federal State into a Unitary State with the name "The United Republic of Cameroon" (Percival, 2008: 10). Due to the fact that freedom of speech and expression of private opinion was not guaranteed under the Cameroon legal system, the newly proposed constitution was voted without objection by an overwhelming majority in Parliament and became a reality through the Referendum of 20th May 1972. By these political manoeuvres, Southern Cameroonians came to the conclusion that the purported Federation invoked at the time of reunification was a post-colonial tool to suppress and possibly eradicate the Anglophone culture (Percival, 2008: 10).

The 1972 Constitution was amended to include the position of a Prime Minister who shall become the constitutional successor of the President of the Republic. Further constitutional amendments in 1984 changed the country's name from "The United Republic of Cameroon" to "The Republic of Cameroon". In the opinion of West Cameroonians, Law No. 84-1 of 4 February 1984, was irrefutable evidence that the original intention of the proposed 1961 union was to absorb Southern Cameroon and not to treat with them as equal partners in the condominium (Percival, 2008: 10). This was evident in all spheres of the country's political, economic and social administrative setups. Subsequently, Southern Cameroonians were neither represented in the country's political decision making processes nor did they fully enjoy the economic output of the country's natural resources. The continuous suppression of the Anglophone's sub-system resulted in the birth of separatist movements that have today organized themselves as civil society organizations fighting against Anglophone marginalization (Emeh, 2017).

Uneven partitioning of resources provoked 'Civil Disobedience'

Cameroon was designed as a centralized unitary state under the 1972 Constitution the result of which, the country's administration was centralized in Yaoundé. By this administrative centralization, almost all ministries and government departments, including manufacturing industries and companies were centred in Yaoundé (Sikod and Teke, 2012). This administrative structure was particularly not favourable to Anglophone Cameroonians given that French language was a principal barrier and resources extracted from the Anglophone section was transferred for processing in Yaoundé. This created an administrative gap for which, resources were mostly exploited from the Anglophone regions, but processing and subsequent distribution for commercial purposes was done in Yaoundé and Douala (Emeh, 2017). In an attempt to remedy the situation, the 1996 Constitution provided for administrative decentralization to reach the door steps of majority Cameroonians, both English and French Speaking, the economic benefits arising from the country's available resources (Cameroon Constitution 1996, Article 1(2)).

Whereas, the said administrative decentralization articulated under the 1996 Constitution raised the hope of Southern Cameroonians towards a system of autonomy where values and cultural heritage would be restored, the reverse became a reality as decentralization was never achieved and Anglophone marginalization attain its climax (Emeh, 2017). Out of the five ministries concern with education which of course is a means of transmission of knowledge and culture, none of the ministers is Anglophone and none even qualifies for the position of a deputy or Secretary of State.

National Entrance Examinations into Schools that develop the country's human resource capacity are set per the French Subsystem of Education which of course makes it very difficult for the Francophones and Anglophones to compete on a level platform. Besides, majority members of these Examination Boards in Anglophone regions are Francophones all in effort to minimize the Anglophone interest, the reverse of which is never true for the Francophone regions (Emeh, 2017). These and many more gave the impression of a calculated attempt to kill the Anglophone culture.

In the deployment of human resource personnel's, there is an overwhelming inequality gap in the distribution of post of responsibilities between Anglophones and Francophones. Out of 36 ministers called upon to defend their yearly budget in December 2016, only one was Anglophone. Also, it seems strategic ministries have been reserved for francophone ministers only and Anglophones do not qualify to become Ministers or Secretary of State under these ministries. These include but are not limited to the ministries of Defence, Finance, Territorial Administration and Economy (Emeh, 2017).

Beside inherent administrative weaknesses perceived in the ministries and related government departments, The Association of Common Law Lawyers and the Teachers Trade Union raised a number of issues affecting the legal and education departments of the English Subsystem. The lawyers complained that the majority of Magistrates in the Anglophone regions are disproportionately Francophones who do not understand the English Language. Hence, most of their cases are being conducted and judgments released on the basis of the Civil Law jurisprudence as opposed to the Common Law tradition (Emeh, 2017). The OHADA Uniform Code governing commercial activities in Cameroon was written basically in French yet applicable to both the English and French sub-systems. Therefore, the lawyers argued that such attempts were meant to absorb the English sub-system and dissolve the Anglophone identity.

Teachers also complained that increasing number of Francophone principals and teachers alike, have been posted to Anglophone schools with little or no ability to put the English language into practice. As a consequence, they end up teaching in a language that is neither English nor French (pidgin) (Kindzeka, 2016). Because language is a medium of instruction through which the student undergo transformation, it is believed that the act of using an unfamiliar language to transmit academic information's only helps to un-teach rather than teach the students. Therefore Parents and teachers from the Anglophone regions felt disappointed by this display of disrespect for the Anglophone academic sub-system.

The complainants also expressed discontent towards the poor infrastructural setups, including poor road networks in the North and South West Regions of the Country and the mismanagement and ruin of relevant companies like the West Cameroon Marketing Board, West Cameroon Cooperative Movement, Cameroon Bank and many more (Emeh, 2017). Oil revenues have been patronized by those in power to accommodate their personal ambitions and those of their allies. In addition, major agro-industrial enterprises, especially the Cameroon Development Cooperation (CDC) and Pamol du Cameroun Ltd (Pamol), are being sold or their headquarters moved elsewhere (Emeh, 2017). These and many more prompted the submission of a memorandum to the presidency by the Association of Common Law Lawyers and the Teachers Trade Union, highlighting some of the issues to be addressed by the President of the Republic, the failure of which would result in further actions as promised by the complainants (Emeh, 2017).

In the president's State of the Nations Address for the year 2016, he waived the most important and long awaited question regarding Anglophone marginalization. Rather, the president told the nation that the purported Anglophone problem put forth by Common Law lawyers and teachers was a fallacy. He refused acknowledging the presence of an Anglophone problem (Emeh, 2017). The president further insisted that he took the oath of office as president to defend a "one and indivisible" Cameroon as provided for under Article 1(2) of the 1996 Constitution. Whereas the said "one and indivisible" Cameroon is clearly stated under Article 1(2) of the constitution, the same section provides for "administrative decentralization" which has been waived by the president. The continuous silence on the part of the president and top government officials frustrated the civil society of Anglophone Cameroonians. Hence, the teachers and lawyers flamed out such frustrations by disregarding their functions to paralyze the educational and legal sectors of the English Subsystem. These actions gained support from the civil society of Anglophone Cameroonians and subsequently resulted in massive civil disobedience that has left the country in a state of political uncertainty.

Finding common ground(s)

The silent and ongoing political turmoil affecting the English Speaking Regions of Cameroon has not only paralyzed the academic and legal sectors of the English Sub-system but as well, it has led to serious economic hardship as the region is partially disconnected from the rest of the world. Hundreds of English Speaking Cameroonians have been arrested and detained in the Yaoundé Kondengui Central Prison (Emeh, 2017). The government seemed to have launched a campaign of terror against Anglophone Cameroonians due to the fact that legitimate complaints affecting their fundamental human rights have been raised. While it seemed such showcase of political hegemony still continue in the region, one question remains! Will the government's continuous suppression and violation of fundamental human rights of English Speaking Cameroonians bring solution to the country's socio-political and economic issues? If not, what then will be the way forward?

Human rights activists have recon that atrocities do not weaken the opponent's ambition to continually fighting for a change. Rather, it fuels their fury and increases their combat techniques. It is important therefore to engage in to meaningful and constructive dialogue as an alternative to violence in the face of turbulence (Shelton, 2015: 438). On their part, Conflict Resolution Activist have identified that effective resolution entails proper assessment of the root causes of every conflict. In doing so, it becomes easier to identify joint and separate interests of conflicting parties in the face of a crisis. Through constructive dialogue, such interests can positively inform one another and also motivate the zeal of conflicting parties towards finding a lasting solution to their problems. From this premise, one can say for sure that meaningful and constructive dialogue can serve

323

as an alternative to violence in the face of turbulence (Kaufman and Williams, 2010: 79).

It is hoped that the political crisis in Cameroon could have been resolved if the government had considered engaging the leaders of the Teachers Trade Union and the Association of Common Law Lawyers in to constructive and meaningful dialogue with the view to addressing at least some, if not all of their concerns. Through a number of governance issues affecting the English Sub-system, the complainants requested for re-installation of the federal Constitution of 1961 (Emeh, 2017). Besides government denial of the existence of an Anglophone problem, the president continually maintain his constitutional obligation to defend a "one and indivisible Cameroon" as stipulated under Article 1(2) of the 1996 Constitution. For the law to gain its full meaning as intended by the draftsman, it must be interpreted in completion and not in patches. Whereas Article 1(2) of the 1996 Constitution provides for a "one and indivisible" Cameroon, it as well provides for "administrative decentralization" to grant separate administrative autonomy to the ten regions of Cameroon. If the quest for Federalism is denied on the basis that it is unconstitutional, at least, administrative decentralization clearly stipulated under the constitution should be utilized by the government as the starting point for a meaningful and constructive dialogue. It is hope that the Anglophone problem can be resolved through this means which has rather been undermined for political reasons.

Conclusion

Conclusively, it can be said that the solution to Cameroon's crisis is at hand but, the government searches for it afar. Relevant constitutional jurisprudence capable of bringing the crisis to an end has been ignored for obvious political reasons. If Article 1(2) of the 1996 Constitution is given priority, then it should be applicable in the broader sense. The narrow approach will only cause more problems for the country as Anglophone Cameroonians have risen on their feet's to ask for what is constitutionally permissible and rightly theirs. By such constitutional fulfilment, long standing socio-political and economic issues will be resolved for the benefit of the entire republic of Cameroon. It is acceptable that numerous constitutional amendments have not solved Cameroon's political crisis. This is because politics is always given preference over the law (Emeh, 2017). In this regard, the country needs no further constitutional amendments, for the solution to its problem is already printed under Article 1(2) of the 1996 Constitution. Whichever method used by the government to resolve the crisis in Cameroon, the solution lies under Article 1(2) of the 1996 Constitution of Cameroon.

Bibliography

Amin, A. A. (2008). *Developing a Sustainable Economy in Cameroon.* Africa Books Collective: 126.

Ashley, R. (2005). 'The Policy Terrain in Protected Area Landscapes: How Laws and Institutions Affect Conservation, Livelihoods, and Agroforestry in the Landscapes Surrounding Campo Ma'an National Park and The Dja Biosphere Reserve, Cameroon.' Tropical Resources Institute, School of Forestry and Environmental Studies, Yale University: 9.

Ayim, M. A. (2010). *Former British Southern Cameroons Journey Towards Complete Decolonisation, Independence and Sovereignty: A Comprehensive Compilation of Efforts.* Vol. One, AuthorHouse: 66.

Belle, W. N. (2016). 'Why you must visit Cameroon, Africa in miniature. Available at;
https://www.africanexponent.com/post/8100-cameroon-african-in-miniature.[Accessed 18 March 2017).

Cameroon Mining Guide (2014) KPMG Global mining Institute. Available at; http//:kpmg.com/mining. [Accessed 18/03/2017].

Cameroon population 2017, available at;
http://countrymeters.info/en/Cameroon.[Accessed 18 March 2017.

Chiabi E. (1997). *The making of modern Cameroon.* Volume 1. Lanham, MD: University Press of America.

Constitution of the Republic of Cameroon (1961). Law No. 61/24 of 1st September 1961 revising the Constitution law of 4th March 1960.

Constitution of the Republic of Cameroon, (Referred to as Cameroon Constitution, (1996).

Law No. 96-06 of 18 January 1996 to amend the Constitution of 2 June 1972.

De Bruyn, C. (2010). 'Africa Aura sees potential for significant iron ore project in Cameroon. Creamer Media (Pty) Ltd.' Available at; http://www.miningweekly.com/article/african-aurasees-potential-for-significant- iron-ore-project-in-cameroon-2010-09-21.)[Accessed 18 March 2017].

Emeh, W. (2017). 'Ticking time bomb of Anglophone Marginalisation: The facts and the farce. *Cameroon Panorama*, January (edn.), No. 702.

Geovic Mining Corporation (2010a). 'Republic of Cameroon-Africa profile. Mining Corp.' Available at; http://www.geovic.net/cameroon_profile.php.)[Accessed 18 March 2017].

Geovic Mining Corporation (2010b). 'Republic of Cameroon-Nkamouna: Geovic Mining Corp.' Available at; http://www.geovic.net/projects.php.) [Accessed 18 March 2017].

Geschiere, P. (1993). 'Chiefs and colonial rule in Cameroon: Inventing chieftaincy, French and British style.' *Journal of the International African Institute*, volume 63, No. 2: 151-175.

Kaufman, J. P. and Williams, K. P. (2010). *Women and War: Gender identity and Activism in Times of Conflict.*: Kumarian Press: 79.

Kengaum *et al.* (2016). 'Cameroon's forest policy within the overall national land use framework: from sectorial approaches to global coherence? *International Forestry Review* 18 (Supplement 1): 4-13.

Kindzeka, M. E. (2016). 'Lawyers, Teachers in Cameroon Strike for More English in Anglophone regions.' Available at; http://www.voanews.com/a/lawyers-teachers- strike-cameroon-more-english-anglophone-regions/3616197.html [Accessed 19March 2017].

Kiye, M. E. (2015). 'The Repugnancy and Incompatibility Tests and Customary Law in Anglophone Cameroon. *African Studies Quarterly*, Volume 15, Issue 2: 86.

Legend Mining Ltd., (2010). 'Legend exercises its right to acquire 90% interest in Cameroon project.' Available at; http://legendmining.com.au/cameroon-project/.[Accessed 18 March 2017].

Linder, J. M. (2008). 'The impact of hunting primates in Korup National Park, Cameroon: Implications for primate conservation. *ProQuest Publications Online*: 216.

McCall, M. and Minang, P. (2005). 'Assessing participatory GIS for community-based natural resource management: claiming community forest in Cameroon. *The Geographical Journal*, Volume 171, No. 4.

Mega Uranium Ltd. (2010). 'Mega provides update on exploration in Cameroon: Mega Uranium Ltd.' Available at; http://www.megauranium.com/news_room/2010/index.php? &content_id=380.) [Accessed 18 March 2017].

Mengang, J. M. (1995). 'Evolution of Natural Resource Policy in Cameroon. Yale F&ES BULLETIN, No. 102. Available at; https://environment.yale.edu/publication-series/documents/.../0-9/102mengang.pdf [accessed date 18 March 2017].

Musa, Tansa. (2010). 'S. Korea's C&K signs Cameroon diamond convention. *International Business Times,* July 9. Available at; http://www.ibtimes.com/articles/33874/20100709/s-korea-s-c-k-signscameroon- diamond-convention.html.) [Accessed; 18 March 2017].

Newman, H. R. (2012). *The mineral industries of Cameroon and Cape Verde*. 2010 Mineral Yearbook, Cameroon and Cape Verde. Place of publication: Publisher.

Nfor, N. N. (2016). *Urgency of a New Dawn: Prison Thoughts and Reflections*. Langaa RPCIG: 176.

Ngang, F. D. (2015). 'The contribution of community-based natural resource management to livelihood conservation and governance in Cameroon. A comparative assessment of three community forest in Fako Division. Pan African Institute for Development – West Africa (PAID-WA).

Ngoh, V. J. (1979). 'The political evolution of Cameroon, 1884-1961.'Dissertations and Theses. Paper 2929. Available at; http://pdxscholar.library.pdx.edu/cgi/viewcontent.cgi?article=3936&context=open_a ccess_etds [Accessed 18 March 2017].

Ngwafor, E. N. (2000). 'Customary law versus statutory law: An unresolved second millennium moral quagmire. *Int'l Surv. Fam. L.* 55.

Njeumo, A. (2001). 'The development of community forest in Cameroon: origins, current situation and constraints.' Rural Development Forestry Nature Paper 25b.

Njikam, O. (2003). 'Trade reforms and efficiency in Cameroons manufacturing industries.' African Economic Research Consortium, Research Paper No. 133.

Percival J. (2008). *The 1961 Cameroon Plebiscite: Choice Or Betrayal:* African Book Collective: 10.

Schroth, G., G. Fonseca, C. A. Harvey, C. Gascon, H. Asconcelos and A.M. Izac (eds). (2004) *Agroforestry and Biodiversity Conservation in Tropical Landscapes.* Washington: Island Press.

Shelton, D. (2015). *Remedies in International Human Rights Law.* Oxford: Oxford University Press: 438.

Sikod F and Teke J. (2012). 'Governance and Economic growth in Cameroon.' Africa Economic Research Consortium, Nairobi, AERC Research Papers 250.

Sundance Resources Ltd. (2010). 'Mbalam project MOU with China rail—Africa: Sundance Resources Ltd.' Available at; http://www.sundanceresources.com.au/IRM/Company/Show Page.aspx/   PDFs/1749-15844879/MbalamProjectMOUSignedwithChinaRailAfrica.) [Accessed 18 March 2017].

Thomas *et al.* (2004). *Getting biodiversity projects to work: Towards more effective conservation and development.* Colombia: Colombia University Press: 211.

Chapter Eleven

Aligning the Mining Sector with Sustainable Development in Namibia

Michelle Munyanduki

Introduction

In retrospect, mining activity began officially in 1855 in Walvis Bay however Social Corporate Responsibility as a practice only surfaces over a century later in the 1980s.[27] Littlewood describes the nature of SCR as practiced by mining companies in the 1990s to the 2000s as green wash.[28] On the other hand for the longest time mining activities have posed a risk on the environment hence calls for rehabilitation to restore ecosystems. However it must be acknowledged that much of the improvement in practice can be attributed to greater public scrutiny from pressure groups and the media.

This chapter provides an evaluation on how Namibia currently deals with the social and environmental aspects of sustainable development with a particular focus on the corporate social responsibility (CSR) and rehabilitation in the uranium mining industry. Thus the central question is to what extent is the current status of the mining industry aligned with sustainable development?

At this point key terms for definition are firstly, *Sustainable development*, which generally understood, means "development that meets the needs of the present without compromising the ability of future generations to meet their own needs".[29] Explained more

---

[27]BDO. 2016. Mining in Namibia Available at www.bdo.com.na; last accessed on August 15 2017

[28] Littlewood, D. 2011. CRR 2011 Conference Paper Corporate Social Responsibility (CSR), Development and the Mining Industry in Namibia: Critical Reflections through a Relational Lens

[29] World Commission on Environment and Development's (the Brundtland Commission) report Our Common Future (Oxford: Oxford University Press, 1987).

precisely, the *International Council on Mines and Minerals* (ICMM) states that; "in the mining and metals sector ... investments should be financially profitable, technically appropriate, environmentally sound and socially responsible".[30] Sustainable development as a concept stands on three legs as illustrated below.

Secondly, *Rehabilitation* is the overall, avoidance of pollution of the water, soil and air. It involves the optimization of the use of natural resources and energy and minimization of any impact from the site and its activities on people and the environment. In so doing, it includes considerations of sustainability, bio-diversity and ecology in guarding against environmental impact.[31]

Lastly, *Corporate Social Responsibility* (CSR); refers to voluntary actions undertaken by mining companies to either improve the living conditions (economic, social, environmental) of local communities or to reduce the negative effects of mining projects. By definition, voluntary actions are those that go beyond legal obligations, contracts, and license agreements although evolving legal requirements are leading towards increased regulation of CSR worldwide.[32]

Since the main purpose of this chapter is to evaluate, the criteria of evaluation shall be the degree of 'alignment with sustainable development'. To satisfy this criterion it is submitted that two elements need to be satisfied; there should be clear law, this law must further be binding law and a monitoring system to ensure compliance to the law needs to be available.

Before evaluation of the degree to which the mining sector is aligned to sustainable development, the first port of call is for one to derive an appreciation of the significance of mining in general by reflecting on the statistics. Currently, 50% of exports and 11.9% of Gross National Income (GNI) are derived from the mining industry and in 2014 government recouped N$3.76 billion in tax and royalties

---

[30]International Council on Mining and Metals.
[31]Namibia Uranium Association. 2016. *Sustaining Global Best Practices in Uranium Mining and Processing: Principles for Managing Radiation, Health and Safety, Waste and the Environment.* Available at www.namibianuranium.org ; last accessed on 15 August 2016
[32] www.miningfacts.com

alone.[33] Hence, it is no exaggeration to assert that mining is the backbone of the Namibian economy. Apart from the notable revenue contribution, the industry employs about 8835 permanent, 716 temporary and 9423 contract employees.[34] Even so, it is submitted that through SCR communities have benefited to the extent of dependency from mining activity.

It comes as no surprise that in Namibia mining is discussed by government more in line with its economic contribution and or benefits. As such, matters relating to the economic aspects of mining are clearly outlined in the *Minerals Act*;[35] for instance it reserves the entire *Part 16* of the *Act* to financial matters, dealing directly with issues of royalty payments, penalties, security for payment and proof of payments. Unfortunately, the social and environmental aspects of the mining which inform sustainable development attract less attention.[36] This position is evident in the mining legal framework.

At this juncture I must highlight *that Article 100* read with *Article 95 (i)* of the Constitution, has the effect that the state being the owner of minerals has a mandate to utilize resources in a sustainable manner for the benefit of all Namibians.[37] From a social perspective, the larger percentage of people for which the state holds these minerals benefit scantly from revenue derived from mining.[38] In addition, the environmental aspect of mining is inadequately regulated with the effect that matters such as rehabilitation are self-regulatory. Unfortunately, to a large degree, this is because Namibia lacks adequate monitoring tools attributed to limited human capital. Thus this renders the policy of self-regulation ineffective.

It is submitted that the law plays a significant role in attaining sustainable development, for how else can a state develop sustainably without setting out clear cut-obligations and boundaries in an economically centred industry as mining. Further outlook identifies that the law that regulates mining activities must address the social

---

[33] Chamber of Mines Namibia Annual Report 2015, p7
[34] Ibid.
[35] No. 33 of 1992. Sections 114- 120
[36] United Nations. 2016. Sustainable Development Goals. Available at www.un.org; last accessed on 15 August 2016
[37] The Constitution of Namibia 1 of 1990
[38] Namibia has a Gini coefficient of 61.3

and environmental issues with as much clarity and gravity as it does the economic issues (such as royalties and tax) for the purpose of sustainable development.

Uranium Mining and the Society: Corporate Social Responsibility

It must be highlighted from the onset that government does not require companies to contribute towards CSR in its legal framework.[39] Although CSR programs have sometimes been viewed as part of a company's public relations strategy, they are now increasingly recognized as a serious effort to deliver sustainable benefits and to improve the well-being of people and communities in which miners operate.[40]

While the Environmental Management Act[41] indicates that the Namibian people should benefit from the exploitation of resources in their areas; the Act does not elaborate on what this actually means. However to fill this vacuum on interpretation, the Act refers to international best practices as guiding principles. But one needs to understand that even international best practices are merely advice to the state and not the company.

On the other hand, the *Namibian Uranium Association* (NUA) as the mother body of the uranium industry accepts international guidelines as designed by the World Uranium Association (WUA) to guide the industry. As such the *World Uranium Association Policy Document (WUAPD)* is the first point of reference in the uranium industry in regards to CSR.[42] Under this document the *Principles of Uranium Stewardship,*[43] indicate that companies should contribute to the social and economic development in the areas they operate in. The same message of involvement in the development of the communities is conveyed by the ICMM in their *Sustainable Development*

---

[39]Alberto, Z. 28 September 2016. CSRR in the mining sector. (M. Munyanduki, Interviewer)
[40]Principles of Uranium Stewardship,
[41] Section 3
[42] Namibia Uranium Institute.
[43] Principle 4

Principles.[44]However these are guidelines and are thus not legally binding no matter the extent of detail displayed. As a result no legal obligation on the mining companies can ensue from them.

In light of this, currently in the uranium industry corporate social responsibility is carried out on a self-regulatory basis.[45] This means that companies formulate their own strategies to contribute to the social and economic development. Generally the Chamber of Mines report indicates that this is mostly carried out through donations to community projects, training programs and bursary awards.[46] However what is reported are activities that the companies have voluntarily decided to contribute towards and there is no verification of the accuracy of these reports.

Rossing CSR

For the lack of time and space this chapter does not go in depth with all the Rossing contributions towards CSR but identifies a few examples necessary to substantiate arguments herein. On CSR, Rossing gives a detailed account in its annual reports going beyond what is done by its counterparts. In principle, Rossing asserts that its CSR is "not a philanthropic endeavour but a core business interest aimed at maintaining sustainable and mutually beneficial relationships" with stakeholders.[47] From as early as 1978 Rossing established a foundation run by a board of trustees to further its CSR.[48] In addition to this, it is a member of the Erongo Development Fund (EDF). The latter is an independent and financially prudent organisation involved in community development projects.[49] Through these channels and at times directly through the company, Rossing executes its CSR.

---

[44] Principle 9

[45] Minerals Policy 2002 5.3

[46]Chamber of Mines of Namibia Annual Report 2015

[47] Rossing Limited. 2016. *Rossing Uranium Limited Report to Stakeholder 2015.* Available at www.rossing.com; Last accessed 14 August 2016, p32

[48] Rossing Limited.

[49] Namibian Uranium Institute. 2016. *Namibia Uranium Institute Annual report 2014/2015*, p16Available at www.namibianuranium.org.na; Last accessed 14 August 2016.

In 2015, Rossing made a contribution of N$18 million (approximately 1% of a turnover of N$1.841billion in 2015) through the company directly or the foundation as part of their CSR.[50] This covers financial support towards various initiatives in art, culture, agriculture, education and the environment.[51] Their annual reports give a comprehensive account of their CSR.

From as early as 1990, Rossing partnered with the Ministry of Education, Arts and Culture.[52] This partnership led to the establishment of the mathematics, science and English centres in Gobabis, Swakopmund and Windhoek. They were designed to address the issue of poor performance in these subjects among the local students. To support this initiative, the centres include libraries which are at the disposal of the communities. Even so, Rossing has scholarship, apprenticeship and part-time study opportunities for the locals. It is clear that their contribution to education in the community cannot be overemphasised. Their contribution was likewise extended to the Orphans and Vulnerable Children's centre in 2015. Through the company's employee volunteer program, Rossing employees painted the centre.

Evaluation of the sustainability CSR

To this end, although done on an ad hoc basis, it is imperative to highlight that Rossing sets the standard in the uranium industry of what it means to be a good corporate citizen as far as Namibia is concerned. It somewhat represents a general understanding of what could generally be understood as the fulfilment of CSR according to international best practice in the Namibian context.

However, an in-depth analysis indicates the requirement of an increased alignment of the current state of affairs with sustainable social and economic development. Thus one must enquire, as

---

[50]Namibian Uranium Institute. 2016. *Namibia Uranium Institute Annual report 2014/2015*, p16 Available at www.namibianuranium.org.na; Last accessed 14 August 2016.

[51] Ibid, p59

[52]Rossing Limited. 2016. *Rossing Uranium Limited Report to Stakeholder 2015*. Available at www.rossing.com; Last accessed 14 August 2016.p33-43

regulated by the international guidelines and implemented through self-regulation, just how sustainable current CSR is. These questions must be understood in light of the aim of CSR which is to benefit the communities in which the corporates operate. The questions that arise at this point of the discussion are; what contributions from the corporate world benefit the communities in the long-term and in what manner can CSR be executed to ensure sustainability?

At this interval a few issues can be identified. Firstly, the execution of CSR in addition to varying from one company to another are executed on an ad hoc basis. This incredibly reduces the certainty of corporate contribution as part of their CSR. As the government policy requires self-regulation the matter of CSR is left in the hands of the corporates to contribute what they, from a 'subjective' point of view, deem necessary for the community's social and economic development. This whittles down the oversight by government over the corporates; a phenomenon that can become problematic in holding the companies accountable.[53]Even so the ambiguity contained in the earlier mentioned guiding policies only makes it more difficult for the mining sector to make use of them.

Furthermore Rossing decides who to partner with in pursuance of this mandate. As a result, while companies like Rossing are active some essentially take a back seat. In essence, there is an evident lack of uniformity in the implementation of this duty. This can be attributed first to the fact that, the government, in addition to allowing self-regulation, has vague rules guiding CSR. In addition to this, for the reason that the law does not place emphasis on this duty, so do the corporates. The WNA guidelines referred to above fail to highlight the importance of CSR but also do not define what "contribution to the social and economic development actually involves".

The Chamber of Mines Uranium Association has the responsibility to ensure that companies self-regulate but the fact that it is funded by the mining industry adds a flaw to the system of regulating the industry. Moreover, the absence of sanctions for non-

---

[53]Majer, M. 2013. *The Practice of Mining Companies in Building Relationships with Local Communities in the Context of CSR Formula.* Journal of Sustainable Mining. Volume 12, Issue 3, 2013, Pages 38–47

compliance or a clear disincentive to the CSR mandate renders the exercise ineffective. For example Rossing report to its stakeholders indicates that in the years 2011-2013 no funds were distributed through the Rossing Foundation.[54] For this reason it can be argued that companies perform their CSR mandate as and when it is convenient to them.

However above all of these issues, it must be acknowledged that the custodian is the state. International best practices are handed to the state and therefore it is for the state to ensure that they add legal enforceability of those practices.[55] Given the broad nature of international best practices, it is the duty of the state to ensure that mechanisms are in place to ensure that the necessary contribution is made. This is because not all mining companies have the same corporate values as Rossing in implementing their CSR. These companies will essentially need to be forced to contribute to their communities but above all they will need clear set binding standards for an effective contribution.

Uranium mining and the Environment: Rehabilitation

On the environmental end of mining progressively, mining companies are making efforts to reduce the environmental impact of mining and minimize the footprint of their activities throughout the mining cycle, including working to restore ecosystems post-mining.[56]

According to international standards Uranium mining must be conducted with due consideration of the environment for the purpose of sustainable development.[57]However in practice attaining a balance between the need to protect the environment and to gain economically from exploitation activity is no easy task.

---

[54] Rossing Limited. 2016. *Rossing Uranium Limited Report to Stakeholder 2015.* Available at www.rossing.com; Last accessed 14 August 2016, p59
[55] Brand, D & Heyns, C. 2005. Socio-economic Rights in South Africa. Pretoria: Pretoria University Press, p13
[56]Burke, A. 2007.*Eleven Steps to rehabilitation in the Succulent Karoo and Namib Desert.* Environmental Science and Namibia Nature Foundation. Oranjemund & Windhoek, p.24.
[57] Ibid.

As mentioned earlier, the term rehabilitation refers to those steps taken to repair the environment from damage and includes decommissioning as well as ecological restoration.[58] Since the Ministry of Mines and Energy issues mining licenses, an environmental clearance certificate is a prerequisite.[59] This certificate requires that in cases where damage to the environment cannot be avoided rehabilitation plans must be in place.

In Namibia, there is no clear legal obligation to rehabilitate a mine. However, as it is mentioned in the Environmental Management Plan, the company is legally bound to the plan it lays out. Be that as it may, the *Minimum Standards* for *Rehabilitation and Exploration Sites* as established by the NUA explains that the rationale for rehabilitation is "to reduce visual impact, prevent pollution and assist disturbed areas to reintegrate with the ecosystem".[60] Intrinsically, there is a general duty to rehabilitate and a duty to report any damage to the environment.[61] Unfortunately these standards are to a large extent too general to ensure adequate rehabilitation and environmental protection especially under the current self-regulatory framework. [62] Again for the reason that they constitute guidelines and are not embodied in a legal document makes it difficult for the state to enforce.

Firstly, the Minerals Act stipulates that in addition to providing an EIA that the company must provide an EMP setting out the steps to be taken in order to revive the environment from the ensued damage.[63] The Act precisely instructs the mining companies to take necessary steps to remediate the environment.[64] However, the vague wording makes its utility to the industry minimal. In *section 130,* the companies are directed to employ *continuous* rehabilitation to control the effects of exploitation activity. The term continuous in this context implies therefore that the law does not expect an operator to only rehabilitate at the end of the activities but rather to engage in a

---

[58] Ibid.

[59] Minerals Act

[60] Minimum Standards for Rehabilitation and Exploration Sites,2014

[61] Ibid.

[62] Ibid.p3

[63] Minerals Act 33 of 1992 Section 50 f (i) and (ii)

[64] Ibid. section 54(3)

constant exercise of repair of any harm done. However for the lack of detail and specification of the manner in which this is to be done renders the issues of rehabilitation ineffective.

This said, the Mining Policy insists on compliance with the international guidelines on rehabilitation.[65] It states that;

> Government will ensure compliance during rehabilitation with national policies and guidelines and where appropriate and applicable with global best practice and with relevant stakeholders to investigate the established financial mechanisms for environmental rehabilitation and aftercare.[66]

To this end, by Minimum Standards as established by Namibia Uranium Association guide the uranium industry on the issue of rehabilitation. These follow the international standards as established by the WNA but go a step further by creating an adapted version that precisely matched the Namibian context. These standards again, are said to represent the most practical interpretation of current knowledge based on experiences of practitioners and scientists.[67] Furthermore, on the crucial matter of funding for rehabilitation, the Chamber of Mines Code of conduct deals to a greater extent as compared to the Act,[68] with rehabilitation. They direct that attached to the environmental clearance certificate must be a financial guarantee in the form of an independently managed financial instrument to cover the costs of any likely impact to the environment attributed to exploitation activities.[69] While the Chamber is the mother body of mining, it is not an institution established by an Act of parliament but rather a *voluntary association*; as such their code is not legally binding. In fact the code appeals to the members to comply

---

[65] Section 5.3
[66] Minerals Policy 2002 Section 5 (3)
[67] Namibian Uranium Institute. 2014. *Minimum Standards for Rehabilitation and Exploration Sites* Available at www.namibianuranium.org.na; Last accessed 23 August 2016
[68] No.7 of 2007
[69] Section 5.2

which should not be the case for an issue so crucial to the protection of the environment.[70]

Rossing rehabilitation

From an environmental perspective, Rossing retained its ISO 14001 certification in 2015.[71] This is a standard which seeks to minimize environmental impacts from mining and encourage compliance with existing environmental law and policy through formal audits by external institutions.[72] Uniquely it has an on-going rehabilitation project of an erosion protection and sediment retention structure.[73]

The Rossing reports that it projects to end operations in 2025.[74] To this end, the company has put in place a rehabilitation plan for the closure phase. Important to note at this point is the fact that the open pit measures 3km by 1.5 km and is 390m deep. However Rossing has clearly displayed no intention of refilling this pit. Thus in 2025 it will remain as a mining void. However there are plans to cover the Tailing Storage Facility with waste rock to prevent dust emissions and storm water erosion. In addition, tailing seepage continues to be recovered but as opposed to reusing it for mining it is allowed to evaporate. Furthermore, there are plans to demolish and remove the entire infrastructure and decontaminate it before it is sold to third parties.

From its report, Rossing displays an affirmative stance in their rehabilitation compliance plans. Moreover, what makes their position more concrete is that in addition to their closure plan is a supporting financial guarantee to fund the execution of the rehabilitation plan as found in the *Rossing Environmental Rehabilitation Fund*.[75] Although there is no legal obligation in law, this reconciles with the Chamber of

---

[70] Chamber of mines Code of Conduct, 2010, introduction section

[71] Chamber of Mines. Annual Review.p45

[72] Renkhoff, N, A. 2015. Evaluation of Nuclear Legislation: The issue of rehabilitation of Uranium mining sites in Namibia. EJOLT report 22, p18

[73] Ibid.p59

[74] Rossing Limited. 2016. *Rossing Uranium Limited Report to Stakeholder 2015*. Available at www.rossing.com; Last accessed 14 August 2016,p45-53

[75] Ibid.p53

Mines Code of Conduct discussed above but attributed to the company policy which has allowed the company to retain its ISO14001 certificate. In addition, the corporate legal Counsel for Rossing explains that their fund is managed independently thereby reducing the risk of absorbing funds during financial difficulties.[76] To put this into perspective, the closure plan is estimated to cost N$1.4 billion, to date a balance of N$505 million stands.[77] This means that a deficit of N$895million remains standing. Assuming all things constant, that the mine is to halt operations in 2025, this means that an additional 10 years remain to assure the closure plan is fully funded. In essence, N$89 million per year will need to be injected into the fund until 2025 for the closure plan to be fully realized.

Evaluation of the sustainability of Rehabilitation

In light of the above, it can be submitted that a gap in law on the issue of rehabilitation of mines is a major concern hindering sustainable development. Presently there is no binding and clear law on the matter. However, it is submitted that although rehabilitation is self-regulated and in the absence of a binding law, it can also be implied. To put this clearly one needs to be cognizant of the Minerals Act,[78] which states that the mining company shall;

Exercise any right granted to him or her in terms of the provisions of this Act reasonably and in such manner that the rights and interests of the owner of any land to which such license relates are not adversely affected,[79]

It is clearly identified that by the use of the word 'shall' the section lays out a mandatory legal provision.[80] Although vague in text the rights and interests related to the owner in the mining context can be interpreted as the rights and interests of the Erongo community to a sustainable environment. Thus while it is inadequate to merely have

---

[76] Alberto, Z. 28 September 2016. *Rehabilitation at Rossing Mine.* (M. Munyanduki, Interviewer)
[77] Rossing Limited, p53
[78] No. 33 of 1992
[79]section 50 1 (a)
[80]Botha, C. (2005). *Statutory Interpretation: An Introduction for Students* (3rd Ed). Cape Town: Juta & Co, Ltd.

a rehabilitation plan, significantly, an omission to execute an *effective* rehabilitation plan is in fact a violation of this section.[81] To clarify what effective rehabilitation means it is paramount to refer back to its purpose as mentioned above; which is to reduce visual impact, prevent pollution and assist disturbed areas to reintegrate with the ecosystem.[82] These three elements are what in principle any so called rehabilitation plan should aim to achieve and so a plan should be directed towards these three elements.

As mentioned and acknowledged earlier, sustainable mining is no easy task. Rossing's rehabilitation plan though in place has protracted short comings in meeting the purpose of rehabilitation. Although it plans to remove infrastructure and decontaminate equipment before it is sold off, Rossing intends to leave its 3km by 1.5 km and 390m deep open pit as a void mine.[83] This essentially means that by 2025 upon closure, the Erongo region would have been robbed of an area of 3km by 1.5 km and 390m of land. But then again this is no ordinary plain land as it is situated in the Namib Desert; where we find the Doro and Namib Naukluft national parks. The Namib Desert is the centre of tourism in Namibia. Therefore, leaving the open pit will to a large extent negate the aim to reduce visual impact of the mining operation.

Above all, the major issue is that as the holder of the right to a sustainable environment, the state unfortunately allows mining companies to self-regulate. There are bodies such as the Sustainable Development Committee established by the NUA to ensure that uranium mining is done in an environmentally friendly manner (among other aims). However, their lack of capacity to execute their duty is not necessarily because of their apparent bias,[84] but more so because the members are reported to lack the additional expertise in environmental law.[85]

---

[81]To a good environment.

[82]HERSS standards.

[83]Rossing Limited. 2016. *Rossing Uranium Limited Report to Stakeholder 2015*. Available at www.rossing.com; Last accessed 14 August 2016,

[84] The Chairperson of the committee is a representative of uranium mine located in Bannerman's Etango project (considered to be a sensitive area. And the former legal advisors were corporate lawyers working for uranium companies.

[85]Renkhoff, N, A. 2015,p32

It is appreciated that the government took measures in 2011 to address the environmental concerns in the Erongo Region through a Strategic Environmental Assessment. This was followed by a detailed Strategic Environmental Management Plan (SEMP) which endeavours to advice on the way forward in aligning uranium mining activities with sustainable development. However, considering the free-market economic policies endorsed by the World Bank and International Monetary Fund,[86] and followed by the state, concerns are raised in relation to the degree of responsibility the latter expects from companies that are simply 'doing businesses'. It can be argued that a state primarily driven by short-term economic gain, with a short-sight on the consequence of uranium mining would reasonably believe that resource seeking investors that strive to cut on costs of production will actually invest in rehabilitation.

As mentioned earlier, the Chamber of Mines Code of Conduct[87] requires an environmental rehabilitation financial guarantee to fund rehabilitation plans. In accordance to this, Rossing reports in detail of its financial guarantee in its stakeholders' report. However, it omits to report to the Chamber of Mines in the report of this funding. By implication, this indicates that in practice, there is no obligation to report to the state on the financial standing of the rehabilitation financial guarantee. As such this compromises any guarantee of rehabilitation and ultimately puts the environment at risk. The corporate legal advisor for Rossing explains that the obligation to fund rehabilitation should be insisted on from the beginning of operation as this will allow investors to make informed long-term financial decisions.[88]

To these issues, the deputy director of environmental assessment states that there are plans to amend the environmental management act so that all players (new and old) of the mining industry are obliged to plan and fund rehabilitation.[89] In contrast, Rossing legal Counsel

---

[86]World Bank. 2009. Namibia – Country Brief. Washington D.C.

[87] Section 4.3(c)

[88] Alberto, Z. 28 September 2016. *Rehabilitation at Rossing Mine.* (M. Munyanduki, Interviewer)

[89] Saima, M. 28 September 2016. *Rehabilitation of Mines.* (M. Munyanduki, Interviewer)

cautions that a subsequent introduction of law requiring mines to provide funds for rehabilitation may be problematic.[90] This is because at stages like closure mining operations will not be making a profit to fund such programs.[91] The dilemma that the industry-players and government find themselves in as I have just illustrated is one that easily finds its routes in the lack of clearly defined binding law monitored by government for compliance.

Comparative Study: Canada, Manitoba

To this point a discussion of the Namibian state of affairs has been illustrated: going forward Canada forms the comparative study of the chapter. This is because not only is it the second largest producer of uranium but is generally accepted as the case study for best international practices in mining.[92] While the provincial states have the exclusive mandate to regulate mining activities in their provinces, it is highlighted that in the case of Canada, Provinces such as Manitoba have clear laws on rehabilitation and generally on the issue of CSR the central government plays a key role in incentivizing the practice.

Therefore Namibia can learn from Canada's example not only in rehabilitation and CSR but from a broad mining perspective on sustainability. While there is a lot to be desired in the Namibian legal framework, it is important to note in the first place that the *Mines and Minerals Act,*[93] for the province of Manitoba incorporates comprehensive law on rehabilitation. The legal framework of mining in Manitoba takes cognisance of all three pillars of sustainability explicitly. That is the environmental, social and the economic aspects. This is because in the first instance, the Act seeks to define the principles of sustainable development in light of the elements of sustainability in the mining industry.[94] Initially it states that;

---

[90] Alberto, Z.

[91] Ibid.

[92] Kabir, Z, Rabbi, F, Chowdhury, B, M and Akbar, D. 2015. *A Review of Mine Closure Planning and Practice in Canada and Australia* .World Review of Business Research. Vol. 5. No. 3; p140 – 159

[93] CC.S.M.c.M162

[94] Section 2

... decisions respecting the economy and mining activities be *integrated*[95] with decisions respecting protection and management of the environment so that mining activity is commenced with due regard for its impact on the environment and environmental programs or initiatives are instituted with proper regard for their economic impact;[96]

Observing from this section, it is clear that Manitoba seeks to take a more integrated approach in regulating the mining industry. The focus of the act as a whole essentially draws attention to the social and environmental matters that inform sustainability. This is something that evidently lacks, to a large extent in the Namibian Minerals Act.

Rehabilitation

To be more specific on sustainability, the Act defines what rehabilitation is for the mining companies.[97] It states that land that, in environmental terms, is considered to be damaged by mining activity should be rehabilitated.[98]While this instruction is similarly found in the Namibian context, the Manitoba Mines Act goes further by defining the term. It states that;

Rehabilitation" means, in respect of a project site or an aggregate quarry, the actions to be taken for the purpose of

Protecting the environment against adverse effects resulting from operations at the site or quarry ... Minimizing the detrimental impact on adjoining lands of operations at the site or quarry ... minimizing hazards to public safety resulting from operations at the site or quarry,... leaving the site in a state that is compatible with adjoining land uses...[99] In contrast, the Minerals Act,[100] defines the purpose of rehabilitation in broad terms leaving a lot of room for interpretation.

---

[95] My emphasis added
[96] Section 2.2 (a)
[97] Section 1
[98] Section 2.2 (h)
[99] Section 1
[100] No.33 of 1992

It simply seeks that rehabilitation leaves the land in a state that minimize effects of mining and prospecting.[101]

This process of rehabilitation is done progressively in the course of the operation and not at the end.[102] As such the company is mandated to report annually to the director,[103] on the success or otherwise of the rehabilitation process.[104] However what is more striking is that to secure guarantee that rehabilitation takes place, there is a Mine Rehabilitation Fund in which companies pay securities that fund rehabilitation should the need arise.[105] In addition to this there is a provision for the closure plan security which requires the company to make provision for a financial instrument aimed at covering the costs of rehabilitation.[106] On this, while Namibia has an environmental fund, there is no rehabilitation fund or law dictating the allocation of funds by companies specifically to fund rehabilitation.

In addition to this definition, the Mines Act of Manitoba attaches Regulations on Mine Closure.[107] It is these that evidently reflect that Manitoba is committed to ensure the protection of the environment through rehabilitation. While, like Namibia, Manitoba requires closure plans, it goes further by stipulating in its regulations the actual content it requires. Even so, reports are required on an annual basis with information on the nature, extent and adequacy of rehabilitation.

Most importantly are the cost schedule that the company must provide which covers costs of closure, rehabilitation and monitoring progress.[108] However all this, unlike the case of Namibia, needs to be certified by engineers that they are accurate or close approximates of the actual costs of rehabilitation.[109] This essentially displays a sense of diligence and a stance of pro-activeness on the part of the Director

---

[101] section 92

[102] Mines and Minerals Act section187

[103] Equivalent to the minister of mines in Namibia.

[104] Mine and Minerals Act section 190

[105] Ibid. Section 195

[106] Ibid. section 193

[107] Mine closure Regulation 67 of 1999

[108] Section 10

[109] Section 18

of Mines and Minerals to ensure sustainability of mining from an environmental perspective.

Corporate Social Responsibility

This portion of the paper essentially investigates the Canadian national policy on CSR. One must note from the onset that as a global leader in the extractives, Canada has a responsibility to ensure that it sets a good example to the rest of the industry players abroad. Thus what is particularly notable about the Canadian example is that the government not only provides comprehensive guidelines but it goes further into bringing support that encourages the mining industry to contribute towards CSR.[110]

At central government level, there are initiatives aimed at promoting CSR. In 2003, the Canadian Government supported the establishment of an online Sustainability Reporting Toolkit. To further compliance, government went on to establish The National Training Workshops on CSR for Canadian companies.[111] In 2007, the government joined the *Extractive Industries Transparency Initiative* (EITI), a mechanism to publish and verify company payments made to governments and government revenues received from mining (oil and gas).

The Canadian government issued the report on Building the Canadian Advantage: *A Corporate Social Responsibility (CSR) Strategy for the Canadian International Extractive Sector*,[112] which encourages Canadian companies to observe the international Guidelines in their operations at home and abroad. However unlike Namibia where the same is done in issuing guidelines, the task was extended by providing support that encourages compliance.

---

[110]Global Affairs Canada.2016.*Canada's Enhanced Corporate Social Responsibility Strategy to Strengthen Canada's Extractive Sector Abroad.* Available at www.international.gc.ca; last accessed on 29 August 2016

[111] Randall, S.J. 2010, Canada, *the Caribbean and Latin America: Trade, Investment and Political Challenges.* Canadian International Council

[112]Global Affairs Canada.2016. Canada's Enhanced Corporate Social Responsibility Strategy to Strengthen Canada's Extractive Sector Abroad. Available at www.international.gc.ca; last accessed on 29 August 2016

Most recently, *Canadian International Development Agency* and various mining companies from Canada are co-financing CSR projects in developing countries.[113] This brings economies of scale needed for effective CSR. In contrast, in Namibia, there is a lack of this coherent effort by the industry but rather largely CSR is observed on an individual based participation. Thus a good deal simply reflects on the image of one or a few mining companies as opposed to an industry based image.

More so, Canada has the *Office of the CSR Counsellor*, established in 2009.[114] This office has a dual mandate of offering guidance and advice. Thus in cases where conflict is anticipated, its non-judicial role allow it to develop meaningful dialogue and assist in solving issues amicably. The office further plays the role of reviewing current practices by mining companies abroad.[115] The review focuses on the degree of compliance to the international guidelines and those established by the Canadian government.

To this, the Canadian Government again has a *Centre for Excellence* (CfE) in which reinforces the will in mining companies to comply with the strategy. Established in the *Canadian Institute of Mining, Metallurgy and Petroleum* (CIM), the CfE was envisioned as a focal point for the development and dissemination of practical tools and information to a broad range of extractive sector stakeholders. Through its Executive Committee, the CfE constantly allows for regular discussions with stakeholders to identify the needs and establish the common solutions for resources and community development.

Furthermore, the regular update of the strategies implemented for effective CSR allows for the government to learn and improve its standards. This ensures that to a greater degree CSR is appreciated by the industry in their operations.

While, like in Namibia, CSR is viewed as a voluntary practice, in Canada non-participation is made public knowledge with due consequences. It is stated that;

---

[113] Ibid.
[114] Ibid.
[115] Ibid.

Companies are expected to align with CSR guidelines and will be recognized by the CSR Counsellor's Office as eligible for enhanced Government of Canada economic diplomacy. As a penalty for companies that do not embody CSR best practices and refuse to participate in the CSR Counsellor's Office or NCP dispute resolution processes, Government of Canada support in foreign markets will be withdrawn.[116]

Thus the existence of a disincentive for non-compliance to national and international guidelines encourages the companies to partake not only in CSR but in engaging in discussions on effective contributions. In the case of non-participation, government withdraws its support in terms of advocacy and assistance from the aforementioned CSR Office of CSR Counsellor. In addition to this, matters of CSR are considered by government's financing corporation Export Development Canada (EDC), in evaluating the possibility of providing financial support to Canadian mining companies abroad.[117]

Therefore, using the evaluation criterion set out in this chapter it is important to note that while Canada does not necessarily represent a perfect alignment with sustainable development it does exemplify how a state can progress towards sustainable development through clear law that is binding and having an effective monitoring system (independent government agents); one that involves government's hands on involvement in ensuring sustainable development. While Canada like Namibia encourages a free-market economy, the former indicates a more deliberate attempt at aligning their mining industry with sustainable development as reflected in the detail of the law and policy on social and environmental aspect of mining.

---

[116]Global Affairs Canada.2016. Canada's Enhanced Corporate Social Responsibility Strategy to Strengthen Canada's Extractive Sector Abroad. Available at www.international.gc.ca; last accessed on 29 August 2016
[117]Global Affairs Canada.2016.

Conclusion

This chapter has dealt with the issues concerning sustainability in the mining industry with a particular focus on uranium mining as practiced by Rossing Limited. The state seeks to achieve sustainable development in the mining industry but this chapter has shown that its current framework does not effectively ensure that mining activities are environmentally sound and socially responsible. Essentially sustainable development, in an industry so economically driven as mining, is nearly impossible in the absence of clear law that is binding with an effective monitoring system to ensure compliance. While it may be easy to cast blame on the industry players, the role of government in encouraging positive sustainable practices should not be overlooked.

Sustainable development, whether defined precisely, in the mining context or in general terms, stands on three essential elements, the social, environmental and economic. Although self-regulating on the issues of CSR and rehabilitation, this chapter argued that Rossing reflects sustainable practices in mining. While their practices are not necessarily the ideal, their positive action towards sustainable practices is appreciated in this chapter. Even so, this is credited to the company's policy as opposed to the current legal framework on the issues discussed herein.

Nonetheless, apparent in this chapter are the lack of a monitoring tool, and the lack of coordinated effort, in the case of CSR. On the other hand, the lack of monitoring, the inadequate reporting and the absence of legal requirement to guarantee that funds are reserved constitute major issues of concern on rehabilitation. Under these circumstances therefore, there is a greater need to align the uranium mining industry with sustainable development on the social and environmental aspects. The chapter also argued that while there are guidelines uniquely developed for Namibia, their lack of legal enforceability render their utility to the industry minimal.

It is up to the Namibian government however, to align its mining law with sustainable development to ensure that other players of the industry including Rossing are clear on the accepted standard. It goes without saying that a country cannot operate on policy and guidelines lacking legal enforceability but should be regulated by the rule of law as envisaged in Article 1 of the Constitution.

Recommendations

CSR

Based on the international best practices as demonstrated in the Canadian example Namibia should encourage a coordinated industry model for CSR. This will result in increased efficiency of the industry in dealing with government departments. To this, it may be more practical and beneficial for the companies to contribute funds directly to the local authorities which may thus utilise the funds in supporting local projects according to their set out plans. Granted the issue of corruption may be the subject matter for further discussion, establishing a transparent reporting system that involves audits of local authorities may curb this issue

Even so communities will benefit from economies of scale when mining companies contribute jointly than separately. As such amongst themselves may develop a responsibility to contribute towards the combined effort of the industry.

Lastly, establishing sanctions for non-contribution towards CSR will encourage the companies to participate. First of all, a standard needs to be set on what government deems as the minimum contribution which takes cognisant of the quality and not necessarily the quantity of contribution. This can be relevant to financial standing based primarily on turnover rather than net profit given that in some years companies do not yield profits. Having established standards of contribution the Chamber of Mines as well as the Namibian Uranium Institute needs to name and shame companies that exploit resources without making an adequate and sustainable contribution to the communities in which they operate.

Rehabilitation

Rehabilitation is an essential part of the mining process especially in the Uranium mining where open pit mining is conducted. However, rehabilitation should be specifically and not vaguely regulated. In the absence of law, the state needs to follow up on the

EMP with a focus on the degree of compliance of mining companies to their rehabilitation clauses. This constitutes an interim solution in the absence of statute specifically creating a duty to rehabilitate.

Another issue is that rehabilitation needs funding and as such companies in the uranium mining industry need to be guarantee this from the onset. Government must make these guarantees compulsory for the granting of a mining license. This will allow potential investors to plan accordingly. It will be cumbersome to enforce rehabilitation at closure as companies will no longer be making profits to cover rehabilitation costs.

However, the task does not end there; government needs to be actively involved in monitoring the availability of the funds. This essentially involves a move away from the current system where the companies are independently in charge of the fund but rather have the state receive securities as is the case in Manitoba, Canada. This will essentially ditto the risk of companies using the funds in times of financial difficulties.

Bibliography

Law

Domestic law
The Constitution of Namibia 1 of 1990
Atomic Energy and Radiation Protection Act, 5 of 2005
Environmental Management Act 7 of 2007
Minerals (Prospecting and Mining) Act 33 of 1992

Regional law
African Charter on Human and People's rights, 1986
African Nuclear Weapon Free Zone Treaty, 1996
SADC Protocol on Mining, 1997

International law
United Nations General Assembly International Covenant on Economic, Social and Cultural Rights, 1966

United Nations General Assembly Resolution 1803 on the
Permanent Sovereignty over Natural Resources (XVII) of 1962
Treaty on the Non-Proliferation of Nuclear Weapons, 1970

Canada
Mines and Minerals Act,[118]

Bibliography

Burgess, S. (2010). *Sustainability of Strategic Minerals in Africa and the Potential Conflicts and Partnerships.*

Burgess, S. (2010). Sustainability of strategic minerals in southern Africa and potential co Institute For National Security Studies US Air Force Academy Co.

Burke, A. (2007). *Eleven Steps to rehabilitation in the Succulent Karoo and Namib Desert. Environmental Science and Namibia Nature Foundation.* Oranjemund & Windhoek, p.24.

Chamber of Mines Namibia. (2016). *Chamber of Mine of Namibia Annual Report 2015.* Available at www.chamberofmines.org.na ; last accessed 26 August 2016, p57.

Conde, M. (2014). *Radiological Impact of Rossing Rio Tinto Uranium Mine.* EJOLT Report, p15

Cowan, W and Robertson, J. (2000). Mine Rehabilitation in Ontario, Canada: Ten Years of Progress, pp. 1043-1037, Available at www.gov.on.ca/MNDM/MINES/MG/minrehab.html.

Desjardins, J. (2013). *Visual capitalist.* Available at www.visualcapitalist.com; last accessed on 25 August 2016.

Dubiński, J. (2013). Sustainable Development of Mining Mineral Resources. *Journal of Sustainable Mining.* Volume 12, Issue 1, 2013, Pages 1–6.

Frick, C., (2002). *Direct Foreign Investment and the Environment: African Mining industry,* in Conference on Foreign Direct Investment and the Environment: Lessons to be learned from the Mining industry, OECD Global Forum on International Investment, Editor 2002, and OECD: Paris.

---

[118] CC.S.M.c.M162

Global Affairs Canada. (2016).*Canada's Enhanced Corporate Social Responsibility Strategy to Strengthen Canada's Extractive Sector Abroad.* Available at www.international.gc.ca; last accessed on 29 August 2016.

Jeff Desjardins. (2013). Uranium: *The Metal of Tomorrow.* Available at www.visualcapitalist.com; last accessed on 15 August 2016

Jenkins, R., (2005). Globalization, Corporate Social Responsibility and poverty. *International Affairs*, 81(3): p. 525-540.

Kabir, Z, Rabbi, F, Chowdhury, B, M and Akbar, D. (2015). *A Review of Mine Closure Planning and Practice in Canada and Australia* .World Review of Business Research. Vol. 5. No. 3; p140 – 159

KPMG International. (2014). *Country Mining Guide.* Available at www.kpmg.com; last accessed 25 August 2016.

Ministry of Mines and Energy. (2010). Strategic Environmental Assessment for the central Namib Uranium Rush. Ministry of Mines and Energy, Windhoek, Republic of Namibia.

Moran, K. (2015, December 1). Uranium Outlook 2016: Supply Deficit in the Cards. Retrieved August 23, 2016, from Investing News Network: http://www.investingnewsnetwork.com.

Moran, K. (2015, September 14). Invest News network. Retrieved August 23, 2016, from Invest News Network website: http://www.investnewsnetwork.com.

Namibia Uranium Association. (2016). *Sustaining Global Best Practices in Uranium Mining and Processing: Principles for Managing Radiation, Health and Safety, Waste and the Environment.* Available at www.namibianuranium.org; last accessed on 15 August 2016.

Namibian Uranium Institute. (2014). Minimum Standards for Rehabilitation and Exploration Sites p16 Available at www.namibianuranium.org.na; Last accessed 14 August 2016.

NASA Earth Observatory. *Rossing Uranium Mine: Image of the day.* Available at www.earthobservatory.nasa.gov; last accessed on 27 August 2016.

Pietrezella, M. (2013). *Mining and Sustainability? Systems and Stakeholders of Uranium Mining in Namibia.* Assessed at www.diva-portal.org on 23 August 2016.

Porter, M. and M. Kramer, M. (2006).*Strategy and Society: the Link between Competitive Advantage and Corporate Social Responsibility.* Harvard Business Review.

Randall, S.J. (2010). *Canada, the Caribbean and Latin America: Trade, Investment and Political Challenges.* Canadian International Council.

Renkhoff, N, A. (2015). *Evaluation of Nuclear Legislation: The issue of rehabilitation of Uranium mining sites in Namibia.* EJOLT report 22, p18.

Rossing Uranium Limited. Available at www.rossing.com: last accessed on 28 August 2016.

Taylor, J & Green, K, P. (2016). *Fraser Institute Annual Survey of Mining Companies, 2015.* Fraser Institute. Available at www.fraserinstitute.org; last accessed on 15 August 2016.

United Nations. (2016). *Sustainable Development Goals.* Available at www.un.org ; last accessed on 15 August 2016.

World Bank and International Finance Corporation. (2002). *Large Mines and Local Communities: Forging Partnerships, Building Sustainability.* International Finance Corporation.

World Bank. (2015). February 5). Building Negotiating Capacity in Africa to Make the Most from Mining. Retrieved July 31, 2016, from The World Bank: http://www.worldbank.com.

World Commission on Environment and Development's (the Brundtland Commission) report Our Common Future (Oxford: Oxford University Press, 1987).

World Nuclear Organisation. (2016, August).Uranium Namibia. Retrieved August 29, 2016, from World Nuclear Organisation: http://www.world-nuclear.org.

World Uranium Association. Uranium Production. Available at www.world-nuclear.org; last accessed on 15 August 2016.

World Uranium Association. (2016). What it Uranium and How does it work. Available at www.world-nuclear.org; last accessed on 15 August 2016.

World Uranium Association. (2016). What it Uranium and How does it work. Available at www.world-nuclear.org; last accessed on 15 August 2016.

Chapter Twelve

Exposing the Emperor's Flawed (Neo-)colonial Template:
Charting a Contemporary Regulatory Framework for Africa's Mining Sector

Tapiwa V Warikandwa & Artwell Nhemachena

> *Africa, is a massive "crime scene" and it is up to us to preserve the evidence, document it, and find the critical "teaching moments" that can inform us and the coming generation. After all, the biggest success of the imperial project in Africa was the conquest of our minds. There is much work to be done* (Anonymous).

Introduction

Africa's endeavours to transform its mining sector to ensure that it benefits indigenous Africans have not been a success (Bourgouin, 2011: 526; Magure 2012: 67). The lucrative mining sector has continued to benefit foreign investors and their countries of origin at the expense of the indigenous Africans who are supposed to be the principal beneficiaries of the natural resources extracted from the resource rich continent (Murombo, 2013). At the centre of failed attempts to transform the mining sector in Africa has been the colonially induced closed society features which render a framework for integrating the mining sector coherently and firmly into Africa's economy and society complex, if not impossible (Miller, Desai & Lee-Thorp, 2000). Emphasis of the emperor's template on mining has been the continued focus on the direct export of strategic raw materials to developed countries at the expense of value addition (Wertmann, 2000). The application of Ricardo's Comparative advantage theory in the African context gives the impression that Africa must continually supply raw materials because they are not technologically advantaged.

The pattern of trade in raw and processed materials can be justified by differing endowments of skilled workers and land (Phimister, 1974). As such, since Africa allegedly has a lower level of skilled workers per acre, it will tend to import manufactured goods and export raw materials. For Africa to realise value-addition in the mining sector, it must invest in the production of skilled human capital. Such human capital investment can be realised through the education and/or training of Africans so that they acquire the requisite skills aimed at growing the processing industry in Africa. There are so many universities in Africa which have trained graduates in the engineering and manufacturing sectors for over twenty five years. Some of these graduates have been trained in the West yet they can hardly influence development on the continent. It must be questioned if the type of education they have acquired is suitable for fostering development and economic growth in Africa. The template for education has been laced with dominant Western theories of education whose capitalist content does not promote growth in Africa but promotes the further exploitation of the continent (Warikandwa, 2013). The Western educated African graduates play a central role in the exploitation of their own continent through the deployment of their newly found and celebrated anti-Africa education (Warikandwa, Nhemachena & Mpofu, 2017). This celebrated crop of graduates simply applies western ideologies at the expense of their fellow Africans and their own future; a development akin to cutting the branch that has for long been preventing the same parties from falling (*Ibid*). Raw materials exported from Africa are then processed and sold back to Africa at extortionist prices, a process which has further underdeveloped Africa. The emperor's mining template informed by colonial business and educational practices has to be challenged and substituted by a model which allows for greater beneficiation for indigenous Africans from the natural resources extracted from their land.

A flawed colonial business model

Mining laws at independence, in most African countries, vested ownership and operation rights to foreign companies (Van der

Schyff, 2012; *Bengwenyama Minerals Pty Ltd and others v Genorah Resources Pty Ltd and Others* CCT 39/10 (2010) ZACC 26). These foreign companies extracted natural resources in Africa in their raw state, imported inputs required to carry out mining activities and externalised the proceeds and profits realised (Murombo, 2010). The foreign companies would only retain capital meant to sustain business operations in the country of extracting mineral resources (*Ibid*). As such, even though mining is a major source of revenue obtained through taxation and royalties, with statistical data on trade being dominated by mineral exports, fabricated reports were made of what African countries benefitted from the mining process. This picture was recently reflected in Namibia when the country's Minister of Mines and Energy, Mr Obeth M. Kandjoze robustly cautioned foreign investors in the diamond sector to ensure that Namibians benefit from the extraction and trade in minerals mined in the country (Kandjoze, 2017). His remarks emanated from the fact that regardless of the existence of an Agreement on Diamond Sorting, Valuing, Sales and Marketing (DSVSMA) signed in May 2016 with De Beers (a mining company established in the colonial era), which aimed to ensure that Namibians benefit from the exploitation of their natural resources, more than foreign investors, not much had changed (*Ibid*). Foreign companies continued to pursue exploitative economic models which undermined the Namibian Government's initiatives to ensure increased beneficiation and equality in the country using the mining industry as a tool for economic transformation. The DSVSMA's key outcomes are:

a)   To increase the Local Offer Threshold to a price indexed annual amount of US$430 million;

b)   To ensure that the diamond sector has a significant positive impact on the growth and long-term sustainability of the Namibian cutting and polishing industry;

c)   Increase opportunities for job creation and skills transfer, investment in technology and infrastructure; and

d)   Further integration of Namibians into the economic mainstream and empowerment of the same (*Ibid*).

However, regardless of the fact that the Namibian Government, like most African governments, has been working feverishly to ensure downstream beneficiation from proceeds of the diamond industry and close the inequality gap in the country, foreign companies have continued to export raw materials without value addition. In some cases, the exports of raw materials have been 100% without any local production being realised (*Ibid*).

The Emperor's flawed template

In the 1960's African countries that had just attained their independence from colonial rulers began to nationalise their mining industries and set up state-owned mining enterprises (Makoni, 2014; Leon, 2009). Nationalisation offers broader benefits to everyone in the country and has trickle down effects if properly implemented (Warikandwa & Osode, 2017). Other countries elected to take significant shares in existing foreign owned mining companies. The overall objective of these plausible initiatives was to increase the State's revenue base. However, due to the fact that the colonial empires from which the foreign owned companies originated from were not willing to cede their mining interests to the African countries, the results from the State mining enterprises were not remarkable (Libbay & Woakes, 1980). Foreign mining companies continued to reap the greater rewards from mining practices in Africa, as is the case to date. This was attributed to the fact that the management of the mining companies was dominated by expatriate personal whose interest was to benefit their countries of origin. Procurement of mining equipment remained external to the African countries hence the revenue generated from the mining activities continued to be externalised with little or no benefits accruing to the host nations. State revenue no longer served the developmental interests of Africa countries but that of the developed countries from which the foreign companies originated from. The net outcome of this development was that mining in Africa, even if it was under State control remained a closed society business venture for the foreign owned mining companies.

It was therefore not surprising that in the 1980s, African mining declined (Libbay & Woakes, 1980). To remedy this decline, African solutions were not adopted. Instead, a neoliberal economic institution, the World Bank, undertook a study whose findings centred on proposing liberal reforms designed to grow the African mining industry through attracting Foreign Direct Investment (FDI) (Warikandwa, 2012). To attract FDI, African countries were advised by the World Bank to change their mining regulatory regimes so as to realise the following outcomes:

a)   Assure investors of the protection of their mining investments in host countries;

b)   Promote free market policies characterised by little or no State participation in the mining sector;

c)   Liberalise the exchange rate policy and exchange controls; and

d)   Introduce tax regimes which are more competitive in comparison to those prevailing in other developing countries, especially in South America (Warikandwa, 2012).

As expected, the World Bank's neoliberal reforms provided a fertile and/or conducive business environment for foreign companies investing in Africa's mining industry (Warikandwa & Osode *Speculum Juris* 2014). The results of the reforms brought about by the World Bank mirrored those realised in South America after the adoption of the Washington Consensus (*Ibid*). However, as is the norm with the neoliberal economic order, it does not consider the protection of human rights and the developmental interests of African people and their governments respectively (Warikandwa & Osode, *Law Development & Democracy* 2014). As such, foreign companies focused on maximising profits (Warikandwa & Osode *Law Development and Democracy* 2014; Warikandwa & Osode *Comparative International Law Journal for Southern Africa* 2014) and placed little or no emphasis on a need to contribute to the socio-economic development objectives of African countries (Warikandwa & Asheela, 2016). African countries were thus not getting the best from the exploitation of their mineral resources. Civil society organisation began to criticise foreign owned mining companies regarding their business operations in the African mining industry.

Instead of enlarging the share of returns realised from the exploitation of African mineral resources, the World Bank introduced competition between African countries to attract foreign investment (Warikandwa, 2012: 179). This approach led to the "race to the bottom" syndrome in which African countries employed weak regulatory standards in their business and labour laws to attract investors (*Ibid*). The lowering of the regulatory standards which is now known as regulatory flexibility, popularised by the World Bank's ease of doing business index also brought about another related business practice regarded as the "beggar thy neighbour" syndrome. In this regard a country would lower its regulatory standards to attract a foreign investor already operating in another country into its jurisdiction. The Ramtex case of Namibia in which an Asian company closed its operations in South Africa after being lured by the Namibian Government is an example (Jauch, 2006; Warikandwa, 2012: 324).

In 1995, the Namibian Government introduced the Export Processing Zones Act. The Act provided foreign investors incentives such as tax holidays, exemption from import duties on imported intermediate and capital goods, and free repatriation of profits in order to lure them into the country (Jauch, 2006). The Namibian Government also provided that the Labour Act of 1992 would not apply to export processing zones. Such labour market regulatory flexibility informed by the World Bank was meant to create employment whilst realising lower costs of doing business for foreign investors (Warikandwa, 2012: 324). Whilst Ramtex was not a mining company, the facts and circumstances informing the case are consistent with those prevailing in FDI related practices on the continent. Jobs were lost in South Africa as a result of the withdrawal of Ramatex's investments in South Africa. Whilst almost 7000 jobs were created in Namibia, the same jobs were to be lost after the company suddenly ceased its operations in Namibia in 2008 (Zapini, 2008). Of the 7000 jobs created, 2000 were for migrant workers from Asia. Further, the Namibian Government offered Ramatex an incentive package which included subsidised water and electricity, a

99-year tax exemption on land use as well as over N\$100 million to prepare the operational site, including the setting up of electricity, water and sewage infrastructure (Cappucio, 2006). Such developments are significantly problematic in Africa as the end result of the race to the bottom and the beggar thy neighbour construction is that African States give up their economic gains and lose out on opportunities to formulate policy and regulatory options that have long-term developmental goals as their central agenda.

Should the colonially induced mining regulatory and policy systems continue to subsist, African countries will not realise their development goals. They will lose a good opportunity to maximise on the benefits of a global demand for natural resources, in particular metals and minerals. Africa will also lose on the opportunity to negotiate for better terms for their natural resources, a development which could catalyse economic growth and reduce poverty on the continent. Africa's mining policies must be regularly reviewed and regulatory framework revised (Murombo, 2010). Such revision of policies and revision of mining laws must be measured against the broad and long-term developmental goals for African countries (Magure, 2012). It is evident that the contradiction in terms of African mining in the contemporary era lies in colonially induced structural deficiencies. Such structural deficiencies have been adopted by corrupt and greedy African leaders who care little about the best interests of their citizens but hold power on behalf of their foreign handlers. South Africa's Jacob Zuma and Zimbabwe's Robert Mugabe are prime examples of African leaders who have disregarded the interests of their citizens in favour of engaging in mining transactions which do not benefit their countries (Warikandwa & Osode, 2017). Jacob Zuma's questionable relations with the Guptas in the gold and energy mining sectors and Robert Mugabe's relations with Chinese companies in the diamond mining sector have seen illicit deals being entered into with no benefit accruing to ordinary citizens and the State (Warikandwa & Osode, 2016). Such practices by corrupt African leaders, their cronies and foreign investors serve as reason why the mining industry has significantly weak links with the rest of the national economy.

Operations of African mines and in selected instances, their ownership, vest in foreign companies with most minerals being exported in their raw state whilst the industry imports most of its industrial inputs from Western or Asian companies. There is no value addition on the minerals extracted and no beneficiation for communities in which raw materials are extracted. As a result not many benefits are accruing from mining to African states. Instead, there are negative impacts of mining that are being realised in Africa. The next section discusses the negative impacts of mining in Africa under the current regulatory and policy regime.

Negative effects of mining in Africa

Africa is not significantly benefiting from the extraction of its mineral resources by foreign companies (Tapula, 2012; Mabuza, 2012; Ndebele, 2012). Should this negative development not be addressed, there will be no development driven by the exploitation of minerals in Africa. Only foreign companies and their countries of origin will continue to benefit at the expense of the poor Africans (Twala, 2012). Greedy African leaders will also continue to obtain short term benefits with no short or long-term benefits being realised for the ordinary Africans (Msomi 2012). If the adverse social and environmental impacts of mining are not properly managed, the significant disruption to livelihoods and social fabric of African communities neighbouring the mines will continue to counteract any positive contributions that mining makes on the continent.

Whilst negative impacts of mining are unavoidable, in certain circumstances, the appropriate prevention and mitigation measures could assist mining companies to lower their cost of doing business and build relationships with the disgruntled African communities (Van der Berg & Koep, 2016). Mining in Africa can no longer be business as usual as transformation has to take place in the mining sector in the best interests of Africans. Namibia's Minister of Mines emphasised the importance of ensuring that mining companies should benefit indigenous people in the communities that they operate in (Kandjoze, 2017). The continued failure to benefit local communities explains the reason why the militarisation of mining sites is now becoming a common feature in Africa. A prime example is that of the Marikana debacle which saw mine workers striking against Lonmin a British owned company due to its poor wage policies and failure to realise its corporate social responsibility objectives in the community in which it mines (Warikandwa, 2013; Twala, 2012). If mining companies had good community relations, participatory and transparent corporate governance processes would be realised and communities would be responsive to the business practices of the foreign investors. Such good corporate governance would be underlined by the enforcement of labour, environmental and human rights standards (Warikandwa & Osode, *Law Development and Democracy* 2014; Warikandwa & Osode, *Comparative International Law Journal of Southern Africa* 2014, Warikandwa & Osode, *Speculum Juris* 2014, Warikandwa & Osode, 2017, Warikandwa, 2013). The adverse impacts of mining are discussed below.

Undesirable social effects of mining

Mining has many negative social impacts. Mining operations normally induce the resource curse or Dutch disease syndrome. African countries tend to rely heavily on mining at the expense of other business activities such as agriculture. Countries like Nigeria and Equatorial Guinea have fallen into the category of African countries crippled by the resource curse. A community in which a specific mining activity takes place becomes vulnerable should a mining company which they were heavily dependent upon closes or scales down its operations. Due to a change in land use, poverty levels are also increased because subsistence agriculture activities cease as everyone focuses on mining. This is a significant departure from the pre-colonial mining practices in which mining was not permitted to infringe upon other societal activities such as agriculture (Botchway, 1995: 299). Furthermore, communities are displaced to give way to mining activities. Such an approach often translates to tensions between the communities, farmers and the mining companies. Often, the mining companies and relevant government authorities make promises to compensate families disrupted by relocation. However as often the case is, failure to compensate or inadequate settlement leads to permanent sources of tension between the mining companies and the communities. The Chiadzwa and Marange diamond operations are a case in point. Local inhabitants of the aforementioned areas were forcibly relocated to give way to Chinese mining companies such as Ainjin which wanted to mine diamonds in the areas. Regrettably, none of the diamonds mined benefitted the displaced people or indigenous Zimbabweans as over 15 billion United States dollars was unaccounted (Warikandwa & Osode, 2017; Warikandwa & Osode, 2016). Most of the money obtained from the mining operations was externalised. All the negative outcomes of mining pointed out in this paragraph lead to inequalities within communities between direct beneficiaries of mining and those who do not. Tegeta mining in South Africa is also another example of how the forcible relocation of community members due to mining activities leads to unending tensions between the mining company and the community.

The tensions emanating from unfulfilled relocation compensation obligations are worsened by the influx of immigrants or outsiders into the communities in which mining is taking place. In Southern Africa, most mining areas have attracted cheap migrant labour which is regarded as a cost cutting measure as such migrants are willing to work for lower remuneration as compared to local people. This has often destabilised internal community power relations and often aggravated tensions between mining companies and the communities. This serves as reason why South Africa has been home to many barbaric xenophobic incidents in the recent past years. Equally, in Nigeria in the Niger Delta, the existence of violent unemployed youths and militias can be attributed to feelings of loss of community assets and perceptions of exclusion from benefiting from the extraction of natural resources in the country.

Regulatory challenges posed by mining

Most mining in Africa is conducted by foreign companies. Article 6 of the Protocol of Mining in the Southern African Development Community (SADC) places emphasis on the exploration of mineral resources in the region by the private sector. Article 6 titled Promotion of Private Sector Participation provides as follows:

1.	Member States shall adopt policies that encourage the exploration for and commercial exploitation of mineral resources by the private sector.
2.	Member States undertake to develop a mechanism that will enable the private sector's continued participation in the sector.
3.	Member States shall strive to create a favourable environment for attracting local and foreign investment to the region and to the mining sector in particular.

Article 6(1)-(2) places so much emphasis on a need to create business environments which are conducive for the business operations of foreign investors. There is no indication that SADC countries aim at focusing on value addition driven by local businesses serve for the provision in Article 6(3) which is mentioned together with foreign investment as key objectives. With radical changes in the global economic environment causing intense competition between countries to attract FDI, African countries have embarked on structural reforms to be more competitive. Article 4(5) of the SADC Mining Protocol provides that:

1.	Member States shall promote, strengthen and rationalise the utilisation of existing facilities and those to be developed in future.
The development of mining facilities, which often is done through capital investments from foreign owned companies, is believed to foster competitiveness. Such competitiveness includes African governments ensuring the security of tenure for foreign investors and the provision of national geo-scientific data to further stimulate exploration and mining. However, such regulatory reforms ignore the present reality that African countries are exporting most of their raw mineral resources with little value addition. The net implication of this development is that the full potential benefits to African countries are not being realised (Whitmore, 2006). It is therefore important that African governments explore opportunities for value addition to mineral resources in order to maximise beneficiation.

Whilst policy and regulatory measures might be in place to ensure that mineral industry investors sufficiently account for social and environmental impacts of mining, two issues still come to the fore. These are:

a.   The lack of capacity of African governments to enforce the social and environmental laws; and

b.   Regulatory evasion by mining companies through collusion with corrupt African government officials.

African governments have focused on the immediate social and environmental impact of a programme as opposed to its long-term ramifications. At the centre of this short sighted approach has been a dearth of qualified professionals with a wide range of skills required to address Africa's challenges in the mining sector. For example, in the legal fraternity, very few universities train mining law experts. As a result, those who seek to acquire training in mining law have to turn to developed countries to acquire legal training in mining. Such countries are often former colonisers of the country of origin of the students seeking mining law education. Article 4(1) of the SADC Mining Protocol provides that, "Member States shall co-operate in developing and upgrading the technological capacity of the human resource in the mining sector of the region." As such, there is nothing inherently wrong in seeking to further one's studies in Western countries to upgrade human resource technological capacity. However, the form of training acquired in realising the technological capacity is a cause for concern. The education acquired does not address the historical and social contextual demands of African countries. The education system is modelled on a capitalist template which perpetuates the exploitation of African countries by Western and Asian countries. Such capitalist education places emphasis on free market policies, regulatory flexibility and the continued export of African raw materials to the Western countries. Raw materials and cheap labour are regarded as Africa's competitive advantage. What advantage is this which leads to poverty?

What is overlooked in this system of education is that value addition will reap rich rewards for African countries and eradicate poverty. It does not make sense for Nigeria to run out of petrol and diesel yet it produces millions of crude oil daily for shipping to Western countries to be refined. Equally, it does not make sense that Zimbabwe lost over 15 billion United States dollars in potential revenue which could have been earned from diamond mining ventures by Chinese companies yet it is suffering from a liquidity crunch (Warikandwa & Osode, 2017; Warikandwa & Osode, 2016). Countries like Namibia are suffering the same fate with most of their raw mineral resources from the diamond sector being externalised with little or no gains for the local communities. Western trained African graduates are regarded as paragons of virtue who epitomise the apex of knowledge. Sadly the same graduates perpetuate poverty in Africa and are often used by Western institutions in return for a fortune (Warikandwa, Nhemachena & Mpofu, 2017). Such graduates are oblivious to the further impoverishment of Africa that they are engineering. Education must emancipate a person and communities and not be used as a tool for enlarging poverty in Africa.

For institutions that offer mining law in Africa, little regard is paid to the significant lessons that could be drawn from the regulation of mining through customary law in pre-colonial Africa. Emphasis is placed on the regulation of mining in colonial and post-colonial Africa. Mining law education in Africa ignores the community-based mining practices that prevailed in pre-colonial Africa. This serves as reason why in modern mining law education the world embraces concepts alien to the African Ubuntu driven mining practices such as the polluter pays principle and the neoliberal economic order. The polluter pays principle contradicts the environmental objectives set out in Article 8 of the SADC Mining Protocol which provides that: "Member States shall promote sustainable development by ensuring that a balance between mineral development and environmental protection is attained." Continued environmental degradation due to mining as informed by neoliberal capitalist practices is a process that has condemned Africa to further impoverishment. Unless the current flawed mining law education curriculum borrowed from the naked emperor is not changed, Africans will never realise development through the mining sector. Education must not be acquired for the sake of "just being educated". Education must be acquired to address the challenges being faced by communities. Place based education in mining law modules must be emphasised upon.

A revised Africanised curriculum which seeks to realise a balance between the globalisation agenda and African developmental interests must be formulated as a matter of urgency. African people are paying fortunes to educate their children in Western countries. The same Western countries impose conditions that such graduates must go back and serve their communities with an education that is ill-suited to such economies. Colonial education still remains a reality in our schools and institutions of higher education. Unless we unyoke ourselves from such, impoverishment will underline Africa's existence. Even noble initiatives such as the Mining, Minerals and Sustainable Development Project adopted in the 1990s will not be of any significant value to Africa if there is no policy and mindset shift from capitalism to a Pan-African mining agenda.

It is interesting to observe that in so far as concepts such as rehabilitation and corporate social responsibility are concerned, there are scant laws governing such key issues. Mining companies engage in such practices on a largely voluntary basis. All this is done in the name of promoting the ease of doing business in Africa and attracting FDI. The health of African people is compromised and natural resources which are supposed to ensure growth of African economies and realise employment for the unemployed continue to be externalised to sustain development for the already developed Western countries and lately fast developing Asian countries. Such an unsustainable development agenda has to be changed if there is any hope of Africa industrialising and eradicating poverty.

Limited public participation in mining activities in Africa

In pre-colonial Africa, the concept of Ubuntu ensured that community members had a collective responsibility towards mining practices employed (Botchway, 1995). Kings and chiefs would consult their subjects as regards the suitability of certain mining practices *vis-à-vis* community health and environmental interests (*Ibid*). However, capitalism as represented by captured African heads of States has supplanted the role the ordinary Africans play in determining suitable mining practices to be pursued in their communities (Magure, 2012; Murombo, 2010). The potential profits to be realised from exploiting mineral resources in African communities are deemed as more significant to human life. This serves as reason why non-derogable human rights such as the right to life are violated in pursuit of mineral resources. The blood diamonds of Sierra Leone, Liberia, the Democratic Republic of Congo and the Marange and Chiadzwa diamond fields of Zimbabwe are prime examples. Communities are often displaced with little or no compensation. Their health concerns are disregarded as the case has been in the Tegeta coal mining activities in South Africa.

Public participation is central to determine whether or not a mining activity should continue if continuing to do so would compromise the community social and environmental interests. Public participation in deciding on the pursuit of mining activities is important because:

a. Local knowledge about specific communities in which mining activities are earmarked provides significant information about environment and social issues often overlooked by mining experts; and

b. Community participation in mining activities legitimises the mining project and reduces chances of tensions between mining companies and the communities.

However, it is common practice in Africa that communities are often ignored (Magure, 2012; Matsyak, 2010; Murombo, 2010). The social and environmental obligations of mining companies to the communities in which they operate in are undermined in pursuit of profiteering. Western and Asian mining companies often regard Africans as entities that have no entitlements and therefore not worth respecting (Warikandwa, Nhemachena & Mpofu, 2017).

Communities have often complained about foreign mining companies not giving back to the communities in which the extract mineral resources (Twala, 2012). African communities often expect foreign companies to employ their unemployed youths yet this is hardly the case. It is now the norm that mining companies retrench workers on account of reducing operational costs and a "weak global economic environment". Mechanisation has seen machines replacing human beings in certain sections of the mining production chain. Privatisation has also led to job losses hence one is prompted to ask what benefits foreign investor driven mining activities bring to ordinary Africans.

Flexible regulation of employment laws which gives rise to "flexible working" conditions also undermines African workers' right to fair labour practices (Barker, 2007; Warikandwa, 2012). In particular, the International Labour Organisation's "decent work" agenda is significantly undermined. The International Labour Organisation's decent work agenda focuses on realising security in the workplace, payment of fair wages, offering social protection for workers' families, freedom of expression for workers, amongst other things. Mining companies should abide by national employment laws and abide by the ILO's international standards (Warikandwa, 2012). However, as has become the norm in Africa, governments lack the capacity to implement international standards and are reluctant to challenge foreign investors over their employments standards (Warikandwa & Osode 2016). Again ordinary Africans suffer at the expense of the business interests of foreign investors.

Weak policy implementation

Africa has consistently failed to come up with a holistic minerals policy. Such a policy has to consider the benefits of export earnings, taxes, jobs, revenues, amongst other things and environmental and social costs to communities. The idea behind the holistic policy is to ensure that mining guarantees development for Africa rather than be an impediment to sustainable development. Most constitutions and enabling pieces of legislation in African countries contain provisions which seek to address key developmental changes at local and national levels. To achieve such objectives, policies must be formulated to ensure that mining companies operate in an environmentally and socially responsible manner. Human rights and basic core labour standards must be protected. However, as often has been the case, human rights have been disregarded in pursuit of mining gains (Warikandwa & Osode, 2016). Western and Chinese companies have been fingered for promoting human rights violations and not adhering to a need to protect core labour standards (*Ibid*). At the centre of such dastardly deeds are policies which disregard the importance of human rights protection in favour of profit making (*Ibid*). This short sighted approach to fostering economic growth is not plausible. African countries must change their approach.

Social effects of mining

Mining has many potential benefits to Africa (Tapula, 2012). These include generating revenue for African countries through taxes and royalties. However, it is also acceptable that mining has negative effects on communities. In most instances where mining has to take place, communities are displaced. Those who rely on the land for subsistence farming often lose their means of livelihood. Promises for compensation are often not honoured or the compensation is inadequate to address the losses incurred. The disruption of livelihoods often translates to an increase rather than reduction in poverty as subsistence agriculture is damaged (Amin, 1972). There are also increases in inequalities in communities as some people from the mining companies' activities whilst others do not. Communities are also left vulnerable when the mines close down because they would have on the mining operations for economic sustainability.

Environmental effects of mining

Article 8 of the SADC Mining Protocol makes provision for member states to promote development by ensuring that a balance is struck between environmental protection and mineral development. However, negative environmental effects are still being realised in the Southern African region as is the case in most African countries. The toxic substances and chemicals from the mining process have often led to the radical stripping away of the natural environment. Certain mining practices such as open cast mining have often resulted in ecosystem disruption, deforestation, air pollution, land degradation and soil erosion.

371

It is also important to observe that mining activities have negative impacts which go beyond the mining area itself. To this end, the environmental effects caused by mining have socio-economic effects as the livelihoods of the community inhabitants are significantly disturbed (Van den Berg, 2015). The subsistence farming activities that normally provide the required food and cash generating opportunities are significantly disturbed. Furthermore, months or years after mining activities have ceased, the negative effects of mining on the environment still remain being felt. Thus far, the environmental legacy of mining in Africa is that of unfilled dongas which pose significant harm to people, wildlife and domestic animals. Practices such as rehabilitation which aim at addressing the environmental effects of mining are often voluntary and not strictly regulated. It is to the discretion of the company and the host government to decide if such company wishes to rehabilitate the environment or not. In some cases, the hazardous environmental conditions are maintained in the name of making the donga infested area a historical monument. This is the case with Rossing Uranium mine in Arandis, Namibia, where the Namibian Government signed an agreement with the mining company not to rehabilitate the area because they wanted it to be a tourist attraction site.

The mining sector's contribution to broad-based development in Africa

For mining in Africa to better contribute to broad-based development, there is need to integrate it into people oriented national and regional economic policies (Warikandwa & Osode, 2017; Murombo 2010; Magure 2012). Such policies should be development oriented hence investment must be attracted and planned in a strategic manner. Emphasis must be placed on human capital investment and technological development. The minerals policies of African countries must be integrated into the national and regional development policies so as to move away from the exclusive mining practices to the inclusive mineral extraction processes. Such an approach will promote minerals beneficiation before export. Beneficiation has the capacity to contribute to significant economic growth and diversification (Kandjoze, 2017). This approach is likely to create jobs for the unemployed Africans and increase the revenue base of African countries.

Another central concept to promoting broad-based development in Africa is the need to ensure that mining companies contribute to corporate social responsibility (CSR) (Hopkins, 2007). Mining companies must contribute to the wider developmental objectives of the countries in which they extract mineral resources (De Boeck, 1998). The Pan-African investment code sets the tone in this regard. CSR must be entrenched in national mining policies and laws. Sadly, mining companies often do not regard contributing to social responsibility as a significant component of sustainable business (Dumett, 1998). The development of mines must be seen as an opportunity to improve conditions in communities in which mining activities are taking place. Failure of mining companies to contribute to the development of the areas in which they operate in is likely to lead to militarisation of such communities to fight against such companies. The Marikana community in South Africa is a classic example of how failure of companies to practice CSR can have negative effects on business (Twala, 2012). Central to CSR are the following principles:

a)   Mining companies' implementation of effective and transparent engagement, communication and independently verified reporting arrangements with stakeholders such as the community;

b)   Contributing to environmental protection;

c)   Contributing to the social, economic and institutional development of communities in which the mining companies operate in;

d)   Integrating of sustainable development considerations within the mining companies' business decision making processes; and

e)   Upholding human rights and respecting cultures, customs and values of African people in dealings with employees and ordinary community members.

Artisanal and small scale mining must also be regarded as legally protected business practices which can be used to improve rural livelihoods. The aforementioned mining practices have the potential to stimulate entrepreneurship in a socially responsible manner and can easily promote local and integrated national development and regional cooperation amongst African countries. African countries lack policy and legal frameworks which are flexible enough to accommodate artisanal and small-scale mining. Emphasis is placed on large-scale mining which is often conducted by foreign investors who externalise proceeds from mining. This leaves little or no beneficiation for poor African people. It would therefore be useful if the African mining regime would regularise informal artisanal mining through assuring a legal regime that gives artisanal miners mining rights which are secure. Artisanal and small scale mining are prevalent in Africa. They are used to sustain livelihoods and significantly contribute to national economies. Mining, in all forms, can contribute to economic and social development.

Recommendations

Africa must change its approach to regulating mining activities on the continent. A new regulatory regime must be adopted which is transparent and equitable. Such regulatory regime must set the basis for the optimum exploitation of mineral resources to promote socio-economic development and broad-based sustainable growth. The following is therefore proposed:

1)   A Pan-African mining code must be adopted to act as a catalyst for broad-based growth and development in Africa. Such mining code must focus on mineral beneficiation and value addition of mineral products in Africa.

2)   New harmonised mining laws for Africa must be adopted. Such laws must legalise artisanal mining and enforce CSR. Africa's mining sector must harness the potential of artisanal mining and small-scale mining to stimulate local/national entrepreneurship, improve livelihoods and advance integrated rural social and economic development.

3)   Emphasis on mining in Africa must now focus on human capital investment. Africans must acquire mining skills, management

skills and become owners of mines. The current arrangement where foreign mining companies continue to monopolise Africa's mining sector leaves Africa susceptible to manipulation by the West and Asia. State capture will continue to be the norm as Africa is not independent but dependent on the West and Asia for the sustainability of its mining ventures.

4)　　　Mining modules in institutions of higher learning must be changed to suite the African agenda. The education template is currently flawed and stands to sustain the bleeding of Africa's mining sector in the best interest of the West and Asia. Africans must acquire valuable education which will allow them to counter capitalist agendas and not to perpetuate them. The current curriculum in mining law, in particular, is Western oriented and does not equip the African students with the necessary skills required to realise transformation in Africa. Pre-colonial mining should be taught in mining law modules. This will provide Africans with the valuable knowledge of how pre-colonial Africans exploited their mineral resources and traded in finished products and not raw materials.

Conclusion

The minerals sector in Africa still remains a fundamental component for realising sustainable development on the continent. Africa has the world's largest mineral reserves which the West and Asia desire to continually access. These mineral reserves are largely unexplored and offer unique opportunities for Africa to realise significant economic growth. There is an undoubted demand in the minerals resources from Africa. This serves as reason why Africa is constantly being courted by suitors who are looking for reliability and security of supply of mineral commodities. All the suitors have a clear and focused strategy on what they want from Africa; to exploit African resources and maximise on their gains at little or no cost. Their interest is not on the welfare of poor Africans or the development of the continent. It is in this regard that Africa has to develop a coherent strategy in response to the exploitative agenda set by the foreign investors as assisted by global monetary institutions such as the World Bank and the International Monetary Fund.

Africa must leverage the increased competition for its natural resources and maximise on such opportunities to realise development. However, for this to happen there is need for a paradigm shift. Africans must realise that they are capable of running the mining industry on their own without relying heavily on the West and Asia. Investing in a Pan-African mining education and regulatory regime would be the starting point. This should be accompanied by the eradication of corruption through adopting an Ubuntu driven corporate governance agenda. It is evident that the emperor is naked and seeks no good for Africa and its people. Africa must take this point of realisation as a starting point. Artisanal miners must be protected at law and foreign investors must be seen to contribute to African development in the short-term. In the long-term, mining education must empower young Africans to have the knowledge to run mines without reliance on the West and Asia. Africa has the potential to generate significant revenue to run its own mining projects. It is hypocritical to contend that Africa has no capital to run capital intensive projects such as mining yet foreign investors run mining projects using capital generated from the exploitation of mineral resources from Africa. If there was no money in the mineral sector of Africa which allows foreign investors to break even in their business operations, why are all roads consistently leading to Africa? Africans must wake up and smell the coffee! Technological growth must be realised in Africa to ensure that no raw materials from the mining sector on the continent are exported without value addition. The West and Asia must buy finished products and not raw materials from Africa.

Bibliography

Amin, S (1972), "Underdevelopment and dependence in Black Africa-origins and contemporary forms", *The Journal of Modern African Studies*, volume 10(4) pp 503-524.

Barker, F (2007) *The South African Labour Market: Theory and Practice*, Pretoria: Van Schaik.

Botchway, FNN (1995), "Pre-colonial Methods of Gold Mining and Environmental Protection in Ghana," *Journal of Energy and Natural Resources Law* volume 13, pp. 299-311.

Bourgouin, F (2011), "The politics of large-scale mining in Africa: domestic policy, donors, and global economic processes" *The Journal of The Southern African Institute of Mining and Metallurgy*, volume 111, p 526.

Cappucio, S (2006), "Labour and Environment: A natural synergy" available at
http://www.unep.org/labour_environment/TUAssembly/case _studies/Cappuccio-ITGLWF.pdf (accessed 9 April 2017).

De Boeck, F (1998), "Domesticating diamonds and dollars: Identity, expenditure and sharing in Southwestern Zaire (1984-1997)" in Peter Geschiere and Birgit Meyer (Hg) *Globalisation and identity: Dialectics of Flows and Closures*, Development and Change volume 29(4) pp 777-810.

Dumett, RE (1998), *El Dorado in West Africa. The gold-mining frontier, African Labour, and colonial capitalism in the Gola coast, 1875-1900*, Ohio University Press: Oxford.

Hopkins, M. (2007) *Corporate Social Responsibility and International Development: Is Business the Solution?* Earthscan: London.

Kandjoze, OM (2017), "Keynote address at Minister's Engagement Session with the Diamond Industry" Hilton Hotel, Namibia, 27 March 2017.

Leon T (2009), "Creeping Expropriation of Mining Investments: An African Perspective" Journal of Energy and Natural Resources Law pp 33-40.

Libby R and Woakes M (1980), "Nationalisation and the Displacement of Development Policy in Zambia" African Studies Review pp 33-50.

Mabuza, K (2012), "Striking Miners dare police to 'Finish us off'", *Sowetan*, 17 August.

Magure, B (2012), "Foreign Investment, Black Economic Empowerment and Militarized Patronage Politics in Zimbabwe" *Journal of Contemporary African Studies* pp 67-82.

Makoni, PL (2014), "The Impact of the Nationalisation Threat on Zimbabwe's Economy" Corporate Ownership and Control pp 160-179.

Matyszak, D (2010) "Everything You Ever Wanted to Know (And Then Some) About Zimbabwe's Indigenisation and Economic Empowerment Legislation but (Quite Rightly) Were Too Afraid To Ask" available at http://researchandadvocacyunit.org/system/files/Everything%20you%20ever%20wanted%20to%20know.pdf (accessed 9 April 2017).

Miller, D., Desai, N., and Lee-Thorp Julia, (2000), "Indigenous Gold Mining in Southern Africa: A review" *South African Archaeological Society Goodwin Series*, volume 8, pp 91-99.

Msomi, S (2012), "COSATU elite losing touch with rank and file", *Sunday Times*, 19 August.

Murombo T (2010), "Law and the Indigenisation of Mineral Resources in Zimbabwe: Any Equity for Local Communities" *Southern African Public Law* pp 568-589.

Murombo, T (2013) "Regulating Mining in South Africa and Zimbabwe: Communities, the Environment and Perpetual Exploitation" *Law, Environment and Development Journal* pp. 31-49.

Ndebele, N (2012) "Liberation betrayed by bloodshed", *City Press*, 26 August.

Phimister, IR (1974), "Alluvial Gold mining and trade in nineteenth-century South Central Africa", *The Journal of African History*, volume 15(3), pp 445-456.

Van der Berg, M and Koep, P (2016) "Mining and energy in Namibia" in Olivier C Ruppel and Katharina Ruppel-Schlichting (eds) *Environmental law and policy in Namibia*, 3rd edition, Hanns Seidel Foundation: Namibia, p 211.

Van der Schyff, E (2012), "South African Mineral Law: A Historical Overiew of the State's Regulatory Power regarding the exploitation of minerals", *New Contree: A Journal of Historical and Human Science of Southern Africa* p 131.

Warikandwa, TV (2012), "Enlarging the place of human rights and development in international trade regulation: An evaluation of the problems and prospects of incorporating a social clause in the legal framework of the World Trade Organisation" Doctor of Laws degree thesis, University of Fort Hare, p 159.

Warikandwa, TV (2013), "Linking Trade to Core Labour Standards to Limit Labour Unrest: A South African Perspective" *Transformer, volume* 19(1), p 31.

Warikandwa, TV and Asheela, NV (2016), "Economic Transformation and Investment Security in Namibia: An Appraisal of the National Equitable Economic Empowerment Framework Bill" *University of Namibia Law Review,* volume 3(1), p 53.

Warikandwa, TV, Nhemachena, A and Mpofu, N (2017), "Double Victimisation? Law, Decoloniality and Research Ethics in post-colonial Africa", *Africology: The Journal of Pan African Studies* volume 10(2), (forthcoming April 2017).

Warikandwa, TV and Osode, PC (2014), "Legal Theoretical Perspectives and their Potential Ramifications for Proposals to Incorporate a Social Clause into the Legal Framework of the World Trade Organisation" *Speculum Juris,* volume 28(2), p 41.

Warikandwa, TV and Osode, PC (2016), "Chinese Companies' Trade Practices and Core Labour Standards: A South African, Zambian and Zimbabwean Perspective" *African Nazarene University Law Journal (Published by JUTA),* volume 4(1) p 102.

Warikandwa, TV and Osode, PC (2017), "Regulating against business 'fronting' to advance black economic empowerment in Zimbabwe: Lessons from South Africa" *Potchefstroom Electronic Law Journal,* volume 20, pp 1-43.

Werthmann, K (2000), "Gold rush in West Africa: The Appropriation of 'natural' resources: Non-industrial gold mining in South-Western Burkina Faso", *Sociologus,* volume 50(1) pp 90-104.

Whitmore A, (2006), "The Emperor's new clothes: Sustainable mining?" *Journal of Cleaner Production,* volume 14(3-4) pp 309-314.

Southern Africa Development Community Protocol on Mining, 1997.

Tapula, T (2012), "Making the Mining Charter go further towards genuine empowerment", *Diplomatic Pouch,* 25 July.

Twala, C (2012), "The Marikana Massacre: A Historical overview of the Labour unrest in the mining sector in South Africa" *Southern African Peace and Security Studies Policy Brief* volume 1(2) p 61.

Van den Berg, HM 2015, "Regulation of the upstream petroleum industry: A comparative analysis and evaluation of the regulatory frameworks of South Africa and Namibia", Unpublished PhD-thesis, University of Cape Town.

Zapini, D (2008), "Developing a Balanced Framework for Foreign Direct Investment in SADC: A Decent Work Perspective" *Monitoring Regional Integration in Southern Africa Yearbook* Chapter 5.